Moreton Morrell

management
consultancy

management consultancy

JOE O'MAHONEY

OXFORD
UNIVERSITY PRESS

OXFORD

UNIVERSITY PRESS

Great Clarendon Street, Oxford OX2 6DP

Oxford University Press is a department of the University of Oxford.
It furthers the University's objective of excellence in research, scholarship,
and education by publishing worldwide in

Oxford New York

Auckland Cape Town Dar es Salaam Hong Kong Karachi
Kuala Lumpur Madrid Melbourne Mexico City Nairobi
New Delhi Shanghai Taipei Toronto

With offices in

Argentina Austria Brazil Chile Czech Republic France Greece
Guatemala Hungary Italy Japan Poland Portugal Singapore
South Korea Switzerland Thailand Turkey Ukraine Vietnam

Oxford is a registered trade mark of Oxford University Press
in the UK and in certain other countries

Published in the United States
by Oxford University Press Inc., New York

© Joe O'Mahoney 2010

The moral rights of the author have been asserted
Database right Oxford University Press (maker)

First published 2010

British Library Cataloguing in Publication Data
Data available

Library of Congress Cataloging in Publication Data
Data available

Typeset by MPS Limited, A Macmillan Company
Printed in Italy on acid-free paper by Lego SpA

ISBN 978-0-19-957718-7

10 9 8 7 6 5 4 3 2

To the Middlesex Mile Champion, 1960 and 1962,
and Ma

ACKNOWLEDGEMENTS

This book reflects and draws on research projects, publications, and interviews that I have undertaken over the last four years. Some of this research has been funded by the Advanced Institute of Management, the Economic and Social Research Council (RES 331–27–0071), and the Cardiff Business School Seedcorn Fund. For this financial support, I am very grateful.

The greatest help in writing the book came from my family: Katherine, Elizabeth, Ellie, Mary, Jane, and Kevin O'Mahoney. Their ideas, criticisms, and copy-editing were invaluable and of a much higher standard than my own. I would also like to thank Per Voll for his help with Chapter 7. I also acknowledge the support of my editors at Oxford University Press, Nicki Sneath and Alex Lazarus, who have been consistently outstanding in their work and support. In addition, the comments of four good friends improved the text considerably: Thorsten Barthel, Colin Moughton, Aidan Davies-Webb, and Daniel Muzio. I should also thank all of my MBA students whose critique of my course and my cases has allowed it to evolve, especially David Tse.

In addition, the book has benefited greatly from the contributions from various experts in the field who took time out of their busy schedules to pen their perspectives on the industry. I would also like to thank Graham Briscoe, Alan Leaman, Hamid Atiyya, Deborah Fleming, Graeme Pauley, Andrew Sturdy, Peter Hill, Fiona Czerniawska, Lynda Purser, Ian Brodie, and Roger Singer. I am also grateful to all the contributors to this book who gave their time and knowledge without hesitation. Additionally, without three outstanding mentors, I would not have understood how either consultancy or its analysis should work: Mike Sturrock, Rick Delbridge, and Simon Forge.

Finally, and most importantly, thank you to my wife, Hannah, who excused the unfortunate timing of this book coinciding with our first year of marriage and provided me with all the support I could have asked for.

J.O.

CONTENTS

DETAILED CONTENTS

PART 2

The Practitioner Perspective

6 Consulting Tools, Skills, and Techniques   179

PART 3

The Critical Perspective

PART 4

The Career Perspective

GUIDE TO THE BOOK

There are many key features included in the chapters of *Management Consultancy* that are designed to help you to both learn, and organize information.

Chapter Objectives
This chapter introduces the reader to the purpose, stru
book. Specifically, it states that the book:

■ Attempts to provide the student with four key perspe
  industry: a description of what management consulta
  it is done, an analysis of the critical, ethical, and socia
  and, finally, a guide to the consulting career.

■ Provides a mix of case studies for students to grappl
  small, illustrative cases are provided as discussion p

Chapter Learning Objectives

Each chapter opens with a bulleted outline of the main concepts and ideas. These serve as helpful signposts to what you can expect to learn from each chapter.

Case Study

Johnson and Johnson

With sales of $53n in 2006 J&J faced massive procurement costs
es. In their procurement of consultants there was little central
with regard to small projects. More importantly, the differing de
els meant that advice was not given to managers on rates that
ects were often badly managed, and the wrong consultants wer
per cent of reported spend for consultants was for vaguely defi
   After a review of best practice and a gap analysis, J&J created
new system:

Case Studies

Each chapter contains at least two short case studies designed to place the content of that chapter into a practical context. Each chapter in Part II is further followed by an in-depth case study designed to help you put the theory of the chapter into context.

Student Exercise: Design your Own Consultancy

It is July 2011. You and nine of your consulting colleagues in Co
and start up your own management consultancy. You will speci
the financial services sector. A non-competition clause between
employer means that you cannot "poach" any of its clients. A fri
with a large bank has offered you a lucrative contract which you
business to keep ten of you busy for at least six months. You will
between the ten of you which you think you can just about affor

1   What are the main activities you will engage in as a consulta
    important activities.

2   What will your main costs be? Estimate these costs.

Student Exercises

A variety of student exercises, ranging from group activities through to individual work are provided throughout the book, and are relevant to each chapter.

PRACTITIONER INSIGHT

A Positive Force for the Economy

Alan Leaman, Chief Executive of the MCA
(Management Consultancies Association)

Practitioner Insights

Short pieces follow each chapter, written by consultants and industry representatives, and provide you with different and often conflicting views on the chapter topics.

ally non-existent (Maister 2003). However, in firms with more pa
will be greater emphasis on developing and promoting talent, wh
strategy partnerships tend to have an "up or out" policy: they do
junior consultants blocking those who might make it further up t

----
Leverage is not just an outcome, it is a strategy, a performanc
for the company.

—EO, medium-s

As we explore the different aspects of consultancy practice we
of the importance of leverage.

Practitioner Quotes

Each chapter contains quotes from practitioners to help illustrate points throughout the text.

approached things differently. Try to agree on the best route for

Discussion Questions

• What are the steps in the consulting life-cycle?
• How do consultancies sell to potential clients?
• What forms of data collection might a consultant use?
• What is the difference between inductive and deductive rese
• What components should a delivery plan include?

End of Chapter Discussion Questions

Discussion questions have been included at the end of every chapter to prompt further investigation.

■ Chapter Summary

This chapter has provided an overview of the consulting indu
and segmentation. It has shown:

• how consultancies grew on the back of a growing industria
  management expertise.
• that, in the last twenty years, the industry has changed in r
  crises, sophisticated clients, and the development of IT and
• that there are varied and competing explanations for unde
  consultancies exist.

Chapter Summaries

Each chapter ends with a précis that summarizes the most important arguments developed within that chapter.

Further Reading

There are surprisingly few good texts that examine the relations
consultants. From the academic side, one of the most influentia
Fincham (1999), which highlighted the contingent and influen
between the client and the consultant. A strong but under-cited
Dealing with Confidence, a deeply analytical collection of essay
clients and various management advisory companies by Furust
area, it is worth keeping an eye open for work by Tim Clark, And
Whittle, all insightful commentators in this area.

Outside of academia, the best work in the area is by Fiona Cze
practitioner insights with strong analysis. Her book entitled The
researched argument that "trusted advisors" are no longer enou

Further Reading

An annotated list of recommended reading on each subject will help guide you further into the literature on a particular subject area.

HOW TO USE THE ONLINE RESOURCE CENTRE

www.oxfordtextbooks.co.uk/orc/omahoney/

There is a wide range of web-based content for tutors and students to support this text. Students can go to the Online Resource Centre to find web links, a comprehensive glossary and online appendices for the text. Tutors will be able to access a suite of customizable PowerPoint slides, which can be used in lectures and seminars, alongside a bank of exercise solutions and answers to cases, as well as suggestions for group projects and discussion questions.

All of these resources can be incorporated into your institution's existing virtual learning environment.

■ For Lecturers

PowerPoint® Lecture Slides

A suite of PowerPoint slides has been included for use in your lecture presentations. They are fully customizable so you can tailor them to match your own presentation style.

Case Commentary and Answer Guidance

To support the many case studies included in the book, the author has provided a commentary and answers to the questions posed within the text.

Exercise Solutions

A suite of answers are provided to the student activities in the text.

Suggested Group Projects

A collection of group activities provide you with a wide range of seminar and assessment resources.

Suggested Discussion Questions

An additional suite of discussion questions are also provided for use in your teaching.

■ For Students

Annotated Web Links

Links to relevant websites direct students towards valuable sources of information, as well as professional associations.

Glossary of Terms

A glossary of terms is presented in an accessible format to help revise key terms and concepts.

Appendices

To complement this text, useful material to aspiring consultants such as a sample covering letter, and a consultancy contract are provided online for your reference.

Chapter on 'Typical Clients'

An additional brand new chapter, not featured in the book, is available to download for free.

1

Introduction

Chapter Objectives

This chapter introduces the reader to the purpose, structure, and style of the book. Specifically, it states that the book:

- Attempts to provide the student with four key perspectives on the consulting industry: a description of what management consultancy is, a guide to how it is done, an analysis of the critical, ethical, and social views on the industry, and, finally, a guide to the consulting career.

- Provides a mix of case studies for students to grapple with. In each chapter, small, illustrative cases are provided as discussion points, whilst at the end of each chapter in Part 2, longer cases are provided for in-depth discussions. Part 4 also contains a number of cases similar to that used by consultancies for recruiting graduates.

- Introduces the views of a number of global experts and stakeholders in the consulting industry. These come from a number of perspectives and provide students with contrasting voices and opinions about the industry.

These features enable the book to act as a comprehensive introduction to the consulting industry for students, graduates, consultants, and those interested in becoming a consultant. In addition, the Online Resource Centre contains an extended library of web-links, references, presentations, case-study solutions, and an additional chapter.

■ The Management Consultancy Phenomenon

If growth and influence are a measure of a successful industry then few have more claim on the top position than that of management consultancy. In 1980, revenues from the consulting industry were estimated at $3bn (Kennedy Inf ormation 2002). By 2008, this figure had reached $330bn, an increase of over 10,000 per cent in less than thirty years (Kennedy Information 2009).

Even more remarkable has been the impact of the consulting industry on society. This does not only concern graduates, who now put consultancy as their number one career choice (Chung et al. 2008), or even businesses, where the spend on consultants in single out-sourcing or IT development projects can run to hundreds of billions of dollars. Consultancy has had an impact on every one of us, from the structures of government and the provision of education, to the very language that we use and the way that we think about the world.

If the statement above seems incredible, it should not. In the last ten years the influence of consultants in the actual governance of countries across the Western world has increased exponentially. As government spending on consultants has risen by 1,000 per cent over the last ten years (IPSOS/MORI 2007) consultants have fostered increasingly close relationships with senators, ministers, and senior public officials in an attempt to influence political agendas and spending strategies (Craig and Brooks 2006). The resulting projects on modernisation, e-business, and new public sector management have cost governments hundreds of billions of pounds with highly varied levels of success (Saint-Martin 2004).

A clear consequence of this success has been the growing dominance of the managerialist practices and discourses in areas which were previously immune, ranging from sectors such as education, charities, 'the arts', and health to whole economies in the developing world. This "colonisation" effect has prompted many academics to term consultants "missionar-ies" (Wright and Kitay 2004) charged not with religious, but with corporate fervour, in their attempts to transform supposedly archaic systems into modernised management practice.

The influence of the consulting industry can also be evidenced in the remarkable spread of the management innovations that have been invented and disseminated by consultan-cies and consultants, which amount to hundreds of thousands of concepts that organi-sations across the globe use. These include Total Quality Management, Business Process Re-engineering, Core Competences, Growth Share Matrix, and the 7-S Framework. As we discuss later in Chapter 8, the actual benefit of such concepts may be a moot point, but the impact they have had on clients, their employees, and society at large cannot be denied.

■ The Backlash

The success of the consulting industry in terms of revenue generation, growth, and influ-ence has, in recent years, created a backlash amongst many journalists, academics, and government watchdogs. The complicity of the consulting industry in the collapse of the dotcom industry as well as high-profile companies such as Enron, WorldCom, and Par-malat marked a turning point in public attitudes towards the industry. Amongst journal-ists, titles such as *Plundering the Public Sector* (Craig and Brooks 2006) and *House of Lies*

(Kiln 2005) point the reader to a murky world of backroom deals, failed projects, and excessive fees, all paid for by the public purse.

These concerns were reiterated, albeit in a more restrained manner, by government watchdogs, such as the Securities and Exchange Commission (SEC) and the Congressional Budget Office (CBO), in the USA, and the National Audit Office (NAO) and the Financial Services Authority (FSA) in the UK. Such watchdogs have increasingly warned against the rising costs of consultancy projects in the public sector, conflicts of interest between audit companies and consultancies, and, in the last few years, the complicity of reward consultants in setting the pay of CEOs.

Academics have long been interested in the consultancy industry for its persistent growth rate, its use of partnership models, and its influence on the wider economy. However, from the 1990s onwards, academic analyses increasingly incorporated a critical perspective. Such studies, especially in Europe, have critiqued consultants for selling fads, exploiting managers, introducing redundancies to organisations, and having conflicts of interest (Newell et al. 2001; Kieser 1997). There has also been a growing interest in the impact of the intensive consultancy lifestyle on consultants themselves (O'Mahoney 2007).

Whilst experiencing a deluge of criticisms from all sides, the consulting industry is itself facing a number of challenges to its growth and profitability in addition to the day-to-day struggles of competition. First, the 2009–10 recession witnessed the first reduction in consulting growth since the dotcom bust eight years earlier creating declines in profits that "will not return to 2008 levels until 2012" (Kennedy Information 2009). Second, the growing sophistication of clients and the increasing use of procurement experts for purchasing consultancy services has put pressure on fees, which in turn decreased profit margins across the industry and led to declining productivity (Brett Howell 2009; AMCF 2009; Sako 2006). This pressure on fees has also led to a third challenge, which is attracting talent. As profits have declined, so too have the salaries that can be offered to consultants. This in turn means that in the "war for talent" consultancies are more and more likely to lose out to investment banks when recruiting from the top business schools (O'Mahoney et al. 2008).

Whether or not consultancy is at a crossroads or whether the recent crisis is a mere blip on the path to greater growth is difficult to tell. However, for students, academics, journalists, and consultants, the industry still offers exciting and interesting opportunities in the fields of theory, practice, and analysis.

■ Perspectives on Consulting

As implied above, the consulting industry is beset by differences of opinion and perspective. Some students, and academics, for example, simply wish to understand more about the basics of the industry. This point of view, which can be called the Descriptive Perspective, is often covered by professors and tutors in the first few lectures when they give an overview of the industry. They tend to cover questions such as:

- What is, and isn't, management consultancy?
- How do the different forms of consultancy differ and why?
- Why did the industry emerge and how has it changed in recent years?

Some students may have already entered the industry, or are in a managerial role, and seek to better understand what consultants do. This view, termed the Practitioner Perspective, focuses on ensuring the better use of consultancy in organisations and is often, though not always, the main focus of courses on consultancy. This Practitioner Perspective is more interested in practical and operational issues such as:

- How should clients deal with consultants?
- What tools and techniques do consultancies use?
- How should one run a consultancy firm?

Many courses, especially at universities, also incorporate a Critical Perspective which aims to analyse and understand the industry by applying explanatory theories. The Critical Perspective tends to ask questions such as:

- How does management consultancy interact with its social, political, and economic environments?
- What theories can we use to better understand the dynamics of the industry?
- How can consultancy be ethical?

Finally, some courses, and certainly most students, wish to learn about the Career Perspective. Getting into a consultancy requires knowledge that is very different from standard graduate jobs, and students are naturally interested in landing a job in one of the most varied, challenging, and well-paid professions. This Career Perspective asks questions such as:

- Which firms should students apply for and at which grade?
- How should students apply for a job?
- How can students maximise their chances of success?

■ This Book

As a management consultant who joined academia a few years ago, it was surprising to me that my Business School didn't offer a course on Management Consultancy for our MBA students. After volunteering to create one, I did a thorough review of existing courses and books and found that most were firmly located in one or two, and more rarely three, of the perspectives described above. This meant that, in many courses, students were provided with a consultancy "tool-kit" but were not given the critical skills to understand the industry in its wider context. In other courses, consultancy would be analysed and critiqued as a sociological phenomena, but students were left at a loss when it came to applying for jobs or understanding what consultants actually do. As a result, I decided to write my course material from scratch based on my experience as a consultant, my research on the consulting industry, and several literature reviews that I had conducted around the industry.

The course became the most popular MBA elective in the Business School, attracting some 180 students in its first year, and received some of the highest student ratings. Additionally, many of the graduates had great success in applying to top consultancies around the world.

Key to the success of the course was the importance of understanding consultancy from several points of view. When several students suggested that the course could be usefully turned into a book, it was these perspectives that I felt would be of most use to others.

The rest of the book, therefore, is split into four sections, each dealing with a different perspective on the industry:

Part 1: The Descriptive Perspective

This provides an overview of the industry. In Chapter 2, the definitions, history, trends, and structure of the industry are described. It also provides a description of the different forms the industry takes around the world. In Chapter 3, the different types of consultancy are outlined and differing business models, sectors, and services are introduced.

Part 2: The Practitioner Perspective

There are four chapters in this section, reflecting the prominence that many courses give to the Managerial Perspective. Chapter 4 focuses on clients: why and how they use consultants and what their changing needs are. Chapter 5 focuses on consulting work: it introduces the consulting life-cycle and examines the sales, research, and delivery of consultancy work. Chapter 6 continues this focus on consultancy work by examining the tools, methods, and skills that consultants employ in effecting change in client companies. Chapter 7 explains more about the consultancy firm, especially the unusual partnership structure that many firms adopt, and shows how such firms operate. After each one of the chapters in this section, students are provided with a detailed case study to tackle.

Part 3: The Critical Perspective

This section of the book focuses on a sociological, political, and ethical critique of the industry. Chapter 8 introduces the students to the main sociological and philosophical themes that academics use in understanding the wider picture of consultancy. Chapter 9 builds on this basis and provides a rich sociological examination of ethics in the consulting industry, arguing that academics need to focus more on macro-level institutions as well as micro-level dilemmas when discussing ethics.

Part 4: The Career Perspective

This final part introduces the student to the unusual and challenging world of the consultancy career. Chapter 10 outlines, in detail, the standard application process for consultants and explains how a student can maximise their chances of success. It also goes on to explain how consultants move up the firm and what happens when they decide, or are forced, to exit the company. Finally, Chapter 11 provides students with an overview of case interviews: a method of recruitment unique to the consulting industry. It also provides a number of case interviews for students to practise.

To add to the theme of different perspectives in this book, I have invited a number of leading industry commentators to write short pieces reflecting their views on the industry.

You will notice that these pieces are quite different and even disagree with each other in places. This is, I believe, a good thing, in that it reflects the incredible diversity and variety of views on one of the most powerful industries in the world. In addition, where appropriate each chapter contains small illustrative cases, examples, and quotations from practitioners. At the end of each chapter there is a student exercise and discussion questions. The Online Resource Centre has additional cases for discussion, a set of links to online material, an extended bibliography for research, and an additional chapter on the different types of clients that consultancies encounter.

■ A Note on Sources

Surprisingly, reliable information on the global consulting industry is hard to come by. Those reports which are available often differ by up to 20 per cent in their reporting of industry revenues, employment, or profits. Figures are notoriously unreliable due to different governments and research institutes having different definitions about what counts as management consultancy. To make things worse, the largest research company in the industry, Kennedy Information, is reluctant to share its findings with the academy and many of the most famous consultancies are privately owned and refuse to provide anything but the most basic information to analysts. For this reason, some figures in the book may contradict others and, in some cases, educated guesses and approximations have needed to be used where hard data as not available.

References

AMCF (2009). *Operating Rations for Management Consulting Firms*. Association of Management Consulting Firms.

Brett Howell Associates (2009). *Financial Benchmarks: Management Consultants Survey*. BHA.

Chung, E., Herrey, P., and Junco, E. (2008). *Vault Career Guide to Consulting*. Vault.com.

Craig, D., and Brooks, R. (2006), *Plundering the Public Sector*. London: Constable.

IPSOS/MORI (2007). *Paying More and Getting Less: What Clients Think about Consultancy*. Report for Ernst and Young.

Kennedy Information (2002). *The Global Consulting Marketplace: Key Data, Forecasts and Trends*. Fitzwilliam, NH: Kennedy Information Inc.

——(2008). *The Global Consulting Marketplace: Key Data, Forecasts and Trends*. Fitzwilliam, NH: Kennedy Information Inc.

——(2009). *The Global Consulting Marketplace: Key Data, Forecasts and Trends*. Fitzwilliam, NH: Kennedy Information Inc.

Kieser, A. (1997). Rhetoric and Myth in Management Fashion. *Organization*, 4 (1): 49–74.

Kiln, M. (2005). *House of Lies: How Management Consultants Steal your Watch then Tell you the Time*. New York: Imported Little.

National Audit Office (2006). *Central Government's Use of Consultants*. 13 December.

Newell, S., Swan, J., and Kautz, K. (2001). The Role of Funding Bodies in the Creation and Diffusion of Management Fads and Fashions. *Organization*, 8 (1): 97–120.

O'Mahoney, J. (2007). Disrupting Identity: Trust and Angst in Management Consulting. In S. Bolton (ed.), *Searching for the H in Human Resource Management*. London: Sage.

O'Mahoney, J., Adams, R., Antonacopoulou, E., and Neely, A. (2008). *A Scoping Study of Contemporary and Future Challenges in the UK Management Consulting Industry*. ESRC Business Engagement Project: AIM Research.

Saint-Martin, D. (2004). *Building the New Managerialist State*. Oxford: Oxford University Press.

Sako, M. (2006). Outsourcing and Offshoring: Implications for Productivity of Business Services. *Oxford Review of Economic Policy*, 22 (4).

Wright, C., and Kitay, J. (2004). Spreading the Word: Gurus, Consultants and the Diffusion of the Employee Relations Paradigm in Australia. *Management Learning*, 35: 271–86.

A Positive Force for the Economy

Alan Leaman, Chief Executive of the MCA (Management Consultancies Association), UK

Strength in diversity is a phrase I often use when talking to audiences about the UK management consulting industry. You only need look at the varied membership of the MCA to see what I mean. Under the banner of management consultancy, you will find a rich assortment of different types of company, both large and small.

For purposes of analysis we divide our members into six segments, based on the range of services that companies provide.[1] The history of management consultancy, particularly its links with the IT industry, financial services, accounting, and engineering, has created a fascinating patchwork of firms, all part of the management consulting family but often with distinctive offerings.

So what holds them all together? What do they have in common?

In the MCA, we have defined management consultancy as "the creation of value for organisations through improved performance, achieved by providing objective advice and implementing business solutions". And we have strict membership criteria to ensure that this definition sticks.

The *value* for clients comes in the form of increased business opportunities and performance, improved efficiency, or reduced costs. The return on the investment in consultancy is often difficult to measure precisely—some of it comes in the "soft" form of improved leadership or strategy. And, since consultancies increasingly work in close partnership with their clients, it is often difficult and counter-cultural to try to apportion credit between the two.

At the MCA we are working on ways of calculating the value that is generated for business and the taxpayer by the industry as a whole. It is vital to do so, since the industry has many critics, in the media and elsewhere, but also because clients and decision-makers need to understand better the role that consultancy plays.

---

1   1. Pure management consulting only 2. Management consulting, accounting, tax, and corporate advisory firms. 3. Management and IT consulting firms. 4. Management and engineering consulting firms. 5. Management consulting and outsourcing firms. 6. Combined management consulting, IT systems development and outsourcing/managed services firms.

We know that the vast majority of clients value the contribution of their consultancies—because they report high levels of satisfaction and continue to use them. Our aim is to provide a widely understood measure of that value so that the return is better appreciated.

We emphasise the objective nature of the *advice* that consultants provide because this is one of the essential qualities of the industry. Clients normally look to consultants because they need an outside view or perspective. Equally, they want assurance that the advice is genuinely in their best interests and not influenced by other commercial priorities. The independence and objectivity of management consultancy is key, even if it leads on occasion to consultants having to deliver some unwelcome messages to their clients.

Consultancy is also, of course, about delivery and achievement. The days when consultants would simply analyse a problem, prepare a report, and, perhaps, offer recommendations have largely passed. Clients need *solutions* as well. A consultancy's role is increasingly to see that its recommendations are implemented. Programme and change management skills are much valued. And they often share the risks with their clients through how they are paid for the work, so that there is an explicit shared interest in making sure that the project is a success.

A government-sponsored report recently described the UK management consulting industry as a "world leader".[2] The UK-based industry has a high reputation around the world, and many MCA member companies are significant exporters of consultancy services, winning business abroad worth nearly £1bn in 2008. The industry as a whole generates fee income of around £9bn and employs more than 55,000 people.[3] It has many years of double-digit growth under its belt. Consultancy is an increasingly important part of the UK's professional services sector.

To maintain this position and to grow it further, the industry now needs to build a solid, mature, and popular reputation for quality service and value for money. The MCA is playing a key role here. It is our job, as the representative body for the whole industry, to articulate and communicate the value of consulting and to engage with key audiences on the industry's behalf.

One way we do this is by promoting the contribution that management consultancies can make to public debate on many of the key topics of the day. There are many issues where management consultants have a distinctive and important voice that needs to be heard: how to respond to the economic downturn and prepare for a recovery; environmental sustainability and the threat of climate change; the bonus culture and executive remuneration; the future of public services as public spending constraints tighten; the future of financial services following the credit crunch and the arrival of new forms of regulation. There are many more. In all these cases, I find that management consultants are often leading the policy and operational thinking.

As advocates for high standards of professionalism and integrity, the MCA has also recently launched a Code of Practice for our member companies.[4] Each company must explain how it complies with these principles and is subject to an audit process. Through

---

2   Professional Services Global Competitiveness Group report, March 2009.
3   MCA: A positive voice for the economy, May 2009.
4   www.mca.org.uk/codeofpractice.

this process, we are generating and sharing best practice in the industry. This initiative has been widely welcomed.

Our annual Management Awards and Consultant of the Year Awards[5] celebrate and encourage excellence in the industry. In each, consultants are recognised because their clients really appreciated their work; they went the extra mile and really delivered. These awards give the industry a back catalogue of outstanding work. One of our aims is to ensure that management consultancy continues to attract high-quality and talented recruits to our industry.

It is easy in the busy, competitive, and challenging world of consultancy to forget that every industry is nowadays under far greater scrutiny than ever before. There are more questions and the pressure to provide answers is growing all the time. Companies and whole industries thrive on their reputations as well as the bottom line.

It's one reason why representing the management consultancy industry is such a fascinating job!

---

5   www.mca.org.uk/awards.

PART I

The Descriptive Perspective

2

The Consulting Industry

Chapter Objectives

This chapter provides an overview of the consulting industry. Specifically, you will learn:

- What management consultancy is, and why it exists.

- The history of the consulting industry.

- The institutions of consulting.

- The variation in consulting markets around the world.

The chapter starts with the basics: what consultancy is, its history, and the recent trends in the market. It then moves on to explain why consultancy exists at all, what institutions sustain it, and the main ways in which events like the dotcom crash, the IT boom, and the credit crunch have affected the industry. Finally, the chapter examines consultancy across the world, both in terms of the markets and also how consultancies operate in each region.

■ The Basics of Consultancy

What is Management Consultancy?

The answer to the question above appears, at first glance, to be simple. Surely, management consultancy is where someone is paid to give expert advice on management? This is true, but, as we will discuss later, if this definition was strictly applied then around 50 per cent of people who now describe themselves as management consultants would no longer be classified as such.

The mainstream view of management consultancy is perhaps best summarised by the Management Consultancies Association (MCA):

> The creation of value for organisations, through the application of knowledge, techniques and assets, to improve business performance. This is achieved though the rendering of objective advice and/or the implementation of business solutions.

In this definition, one can identify three sequential steps that consultants could undertake in engaging clients:

- Identifying a problem, e.g. company X's people costs are too high.
- Researching and recommending a solution, e.g. proposing the use of software Y instead of Z.
- Helping implement that solution, e.g. building an IT system to automate the payroll function.

Much of the consultancy work students typically read about is strategy consulting, which is generally concerned with categories 1 and 2. However, unless the student is fortunate enough to work at one of the strategy houses, such as McKinsey's or Bain, the chances are that they will not do the blue-sky visionary work which many associate with the industry.

It is much more likely that a typical graduate will be working on step 3—helping to implement a solution that other people have chosen; for example, redesigning business processes, writing software requirements, or ensuring systems compliance. Indeed, in recent years, some "pure" consulting firms have complained that the definition of consulting is becoming diluted with IT, outsourcing, and tax employees who, they argue, do not "consult" but "do".

Even further away from what some might call "real" advisory consultancy are the big outsourced projects where clients hand over the running of their non-core processes, such as call centres, application hosting, or systems maintenance, to companies like IBM and Accenture to run on a permanent basis. These are not consultancy services themselves but are often run by consultancy companies who perform both the advice on how to structure the solution and implement the solution itself.

Figure 2.1 illustrates the different types of consulting and where the boundaries are drawn by the MCA.

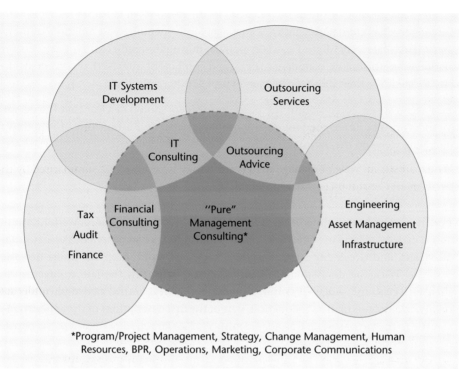

*Program/Project Management, Strategy, Change Management, Human
Resources, BPR, Operations, Marketing, Corporate Communications

Figure 2.1. Boundaries of management consulting
Source: Czarniawaska 2007.

The MCA's definition of consultancy is one that rests upon emphasising the consultant's utility to the client and is, therefore, a highly managerialist account. It is also important to bear in mind that the manager's perspective is not the only one. As we shall discuss further in Chapter 8, there are many other depictions which portray consultants as:

- Political agents: from this perspective, consultants are seen as actors that shape and institutionalise agendas and discourses. The role of consultants in bypassing the civil service in the UK to promote new forms of management is an example of such activity which is explored later (Saint-Martin 1998).

- Fashionistas: in the academic literature, consultants are seen as central to the creation and dissemination of management fashions. This view emphasises the ideas that are generated, the networks through which they are spread, and the interactions with clients that make them receptive to fashionable ideas (Abrahamson 1996; Kieser 1997).

- Missionaries for capitalism: in this view, consultants are seen as part of a wider neo-liberal agenda of "financialisation" in which free trade, privatisation, and re-regulation are imposed upon developing countries. Analysts point to numbers of consultants that work on such projects as part of government aid and World Bank interventions where support is linked to the deregulation of local economies (McDonald and Ruiters 2005; EAC 2006).

- Fraudsters: in some of the more populist critical accounts of consultants, consultants are depicted as charlatans that trick managers into spending vast amounts of money on advice that rarely works. Especially popular during the credit crunch, such accounts emphasised the bribes, confidence tricks, and conflicts of interest that consultants foster to maximise their income (Craig and Brooks 2006; Craig 2005).

These views are explored later in the book, but readers should be clear that the perspective that consultants are good for organisational effectiveness is only one of a number of competing views on the industry.

The History of Consulting

There has never been a time in recorded history when the rich and powerful have not needed expert advisers of some description. Biblical kings had prophets, Persian sultans had viziers, and Greek city states had the Oracle at Delphi. Even the Mafia had their *consigliere*. With the development of industrial capitalism in the late eighteenth and nineteenth centuries, a new class of wealthy factory owners needed advice on how best to organise the systems of mass production. One of the first descriptions of the application of expertise to the factor system was Adam Smith's (1776) famous description of the benefits of specialisation in a pin factory:

> But in the way in which this business is now carried on ... divided into a number of branches ... One man draws out the wire, another straights it, a third cuts it, a fourth points it, a fifth grinds it at the top for receiving the head; to make the head requires two or three distinct operations ... in this manner, divided into about eighteen distinct operations ... I have seen a small manufactory of this kind where ten men only were employed ... they could, when they exerted themselves, make among them about twelve pounds of pins in a day.

The massive increase in demand for industrial products from both a growing middle class and increasingly militarised governments required factories to sustain hundredfold increases in production capacity (Hobsbawm 2002). This in turn required a transformation in both the machinery and the organisation of enterprises that necessitated skills which neither factory owners nor their recently urbanised workers possessed. Instead, owners turned to a growing group of industrial engineers who had developed methods for measuring and improving the efficiency of production systems.

This group, which included pioneers such as Charles Babbage (1792–1871) and Frederick Taylor (1856–1915), focused on the standardisation, measurement, and specialisation of tasks that became known as "scientific management". Companies throughout the USA, Europe, and especially Russia paid considerable sums to firms which would provide teams of engineers both to measure existing practices and to implement the new systems. Such firms were often accounting or engineering firms that used their contacts to sell a new range of management products that made the most of their existing numerical and audit skills (McKenna 2006).

The (considerable) fortunes of the management consultancy industry in the twentieth century are traceable not simply to the growth of large, industrialised corporations but also to the strategic alignment with financial and banking institutions. In the first US firms, consultancies aligned themselves with the more established professions of law, accountancy, and engineering in order to gain credibility. By 1929, there were enough firms to create the first US association, the Association of Consulting Management Engineers (ACME).

The growth of the industry also reflected the legal and economic interventions by governments. For example, the Glass–Stegall Banking Act of 1933 prevented banks from engaging in non-banking activities (including management consultancy) and, therefore, provided a significant spurt of growth to the industry. In their early alignment with banks, financiers, and accounting firms, pure consultancy firms such as AD Little, McKinseys, and Booz gained a strategic advantage enabling them to win exclusive access to significant financial backing and large clients. The crucial importance of this alignment with the finance industry was repeated in the 1960s when the development of consultancy practices by the large accountancy firms (Andersen, PWC, Deloitte, and Ernst and Young) provided a strategic advantage given that such firms had already developed relationships at senior levels with client organisations. This early alignment of consultancies with the financial elite, to some extent, created a barrier to entry for firms that sought to compete with them. To this day, there are few consultancies that have broken the grip of the strategy and audit firms on the board-level relationships that they have monopolised for over fifty years.

During the Second World War, governments actively encouraged the use of consultants to spread effective ideas to the armament and other industries, for example, by exempting consultants from national service (Kipping and Saint Martin 2005). The expansion of consultancies in the post-war era led to the creation of industry bodies to certify consultants, provide best-practice guidance, and advise on ethics. These were known, in both the USA and Europe, as the Institutes of Management Consultancy. These institutes not only acted as lobbying bodies but also as a quality control mechanism refusing membership to consultants which failed to meet their stringent criteria. In both the USA and Europe, there was a growing distinction between the trade associations responsible for representing and promoting consultancy firms and those institutes which sought to certify and register consultants whilst promoting best practice (Curnow and Reuvid 2003). As we shall discuss in Chapter 9, the increasing influence and wealth of consultancies prompted many institutes to call for the compulsory registration and certification of consultants—a call which governments and consultancies have successfully resisted to the present day.

Consultancy 1990–2010

The Growth of the Profession

Until 2009, the consultancy industry had been one of the fastest growing professions, exploding from revenues of $3bn in 1980 to $330bn in 2008 (Kennedy Information 2009). This growth, which has averaged around 10 per cent per annum has been driven by growing demand in the government and finance sectors, exponential growth in demand for IT services, and an unprecedented level of merger and acquisition activity: all areas which require consulting expertise.

These revenues are made up of different consulting services that are offered to clients which are summarised in Table 2.1. From this table you can see that IT Consulting

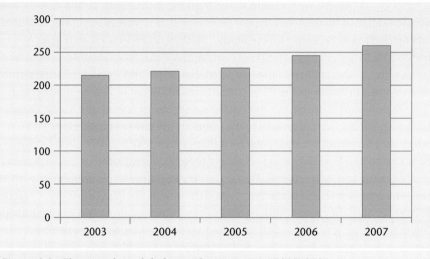

Figure 2.2. The growth in global consulting revenues 2003–2007
Source: Datamonitor (2008).

is now the largest market for consulting companies. It should be noted, however, that this work is mostly IT development (designing, implementing, and integrating new systems) rather than providing strategic advice. Business Advisory Services are usually associated with quantitative analyses such as those found in financial, tax, and decision-making consultancy as are commonly found in audit consultancies such as KPMG and PWC.

Unsurprisingly, given the size of the US and Canadian economies, North America accounts for almost half of the revenue generated from consultancy services, whilst Europe, the Middle East, and Africa (EMEA) lag behind with a just over a third and Asia/Pacific bring in only 11 per cent.

Whilst spectacular, the growth of the industry has not been continuous and, specifically, two major events in 2001–2 and 2009–10 revealed the fragile and highly dependent nature of consultancy profits: the dotcom crash and the credit crunch.

Information Technology Consulting	152.8
Business Advisory Services	86.5
Operations Management Consulting	48.7
Strategy Consulting	27.6
Human Resources Consulting	15.1

Table 2.1. Global consulting service revenues $bn (2008)

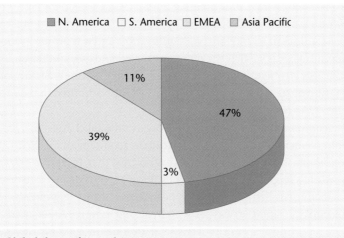

Figure 2.3. Global share of consulting revenues
Source: Kennedy Information 2009.

The Dotcom Crash

In 2000–1 the dotcom bubble finally burst. After years of betting venture capital on the promise of the internet, investors finally realised what many entrepreneurs had already grasped—that there was little reality behind the hype and cut back spending. In 2002, the global consulting industry experienced its first year of revenue reduction after a decade of double-digit growth. To decrease margins and mirror declining demand, consultancies all over the world sacked large numbers of their consultants. Many of these consultants went on to found their own niche consultancies when the economy picked up in 2002. Others jumped ship to join clients, either to set up internal consultancies or to help these companies batter down their consultancy costs.

To make the situation more complex, the collapse in share prices in this period exposed a number of financial scandals where banks, auditors, and consultancies had failed to report, and sometimes encouraged, corrupt financial systems. The fallout forced many auditors (who had not already done so) to divest their consulting arms, led to the introduction of the Sarbanes–Oxley Act, designed to prevent financial mismanagement, and did considerable damage to the reputation of the auditing and consultancy industries (Czerniawska 2007).

However, whilst several companies went bankrupt during this period and there was considerable restructuring, the effects of the crash were not devastating. Growth in the industry slowed rather than reversed, dropping from a massive 17 per cent in 2001 to a relatively paltry 4 per cent in 2002 (Kennedy Information 2004; FEACO 2003; MCA 2003). For an actual reverse in the fortunes of the industry, commentators had to wait only another seven years.

The Credit Crunch

In the 2008–10 recession, consultancies were hit hard by clients cutting back their consulting spend as available credit withered and consumer demand plummeted. Most consultancies made redundancies: Monitor, for example, announced a 20 per cent reduction in its staffing level in September 2008, and KPMG encouraged its staff to take a four-day week or take a short break on 30 per cent pay rather than make redundancies (BBC 2009). Recruitment in 2009 shrunk significantly, and was primarily focused on experienced hires in key areas such as the public sector, oil and gas, and telecoms. In addition, bonuses were also affected. Bain & Co delayed partner bonuses, McKinsey & Company rolled over a third of 2008 bonuses to 2009, and BCG also admitted that partner remuneration had fallen (*The Times* 2009).

As global economic activity in the form of organisational change, mergers, and acquisitions and IT implementation reduced, so too did the requirement for expert advice in these areas. The economic shock to consultancies was so great that, in April 2009, Kennedy Information, the world's largest researcher of consultancy trends, issued a reforecast for global revenues, predicting the first slump in income in recent history (Figure 2.4). The downturn, Kennedy Information reported, was particularly strong in North America and Europe, both of which were reporting a 9 per cent decrease in revenues in 2009, whilst Asia, still buoyed by the growth in China, expected a 3 per cent increase in consulting revenues.

The recession also hit different consulting services in different ways. Particularly badly affected were strategy, operations management, and IT consulting, which are often driven by merger and acquisition work. However, services such as HR advice and process re-engineering were less severely affected as these areas often receive a boost in a recession as clients seek advice on making redundancies and cutting costs.

The New Face of Consultancy?

Consultancy is a highly reactive industry and in the last ten years it has had much to react to. In 2008, I undertook a project (O'Mahoney et al. 2008) which asked partners, directors, and other stakeholders in the consultancy industry what they thought the

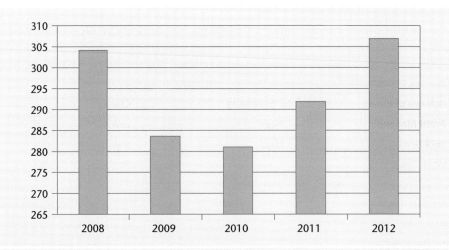

Figure 2.4. The forecast impact of the credit crunch on consulting revenues ($bn)
Source: Kennedy Information Reforecast 2009.

main challenges facing the industry were and how these would change the industry. One of the main findings from the interviews was a move away from blue-sky strategy work where consultants had considerable freedom to innovate towards a more controlled, standardised, and bureaucratic form of work where the client calls the shots. The two strategies have been fairly well defined in consultancies for some time as Personalised approaches where customisation, personalisation, and expertise are dominant, and Codified approaches where commodification, standardisation, and IT systems are dominant (Hansen et al. 1999). These will be discussed further in Chapter 7, but for the time being it should be noted that there appears to be a growing shift between the two types of consulting work (see Table 2.2).

A typical Personalised project would be a short piece of strategy work, perhaps advising a client on the benefits of launching their product in South America. The buyer, often a director who pays for the consultancy from his or her discretionary budget, might have little skill in market assessments or knowledge of South America which gives the consultancy more power in negotiations. Whilst the project may be relatively short, and require only a handful of consultants, it requires considerable skill and knowledge, and consultants with a great degree of flexibility, innovation, and creativity. The charge per hour for this type of work is typically high.

Conversely, a typical Codified project might be a systems integration project in a large company. Here, the client may have already defined the project they require and roughly how much they wish to spend. The recruitment of the consultancy will be a formal process controlled by the procurement department who will compare different consultancies and negotiate costs down. The project will typically last several months and employ dozens of consultants. However, as the work is relatively standardised and commodified, the levels of skill involved are quite low.

	Personalised	Codified
Focus	Strategy	Implementation
Level of Innovation	High	Low
Balance of Power	Consultancy	Client
Profit Margins	High	Low
Skill Level	High	Low
Work Type	Creative	Bureaucratic
Length of Project	Short	Long
Number of Consultants	Few	Many
Client Buyer	Director/Manager	Procurement
Selection Basis	Personal Relationship	Formal Selection

Table 2.2. Personalised and Codified consultancy work

The shift from Personalised to Codified work is the result of three interrelated trends in the consulting market. These are: the rise of IT and outsourcing work, the growing sophistication of client procurement, and the shift from private partnerships to public organisations. These are dealt with, in turn, below.

The IT Market and Outsourcing

Whilst e-business fell temporarily out of favour in 2000–1, the general trend of using developments in IT to cut costs and improve efficiency has continued its growth from the early twentieth century to the present day. The ability of e-commerce, e-business, data-mining, and Enterprise Resource Planning (ERP) to significantly reduce headcount and improve efficiency has offered consultancy an unparalleled opportunity to sell new products to clients. Although "pure" IT start-up consultancies such as Sapient, Razorfish, Scient, and Viant were amongst the first to actively specialise in IT transformation in the late 1990s, the Big Four soon realised that they needed to move into this area. Their opportunity came in 2001 when the dotcom crash decimated the start-up market and bigger players were able to buy up much of what remained.

Systems such as ERP are now relatively standardised products and, combined with educated overseas labour and improvements in communications technology, have encouraged many companies to outsource their non-core services to BRIC countries (Brazil, Russia, India, China). Indeed, as the joint highest revenue earner (with IT) for companies such as Accenture and IBM, recent years would have proved disastrous for many consultancies without large outsourcing projects to maintain their margins.

From its heyday in the late 1990s, the IT market drives much lower margins than it once did, as most systems design, coding, and hosting can be done in BRIC countries and the skills involved are no longer a scarce resource. Most IT work now tends to be a highly standardised and commodified form of organisational change which allows clients easily to compare different consultancy offerings and thus drive down prices. However, despite the lower margins associated with this work, projects are often so large that considerable profits can be made. Projects such as Nestlé's $280m SAP roll-out have made the low margin but high volume IT and outsourcing markets lucrative segments to serve providing one's company has the capital reserves to finance entry into this market.

Client Sophistication

As large consulting projects have become more expensive, clients have become increasingly proactive about managing the processes and costs associated with them. This has occurred in several ways including:

- Using the procurement function to purchase consultancy services. Procurement departments offer a centralised control over purchasing which enables them to ensure that the lowest costs are achieved though bulk buying.

- Recruiting ex-consultants to act as buyers of consultancy services. Ex-consultants are very aware of the complexities, or tricks, in the consultant–client relationship. Thus, the

Firm	Fee income £m	Fee income % change
Accenture	979	15
IBM BCS	753	16
Deloitte	469	16.4
Steria	467	23
PWC	402	39.1
CapGemini	337	5.5
LogicaCMG	310	18
KPMG LLP	274	13
Ernst & Young	254	28
McKinsey & Co	220	18.9
PA Consulting	217	−2.7

Table 2.3. Top consulting firms fee income in 2007
Source: Accountancy Age (2008).

"poacher-turned-gamekeeper" provides clients with "insider" skill and experience when negotiating with consultants.

- Client experience. In the 1980s, few clients had accumulated significant experience in dealing with consultancies. The result was that clients were often unsure about what they really needed and frequently wasted money on unnecessary work. Today, clients tend to have a clearer view of what they require. In the words of one partner I interviewed, "In the old days, clients would come to us asking what they needed to do. Clients now tend to tell consultancies exactly what they need done and the price they will pay for the work."

- Internal consultancies. These are increasingly popular in large firms as a cheaper way of rolling out organisational change and accumulating expertise. Often staffed with ex-consultants, these teams can provide a check, or an alternative, on the work done by external consultants.

Consultants want to avoid the commodification processes that come with procurement because it makes their services easier to compare and drives down costs.

(Analyst, large consultancy)

From Partnership to Public Companies

In his book *The World's Newest Profession* McKenna (2006) shows how the need for a professional identity for consultancies drove the development of the "professional partnership model". Thus, in the 1950s consultancies, especially McKinsey, modelled themselves on law and accountancy firms to boost their own credibility with clients. The partnership model differs from other business models in that:

- The firm is owned by partners rather than external shareholders. This means that there is no board of directors which sits between the interests of the shareholders and the execution of organisational strategy. Instead strategy is decided and implemented by partners who also work as senior consultants, bringing in new business and mentoring younger consultants.

- This form of ownership has implications for the entire strategy and culture of the professional firm. Professional partnerships, in comparison to publicly quoted companies, tend to prioritise values, be less driven by short-term financial gain, have an apprenticeship style of learning, and prioritise personal over technical skills (Greenwood et al. 1990; Richter et al. 2008).

The dominant model of consultancies up until the 1980s, therefore, was the private partnership. However, by 2004, 85 per cent of the largest consultancy partnerships had become publicly traded firms (Adams and Zanzi 2005). Whilst most of the pure strategy firms remain partnerships, the massive growth of consultancies associated with IT and accountancy firms means that the publicly traded firms now dominate revenue generation in the sector. The trend was also exacerbated by the post-Enron spin-off of consultancy arms from accounting firms, the IPO of IT consultancies during the dotcom boom, and the takeover of small partnerships by large firms during periods of economic boom. A final reason for the conversion of partnerships to non-partnerships, provided by Empson (2006), is that increasing levels of litigation made the cost of partnership indemnity insurance prohibitive. However, the evidence for such a statement was not provided.

Whilst the evidence is not conclusive, it appears that pressure to produce short-term shareholder returns in publicly traded companies produces a different type of organisation from that in a private partnership. Greater risks are taken in the pursuit of profit, cultures are more pressurized and competitive, and the strategic horizon is short, rather than long, term (Adams and Zanzi 2005).

The result, then, of the "financialisation" of partnerships, the increasing sophistication of clients, and the rise of large IT and outsourcing projects has been that consultancy work is shifting away from blue-sky strategy work to a more commodified form of implementation where profit margins and skill levels are lower. The corresponding decline in pay and training levels is discussed in greater depth in Chapters 7 and 10.

CASE 2.1

When Definitions Matter

If one examines many of the national associations of management consultancies across the globe, there will usually be a noteable exception to their membership lists. The large strategy consultancies such as McKinsey, Bain & Co, and Boston Consulting

Group are often conspicuous by their absence. At the heart of this lies, according to some reports, a disagreement about what consultancy actually is.

The strategy consultancies were the first consultancies to be established in the world and developed an expertise in providing high-level strategic advice to large organisations. The advice, based on in-depth market research and analysis, still characterises the high-value, strategic work that provides companies like McKinsey with such an elite reputation. Consultancy, in the eyes of these companies, must be advisory, strategic, and board level.

However, if one looks at the definitions used by associations such as the MCA, they often include a phrase such as "the implementation of business solutions". This phrasing means that many companies that do implementation work, such as building IT systems, outsourcing business functions, or structuring finance, can term this work "management consultancy", and appear higher up the lists of "biggest consultancies" that the associations frequently produce.

In an interview with one senior insider, I was told:

> McKinsey and their kind believe that implementation work is not proper consultancy and don't want anything to do with what they perceive to be inferior newcomers such as Accenture, IBM or Cap [Gemini]. It may be a marketing gimmick to emphasise their elite identity of course, but until the associations change their definitions of consultancy, I don't think the strategy consultancies will be applying for membership any time soon.

Out of the following list, what would you categorise as "management consultancy":

* Advising a company on which products it should launch in China.
* Giving a friend advice on their start-up business.
* Designing a customer database system for a bank.
* Running an outsourced IT Support function.

Discuss your answers with a colleague and explain any differences that you have.

■ The Institutions of Consultancy

The consulting profession, like any industry, needs institutions to represent its interests, define best practice, and provide a central point for communications and coordination. Representative bodies are not as strong or as influential as one might expect in consultancy for two reasons. The first is that, unlike many other "expert" sectors, the consulting industry does not have compulsory professional membership. This means that in contrast to lawyers, accountants, or doctors, consultants do not have to be accredited by an external body in order to practise. This, in turn, means that there is no central register of all consultants where policy, rules, and procedures can be specified in exchange for large membership fees. An extended discussion of the implications of this can be found in Chapter 8.

The second reason for the weakness of representative institutions is the power and size of the top consultancies. Consultancy is a top-heavy industry where around the top ten firms account for around 40 per cent of the industry revenue (Kennedy Information 2004). The power and scarcity of these large consultancies puts them in a position where they do not have to rely upon a third party to provide PR, research, benchmarks, or policy advice. This said, there are three types of institutions which should be considered as having some influence on the consulting industry. The first is very specific: the International Council of Management Consulting Institute (ICMCI), which is the consultants' professional body. The second are representative associations such as the MCA and the Association of Management Consultancy Firms (AMCF) which perform (amongst other things) lobbying and publicity services for the industry. Finally, and possibly most importantly, are agencies which represent buyers of consultancy services, such as procurement associations.

Professional Institutes

The ICMCI is the professional body which has charged itself with providing standards for management consultants at a global level. The ICMCI provides an umbrella organisation for the national bodies that respresent consultants and, in total, represents about 30,000 consultants worldwide, which accounts for approximately 2 per cent of all potential members. The body provides a minimum standard for national institutes wishing to join and be accredited. National institutes are then responsible for the recruitment, administration, and accreditation processes. In the UK, this body is the Institute of Business Consulting (IBC), and in the USA it is the Institute of Management Consultants (IMC).

Whilst it is not necessary to have certification to practise as a management consultant, should a consultant wish to be accredited by their national body, it will provide a certification processes which promotes ethical standards and best practice. National associations also tend to provide members access to training courses, online information, and networking events. Increasingly, in a bid to maximise their membership, the national professional bodies for consultancy are letting large consultancies accredit their own staff and focusing their attentions at the level of the firm rather than the individual.

However, whilst the promotion of best-practice and ethical standards in consulting is doubtless a positive exercise, accreditation bodies face a challenge: membership of the national institutes tend to be individuals who are in small businesses or sole-trader consultants, seeking credibility through a larger brand. Consultants who are employed by large consultancies generally don't bother seeking accreditation as their employer provides all the brand they need. The pros and cons of professionalisation are discussed later in Chapter 8.

Professionalisation is a hot topic at the moment. Some people see compulsary professional accreditation as the only way to make consultancy ethical.

(Owner, small consultancy)

Trade Associations

Whilst professional institutes have, at their core, a desire to promote and communicate professional standards for the consultancy profession, the trade associations seek to represent the interests of the consulting industry through lobbying, research, and publicity. In the USA this is the AMCF and in the UK it is the MCA. Additionally, the Federation of Management Consultancy Associations (FEACO) represents around fourteen European countries' associations. These institutions tend to represent larger consultancies and spend a lot of their energy giving the consulting industry a voice in the press. In addition, these institutions often produce useful surveys, such as the AMCF's Operating Ratio report, the MCA's Industry Report, and FEACO's European Consultancy Market survey.

The membership of these associations tends to be larger than professional body institutions, but this is often because membership is at an organisational level and automatically granted to all consultants in that organisation whether they want it or not. Thus, the MCA's claim to represent over 70 per cent of the consulting sector relates only to organisations employing over ten full-time consultants and not, like the IBC, to individual consultants who have personally signed up.

Procurement Institutions

As government spending on consultancies has increased, public organisations have come under increasing pressure from central governments to apply procurement processes to the recruitment of consulting services in a bid to centralise buying and cut costs. In the USA, these are the Procurement Strategy Council (PSC), the Federal Acquisition Institute (FAI), and the Office of Federal Procurement Policy (OFPP), whilst in the UK they are the OGC (Office of Government Commerce) and the Chartered Institute for Purchasing and Supply (CIPS).

This effort has included the production of best-practice guidelines, providing procurement consultancy to the public sector, promoting professional standards in procurers, and providing capability reviews for pubic organisations. The OGC, for example, works with British government departments and with the IBC to produce best-practice guidelines and collaborative groups aimed at clarifying procurement processes.

However, as we shall discuss in Chapter 4, the procurement of consulting services is a very different matter from the traditional markets for procurers such as raw materials, office supplies, and IT equipment. Consultancy services are much harder to compare than, say, pens or paperclips, and the procurer will rarely be in the position to best judge which consultancy is best placed to deliver quality services. For this reason, procurement institutions generally recommend a process that works closely with the actual manager (end user) that is purchasing the services.

CASE 2.2

The German Legal Challenge

In Germany, the professional association for management consultants is called the BDU. Whilst it only represented around 0.4 per cent of consultants, the size of its member firms meant that this accounted for 23 per cent of German consultants.

After the reunification of Germany in 1989, many people set themselves up as consultants to sell advice on privatisation and competition to East German companies with very varied results. This prompted the BDU to campaign for compulsary professionalisation of consultants with formal examinations and registration.

However, in 1997, the request for such a law was rejected by the Minister for Economic Affairs. The reasons given for this decision were threefold. First, that it would unfairly restrict the choices of businesses in who they select as advisers. Second, that this would unfairly restrict the ability of German consultants to sell their skills abroad. Finally, that the law was unnecessary as consultancies used their reputations as guarantors of their quality instead.

Should governments play a role in regulating professions? Why?

Sources: Groß and Kieser (2006); Groß (2009).

■ Why Do Consultancies Exist?

One question which many people fail to ask when studying consultancy is why we need consultants at all. After all, capitalism managed quite well without consultants for a number of centuries. Moreover, outside the USA and northern Europe, consultants are used a lot less. In short, there are a number of factors that influence the ways and number of times that consultants are used. Some of these are outlined below.

Because They Do Things Clients Can't . . .

The standard answer given to the question "why do clients use consultants?" is "to perform some work that the client does not have the skills to do" (e.g. Czerniawska 2002). For example, there is no reason why a firm of accountants will have an expertise in IT; therefore, they are likely to turn to external experts to install and manage their software. Consultants perform all kinds of activities, most of which are described in Chapter 3 and Chapter 5, but, generally speaking, clients look to consultants to give them advice, solve problems, and improve the company. Consultants can do this because, over the years, they develop specialist skills and knowledge by doing things frequently that clients do only rarely (Armbrüster 2006). In a 2006 Management Consultancy Association survey 66 per cent of clients stated that they recruited consultants because their own staff didn't possess the necessary skills. Other high-ranking answers included: to provide original thinking (45 per cent), to get an objective perspective (34 per cent), to fill in for management (17 per cent), to gain access to a methodology (17 per cent), and to validate an internal decision (10 per cent).

In another, differently phrased survey by IPSOS/MORI (Czerniawska 2007) for the MCA, the findings show that, when they select consultants, clients most valued: objective advice (84 per cent), tailored solutions (81 per cent), and close working relationships (78 per cent). They least valued global expertise (44 per cent), the ability to work with other providers (51 per cent), and in-depth sector knowledge (63 per cent). This points to a slightly different area that consultants can help with: providing clients with objective advice. This, as McKenna (2006) points out, has always been an important, if dangerous, feature in the development of management consultancies:

During the 1930s boards of directors shrewdly marshalled the legitimacy of professional opinion, in part through the use of management consultants, to reduce their potential liability in the face of increased regulation . . . The worldwide scandals in corporate governance culminating in the failures of Enron, WorldCom and Parmalat, were a consequence of two decades of surging demand for accounting and consulting services by directors and officers attempting to offset corporate liability for potential managerial malfeasance.

Where management consultants had previously proposed a suggested course of action to be ratified by independent board members the tables were turned during the 1990s when consultants, in practice, became the independent outsiders who endorsed the "internal" board's previous decisions. Management consulting advice, of course, had always been used as a political tool to legitimate executive decisions, but, beginning in the late 1980s, consultants' role in conferring legitimacy began to be more openly employed as a legal hedge against corporate liability. (McKenna 2006: 183)

Whilst useful, the method of asking clients why they recruit consultants is not necessarily going to attain accurate answers. Managers are unlikely to admit, for example, that they recruited consultants to sack people or because they wanted to boost their own internal profile. Whilst it is true that individual managers do, obviously, make decisions about consultants based upon the work that is required, this is only a small part of the logic by which consultants are recruited. The survey and the responses by managers necessarily leave a number of questions unanswered, such as:

- Why do some firms seek to use internal, rather than external, consultants (or vice versa)?
- Why has the use of consultants increased over the years?
- Why are consultants more popular in particular sectors, markets, and countries rather than others?
- What role does history, culture, and psychology play in the selection of consultants?

These and other questions point to the fact that too often, studies focus on the logic of the individual manager that recruits the consultant. The "buyer of consulting services has been more or less explicitly pictured as an individual manager and it has been his/her needs ... that have been in focus as reasons for hiring consultants" (Werr 2005: 93). As well as focusing on the individual manager, an adequate understanding of consultant selection also needs to consider different levels of analysis. This will involve an appreciation of the psychological, sociological, institutional, and organisational processes which underpin the decision to buy.

The sections below examine complementary, yet differing explanations which help us understand more fully why consultants are used. First, transaction cost economics helps illustrate how the cost–benefit analysis of using consultants is much more complicated than some might believe. Second, it is argued that, from an organisational perspective, consultancies can provide a "parallel management" function which is central to ongoing organisational change projects. Finally, it is shown that consultants perform a legitimisation role for clients which helps support managerial projects and also managerial identities.

Transaction Cost Economics

As Adam Smith pointed out, if an organisation specialises in one activity, it can achieve economies of scale which enable it to sell its product(s) on at a profit to companies that need that product. It makes sense, for example, for Ferrari to buy in 100,000 tyres from specialist tyre manufacturers that make millions of tyres rather than make them themselves, because they will be cheaper and better quality from someone who mass-produces them.

As knowledge has become an important commodity in the last fifty years, organisations often require expert knowledge for short periods of time (for example, in creating a strategy or implementing a change). Given the cost of expert labour in developed countries, it often makes sense for these companies to buy in this labour for short periods rather than employ it full time. Moreover, the specialisation in knowledge that consultancies develop (though R&D, training, and experience) means that their "knowledge" products remain up to date and well tested, whereas a full-time employee in a client organisation would not receive such benefits. Thus, McKenna argues:

> within the transaction cost framework, an executive decision on the margin to purchase advice from a consultant is no more outlandish than the decision to purchase machine tools rather than fabricate them internally. (2006: 10)

In his excellent book *The Economics and Sociology of Management Consulting*, Armbrüster (2006) shows that there is a comparison of costs that clients consider when deciding whether to develop skills in-house or to look externally for consultants. These are represented in Table 2.4.

This comparison, Armbrüster argues, will then need to be scaled according to three factors:

• How often the project/task will occur: if a task happens frequently it is likely that the accumulation of fees will make the external consultancy more expensive than the in-house version. The induction process for a new employee, for example, is likely to happen frequently, and is, therefore, likely to be done in-house.

In-house costs	External costs
Hiring new personnel	Fees
Training staff	Searching for consulting firms
Labour costs	Assessing their competencies
Reallocating tasks	Selecting between firms
Monitoring staff	Negotiating, contract drafting
Researching project	Monitoring consultants
	Reinforcing the contract

Table 2.4. A comparison of in-house versus external consultancy costs

- The assets required: assets required for a project may be specialised and costly (for example, implementing an ERP system may require specialised software for development and testing), whilst other assets (for example for customer service training) may be relatively inexpensive and generalised. The cheaper and less specialised the assets, the more likely they are to be found or bought in-house.

- The commodification of the project: this concerns the extent to which a task can be measured and controlled. "The higher the uncertainty of a task the more likely that an in-house solution will be more efficient" (Armbrüster 2006: 47).

There is another, related, factor which Armbrüster does not consider, which should be added to the list:

- The client specificity of the task/project: this concerns the extent to which the task relies on tacit, or hard-to-transfer, client knowledge. For example, an induction process will often be done in-house because the knowledge necessary to do this effectively is often tacit and extremely changeable, thus not particularly open to transfer.

These factors, then, will either encourage a client to develop an in-house capacity for dealing with a task or will drive them to seek expertise outside the organisation. If the project, for example, is a one-off requiring specialised knowledge or technology that is quantifiable (for example reducing 15 per cent headcount through automation) it is likely that a client will turn to external sources. If, however, the project is repeated frequently in the organisation and requires little specialist knowledge (for example, conducting an appraisal) then this is likely to remain in-house.

From a transaction cost perspective, consultancies offer a client certain advantages. As consultancies will repeatedly experience problems that clients will rarely encounter, they build up an expertise in their methods and tools which allows them to offer both economies of scale and economies of scope. The former refers to unit prices becoming cheaper when one activity is repeated. For example, Accenture will be able to license software for systems integration more cheaply than an SME manufacturing company because it will sell so many more of them. The latter refers to services becoming cheaper when several services are offered together and have overlapping economies. For example, consultancies offering BPR, ERP, and automation services will find an overlap of people, skills, and assets, which saves money and time. These savings would not be available to a client who opted to conduct only one of these services in-house. One reason, then, why consultancies are more prevalent in developed economies, such as the USA and Western Europe, is that there are millions of similar projects which allow consultancies to build up economies of scale and scope which simply may not be possible in countries with fewer developed businesses.

Economic Development and Specialisation

Development is a tricky concept as there are many different ways in which an economy can develop. In capitalist economies, the most developed economies are generally those with low levels of agricultural and manufacturing industries and high levels of service industries (such as banking, insurance, and IT) and knowledge workers. There are three main reasons why these types of organisation are more likely to spend on consultancies:

1. They have more money. Profit margins in high-end service sectors such as banking, insurance, and telecoms tend to be high so companies can afford expensive consultancies. Moreover, in the West, these profits tend to be in dollars, pounds, or euros: strong currencies which will buy in expensive consultancies. An operation in Yemen may well be relatively profitable, but paying for McKinseys in riyal might prove prohibitive in most cases.

2. They possess economies of scale. Highly developed economies *tend* to be the home of the largest companies, with few companies outside the USA, Japan, or Europe making it into the Fortune 100. These large companies depend heavily on economies of scale. Thus, if a management consultancy can make just a 1 per cent change to the company's profits, this would amount to several extra billion being posted onto the balance sheets.

3. They have the type of operations that are susceptible to new ways of working. In the banking sector, for example, some organisations, such as the online banks, have managed to move virtually all of their operations online, drastically cutting costs and improving profits. The same is true of insurance companies, virtual mobile operators, and many other businesses.

National Culture

National cultures play an important part in deciding where a CEO will look for advice. As Hofstede (2001) noticed, some countries have cultures which are more collective and less individualistic. These cultures tend to have strong regional, family, and institutional ties which permeate business activities and thus incline decision-makers to turn to their personal network before turning to outside experts. In a recent comparison of EU countries, Crouch et al. (2004) found that countries with higher collective cultures such as Italy and France were more likely to use their strong personal networks for support than more individualistic countries like Germany and the UK that tend to prefer the more formal relationships that consultancies offer.

Furthermore, several countries have cultures and organisations which are more amenable to participative decision-making and therefore may aim to solve problems in-house before turning to an outsider. One may find, for example, that organisations possessing highly trained workers, high trade union involvement, and a participative style of management, such as Sweden, Norway, Denmark, and the Netherlands, rely less on management consultants than countries which have a low-skilled workforce and weak participative management styles such as the USA and the UK.

Political and Economic Ideologies

Linked closely to national culture is the prevailing economic ideology. Economic ideologies, even within a capitalist system, range considerably from relatively neo-liberal economies, such as the USA and the UK, to the north European social democracies, to various forms of market socialism as found in parts of Asia. For the purposes of our discussion, it should be noted that countries with a form of neo-liberalism tend to be more likely to use management consultants. Of course, there are always exceptions, as indeed there should be, to such sweeping generalisations, but there are several reasons to at least postulate a correlation between neo-liberal economies and the use of consultants:

1. Corporate freedom: under neo-liberal governance, organisations are freer to make the decisions they wish, providing these are in the interests of their shareholders. Unions, works councils, governments, and the public in general have few powers of restraint, leaving companies free to engage in mergers, acquisitions, delayering, and any number of other strategies which routinely involve consultants.

2. Privatisation: neo-liberal policies encourage governments to privatise state assets and utilities, policies which routinely involve the use of consultants. A clear example of this is where the World Bank, and Western governments, link financial rescue packages for poor countries to the privatisation of those countries' resources—often recommending the use of consultancies which specialise in these activities.

3. Entrepreneurship: relatively unfettered procedures for start-up companies mean that countries such as the UK and the USA have much higher start-up levels than countries such as Greece or Spain which have quite bureaucratic hurdles in the way of potential entrepreneurs. Entrepreneur-friendly policies not only provide consultancies with a large constantly regenerating market but also enable small consultancies themselves to start up, grow, and adapt quickly to new market conditions.

4. New business models: countries with neo-liberal policies tend to be first to innovate with new business models. New models in 3G telecoms, financial institutions, and e-business were pioneered in the liberal democracies. This not only provides a market for consultancies, but also allows them to create "centres of expertise" which they can then use to spread those innovations around the world.

Government Legislative Institutions

The legal and political framework which envelops consulting practice makes a significant difference to the rates at which the industry expands and contracts. Such direction is occasionally the result of direct legislation. For example, in McKenna's account of the history of management consultancy, he outlines the Glass–Stegall Banking Act of 1933, which prevented banks from engaging in non-banking activities (including management consultancy) and, therefore, provided a significant spurt of growth to the consulting industry. In more recent years, the Sarbanes–Oxley Act (2002) provided management consultants with a vast new market for business process work. Direction also comes from government bodies such as the Securities and Exchange Commission (SEC) in the USA or the Financial Services Authority (FSA) which both successfully put pressure on audit firms to divest their consulting arms in the period 1999–2001.

It is perhaps the *lack* of regulation, however, that makes the most difference to the consulting world. Despite several high-profile scandals in 2001–2, the consultancy industry remains one of the few advisory professions which is still relatively free from institutional constraints. For example, anyone can call themselves a consultant: there are no compulsory exams, qualifications, or procedures that enable access to the profession, nor is there a comprehensive governing body which can strike off unethical individuals or regulate the industry.

Despite the apparent lack of legislative bite the government possesses, it holds considerable sway over consultancies through its power as a buyer of consulting services. Globally, governments account for around 25 per cent of the consultancy market (Kennedy Information 2008), even more if healthcare and defence are added in. This tremendous buying power means that governments can dictate terms to many consultancies in how they bid for business, audit their projects, communicate with public sector clients, and evaluate their successes. Moreover, as governments increasingly use procurement departments to manage the central purchasing of consultancy services, institutions such as the Office of Federal Procurement Policy (OFPP) and the Office of Government Commerce (OGC) increasingly have the purchasing power, not just to drive down costs, but also to impose regulations, processes, and conditions on the suppliers of consulting services.

Labour Markets

The final structural influence on the use, or growth, of consultancies is the types and structure of labour that are available for consultancies to draw on. For advisory consultancy work, for example, in strategy consulting, consultancies draw on highly educated individuals, often from the top business schools. For experienced hires, they look to those who have had cutting-edge experience, preferably in leading blue-chip companies or in other centres of excellence. Until recently, this has meant that recruitment for companies such as McKinsey and Bain & Co came from the top business schools in the West or the Fortune 100, which are predominantly Western companies. For Armbrüster this method of recruitment is as important in what it signals to the market as it is in the quality of labour that is actually recruited:

> management consulting firms signal output quality by input quality ... [they] hire from the most renowned universities and actually obtain better graduates than from other universities, again irrespective of proven educational quality. By hiring from these universities, the renowned consulting firms signal high output quality, can charge higher fees to their clients, and thus can offer higher salaries to their graduates. (2006: 11)

In other words, *even if* Western universities like Harvard, Oxford, or the Sorbonne did not have superior educational training, the fact that they are perceived to do so by stakeholders would mean that consultancies would still have a vested interest in recruiting from them.

Conversely, labour markets where skills are high and labour is cheap, such as India, have traditionally offered consultancies an opportunity for outsourcing or body-shopping, especially when the consultancy has significant operations in both industries. Accenture and

IBM provide good examples. As we will discuss later in the book, changes to countries like India have shifted this model somewhat, but it is true that niche Western labour markets, whether through quality or reputation, still support the development of consultancies better than many other areas of the world.

Legitimisation and Identity

So far, we have examined the economic benefits of using consultants. From this perspective, whilst accepting that the cost–benefit analysis may be relatively complicated, the contribution of consultants is analysed with reference to the balance sheet of the organisation. However, several writers have argued that consultants also offer managers legitimisation for both their ideas and their identities. These arguments will be considered in turn below.

It has long been noted in organisational change and product development literature that companies tend to define new ideas as illegitimate because they do not fit with their existing processes and structures. This is especially so if the ideas threaten power relationships within the organisation (Berger and Luckman 1966; Dougherty and Heller 1994; Heusinkfeld and Benders 2005). Considerable legitimisation work, therefore, needs to be undertaken by managers who wish to introduce change into the organisation. Management consultancies, can create this by providing "outsider" validation and support for an idea (Antal and Krebsbach-Gnath 2001), using rhetoric and discourse to create the image of certainty around projects (Whittle 2005), and by providing drive, energy, and manpower to support the project.

The "political" role of consultants is emphasised by another theme in the literature which highlights the ways in which consultancies are used by clients to seize control over a recalcitrant and uncooperative workforce. In their book *Plundering the Public Sector*, Craig and Brooks (2006) show how management consultants were employed by the UK government to bypass traditional decision-making (through civil servants) and force through a number of unpopular changes. In effect, this created what Saint-Martin termed a "consultocracy" (2004: 20): rule at the expense of traditional managers. This political use of consultants is commonplace in management texts where they write of creating a "burning platform" for change. This means using consultants (or other experts) to report a crisis in an organisation which forces employees to embrace change, often in fear of what might happen if they don't (Kelman 2005: 41). If many of the exposés on the consulting world are to be believed, consultants (and managers) are occasionally required by their clients to manipulate figures in order to make a situation seem worse than it actually is, thus justifying radical cost-cutting measures or changing programmes (Craig 2005).

As well as using consultants as "legitimators" for internal ideas, several academics argue that consultants are also used to provide stability and certainty for management identities in client organisations. This theme is covered in more detail in Chapter 8 but the central idea is that management of complex and open organisations is an uncertain and anxiety-inducing experience. The client manager, therefore, experiences insecurity in terms of their knowledge and their own identities (Whittle 2006). The consultant's image as an expert outsider with access to "real" knowledge provides the illusion of support and certainty to managers in confusing and uncertain times. This focus on identity construction cuts both ways, of course, making it important for consultants to construct their own identities as expert and legitimate sources of knowledge (Kitay and Wright 2007).

■ International Perspectives on Consulting

Global consultancy is a business dominated by the big players. The top five consulting firms in the world take 31 per cent of the global revenues, which means these companies have a significant share in all the major markets of the world. Furthermore, as overseas markets expand, their attraction to the consulting industry grows. The biggest US consultancies now receive more than 50 per cent of their income from overseas contracts (Zeithaml and Bitner 1996) and, even amongst the smaller consultancies, a significant proportion of their work is abroad (Bryson et al. 1997). There is anecdotal evidence from research which the author is currently undertaking that internationalisation of consultancy has hastened since 2009 when consultancy markets in Western countries began to stagnate.

> In a recession, consulting is one of sources of expenditure clients seek to cut. The natural response to this is to seek markets abroad where economic conditions are not so severe. At the moment, we're looking to China, South America and the Middle East.
>
> (CEO, medium-sized consultants, USA, 2009)

International Markets for Consultancy

North America

As the birthplace of management consulting and possessing the largest economy in the world, it should be no surprise that the USA has the biggest population of consultants, the largest consultancies, and generates more profit in the consulting sector than any other country. Early in the twentieth century, the USA accounted for three-quarters of global consultancy revenues (Gross and Poor 2008). However, as other economies have developed and created their own centres of expertise, the US share fell steadily to 47 per cent by 2008 (Kennedy Information 2009). The dominance of the US market and the number of home-grown US consultancies means that, to a great extent, the US industry leads and defines what happens in the rest of the world. When put together with Canada (as many industry reports do) the North American region accounts for around half of global revenues (Table 2.5).

As can been seen from Table 2.5, North America leads in most areas of consultancy, though it is especially concentrated in the public sector, especially defence industries, and consumer goods.

In 2008 the consulting industry in the USA comprised 132,000 companies, employing around 789,000 people (Plunkett 2009) and generating around $157bn in revenues (Barnes 2009). The vast majority of these companies (91 per cent) employ less than ten people, whilst the minority (1.8 per cent) employ over 50 people (IBIS 2009).

Sector	N. America	EMEA	Asia Pacific	S. America
Financial Services	47%	20%	15%	3%
Public Sector	58%	19%	14%	1%
Consumer Goods and Retail	50%	12%	15%	1%
Communication and Media	35%	8%	21%	3%
Energy and Utilities	40%	13%	18%	2%
Healthcare	44%	8%	12%	2%

Table 2.5. Regional concentration in client industries
Source: Kennedy Consulting Research & Advisory (2009).

Unfortunately, the global recession hit the USA particularly hard, due to the concentration of the finance industry, leading to a downturn of around 9 per cent in 2009, a much higher decline than Asia or South America. However, for the foreseeable future, the USA seems in no danger of losing its market dominance in the industry.

Europe

The European consulting market was worth $61.6bn in 2006 according to FEACO, around a fifth of the global market. When we talk of Europe as a market or a home for consultancies, the first thing to note is that the distribution in terms of both business opportunities and organisations is heavily skewed towards Western Europe, especially the UK and Germany. Whilst the UK has only recently overtaken Germany in terms of consultancy revenues, it

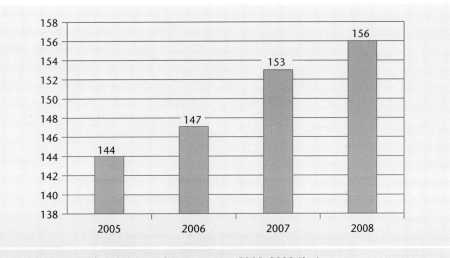

Figure 2.5. Growth in US consulting revenues 2005–2008 ($m)
Source: IBIS (2009).

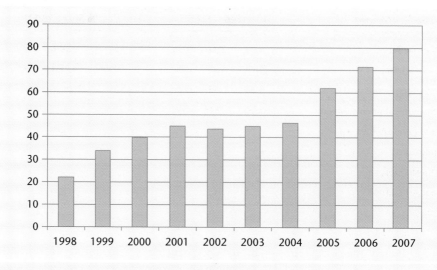

Figure 2.6. Growth in EU consulting revenues (€m)

has traditionally dominated the consultancy industry in Europe as it is home to many of the major consultancies such as KPMG, Deloitte, PWC, and PA Consulting.

The reason for the UK position in the European consulting market is due to the historical strength of ties between the USA and Britain that enabled the transfer of companies, ideas, and people so easily in the first half of the century when consultancy was developing (McKenna 2006). It should also be noted that the British have tended to follow the neo-liberal policies of the USA which appear to encourage the adoption of management innovations and the use of consultants. Finally, the UK has the largest financial sector outside America and therefore possesses a large number of wealthy clients likely to spend heavily on consultants. Given such favourable conditions, it is unsurprising that, until 2008, British consulting companies evidenced double-digit growth for over ten years.

The German economy was hit hard by the integration of East Germany with the West in 1990. However, in recent years, market opportunities, for example around the privatisation of public utilities and the growth in government projects, have offered a number of opportunities for consultancy work to expand.

Whilst northern European countries (Scandinavia, Benelux, Germany) share some similarities with the Anglo-Saxon model of management, supporting highly developed industries, much of the rest of Western Europe rejects the short-termist dominance of the market for cultural or social reasons, or does not possess sufficiently large or developed economies to support significant markets for consultants. Even countries with large GDP such as France or Italy do not possess cultures which encourage large-scale use of management consultants, especially when IT consulting is removed from the equation. As a result, France has around a third of the UK expenditure on business services.

Moving to Eastern Europe and Russia, whilst the market there is still small, it is growing rapidly, especially in outsourcing advice and the deregulation of public utilities. The

Country/region	Fees ($m)	% Share of EU
Germany	23.6	38.6
UK	16.7	27.3
France	5.9	9.6
Spain	2.9	4.7
Scandinavia	2.4	3.9
Italy	2.3	3.7
The Netherlands	2.1	3.5
Eastern Europe	1.6	2.6
Austria	1.5	2.4

Table 2.6. European market for consulting services (2006)

transition from Communism has caused Eastern Europe considerable economic problems both in accessing the business expertise necessary to create high levels of GDP and in terms of creating a market that can afford Western consultancy expertise. However, the developing wealth of specific sectors, such as oil, gas, and utilities, has generated a growing interest in the area from consultancies. According to the Kennedy Institute, the East European market (excluding Russia) accounted for around $4bn in consultancy fees in 2007. Russia, which faces similar economic problems to those in Eastern Europe, grew its consulting market from $650m in 2004 to $2.7bn in 2007 (Step Consulting 2006; www. raexpert.org). This massive increase is partly due to the challenges of modernisation that Russian businesses have faced in the new millennium, but is also due to the growth of a large middle-class consumer market demanding Western forms of goods and services.

Asia

The Asia Pacific and China (APAC) consulting market is the fastest growing in the world and was less affected by the 2008–10 recession than Western countries. Kennedy Information estimates the Asian market will exceed $60bn by 2011. Although Japan is still the largest market for consulting work, India and China are expected to overtake it by 2010. However, the growth of Indian and Chinese economies is now old news and most large consulting firms now have a significant part of their business based there. As a result, competition has intensified and margins are being put under pressure, even in the booming Indian economy.

Recruiting in places like India can no longer be seen as an easy way of recruiting cheap labour or providing body-shopping services. We need these recruits for their skills and their knowledge. It's a strategic choice.

(Director, large outsourcing consultancy)

The Asian, and particularly the Indian, market has traditionally been known for low-skill, low-cost outsourcing and IT deals for consultancies that have tapped into the relatively cheap forms of consulting labour, to offer cut-priced services for Western companies. However, this characterisation is no longer valid. As the Asian economies have matured, there is an increasing home market for strategic and change management offerings which have demanded high-end consulting skills from both Western and home-grown consultancies. This has led, from 2005 onwards, to double-digit growth in strategy, operations management, and HR consultancy, specialisations traditionally associated with higher value advisory work in Western countries.

As companies have grown, both Indian and Chinese clients have moved from questions of internal organisation, such as "How do we manage growth?" or "How do we organise internally?", to a more aggressive, external focus, with questions such as "Which US companies should we take over to best expand internationally?" This is providing a source of growth for those consulting firms interested in the highly lucrative markets of strategy, M&A, and finance consulting. Unsurprisingly, it is the finance industry that can best afford such consulting services, contributing around 40 per cent of consultancy income in Asia.

The expansion of the Asian market, however, has not only been exploited by Western companies. The growth of Asian economies also means that the number and size of home-grown consultancy businesses has likewise developed. Thus, whilst Western MBA graduates have been seeing job offers pulled back and starting salaries slashed, India's top MBAs have seen their starting salaries jump by over 20 per cent each year (MBA Universe 2008). Increasingly, companies set up to take advantage of Indian labour and IT markets have begun to move upstream into the value consultancy market. Thus, Tata Consultancy Services, Infosys Technologies, and Wipro Technologies will, according to a recent report (Gartner 2008), overtake existing giants such as IBM Global Services, Accenture, and EDS by 2011. All three companies have been busy buying up companies in Europe and the USA to aid their reach. Detractors of this growth rightly point out that outside IT and outsourcing, these firms have failed to develop the thought leadership necessary to get a strong place in the high-end consulting market, but with their near-exponential growth and internationalisation, this surely cannot be far off.

The Middle East

The first consultants in the Middle East arrived as colonial advisers who helped local bureaucrats organise their ministries. When independence was achieved, many of the advisers were sought out to help organise work practices in local organisations. There was also considerable exchange of consultants between Arabic countries as the less developed sought to learn from the more developed how best to exploit their natural resources. However, for the most part, advisers on business practices came from the West: in Saudi Arabia, for example, management consultants sponsored by the Ford Foundation led a development project in the 1960s. One of the outcomes of their efforts was the establishment of a Saudi consultancy organisation, the Institute of Public Administration, in Riyadh (Atiyyah 1992, 2009).

Since this period, though, the Middle East has been the fastest growing regional market for management consultancy. This is, however, primarily imported consultancy from the West for the energy and finance markets. Consultancy revenues are especially significant in large economies such as Saudi Arabia, the UAE, Israel, Iran, and Kuwait, as well as those smaller countries which have a large GDP per capita because of their oil and trading positions, such as Qatar, Bahrain, and Oman.

The consultancy boom in these areas has been created by a drive towards modernisation based upon the wealth from oil and tourism. This has driven demand from a number of industries, such as financial services, manufacturing, and defence, to outstrip the supply of skills and expertise from the local populations, offering Western consultancies an opportunity to expand their reach. Many of the services offered by consultancies are driven from financial projects such as privatisation of government-owned utilities, mergers and acquisitions, and tax advice. For this reason, the likes of PWC, KPMG, and Deloitte are dominant players in this region. For more information on some of these states, a good source is PWC's Arab Business Intelligence Report.

A note should also be made about Iraq which has been attracting a growing number of management consultants involved in the reconstruction of the country after the war with the USA and the UK in 2003. As well as specific consultancies involved in security and construction, there are an increasing number of jobs offered in the region to support recruitment, privatisation, and training work. This has tended to be the domain of small, niche consultancies, but as Western markets suffer, it is expected that this will increasingly be of interest to larger players.

■ Chapter Summary

This chapter has provided an overview of the consulting industry, its evolution, structure, and segmentation. It has shown:

- How consultancies grew on the back of a growing industrial sector that required management expertise.
- That, in the last twenty years, the industry has changed in response to economic crises, sophisticated clients, and the development of IT and outsourcing businesses.
- That there are varied and competing explanations for understanding why consultancies exist.
- How different international regions create different markets for consultancies.

Perhaps more than any other industry, management consultancy is defined by its environment. The consulting firms' strategies and fortunes are almost entirely determined by the decisions of the clients, governments, and economies that encapsulate it. For this reason, management consultancy is an exciting yet unpredictable sector to study and work in.

Student Exercise: Design your Own Consultancy

It is July 2011. You and nine of your consulting colleagues in ConsultCo have decided to leave and start up your own management consultancy. You will specialise in data security work for the financial services sector. A non-competition clause between yourselves and your existing employer means that you cannot "poach" any of its clients. A friend of yours who is a director of a large bank has offered you a lucrative contract which you believe will provide enough business to keep ten of you busy for at least six months. You will share the start-up costs between the ten of you which you think you can just about afford.

1   What are the main activities you will engage in as a consultancy? List the five most important activities.

2   What will your main costs be? Estimate these costs.

3   What will your income need to be? How will you ensure this income?

4   A potential investor has offered to put £250,000 into the company. Would you consider their offer? What percentage of the company do you believe would be a fair exchange for this money?

5   What metrics should you use to measure your success?

Optional Question/Assignment:

6   You have decided to accept the potential investor's offer. Create a PowerPoint presentation outlining the key operational features of your company. Ensure you include your main business activities, an organisational chart (including support staff), and your strategy for making money.

Discussion Questions

•   Why has the consulting industry grown so dramatically over the last twenty years?

•   Why do you think the USA, the UK, and Germany have dominated the consulting market for so long?

•   Why is the partnership model under pressure?

•   Do you think the consulting markets will be as big as in fifty years as they are now? Why?

•   What are the pros and cons of being involved in the consulting industry as a new consultant or a partner?

Further Reading

The historical and current structure of the consulting industry has, until recently, been given little attention. The best book on this topic is:

•   McKenna, C. (2006). *The World's Newest Profession: Management Consulting in the Twentieth Century*. Cambridge: Cambridge University Press.

This gives an excellent overview of the industry and the interplay between agency and structure that helped turn it into the beast that it is today.

There are a number of reports which can be purchased to provide up-to-date figures and analysis on the consulting industry. In the UK, the biggest report is the annual *UK Consulting Industry* published jointly by the MCA and PMP. In the USA, Kennedy Information publish a number of reports on the consulting industry both in the USA and globally.

Occasionally, government bodies and NGOs produce reports giving a "state of play" of the consulting industry. The most recent one of these is a report I led for the Advanced Institute of Management (AIM) in 2008 which can be downloaded from the AIM website:

* O'Mahoney, J., Adams, R., Antonocopoulou, E., and Neely, A. (2008). *A Scoping Study of Contemporary and Future Challenges in the UK Management Consulting Industry*.

Other good references that provide an overview of the consulting industry, its evolution, and structures include:

* Aharoni, Y. (1993). *Coalitions and Competition: The Globalisation of Professional Services*. London: Routledge.
* Argyris, C. (2000). *Flawed Advice and the Management Trap*. New York: Oxford University Press.
* Clark, T., and Fincham, R. (2002). *Critical Consulting*. Oxford: Blackwell.
* Crouch, C., Galas, P., Trigilia, C., and Voelzkow, H. (2004). *Changing Governance of Local Economies in Europe*. Oxford: Oxford University Press.
* Hofstede, G. (2001). *Culture's Consequences: Comparing Values, Behaviors, Institutions, and Organizations across Nations*. Thousand Oaks, CA.: Sage Publications.
* Kipping, M., and Engwall, L. (2002). *Management Consulting: Emergence and Dynamics of a Knowledge Industry*. Oxford: Oxford University Press.
* Wood, P. (2001). *Consultancy and Innovation: The Business Service Revolution in Europe*. London: Routledge.

Finally, for a list of the various national councils of management consultancy, one can visit the ICMCI website: www.icmci.org/membership.

References

Abrahamson, E. (1996). Management Fashion. *Academy of Management Review*, 21: 254–85.

Accountancy Age (2008). Long Range Forecast. *Insider Newsletter*.

Adams, S., and Zanzi, A. (2005). The Consulting Career in Transition: From Partnership to Corporate. *Career Development International*, 10 (4): 325–38.

Aharoni, Y. (1993). *Coalitions and Competition: The Globalisation of Professional Services*. London: Routledge.

Antal, A., and Krebsbach-Gnath, C. (2001). Consultants as Agents of Organisational Learning: The Importance of Marginality. In M. Dierkes, A. Berthoin Antal, J. Child, and I. Nonaka (eds), *Handbook of Organizational Learning and Knowledge*. Oxford: Oxford University Press.

Argyris, C. (2000). *Flawed Advice and the Management Trap*. New York: Oxford University Press.

Armbrüster, T. (2006). *The Economics and Sociology of Management Consulting*. Cambridge: Cambridge University Press.

Atiyyah, H. (1992). Research Note. *Research in Arab Countries Organization Studies*, 13 (1): 105–10.

——(2009). Personal communication with author.

Barnes (2009). *US Management Consultancy Services Industry Report*.

BBC (2009). KPMG to Offer Staff Shorter Week. 16 January. www.bbc.co.uk.

Berger, P. L., and Luckmann, T. (1966). *The Social Construction of Reality: A Treatise in the Sociology of Knowledge*. Garden City, NY: Anchor Books.

Bryson, J. R., Keelbe, D., and Wood, P. (1997). The Creation and Growth of Small Business Service Firms in Post-industrial Britain. *Small Business Economics*, 9: 345–60.

Clark, T., and Fincham, R. (2002). *Critical Consulting*. Oxford: Blackwell.

Craig, D. (2005). *Rip Off: The Scandalous Story of the Management Consulting Money Machine*. London: Original Book Company.

——and Brooks, R. (2006). *Plundering the Public Sector*. London: Constable.

Crouch, C., Galas, P., Trigilia, C., and Voelzkow, H. (2004). *Changing Governance of Local Economies in Europe*. Oxford: Oxford University Press.

Curnow, B., and Reuvid, J. (2003). *The International Guide to Management Consultancy*. London: Kogan Page.

Czerniawska, F. (2002). *The Intelligent Client: Managing your Management Consultant*. London: Hodder Arnold.

——(2007). *Paying More and Getting Less*. Ipsos Mori.

Daniels, P. W. (ed.) (2006). *Knowledge-Based Services: Internationalisation and Regional Development*. Aldershot: Ashgate Publishing Ltd.

Datamonitor (2008). *Global Management and Marketing Consultancy*. October.

Dougherty, D., and Heller, T. (1994). The Illegitimacy of Successful Product Innovation in Established Firms. *Organization Science*, 5 (2): 200–18.

EAC (2006). *Trade, Development and Environment: The Role of DFID*. Tenth Report of Session 2005–6. London: Environmental Audit Committee, House of Commons.

Empson, L. (2006). Professionals in Partnership. In J. Craig (ed.), *Futures for Professionalism*. Demos Pamphlet.

FEACO (2003). *Survey of the European Management Consultancy Market*. www.feaco.org.

Gartner (2008). *India-3 are the Emerging Mega-vendors*. 3 July.

Greenwood, R., Hinings, C. R., and Brown, J. (1990). "P2-Form" Strategic Management: Corporate Practices in Professional Partnerships. *Academy of Management Journal*, 33 (4): 725–55.

Gross, A., and Poor, J. (2008). The Global Management Consultancy Sector. *Business Economics*, October.

Groß, C. (2009). Personal email communication with author.

——and Kieser, A. (2006). Consultants on the Way to Professionalization? In R. Greenwood and R. Suddaby (eds.), *Research in the Sociology of Organizations*. Greenwich, CT: JAI Press, 69–100.

Heusinkveld, S., and Benders, J. (2005). Contested Commodification: Consultancies and their Struggle with New Concept Development. *Human Relations*, 58 (3): 283–310.

Hobsbawm, E. (2002). *Age of Empire: 1875–1914*. London: Vintage Press.

Hofstede, G. (2001). *Culture's Consequences: Comparing Values, Behaviors, Institutions, and Organizations across Nations*. Thousand Oaks, CA: Sage Publications.

IBIS (2009). *Management Consulting in the US*. IBIS World Industry Report 54161.

IFSL (2007). *UK Financial Sector Net Exports 2007*. London: International Financial Services. July.

Kellman, S. (2005). *Unleashing Change*. Washington, DC: Brookings Institution Press.

Kennedy Information (2004). CN Rankings: 75 Largest Consulting Firms in the World. *Consultants News*, June: 4–5.

——(2008). *The Global Consulting Marketplace: Key Data, Forecasts and Trends*. Fitzwilliam, NH: Kennedy Information Inc.

Kieser, A. (1997). Rhetoric and Myth in Management Fashion. *Organization*, 4 (1): 49–74.

Kipping, M., and Engwall, L. (2002). *Management Consulting: Emergence and Dynamics of a Knowledge Industry*. Oxford: Oxford University Press.

——and Saint-Martin, D. (2005). Between Regulation, Promotion and Consumption: Government and Management Consultancy in Britain. *Business History*, 47 (3): 449–65.

Kitay, J., and Wright, C. (2007). From Prophets to Profits: The Occupational Rhetoric of Management Consultants. *Human Relations*, 60 (11): 1613–40.

McDonald, D., and Ruiters, G. (2005). *The Age of Commodity*. London: Earthscan.

McKenna, C. (2006). *The World's Newest Profession*. Oxford: Oxford University Press.

MBA Universe (2008), MBA Placement Report. www.mbauniverse.com .

MCA (2003). *The UK Consulting Industry*. PMP.

O'Mahoney, J. (2007). The Diffusion of Management Innovations: The Possibilities and Limitations of Memetics. *Journal of Management Studies*, 43 (8).

——Adams, R., Antonacopoulou, E., and Neely, A. (2008). *A Scoping Study of Contemporary and Future Challenges in the UK Management Consulting Industry*. London: ESRC Business Engagement Project, AIM Research.

Plunkett Research (2009). *Plunkett's Consulting Industry Almanac*. Plunkett Research.

Richter, A., Dickmann, M., and Graubner, M. (2008). Patterns of Human Resource Management in Consulting Firms. *Personnel Review*, 37 (2): 184–202.

Roberts, J. (2006). Internationalisation of Management Consultancy Services: Conceptual Issues Concerning the Cross-Border Delivery of Knowledge Intensive Services. In J. W. Harrington and P. W. Daniels (eds), *Knowledge-Based Services: Internationalisation and Regional Development*. Aldershot: Ashgate Publishing Ltd.

Saint-Martin, D. (1998). The New Managerialism and the Policy Influence of Consultants in Government: An Historical-Institutionalist Analysis of Britain, Canada and France. *Governance*, 11 (3): 319–56.

——(2004). *Building the New Managerialist State*. Oxford: Oxford University Press.

Step Consulting (2006). Russian Consulting Market Review. *Litza Bisnesa*, 7(1): 124.

The Times (2009). Now Even Management Consultants Are Feeling the Squeeze. 19 February.

UNCTAD (2002), *The Tradability of Consulting Services: And its Implications for Developing Countries*. New York: United Nations.

Werr, A. (2005). Taking Control of Need Construction. In S. Furusten and A. Werr (eds), *Dealing with Confidence: The Construction of Need and Trust in Management Advisory Services*. Copenhagen: Copenhagen Business School Press.

Whittle, A. (2005). Preaching and Practising Flexibility: Implications for Theories of Subjectivity at Work. *Human Relations*, 58 (10): 1301–22.

——(2006). The Paradoxical Repertoires of Management Consultancy. *Journal of Organizational Change Management*, 19 (4): 424–43.

Wood, P. (2001). *Consultancy and Innovation: The Business Service Revolution in Europe*. London: Routledge.

Zeithaml, V., and Bitner, M. J. (1996). *Services Marketing*. New York: McGraw-Hill.

Consultancy—Is Behaving Professionally Enough? The Long Journey to Becoming a Profession

Lynda Purser, Director of the Institute of Business Consulting, UK

Consultancy is remarkably diverse and indeed it is used as a catch-all term encompassing a vast range of external services from high-level advice on organisational strategy to financial advice on transactions and contracts; from hands-on support for improvements in operational performance to the implementation and maintenance of new IT systems. These services are provided by organisations which differ hugely in their size and nature: multinational IT services companies, global accountancy-based firms, smaller specialist consultancies, and sole traders. They undoubtedly can't all be the same and indeed some of the large management consultancies are calling their consulting services advisory to distinguish them from the IT and accounting firms.

We can therefore consider consultancy to be an advisory service contracted by and provided to organisations by appropriate specialists who assist in an objective and independent way to identify issues/problems, analyse them, and recommend solutions.

It is clear therefore that such a process will have a significant impact on the organisation contracting for it. The advice given can have major impact on the operation of the organisation and if it is not appropriate or correct it can seriously damage the business. On the other hand sound advice given by an able and experienced practitioner which takes the business forward is invaluable.

Consultancy has in the past century made an important and significant contribution to the global economy. There have been tumultuous organisational transformations, cross-border mergers and acquisitions, major changes in the public sector and corporates. In all of these consultants have been the essential agents of organisational change. Consultants give organisations access to crucial knowledge through their experience and contacts. Consultancy has grown because it represents a powerful solution for the institutional transfer of best practice. It is actually only one of many ways in which this can happen but it has become, through the anti-monopoly legislation of the 1930s in America and then regulatory sanctions, the alternative legal method to transfer knowledge between possibly competing organisations.

By the 1960s consultancy practices had established, institutionalised, and defended consulting from other professional competitors. They developed professional governance structures based on other professions to manage the practice and strong internal cultures. Then as now they promote their corporate culture as the indicator of their core competence.

However, being a profession is more than this. A profession is defined by certain quite specific things. The first is a body of knowledge which defines the profession and which can be gained through professional education and training. In addition a number of years of experience are required and the practising professional keeps continuously knowledgeable about developments in theory and practice. The member of a profession puts knowledge and experience at the disposal of clients and in serving the clients' interests subordinates his own. The whole profession recognises and applies a set of ethical norms which define proper behaviour within the profession. Society recognises the status of the profession and members of the profession apply self-discipline in observing the profession's behaviours. The profession organises itself into a voluntary membership organisation to exercise collective self-regulation over working to an accepted code of professional conduct.

About a century ago consultants operated in several different professional fields and they defined themselves as bankers or accountants or engineers depending on the assignment. Therefore at this time consultants did not see themselves as part of a unified profession. However, they soon began to compete for assignments and began to realise that they were in the same professional area. They became concerned to appear professional as consultants to act both as a barrier to potential rivals from other professions and as a means of establishing a perception of professional behaviour which could generate more assignments and higher fees.

However, at this time and for a couple of decades after it consultants lacked the specific qualifications which defined the older professions. They did not have specialised journals or formalised university education, standards of admission and performance, or a centralised body of knowledge. Without these professional credentials consultants could not (and cannot) constitute a profession. Then as now the leading practices reject proposals to increase the professional standing of individuals at the expense of the power held by the practices.

Consultants decided that objective standards of professionalism were less important than getting the public to think of them as professional and emphasised the similarity between consulting and the established professions. They began to emphasise consultancy's on-going move towards professionalism without having the things which defined it in place, believing that behaving like a professional is as good as being one, and they emphasised the association between consultancy and the established professions, especially law.

Ultimately this use of comparison with well-established professions has resulted in consultancy failing to become a profession. The leading consultancy practices reject the need to achieve full professionalisation, as shown by their relationship with the professional body and its award of certified management consultant (CMC). Most consultancy practices do not require that their consultants obtain the CMC because the certification of individual consultants would weaken the practice's implicit certification of its own consultants. They generally do not believe that individual consultants are all of equal professional standing—an inherent attribute of a profession—with their own consultants. At present without any statutory regulation or full support for the professional body from the larger practices the CMC designation has not become a significant factor. Therefore professionalism is seen as a characteristic of individual practices rather than referring to consultancy as a whole.

However there are significant practices which do believe that the professional approach distinguishes them from others because many practices only give lip service to professional standards. The former practices do recognise the importance of having a professional body responsible for all the components which demonstrate a profession and actively work with them to promote the CMC and professional standards.

During the 1990s consultancy made considerable progress towards professionalisation. It has become the focus of academics across a variety of academic disciplines gaining a serious academic base. There is also a clearer educational pathway with relevant master's-level courses in a number of universities and the degree-level qualifications of the professional body providing a sound underpinning knowledge for prospective consultants. This growing body of academic knowledge and the explicit discussions of ethical lapses are strengthening the case for consultancy to become a profession.

The various recent scandals and emphasis on personal accountability are bringing about a focus on professional values and it could be that this will this time lead to professional status for consultancy. However, there are many consultants especially in the larger practices who see no need for this because they can adopt the style of a profession—language, rewards, client interaction—without the constraints of professional status such as statutory regulation, individual qualification, and professional liability.

So if behaving like a professional works as well as being one why would consultants want consultancy to be a profession? My view is that they will only want this when their clients recognise the need for them to have the characteristics, constraints, and controls of a profession.

3

Types of Management Consultancy

Chapter Objectives

This chapter introduces the different types of management consultancy and seeks to categorise the industry according to different perspectives. Specifically, it:

- Examines different business models of consultancy.

- Explores different consulting services.

- Outlines the different sectors that consulting firms serve.

The chapter will provide a useful overview of the primary characteristics of different categories and will also enable students to better understand where they might best fit should they choose consultancy as a career.

■ Introduction

An awareness of the distinctions between the different forms of consulting is important to demonstrate to clients and employers a general understanding of the industry. It is also important for a consultant's career progression to know which sectors and types of consultancy best suit their own strengths. There is a significant difference in working style and pay between, for example, implementing an IT project in the public sector and doing strategy work in a bank. This is especially true nowadays as many jobs which are described as "management consultancy" are very far from the traditional job description. In an increasingly competitive job market, consultancies are continuously shifting the type of work they do to ensure their revenues remain healthy. If this means reassigning and retraining consultants to do coding, website design, or training, then the employee needs to be aware of what prospects the different forms of work involve.

There are, unsurprisingly, several ways of segmenting the consulting industry and this chapter examines three specifically. There are:

- Business Model: What is the firm's structure and strategy? How does it make money?
- Service: What activities does the consultancy undertake for its clients?
- Sector: What do the firm's clients do?

In the real world, the distinctions outlined below are often blurred and interchangeable—consultancies have to react fast to changing markets and will change their sector, service, and strategy to suit their medium-term needs. Moreover, as we witnessed in Chapter 2, there are a number of long-term trends which appear to be affecting the whole industry: the shift away from strategy consultancy towards implementation work, the increasing scarcity of privately owned partnerships, the increasing power of IT and audit consultancies, and the commodification of consultancy work. The implications of these trends for the segmentation of the consulting industry are also examined over the next few pages.

■ Different Business Models

The differing business models of consulting firms are important because they determine what type of clients the firm will attract, what the consultants' jobs will look like, how they will get paid, and how they are organised. Some of the categories below would not be termed "consultancy" in some surveys. For example, internal consultants, contractors, and body-shoppers would not be classed as management consultants by the consultancy associations either because they are not big enough (contractors), they do not give advice (body-shoppers), or they do not sell their services externally (internal consultants). However, there are always exceptions to such simplistic categorisations and the inclusion of these categories will help readers to understand work which many consultants choose to move from or into.

Hybrid vs. Pure Consultancies

The first distinction to make is between "pure" consultancies that focus solely on consulting work, such as McKinsey, Bain, BAH, and AD Little, and those companies that have added consultancy as an additional competence to complement their other work. For example, audit companies such as KPMG or Deloitte, IT businesses such as Xantus or Axon, and engineering corporations such as Enterprise Consulting or Arup have added consulting to their existing businesses as additional sources of revenue. In many cases, consultancy has become so lucrative that it now provides the dominant source of income in hybrid companies.

Hybrid companies, such as IBM, PWC, and Accenture, tend to be latecomers to consultancy, adding the consulting function onto an existing company. Adding consultancy to an existing business provides a business with an opportunity to cross-sell advisory work to their clients so that the "core" functions, such as engineering, IT, or audit, enable the company to create leads and opportunities for consultancy work. For example, if an IT company undertakes a strategic audit for a client, it may be no surprise if they discover an IT deficiency in their client which could be solved with the use of their IT offerings. This need not be as Machiavellian as it sounds. Specialists in advisory work, whether plumbers, IT consultancies, or chiropractors, tend to see the world from their own perspectives, and the problem-solving methods they use are geared to identifying problems that they can solve. The ability of audit firms, for example, to cross-sell consultancy to their clients means they are now the fastest growing segment, outpacing all other "conventional" consulting service lines (Kennedy Information 2009).

In the late 1990s, the Securities and Exchange Commission in the USA, and the Financial Services Authority in the UK, became increasingly concerned about the conflicts of interest in audit companies that had consultancy arms. Specifically, they had two concerns. First, that the insight an auditor gained from looking at client accounts would allow them to have a better idea of which services a client might purchase. Second, and more worryingly, they believed that an auditor that was receiving large consultancy payments from a client might be under pressure to sign off unsuitable accounts. As a result many of the audit companies sold their consultancy arms in the 1999–2001 period. As we shall discuss in Chapter 9, this was too late for Enron whose collapse can be partially traced to this form of conflict of interest.

Pure consultancies tend to include the oldest, most respected firms (Lerner 2005), which often retain a partnership model of private ownership, though, as we saw in Chapter 2, this has changed over the last three decades. Pure consultancies, which bring in around 10 per cent of the income in the consultancy industry, believe they are trusted more by clients because they have nothing else to sell. The downside to this position is that they tend to be smaller and very dependent on the economy as they have no back-up business to support them in a downturn. In recent years, therefore, pure consultancies have diminished in size and number, with many of them being taken over by larger hybrid companies or simply merging with each other (MCA 2008). As we discuss later, the last ten years have witnessed a drying up of "pure" strategy work as clients are increasingly doing it for themselves. A consequence of this is that "pure" consultancies are increasingly looking for ways to diversify away from a dependency on this type of work.

Niche vs. Generalist

A generalist consultancy is one that offers many services. For example Accenture offers everything from outsourcing to systems integration to strategy work. Having a generalist offering is often useful for consultancies because when one type of work dries up, they can offer something else to balance the loss. For this reason, many of these consultancies employ "generalist" consultants who have easily transferable skills. These consultants are sometimes called "change management" consultants, depending on the employer.

Having been one of these consultants, I can attest to the diversity of projects that one can be deployed on. Within a two-year period, for example, I worked on building a business case of a company interested in 3G, helping implement an ERP service in an airline, supporting the cultural change programme of an acquisition, performing business development for an outsourcing project with a large bank, and contributing to a people project in financial services. Generalist consultants don't necessarily have all the skills required when they start a project. However, they have a strong set of "core" analysis and communication skills and have the ability to learn quickly. Unless the work is of a particularly specialised nature, a good generalist consultant will develop competence within a matter of days. They are more often found in large consultancies where they can be redeployed (or resold) into many different roles. This is useful for large consultancies because it allows them to keep a core of consultants with generalist skills and put them on different projects. Additionally, clients often benefit from the wide experience accumulated by these consultants. Paul Smith, who worked for Bain & Co, argues that many successes occur because generalist consultants take lessons from one industry and apply them in a different area (Smith 2002).

Niche consultancies tend to be smaller and to employ more experienced or specialised consultants. Many of these employ only one or two people and work within a loose network of affiliations of similar consultancies to take on bigger projects. These usually rely on personal contacts and networking for new contracts and often specialise in one service area. Clients like using them because they know the person they are working with, they are often cheaper than large consultancies, and they tend to have more experience than the MBA graduates offered by the likes of Accenture. An interesting paper by David and Strang (2006) argues that the expertise in niche consultancies allows them to produce more reliable and successful work than the generalist consultancies that will bid for a project without necessarily having the skills in place to support it. Of course, an easy way for large generalist consultancies to avoid this trap is by taking over smaller, niche players and thereby gaining access to their skills, clients, and experience.

The dream ticket for a niche consultancy is to be taken over by a large firm because the partners, as the shareholders, often get large pay-outs. However, in order for this to happen, the consultancy needs a strong client list, a number of good partners, who are prepared to stay with the new company, and a history of profitable growth. Takeovers in 2008 hit an all-time high and there are now several companies which provide advisory work to consultancies to make them more attractive to potential buyers (Biswas and Twitchell 2002).

Small vs. Large Consultancies

Due to the paucity of data that is collected at a national level, there are few reliable statistics with regard to the consulting industry. However, where data is collected, for example in the UK and the USA, it is clear that there are significant differences between small and large firms.

In their haste to associate themselves with the big consultancy names, many analysts forget that small- and medium-sized firms make up around 98 per cent of all consulting companies and employ around 78 per cent of all consultants (Brett Howell 2007). However, because the top of the industry is dominated by large companies that employ thousands of consultants in each firm, the big companies bring in more than 50 per cent of the industry's revenue. Smaller consultancies generally generate less income per consultant (Brett Howell 2007).

Furthermore, there is a considerable strategic difference between the large firms such as Accenture and KPMG and the small firms that are usually one-person companies. Large firms foster strong CEO relationships with virtually all the large companies around the globe. They have built a virtual monopoly on the increasingly large change management, IT, and outsourcing projects that generate vast amounts of revenue. The difficulties they face are around attracting talent, competing for the right "space", and resisting commodification (O'Mahoney et al. 2008).

Turnover	No. firms (2000)	No. firms (2004)	% Increase
>£5m	360	485	35
£0.25–£5m	6,100	8,955	47
<£0.25m	43,945	59,805	36
All firms	50,405	69,245	37

Table 3.1. Size and number of UK registered consulting firms (2000–2004)
Source: Office for National Statistics (2005).

No. employees	Market % 2003	Market % 2008
1–4	79.8	82.2
5–9	9.7	8.5
10–19	5.2	4.7
20–49	3.2	2.8
50+	2.1	1.8

Table 3.2. Changing patterns of dominance in size of US consultancy firms (2003–2009)
Source: IBIS (2009).

The challenges small consultancies face are very different from those of large companies. They have difficulty establishing credibility and building contacts, which is why many of them are interested in achieving professional status. They are heavily dependent on the contacts and reputation of their founding members and often disappear when the owner retires or moves on. As with niche consultancies, the golden goose for a small consultancy is to be taken over by a large firm, resulting in large pay-outs for the partners. However, whilst takeovers are at an all-time high in this sector, it is still relatively rare for a small firm to achieve this goal.

Body-Shopping

Body-shopping is when a consulting company or an employment agency sells "bodies" into clients to work as contractors (often software developers). This is a major source of income for many Indian (IT) consultancies who, whilst finding it difficult to win big contracts, still possess a surfeit of skilled labour. Body-shopping can be a quick and easy way to get money for a company that can sit between a cheap, skilled pool of labour and companies that require it, but as profit margins on body-shopping are lower than for consultancy work it needs to be done with a lot of workers for it to be worthwhile. Many large consultancies avoid this type of work because it is not advisory work and doesn't provide a strategic advantage. It is better to use one's consultants as part of a consultancy project than to have them stranded in a client doing mundane operational work in ones or twos. Moreover, the administrative overhead is considerably high for managing such small contracts and the income is often quite low.

Some clients manage their own body-shopping and actively recruit, train, and manage workers from poorer countries. "At any given time during 2000–2001 there were perhaps over one thousand agents specializing in the supply of temporary Indian IT workers across the United States and hundreds in northern California alone, and these agents were managing as many as 20,000 IT workers in the United States" (Xiang Biao 2006). The emphasis on the "body" rather than the "brain" indicates that this kind of work can be monotonous—"consultants" often end up doing coding rather than advisory work.

There is some evidence to suggest that the extremely low wages and semi-legal contract associated with Indian contractors in the 1990s have improved since the US Department of Labor passed legislation aimed at protecting the jobs of American competitors (Aneesh 2006). As with outsourcing, India is increasingly proving itself in the high-end strategy and product development roles that were traditionally reserved for Western companies.

Internal Consultancy

A number of large companies, including Mars, Diageo, IBM, and Microsoft, employ teams of internal consultants. Internal consultants are teams of individuals which are employed by an organisation to perform consultancy services in it. Organisations tend to develop teams of internal consultants if they are frequently experiencing the need for similar projects in different parts of their organisation. This requirement means that it makes more financial sense to develop a small team of specialists rather than constantly hire in external consultants (Armbrüster 2006). Internal consultants, therefore, tend to experience work that is less diverse than external consultants.

However, contrary to the common view that consultants generally implement new ideas and innovations, a recent project (Sturdy 2008) found that internal consultants are frequently used for compliance reasons: ensuring that consistent processes and procedures are being used throughout the organisation. To provide an example, a recent interviewee for one of my research projects runs an internal consultancy in a major manufacturing company ensuring that the reporting processes are consistent and compliant with the Sarbanes–Oxley Act. In effect, the team's job is to force different departments to conform to the edicts issued from the top of the organisation.

The benefit of internal consultants for the organisation is that by employing an internal consultant for £70,000 per year, they save money by not paying an external consultant £1,000 per day—providing, of course, the internal consultant works more than seventy working days on projects that require consultancy skills. Another advantage is in building a team which is relatively independent of company politics and has an "outsider's" perspective on company problems. For this reason, many companies place an emphasis on keeping their internal teams relatively "fresh"—either by recruiting new faces, by sending existing employees on training courses, or by providing them with access to external journals, publications, and reports (Neal and Lloyd 2007).

However, despite the benefits to organisations, there are also two main drawbacks in using internal consultants: first, unless the firm pays an extremely large salary, they are unlikely to recruit the same calibre consultant that one might find at, say, McKinsey. Internal consultancy is often seen as less exciting and varied than external consultancy and having less career-enhancing prospects. For that reason, skilled internal consultants are often hard to keep hold of. Second, internal consultants, because they usually stay with the same client, do not build up the same repositories of skills and knowledge that external consultants acquire (Armbrüster 2006). This often means that their value to the organisation decreases over time.

For the consultant themselves, there are both costs and benefits. A stable, more secure job can seem like a great bonus, especially in a recession. However, the experience and pay will usually not be as rewarding as in an external consultancy.

CASE 3.1

Ball Inc's Internal Consultancy

In common with many UK manufacturing companies, Ball Inc., a manufacturer of precision ball-bearings for machine parts, was facing external pressures. It had grown to a profitable company employing 200 people in the 1980s, primarily by serving the local markets around Birmingham. However, in the 1990s, manufacturing began to decline in the UK, the market shrank, and increasingly, foreign rivals began to undercut Ball Inc. on price.

In 2000, Ball Inc. called in an external consultancy in to help train the manufacturing staff in "lean" Japanese working techniques. This training included continuous improvement, quality management, process re-engineering, and waste reduction techniques. The consultancy decided the best way to achieve this on an on-going basis was to train some of the staff up to train any new recruits that might join the company.

The change programme was a huge success, reducing costs and improving the products, so when the consultancy left, the internal training team decided to spread the "lean" message to other departments. Over a couple of years the five-man team created their own materials and methods, which they believed were an improvement on those taught to them by the consultancy. The team successfully spread the training to other parts of the company.

Whilst this was happening, another manufacturing company in the area, Wharton, heard about Ball Inc's team and approached the MD of Ball Inc. to see if they could hire the team to train their own manufacturing staff. Wharton preferred this arrangement because, in the past, they had had bad experiences with external consultants and their MD refused to use them. The MD of Ball Inc. sent his internal team into Wharton and their down-to-earth attitude and practical manner made them a big hit there.

However, around this time, three things happened. First, the BallCo team approached their MD and suggested that as they were now being charged out to external companies, they wanted significant pay rises. Second, the MD of Wharton was so impressed with the team that he made three of them job offers. Finally, the original external consultancy which trained Ball Inc's team contacted the MD of Ball Inc. and said that he was in breach of contract for selling their techniques to other companies.

- What ethical issues are raised in this case? Who do you think is "right" in each issue?
- What would you do if you were Ball Inc's MD?
- Could this situation have been handled better by any of the parties? How?

Contractors

Contractors are independent workers who generally take on short-term assignments to provide clients with specific skill-sets. They are usually used by clients that need someone to fill gaps in their resource requirement on an individual basis. For example, some large clients might need some coding or testing work done as part of an IT project but don't want to pay a consultancy £1,000 a day for a consultant. Instead, they will often turn to an agency which has a number of contractors on their books. Contractors are usually paid by the hour or the day to work in a company. They work for the client, who pays the agent for their time, and the contractor receives payment from the agency.

For the client, there are a number of reasons for using contractors. First, they might simply not have been able to recruit enough permanent staff with the requisite skill-sets. Second, they may need staff for a short period of time. Third, they may not want to pay the costs of searching for and selecting permanent employees as, for skilled people, these costs can amount to 30 per cent of the person's salary. The client also avoids paying all the additional costs that an employee involves such as National Insurance, pension, and sick and holiday pay. Finally, some clients advertise jobs as "contract to hire", which means they will try a person out as a contractor and, if they like their work, they will take them on as a full-time employee.

For the contractor, there are also a number of benefits. First is that pay is better than that of a full-time employee. Rates will vary from £25 to £80 per hour and the work can involve anything from project management to coding. Second, a typical contractor will rarely stay with a company for more than a year. This means they get to accumulate a lot of varied experiences very quickly. Finally, contracting gives the individual flexibility and autonomy. They don't need to get caught up in company politics because they will probably not be aiming for a career there, and they can change their job whenever they like. I know several contractors, for example, who work from October to April and then take the spring and summer off on holiday.

The downside is that there is little job security, no pension, sick pay, or holiday pay, and the work burden is sometimes greater than that of normal employees. If you are considering contracting, do ensure you set yourself up properly, with a decent accountant, sufficient insurance, and in a tax-friendly company.

Interim Managers

Interim managers are senior executives who provide director-level help to a company on a short-term basis. They are generally very experienced with a specialism that a company may need, either for a short project, or until a permanent replacement is found. Interim managers are in demand during periods of change or crisis, for example when a senior director leaves suddenly or when a merger is taking place. Interim management in 2009 was worth around £500m a year in the UK (IOIM 2009) but is growing much faster than the rest of the consultancy market at around 15 per cent per year. The average length of an interim assignment is 131 days, the average daily rate is around £750, and the public/private sector split is 40/60. The sector with the highest number of interim managers is banking and finance (IPSOS/MORI 2008).

Despite the similarities to consultancy many classifications of consulting do not include interim management because the occupation is much closer to the contractor model: the interim manager usually provides day-to-day management services as an individual contracted through an agency on an individual basis. In contrast, a consultant provides advice, usually on a project basis, as part of a management consultancy. However, in reality, there is often frequent movement and blurring of roles between that of a consultant and that of an interim manager.

■ Consulting by Service

Problems of Classification

The services offered by different consultancy firms vary greatly from company to company and from region to region. However, as mentioned in the introduction, division amongst research companies on categories of consultancy means that comparison across countries and sectors is problematic. Tables 3.3 and 3.4, for example, provide summaries by the two research companies: Kennedy Information and Datamonitor. One can see immediately that Kennedy Information (2008) has, and Datamonitor (2008) lacks, a category of "Business Advisory Services", which includes financial, reporting, and risk consultancy. In Datamonitor's report, this category is subsumed within Operations and Strategy Consulting, pushing the former to a larger market share than would otherwise be the case. Conversely, Datamonitor's report has a section for outsourcing advice which is ignored in the Kennedy Information one.

Service	Market share
IT consulting	46%
Business advisory services	26%
Operations management	15%
Strategy consulting	8%
HR consulting	6%

Table 3.3. 2007 global consulting market share by service (Kennedy Information)
Source: Kennedy Information (2008).

Service	Market share
Operations	36%
IT consulting	22%
Strategy consulting	15%
HR consulting	14%
Outsourcing	13%

Table 3.4. 2007 global consulting market share by service (Datamonitor)
Source: Datamonitor (2008).

Service	Income £m
IT consulting	27
Programme/project management	20
Operations	12
Outsourcing advice	9
Financial	8
Strategy	8
Business process re-engineering	7
Human resources	7
Change management	3

Table 3.5. UK consultancy services and income (2006)
Source: MCA (2007).

Furthermore, if we examine the UK Management Consultancy's survey in Table 3.5, the picture becomes more complicated. Here, programme management accounts for much of what other companies call "Operations Management" and other categories have been split into their sub-components.

The three main categories that subsume most of the categories detailed in these tables can be simplified into strategy consulting, IT consulting, outsourcing, and generalist consulting. The latter category includes operations, process, and programme management consultancy. Below, these main categories are explored in more detail and insights are given into what the work typically comprises.

Strategy

Strategy consulting is universally acclaimed as the sexiest form of consulting and one with which students, job-seekers, analysts, and academics prefer to associate themselves. The strategy firms, such as McKinsey, Bain, and Boston Consulting Group, whilst not the biggest in the world, routinely recruit the best and brightest from the top universities around the world and pay the highest salaries in the industry. A cursory glance at the CEOs of the Fortune 500 reveals a significant percentage of alumni from the top strategy houses which creates a powerful selling opportunity for these well-connected firms.

The reasons for strategy consulting being the best in breed are threefold. First, the niche US strategy firms were some of the first consulting firms to establish themselves early in the twentieth century. This early start meant they could build strong relationships with banks and clients which have developed over the years (McKenna 2006). Without these strategic alliances, it is hard for any other company to muscle in on this lucrative territory. Secondly, strategy definition involves setting the long-term direction of the company. As such it is much more risky and important to get right. A healthy company can easily recover if it implements the wrong software or recruits a weak training company. However, a foolish takeover, a misunderstanding of a market, or the underestimation of the competition can easily cripple a company. As a result, clients are prepared to pay a premium to get strategy right: a few thousand pounds on a consultancy invoice pales into insignificance beside a potential collapse in profits.

Finally, strategy consulting is often used to lever follow-on consulting assignments. Good strategy consultants will use their influence with key directors to line up additional projects concerning the implementation of the strategic plan. For example, after a strategic analysis of a client's market position, a consultancy might recommend that a mobile operator moves into the banking environment. This might then lead to a series of projects developing new software, undertaking market research, and building new products. The consultancy then has the chance to position themselves as the ideal candidate to implement the projects.

However, despite its value, strategy consultancy has declined over the last decade. Globally, revenues reduced from $26bn in 2004 to $24bn in 2009 (Kennedy Information), whilst in the UK revenues declined from £606m in 2000 to £514m in 2007. In the words of Michael Eckstut, a former partner at Booz Allen Hamilton, "the pure-strategy, big-picture stuff is over" (Fortune Magazine 2003). The reasons for this decline are varied, but, as we discuss in Chapter 4, the increasing sophistication of the client means that much of the "blue-sky" work is done in-house, whilst the focus on commodified IT and outsourcing packages means that the main market focuses around implementation.

The "good old days" when you could start with a white board and a room full of CXOs are over. Clients don't want that anymore and are more interested in cutting costs with IT.

(Analyst, consultancy research company)

What Is Strategy Consulting?

At its most basic, strategy consulting is concerned with two questions: where the client should position themselves (the strategy) and how they should get there (the strategic plan). The first of these has been the key to levering lucrative consulting projects since the consulting profession first emerged at the turn of the century. A perusal of all the major consultancies' websites will reveal a multitude of papers, presentations, and research telling potential clients why they should be unhappy with their existing position and what they should do to improve it. In the words of arch-consultant Tom Peters, "if it ain't broke, you haven't looked hard enough. Fix it anyway" (Peters 1988).

Indeed, all the major consultancies have developed tools and frameworks to better analyse their client's strategic position. The Growth Share Matrix, Porter's Five Forces, the Business Strength Matrix, the 4Cs, and countless others were developed primarily to enable a simplification of the uncertainties and complexities which plague strategic decision-making. Such tools can provide the basis of a strategic audit; however, it should also be noted that, contrary to their use on many MBA projects, such tools are virtually worthless unless accompanied by an in-depth statistical analyses of markets, competitors, and consumer trends. Without these, simple lists of qualitative data provide minimal analytical power.

What Should Strategy Consultants Do?

Strategy consultants are supposed to work with the directors of organisations to help them decide on key company decisions such as where to launch new products, which companies to take over, or which territories to move into.

Very often a consultancy will perform a "strategy audit" on a company for its own information. For example, before a partner has a sales meeting with a key client director, analysts will often be asked to perform a strategy audit to find the weak spots of the company: areas where it feels vulnerable and might be induced to spend some extra money.

In theory strategy consultants identify changing markets, technologies, and environments and seek opportunities for companies to increase their shareholder returns or profitability. A key tool that consultants use for this is scenario planning. Scenario planning involves estimating what the world will look like in five years and designing the company to position itself to take advantage of these changes. This might involve issues such as:

- What should BP do if fossil fuels run out?
- What opportunities does global warming offer to insurers?
- How should US businesses respond to the threats from India and China?

These types of scenarios are usually run through in two- or three-day workshops, where directors of the client are facilitated in their discussions by the consultancy, who provides them with information on trends, patterns, and threats. The potential scenarios are then used to generate ideas on how the company can best position itself to maximise its profits. These ideas produce a position which the company would like to move towards. The next task is to produce a strategic plan of how they will get there.

Of course, such strategic documents invariably exist, but on closer inspection, few companies actually use them to plot a future course of action unless the work has been commissioned to support a specific corporate decision. Indeed, in my experience, the common practice in companies of producing an annual strategic plan usually results in the expensive document gathering static in a neglected corner of someone's hard drive. Indeed, many documents named strategic plans often seem more concerned with reporting on the past than the future so it is unsurprising that they have little input into planning.

What Do Strategy Consultants Actually Do?

In reality, most organisations rarely have the opportunity, or take the time, to write their long-term strategies based on such blue-sky thinking. This is because they are constrained by finite resources, current expertise, stakeholder interests, and other path-dependent limitations. Even more significantly, many blue-chip CEOs only have a life-span of three to four years and are thus inclined to focus on short-term wins rather than long-term positioning. For these reasons, most "strategic" work often focuses instead on pragmatic issues which would better be described as "tactical". Typical questions from a client might include:

- Should Tesco take over its nearest competitor?

- Should Ford focus on high-value, niche, or cheap, mass-market cars?

- Should Accenture sell off its Indian operations?

- Should Nokia launch a disposable mobile phone?

Notice that the type of question has changed from "what should I do?" to "should I do this?", thereby limiting the scope for the consultancies to generate endless options. The reality of much of the strategic consulting world is focused on working out the pros and cons of different courses of action rather than generating options for willing clients.

Regardless, the resulting strategic document will usually contain one, or a number of:

- Objectives
  The purest form of strategic planning works on the basis of "what type of company do we want to be", "where do we want to go", "how will we get there", and "how will we know when we've got there".

- Competitor reviews
  These are usually taken as an opportunity to hit the client's vulnerabilities and create a jealous streak. Even if the client is the best in show, they can always be jolted by a statistic which shows how fast the competition are catching up. A key question to ask when undertaking this type of analysis is "on what basis is competitive advantage achieved in this market?" The answer to this question, whether it is company size, product diversity, customer loyalty, or speed to market, will help determine where a company should be focusing its efforts.

- Benchmarking diagrams
  Benchmarking provides metrics comparing the client's performance in certain areas with those of its competitors. Often they can be useful sales tools as they are designed to show the client where their company is lacking. Such an analysis leads itself nicely from stating "your company isn't what it should be" to the proposal of "this is what you can do to fix this".

- Market analyses
  Usually aimed at describing what customers have bought in the past rather than predicting what people will buy in the future, market analyses attempt to identify ncw segments, markets, and opportunities for new or existing products. Typical analyses include:

  ○ "You make product X but don't make product Y which is similar and might sell well."

  ○ "Product X sells well in the USA so let's consider selling it in Canada."

  ○ "Product X has a market but not at the price/value you are selling it."

  ○ "Product X has many competitors—think about diversifying."

- Implementation options
  Once the problems and opportunities for the company have been identified many consultancies go a step further to outline potential recommendations and the cost–benefit associated with these. For example, if the consultancy had identified

that Canada would be a profitable market in which to sell Product X, there are then several ways of achieving this. For example, through direct marketing, a joint venture, taking over a Canadian company, or simply replicating the existing company in the new market. With each scenario, the costs, revenue streams, and strategic implications would be outlined along with a high-level plan for initiating this option.

It should be noted that most of the traditional strategy houses are now moving into the programme management and implementation arenas as the blue-sky/visionary aspect of strategy work is drying up. It is increasingly commonplace to see the niche US strategy houses such as McKinsey touting supply-chain management, cultural change programmes, and project management services.

IT Consulting

After a set-back during the dotcom crash, IT consulting is now one of the fastest growing forms of consulting and was worth an estimated $135bn in 2005 (Kennedy Information 2008) and it was predicted to grow at a rate between 5 and 6 per cent per annum in the period 2005–10. The market is influenced by two key drivers. First by the application of new technologies which provide organisations with opportunities to develop new products, lower costs through efficiency savings, or enhance revenues through quality improvements. Second, by the integration and improvement of existing technologies as companies outgrow, merge, or simply wear out their existing infrastructure.

Consulting and Technology

The first consultancies, such as ADL and McKinsey, had little to do with technology, and this remained the case until it became clear in the 1950s and 1960s that technology could provide companies with a competitive advantage. Thereafter, there was a growing market which aligned a client's business strategy with technological opportunities. This convergence happened in both technology companies, such as IBM and Hitachi Consulting, and consulting companies such as Accenture and Xantus.

Table 3.6 gives a number of technologies which have enabled new capabilities in organisations. These, in turn have allowed new business applications which consultancies now specialise in helping with and developing. Consultants have an unusual relationship with technology. They are rarely involved in its creation or development yet are central to its distribution and application in organisations.

These "core" technologies enable a number of secondary developments and applications which businesses also use. Indeed, usually, it is the secondary applications such as ERP or mCommerce, rather than the enabling technology, that actually provide the real business benefit. Of course, such technologies are not mutually exclusive and actually build on each other to create new opportunities. A simple example of this emerging technology is the mobile phone which now incorporates microprocessors, digital media applications, and the internet.

Increasingly, in the IT consultancy sector, competitive advantage is to be found in discovering and aligning new technologies to enhance business capabilities. Consultancies

Technology	Key enabler	Example business applications
The microprocessor	High-speed data processing.	Accounting software, strategic forecasting, product design and modelling.
Databases	Storage and retrieval of large data fields.	Personnel details, catalogue and warehouse management, CRM.
Digital media	Cheap transportation and reproduction of audio/video.	Content management systems, digital rights management, streaming and download technologies, on-demand television.
The internet	Rapid communication of information.	e-Business, web-design, P2P software, email, information search and retrieval, outsourcing, virtual services.
Mobile telephones	New distribution channel and remote communication.	Remote working, mobile gaming, mobile banking, GPS integration, video-calling.
RFID	Cheap remote monitoring.	FMCG monitoring, supply-chain tracking, security management, warehousing.
Artificial intelligence	Enables machines to use judgement accurately.	Decision-making, automated customer service.

Table 3.6. Technology as a business enabler

that specialise in this sector, therefore, require close relationships with technology entrepreneurs and often fund their own research into new developments in the field.

IT Consulting Work

IT consulting is now the biggest revenue stream of management consultancies and as such deserves special mention here. However, before moving on, it is important to clear up a big misconception about IT consultancy. Many of my students have told me that they can't get involved with IT consulting because they know nothing about IT. However, IT consulting is not about IT—it is about business. The biggest reason IT consulting projects fail is not because the coders or systems analysts get it wrong but because the business fails to control and specify what it wants. This is evident when looking at the diverse reasons companies implement IT:

- To grow the business, e.g. e-business.
- To cut costs, e.g. ERP, Outsourcing.
- To improve services, e.g. Customer Relationship Management (CRM), Business Intelligence.
- For faster communication, e.g. Mobile working, e-marketing.
- Integrating companies, e.g. Systems Integration, Supply Chain Management.

Segment	Description	Daily charge range	Examples
Large systems integrators	These are the large SI and outsourcing firms that also advise on IT implementation. These firms have around 75% of the market. These firms tend to do the management and implementation work.	£400–1,000	Accenture, IBM
Audit houses	Accounting firms are well placed to give advice on IT implementations because they can also offer advice on minimising the tax burden on such systems. These have around 10% of the market.	£600–1,500	KPMG, Deloitte, PWC
Niche strategists	These not only include the strategy consultancies but also niche technology and e-business firms that specialise in this area. These have around 10% of the market.	£800–2,000	Sapient, Avenue A, Diamond
Individuals	These are either consultants or contractors who have enough skill and experience to work independently. In terms of consultants (i.e. not systems analysts or coders!) these account for about 5% of the market.	£250–3,000	James Innes

Table 3.7. The segmentation of the IT consulting industry

Given these motivating factors, it is not necessary for an IT consultant to be an expert in coding or even systems design. Whilst some IT knowledge of what coders and systems analysts do may help you, too much knowledge may also constrain your strategic business thinking.

The IT consulting industry is a diverse and complex area and can be categorised in a number of ways. Let's first break it down by the types of organisations involved. These can loosely be split into four categories as shown in Table 3.7.

It should be noted, of course, it is only the *advising* on IT that counts as consultancy, not the actual implementation. This is an important trap to avoid when applying for jobs at places like CapGemini, EDS, Accenture, and IBM: if you are offered a job as a "consultant", ensure that it will be advisory work and not implementation (unless of course you want to do implementation work). There is a frequent argument between the likes of Deloitte, whose consultants do "pure" advisory work, and firms such as IBM whose "consultants" often do systems development, about whether this work is actually consultancy or not. It is, fortunately, beyond the confines of this book to make a judgement on this.

A related argument that frequently arises in management magazines is whether a company that offers everything from strategy advice to implementation is preferable over one that merely provides advice. The Accentures of the world point to their practical implementation experience and argue that this helps them give better strategic advice. However, the Deloittes and McKinseys of the world argue that the fact that these firms *do* the work means that their advice can be biased. It is better, they suggest, to hire a firm that has no vested interest in pushing its own services. Either way, it should be noted that the vast majority of the work of the big systems integrators is not strategy but systems integration (see Figure 3.1 below). The strategy firms, unsurprisingly, get most of the strategy work (though the accounting houses do their fair share), leaving the middle "management" tier of work to anyone who can fight for it.

In the dotcom boom, the smart money was on companies that specialised in IT such as IXL, Sapient, and Razorfish. These companies exploited their flexibility to get a head start on the bigger consultancies who were sticking to traditional areas such as strategy or HRM. However, when the crash happened, many of these niche companies went bankrupt or were taken over by larger firms. Eventually, the big generalists caught up and, unsurprisingly, all the hype which predicted a new generation of consulting giants proved to be over-optimistic.

IT Consulting Roles

There are several roles involved with an IT project and an understanding of these will help you understand how the parts fit together into a reasonably coherent whole. Consultants are often sold into the business analyst or project management role, because it is these that link the IT to the business.

Figure 3.1. Who does what in IT consulting?

Project	Description	Example	Value
IT Strategy	Understanding how IT can help an organisation get to where it wants to go.	Should a new telecoms company use UMTS or CDMA standards?	High
Architecture	Structuring the high-level components and relationships for an organisation's systems.	How should a bank's firewalls be positioned in relation to its customer data?	High
IT outsourcing	Delegating non-core business processes to third party specialists.	Should the NHS export its call-centre function to an Indian company? How should this be done?	Low
Enterprise software	Providing end to end systems which govern the core of a company's communications and data.	Do HRM and Payroll share consistent information? How is this data to be shared?	Low
Systems integration	Pulling together disparate company systems so they work efficiently and effectively together.	How can a company best integrate its customer database with its order books?	Low
Product development	Creating and designing new software or applications for an organisation.	How can Vodafone create a betting product?	Medium
Information management	Ensuring the right data is in the right place at the right time.	How can accurate predictions be made with regard to customer purchases?	Medium

Table 3.8. Types of IT consulting project

The roles include:

- Business Owner/Product Manager: this person "owns" the project for the business. They ensure that the business is satisfied with whatever is being developed in terms of costs, functionality, and users.

- Project Manager: plans and organises the projects resources (including the people) so that the goals are successfully achieved. The level of project manager varies considerably: in some projects it is a secretarial/administrative role, in others it is a senior manager with responsibility for the budget.

- Business Analyst: finds out the business needs of the project by talking to the various stakeholders and product managers. The business analyst records these requirements and ensures that they are communicated, managed, and prioritised throughout the project. The business analyst attempts to provide a bridge between the business needs and the overall system requirements.

- Systems Analyst: ensures the system design meets the requirements of the project efficiently and effectively. He or she ensures that the structure, data flows, and integration of the system are clear and logical. The systems analyst attempts to provide a link between the business requirements and the actual technological implementation.

- Technical Architect: these are the people who actually get their hands on the technology: the hardware, networks, and components that are required to build the project.

- Systems Architect: focuses on the high-level systems design, mapping how the project components integrate with the wider organisation and ensuring that the overall design is light, logical, and efficient.

- Coders: write the code that the system, product, or application relies upon. In the late 1980s and early 1990s this role could demand high salaries. However, increasingly, this work is being outsourced to cheap overseas providers.

Under many systems development methodologies, the product manager/business owner will help define the business requirements with the business analyst, who will then work with the systems analysts to define what the IT systems should do. This then, structures the work for the coders and the technical architect (see Figure 3.2 below). The project manager and the systems architect act as a link between the project and the rest of the organisation. There are, of course, alternatives to this fairly structured model, but the skills and roles involved tend to remain the same.

IT consulting doesn't require you to know a lot about IT. In fact, the best consultants have not come up from the coding route, because this allows them to focus on the business and what it needs rather than focusing on the technology and what it can do.

(IT consultant, large IT consultancy)

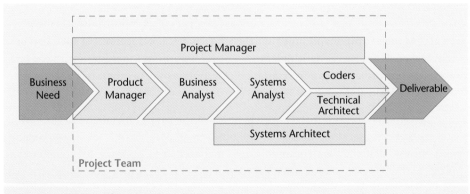

Figure 3.2. The IT Development Project Team

It's the Business, Stupid . . .

There are several reasons why IT consulting interventions fail, but one of the biggest reasons is when they are not driven by clear business requirements. There is a tendency for some students to see IT as a special, unusual, and often mystical art. However, this representation does the success rate of projects no good at all. In reality, IT should be a second- or even third-line support to the business. In other words, once the business strategy has been decided and the marketing, operation, and sales strategies have fallen into line, the IT strategy (along with HR Strategy and Procurement Strategy) should simply support the business aims as effectively as possible. When this prioritisation of the business case is forgotten, IT projects fail. Companies are left with over-complicated products, excessive billing costs, and unmanageable projects.

Clients, especially those unaccustomed to IT projects, will often believe that consultants will come in, deliver the IT, and then leave the system operating itself. In this case, it is the consultants' duty to inform the client that an equal effort needs to be invested in the business processes to support the IT processes with questions such as these:

- Who will maintain the system—when and how?
- What is the security policy—how is it enforced?
- How will changes to the system be managed—and by whom?
- What happens if the server catches fire?

When a consultant presents an IT proposal, it should be treated like any other business proposition. A good client will want to see a quantifiable return on investment over a specific timeline, they will demand penalty clauses for overruns and failures, and will want to ensure that their own staff are trained in how to operate the system. All of these issues present an opportunity for a well-prepared consultant.

To this end, therefore, it is important to understand the business rationale of typical IT projects. For example, Content Management Systems are primarily about adding value to assets, Supply-Chain Management should be concerned with reducing costs, CRM systems should focus on selling more products, and e-business must, at the end of the day, be about profit. In other words, all IT projects are about basic business sense: reducing costs, increasing sales, and maximising efficiency.

For this reason, the business requirements of any IT project must be used as the backbone of the project. Business requirements are the detailed specifications of what the business wants out of a project. These must be collected from the marketing/product side of the business and clearly communicated to any technical consultants working on the project. Requirements need to be prioritised, costed, and categorised (e.g. functional, financial, technical). On its completion, the success of a project will be tested against how many of its requirements have been achieved on time and under budget.

Outsourcing Advice

Outsourcing, the subcontracting of business activities to third parties, was not a common term twenty years ago but now takes up a massive percentage of many consulting firms' revenue. With a net value of around £300bn in 2008, the consultancy (advisory) part of this is worth around £489m, making it the third biggest form of consultancy after IT services and programme/project management. Accenture, for example, receives over 25 per cent of its income from running its outsourcing operations. Indeed, the market is so large that Accenture's CEO believes this percentage may eventually reach 50 per cent. By having up to 35 per cent of their staff in Asia, companies such as IBM, EDS, and Accenture can offer Western firms access to cheap, and increasingly high-skilled, labour in India and China to answer calls, host IT applications, and run business processes.

In recent years, Indian companies such as Tata, Wipro, and Infosys have increasingly taken the battle to the West, building up massive outsourcing contracts and buying up skills and assets in the USA. Indeed, with the increasing skill of Indian labour driving up local costs in India, companies such as Infosys are now buying up call centres and software companies in Eastern Europe and South America—in effect, outsourcing their outsourcing.

Times are changing, however, and with margins getting tighter and the competition becoming more intense, the outsourcing market is not as profitable as it was in the 1990s. With the gigantic start-up costs that outsourcing involves, few consultancies now have the resources to make a late entry into the market. In many definitions of consultancy outsourcing in itself doesn't count as consulting in the same way that systems integration doesn't count. It is generally the advice on outsourcing that counts as consultancy and this is where many companies make their money.

It should also be noted that outsourcing is a catch-all term for a number of activities, some of which include:

- Business Process Outsourcing (BPO): outsourcing processes such as payroll or recruitment.
- Infrastructure Outsourcing: outsourcing the hosting or management of IT infrastructure.
- Application Outsourcing: developing software, then managing its operation and improvement.
- Bundled Outsourcing: disparate activities outsourced to a single vendor.

The same challenges face clients with outsourcing advice as they do with IT advice: should a client choose a consultancy which is independent and has no "solution" they want to sell, or do they get discounted advice from a consultancy who will recommend their own services? It partially depends on the complexity of what they want outsourced and also on the amount of money they have to spend on consultants.

Generalist/Change Management Consultancy

Generalist consultants (sometimes known as change management consultants) usually concern themselves with organisational change of some form. In the last few years, the field of "organisational change" has included:

- BPR.

- Quality improvement/Lean.

- Culture change/change management.

- Human resource management (HRM).

- Operations management.

- Programme/project management.

These types of work are grouped together for several reasons. First, they are usually concerned with the implementation of operational changes to a firm. Second, the consultants who work in these areas will often move between work in these different areas as the skill-sets used, such as training, process management, project management, and communication skills, are common in all these sub-groups. Finally, more recently, these types of projects are well suited to fit with the burgeoning IT consulting business. It is rare, these days, to find large HRM, BPR, or change management projects that do not involve at least some form of integration with IT.

Speaking to recruiters, communication skills and flexibility are the most highly prized skills for generalist consultants. When attempting to implement an organisational change, the generalist consultant needs to focus not simply on doing the work well, but also on overcoming resistance from operational workers, ensuring that other change programmes are kept informed of progress and risks, and channelling relevant information to their line manager, project lead, project manager, and the client. All of this requires the ability to channel the right information to the right people at the right time.

BPR Consulting

Business Process Re-engineering was introduced by Michael Hammer and James Champy in 1993 in their book *Re-engineering the Corporation*. The idea, based on earlier Taylorist and Fordist principles, was that traditional management had focused too much on "vertical"

Segmentation	2005	2006	2007	2008
Programme/project management	880	1,102	1,205	1,230
Operations	419	613	438	520
BPR	418	338	288	377
HRM	292	289	353	343
Change management	127	170	273	284

Table 3.9. 2005–8 income from UK generalist consulting (£m)
Source: MCA (2006, 2007, 2008).

management down departmental lines. What was wrong with this, they argued, was that the things customers were most concerned about were actual horizontal processes which cut across several departments. For example, when a customer places an order, the subsequent activity occurs across several functions such as billing, CRM, manufacturing, ordering, warehousing, and delivery. These activities, Hammer and Champy argued, formed business processes that needed to be mapped, rationalised, and automated as much as possible.

BPR not only provides consultants with a new product, but also with an aggressive language of "slash and burn", "delayering", and "re-engineering" which appeals to the bottom-line concern of clients (Grint and Case 2002). This "violent" approach taken by BPR, especially in the early years, was one reason why failure rates were so high (Coombs and Hull 2007): people were not communicated with, HR was ignored, and decisions were made solely by senior executives behind closed doors.

BPR began to die out in the late 1990s as the dotcom boom took precedence for many consultancies. However, BPR has, in recent years, undergone a bit of a resurgence, for three reasons. First, it seems to be a good way of designing many data management systems (e.g. ERP). Secondly, it provides a solid basis for outsourcing work: it is easier to outsource specific processes, "recruit staff", "pay staff", "manage complaints", than it is to outsource whole departments such as HRM or Finance. Finally, the Sarbanes–Oxley legislation brought in post-Enron was implemented by most firms on a process basis and opened up an entire new market for consultancies with BPR expertise.

... as a change management consultant I was, in the space of one year, asked to work on projects doing BPR, training, e-business, communications work, and cultural change. I had not worked on any of these projects before but was expected to perform as if I had.

(Senior consultant, medium-sized consultancy)

TQM

Total Quality Management (TQM), as commodified by Tom Peters and Rob Waterman, was also built on its predecessors. The basic idea was that by making work more human through teamwork, multi-skilling, and training, workers would be motivated and empowered to develop their own ways of improving organisational practices. In many ways, this was the opposite of the top-down approach taken by BPR as it enabled workers to make decisions and take responsibility (Knights and McCabe 1998).

The idea worked well in Japan, where the movement started, because organisations had a more communicative and participative culture in the first place (McCabe and Wilkinson 1998). It was argued by many academics that implementations in the UK and the USA were more concerned with control and exploitation of the workforce rather than empowerment (Sewell and Wilkinson 1992; Delbridge and Turnbull 1992).

Although the phrase "TQM" has gone out of fashion in many circles, the work on training, quality improvement, teamwork, and bottom-up communication is still very much alive. There is a recent trend, for example, to use quality improvement specialists for *innovation management*. Moreover, the focus on quality initiatives has spread from manufacturing, where it started, to all areas of the economy.

Culture Change Management

Culture change was big in the 1980s and often becomes popular in times of economic boom (as companies' budgets move away from cost cutting towards intangibles that can "add value"). In these days of economic strife and success measures, cultural change is usually reserved for companies that have just been taken over or merged, and want to change the attitudes of their employees to better fit the new environment. Cultural change assignments can involve anything from rebranding and defining mission statements and corporate values at the strategic level, to training, development, and communication projects at an operational level (Schein 2004).

As with many organisational programmes, there are doubts amongst sceptics whether organisational culture programmes actually work or are simply aimed at increasing managerial control over the workforce (Tuckman 1994). Others query whether or not a phenomenon as amorphous as culture can be managed at all, whilst some suggest that high performance produces strong cultures rather than the other way around (van den Broek 2004).

HR Consulting

Organisations frequently state that their "people are their greatest asset"; and such a mantra fitted well with the economic boom when HR consultancy would focus on high investment activities such as training, culture management, and competence development. However, in the last five years, facing economic uncertainty and increasing competition, many companies have done anything in their power to get rid of as many employees as possible through delayering, automation, and outsourcing (Kumar et al. 2002). For HR consultants, this has meant a splitting of the field into HR outsourcing and IT, and more traditional HR consultancy work. The former is primarily concerned with streamlining and standardising the benefits and payroll services that are usually outsourced.

If we examine what is left of HR consultancy once outsourcing and IT work has been accounted for, the biggest sub-group within this field is benefits consulting, followed by talent management. Both of these areas have grown in recent years due to the challenge that clients have of finding, enticing, and motivating the right people. Employees are much more likely to leave their employer than they were twenty years ago and the market for skilled individuals is so competitive that many clients bring in consultancies to help them in this area.

Operations Consulting

Operations consulting can include all or none of the specialisms listed above depending which consultancy you are concerned with. A quick look at those companies which claim "operations consulting" expertise reveals work in BPR, Process Improvement, CRM, Supply-Chain Management, Cost Reduction, Quality Improvement, Lean, and Innovation Management. The only difference I can discern is that consultants who work under the "operations consulting" banner, rather than "change management", tend to have active tenure in industry actually implementing this type of work, rather than being new graduates or MBAs with a couple of years' experience. It is perhaps for this reason that the recent trend of strategy consultancies to move down to operational work has tended to focus on hiring experienced operations experts with niche interests (CRM, Supply Chain, or Lean) rather than consultants with generalist skills such as change management.

Programme Management and Project Management

Programme and project management are different things. Programme management is a high-level process of coordination dealing with several interrelated and complex projects, which requires corporate governance, senior representation, and strategic communication (e.g. launching a 3G company or managing the 2012 Olympics). A programme may contain a number of specified (or yet to be specified) projects. A programme manager may need to define methods, methodologies, standards, and a governance structure: how the architecture of projects will work.

Project management concerns the tactical reporting and control of resources and activities to get a single project done on time and budget. It does not require strategic representation or decisions. A project manager will measure planned timelines and activities against what is actually happening and attempt to manage any slippage. A programme should produce a strategic benefit whilst a project will provide a deliverable towards that goal. This is not to say that project management is less interesting or challenging, but it is often not as well paid. Many people see project management as a learning step on the way to becoming a programme manager. However, it should also be stressed that the pay and attractiveness of each role are very dependent on what project is being managed and how much relevant experience one has accumulated.

Consulting Specialisms

There are, of course, many more types of management consulting, and consultancies constantly look at the market to find new opportunities to make money. Many specialisms are very lucrative as they require niche skills. For example, merger and acquisition consulting often requires not only strategic, but also legal and financial skills and, as a result, is highly paid. In order of income to the consultant, consulting specialisms include:

- Mergers and Acquisitions.
- Private Equity.
- Compliance.
- Marketing and Sales.
- Environmental.

Some of these categories are not counted as "management consulting" by analysts because they do not consult on management *per se* but rather provide advice with regards to other forms of business specialisms.

■ Consulting by Sector

Consultancies, especially the large ones, usually organise themselves around different sectors. This allows them to deploy consultants in specialist areas, accumulate expertise, and direct their sales efforts accordingly. Of course, much of the work that is performed by consultants is similar across sectors. However, the cultures, strategies, and operations of different sectors vary incredibly. Some services (for example strategy or process re-engineering) differ from sector to sector and require specialist knowledge; others (such as coaching or project management) may not be so unique and can be applied in many different sectors in the same way.

The consulting income derived from different sector specialisms is highly dependent on the legal and political environments of each sector. Whilst the dotcom boom, for example, led to a huge investment in retail business and start-ups, the fallout of the 2002 Sarbanes–Oxley Act resulted in an explosion in consulting in the Finance Sector. Following the sale of 3G licences in 2000, Telecoms consulting grew exponentially, whilst in the UK the 2004 Gershon Review sent public sector spending through the roof.

In Figure 3.3 the main sectors are listed in order of size. Loosely speaking, finance and telecoms are better paid than government and utilities work. Another point to note is that often consultancies may package these sectors up in different ways: for example, sometimes pharmaceuticals are combined with health.

Finance and Banking

Traditionally, the banking and finance industry has possessed vast financial resources and thus typically provides around a third of all consulting income. Indeed, when I joined my

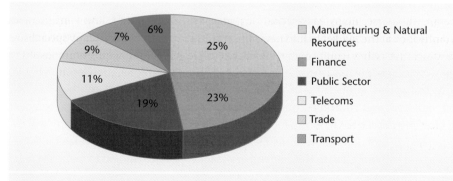

Figure 3.3. Global end users of consultancy (2007)
Source: Gross and Poor (2008).

first consulting firm, I was told that if I was concerned with high wages in consultancy I couldn't do much better than being a strategy consultant in the finance industry. Much of this spending in the last ten years has focused on massive IT projects such as creating online banking, internet-based trading, and e-payment systems. The supporting work in database management, security, and outsourcing has provided consultancies with steady income streams for many years.

However, during the credit crunch, the banking and finance sector cut back on spending as banks were forced to keep greater cash reserves against their lending levels. This meant a cutting back in both IT and consultancy spending by banks which had already begun to affect balance sheets of the large consultancies by 2009. The impact of this cut-back is geographically skewed, as up to 50 per cent of global financial consultancy is performed by the large audit consultances which are all based in the USA and Europe (Kennedy Information 2009). To make things worse, some analysts feel that the profits of the banking sector will be subdued for the long term as government regulation, consumer pressure, and competition from new entrants provide limitations on the bank's ability to generate revenues.

It is important, however, to see the woes of financial services consulting in context. The sector has witnessed a substantial year-on-year increase in income for over a decade now and even if the current decline is as much as 20 per cent, this will still only match revenue levels five years ago. Additionally, when talking to consultants in this sector, several have pointed out that government legislation and the restructuring of firms will lead to a short-term increase in strategy, merger and acquisition, and compliance consulting in the area.

Telecoms/Entertainment

Telecoms and communications consulting boomed in the early 2000s due to the explosion in broadband computing and the sale of 3G licences. This was driven primarily by companies cutting out costs through the implementation of telemetry, and mobile computing, and other companies exploiting digital content (e.g. films, music, documents) through complex content management systems.

The idea behind much of the digital boom has been to make the most of digital assets the company has purchased (unpleasantly known as "sweating assets"). If you imagine you have a photo of a football goal, or a news clip, on your servers at work that you think has value to your customers, this becomes an asset, which needs to be exploited and served to as many customers, on as many different platforms (e.g. TV, internet, mobile), as possible. For this to happen, content needs to be managed cleverly so that it can be searched, stored, retrieved, and controlled to maximise its value. Obviously the more automated and efficiently these transactions happen, the more profitable a digital company will be. Additionally, as more and more firms make use of video-conferencing, video-blogging, podcasts, and corporate TV, so the demand grows for expertise required to make the most of such digital assets.

Increasingly, telecoms and communications consulting are combined with "Media and Entertainment", as content (such as television, films, and music) becomes "multi-platform" and the lines between different methods of delivery become blurred. To be a consultant in this area, one does not have to be an IT expert but one will require a rich understanding of how digital content and applications link to business objectives. This requirement should not put students or graduates off from applying to this sector as it can be an interesting area and the skills developed are easily transferred to other settings.

The Public Sector

Globally, the public sector accounts for around $57bn (Kennedy Information 2008) which represents 19 per cent of consultancy revenues (Gross and Poor 2008). This figure excludes healthcare which, in some countries, can bring the total public spend on consultancy up to nearly 30 per cent. Whilst the proportion of total consulting spend ranges from 43 per cent in Greece to 5 per cent in Portugal (FEACO 2006), globally, public sector spending on consultants has rocketed. In the UK, for example, the market grew in double digits each year 2002–5, increasing revenue from £600m in 2001 to £1.58bn in 2005 (MCA 2006).

There are two main reasons for this increase. First and foremost is cost. Across the world, governments are attempting to cut costs by implementing ambitious IT projects to enable activities such as tax payments, licence applications, and passport applications to be done online. These types of projects tend not to be subject to economic cycles and thus provide consultancies with essential income during economic slumps. Second, many new governments face strong resistance from their own civil servants and public sector workers to proposed reforms. Some analysts have argued that governments use consultants as a way to bypass traditional government decision-making and enforce faster reforms (Craig and Brooks 2006; Saint-Martin 2004).

It is also likely that public sector spending will increase in the 2009–11 period for two main reasons. The first is that, during the credit crunch, several governments committed to stimulate their economies by increasing spending on public projects. Whilst this commitment had the near-universal effect of dramatically increasing government borrowing it also guaranteed increased spending on consultants. The second reason for the increase is located in the USA where the inauguration of Barack Obama in January 2009 committed the country to transformation of public policy in many areas. Traditionally, such significant change is usually associated with considerable support from consultants to aid with advice and implementation.

CASE 3.2

The UK Government's Use of Management Consultants 1999–2008

In 1999, facing spiralling costs in the public sector, the UK government spending reviews (HMT 1999) noted the savings that the private sector had made through e-commerce and BPR, and pushed its own departments for similar savings through e-government. A number of large projects aimed at automating, outsourcing, and streamlining were initiated in the early 2000s which used consultancy expertise to design, implement, and often run these systems. This trend was exacerbated by the Gershon Review (2004) which set the target of £6.45bn in efficiency savings though the introduction of e-business, devolution of decision-making, the use of best-practice processes, and a reduction in bureaucratic headcount. Much of this work involved the use of consultants, brought in to implement IT systems and re-engineer government departments.

However, many projects, such as the ID Database, the Passport Office, and the NHS database, resulted in high-profile failures, overruns, and spiralling costs which led to criticisms from government watchdogs such as the National Audit Office (2006) and the Public Accounts Committee (PAC 2007). The result has been a government effort to regulate and control expenditure on consultants through the use of several mechanisms including greater rigour in procurement. More and more government departments are turning to recruiting ex-management consultants to their procurement departments to batter down consultancy fees.

A corresponding tightening up of the procedures governing the use of consultancies by government procurers led by the Office of Government Commerce (OGC) has ostensibly resulted in improvements in the selection and control of consultants. The double-digit percentage increases in income from this sector finally fell away in 2005–8 and, whilst significant projects still exist, this trend looks likely to continue for the foreseeable future.

- Why do you think that the public sector is perceived as failing to control its consultancy spending?
- Why do you think the UK spends more on consultancy than any other European country?

Health

Sometimes combined with pharmaceuticals, life sciences, and medical manufacturers, health is one of the fastest growing and most politically sensitive areas for consultancy involvement. Globally, the healthcare consulting industry was worth $34bn in 2008 (Kennedy Information 2009); however, consulting interventions are globally diverse and highly entwined with the structure of ownership of healthcare provision in each country. In many countries, such as the UK, the health industry is inextricably entwined with government which is responsible for the majority of care provision. However, in other countries, such as the USA, the majority of care is provided privately, through insurers.

Traditionally, the provision of healthcare by governments meant that their spend on consultants would be low. However, over the last ten years, governments have attempted to minimise their expenditure in this area through the implementation of "modern" management techniques and IT programmes with the consequence that spending on consultancies has rocketed in the last decade. One of the consequences of this programme of reform is that healthcare in Europe, where government provision is the dominant model, now accounts for a greater percentage of global consulting revenues than any other sector.

With constantly changing technology, complex private–public relationships, and massive demand from consumers, healthcare poses difficult managerial problems to both public and private providers and their consultants. In the UK, for example, the NHS spent over £500m on management consultants in 2007, a figure that exceeds £1bn when IT projects are included (MCA 2008). To some extent, healthcare follows the trajectory of any other consumer service in attempting to engender high-quality service from low-cost provision. However, the involvement of government and the keen interest of the general public mean that the involvement of highly paid consultants being funded from the public purse is an emotive issue.

Outside healthcare provision, the pharmacology industry and bio-sciences have been one of the financial success stories of the last twenty years, with investment and venture capital poured into the sector. Consultants have been a key beneficiary of this investment, helping start-ups, takeovers, and flotations as well as providing advice on market changes, strategy, and innovation management.

Utilities, Energy, Mining, and Infrastructure

This sector (often split up into its component parts) rests on a business model of making money from extracting, managing, trading, and transporting assets. Whether consumers or wholesalers ultimately pay for the assets, the two key challenges for this sector are the same: the efficient transportation of assets at minimum cost and the meta-management of the assets, which includes the forecasting, trading, and risk management. Additionally, companies in this sector often work within an increasingly stringent legal, political, and social framework where issues such as environmental awareness, political lobbying, and risk management are central to general business operations.

As well as all the usual operations projects such as outsourcing, IT implementations, and restructuring, consultancies involved in this area emphasise strategy, lobbying, risk management, and change management as additional weapons in their arsenals. There is also a sizeable business supporting trading, capital markets, and futures markets with reference to the utilities and energy sectors.

FMCG, Retail, and Consumer Business

This sector goes by different names depending on the consultancy. McKinsey's, for example, call it "Consumer Packaged Goods". FMCG (Fast Moving Consumer Goods) specifically refers to consumer products that are frequently replaced (such as toothpaste) and are made by companies such as Nestlé and Unilever. A sub-section of this market is Fast Moving Consumer Electronics (FMCE) which are small, frequently replaced electronic items such as MP3 players and camera phones.

Within this field consultants undertake a number of different activities:

1. Defining the strategy: which products should be produced? How are new products created and innovated? Is the product life-cycle well managed? Is the product portfolio well integrated? Answering these questions might include market research, innovation training, and competitor analysis.

2. Cutting costs: is the manufacturing process lean and light? Are the right parts of the value chain outsourced? Is speed to market as fast as possible? Is the supply chain efficient and cheap?

3. Maximising income: are products being sold to the right people in the right locations at the right price? Can different products be bundled together or cross-sold to different markets? How can addition sales or higher prices be supported? Are there new products that might generate higher profits?

Consumer goods work has traditionally been reasonably flush with money (less so than finance but more so than manufacturing). However, in recent years, with the recession and the rising cost of raw material, the industry has felt a squeeze on profits. The bad news for consultancies has been limited by the tendency for firms to call in consultants to look for ways of minimising damage to the balance sheet and to find prices that will maximise their sales in a recession. The business axiom of making goods cheaply and selling them at high margins is the basic operating principle of this sector, but this simplicity belies the complexity of highly complex statistical analyses that are undertaken to better understand consumer spending patterns.

Manufacturing

The decline of manufacturing in Europe and the USA over the last twenty years means that this sector remains one of the weaker areas in the domestic market. In 2007, the UK sector was worth £189m, representing just over 3 per cent of the total market (MCA 2008). However, the growth in the outsourcing of manufacturing to BRIC countries and increased consumer demand from emerging economies means that companies still spend significant sums on consulting services. When not advising on new markets, outsourcing, and supply-chain management, consultancy work in manufacturing tends to focus on innovation, procurement, CRM, and the deployment of "Japanese" work practices (Kaizen, TQM, lean, or JIT). Most major consultancies agree that cost reduction is the primary driver for this competitive sector.

This sector is often broken down further into automotive and aerospace specialisms which are relatively large sub-sectors requiring specialist knowledge of unique markets and operational challenges.

Not for Profit/Social Sector

The charity sector (one of the smallest markets for consultancies) has a traditional image of being run on a more informal basis than many other sectors. However, some years ago, many charities realised that by paying experts in management and marketing to enhance the charity's operations, the improvements would at least cover the costs of the fees. It is for this reason, for example, that charities are using increasingly sophisticated (and aggressive) fund-raising techniques and management strategies.

The needs of charities are much the same as any business: cost reduction, income maximisation, and powerful sales and marketing processes. However, charities are a special case, not simply because their governance and accountability structures are more rigid than other firms, but also because their guiding principle cannot be "profit at any cost". Ethical treatment of employees, service providers, and the environment have to be (and have to be seen to be) crucial for charitable operations.

Environmental

Environmental consulting, whilst a tiny market for consultancies (£77m in the UK in 2008), is one of the fastest growing sectors and covers a myriad of different skill-sets and activities including carbon-trading, energy management, impact assessment, and PR. During the period 2006–7, the consulting services for this sector grew by 186 per cent (MCA 2008).

However, despite increasing discourse about the environment, there are, as yet, few rigorous products for consultancies to sell in this field. Much of the money in this area is spent on engineering and energy consultancies who reduce, manage, and trade energy use. The market for management consultants is still quite undefined.

■ Chapter Summary

This chapter has described the different segmentations of the consulting industry and outlined some of the trends which have affected these sectors over recent years. Some key facts to note are:

- The move to the "middle": strategy consultancies are moving downstream and doing management work, whilst IT and outsourcing consultancies are trying to move upstream into the same area.

- Consulting with everything: many companies have added consulting divisions in an attempt to maximise economies of scope, help setting a client's purchasing agendas, and lever more business. Thus, increasingly IT, finance, and manufacturing companies are offering consultancy services to boost their revenues.

- Under pressure from the public, the government has encouraged procurement departments to negotiate down consultancy expenditure. This trend has been copied by the private sector and is responsible for driving down both consulting fees and profit margins.

- Banking and finance account for most of the income in private sector consulting, but public sector has grown enormously over the last ten years, especially in IT consulting.

Student Exercise: Forecasting the Future

A key skill of consultants is to be able to perform a strategic analysis. Often this involves forecasting what the future will bring to a sector or an industry based on specific assumptions and giving advice on the basis of those scenarios.

Based upon what you know of existing trends in the consultancy industry what forecasts can you make about the next ten years? If you were leading KPMG's advisory business:

1   What trends would be central to their strategic planning?

2   What are the key opportunities and threats in the market and amongst competitors?

3   What are the top three business scenarios that you would plan for? What would your plans be for each?

Discussion Questions

• What different business models can you identify in the consulting world? Which do you think makes the most money, both per consultant and in total?

• What issues do different forms of definitions and classifications present to the researcher of consultancy? What could be done to ameliorate the situation?

• What sectors and services would you be most interested in becoming involved with and why? What do you think the main growth areas will be over the next five years?

Further Reading

The biggest and most important survey of consultancies in the world is routinely undertaken by Kennedy Information. However, their reports are prohibitively expensive for all but the wealthiest companies. For a cheaper overview of the industry one can find reports by Datamonitor, IBISworld, and Forrester. However, if you are a student or a government researcher, there is considerable free information available on the web. I would refer readers to the links available on the OUP Online Resource Centre for this book.

In the UK the best report is conducted annually by the MCA and it available from their website www.mca.org.uk. The report, usually written by Fiona Czerniawska and her colleagues, can be obtained for around £500 for members. Both the MCA and the IBC offer significant amounts of free information on their website. If a paid-for report is out of your price range then there is a plethora of information available online. However, it should be noted that the MCA report excludes consultancies that have less than ten employees.

The European Federation of Management Consultancies Associations (FEACO) provides an annual survey which can be purchased for around £80, but provides previous years' surveys free of charge (www.feaco.org). Similarly, for the UK, International Financial Services also do an annual survey in their City Business Series, which is free of charge (www.ifsl.org.uk). Other sites, such as www.top-consultant.com offer a searchable discussion forum where consultants, MBAs, and graduates discuss everything from working as a female consultant in Dubai to advice on getting into McKinsey.

There are virtually no books on consultancy which provide a detailed, up-to-date guide to industry segmentation. However, the two below are worth a look:

• Curnow, B., and Reuvid, J. (2003). *The International Guide to Management Consultancy*. London: Kogan Page.

• Sadler, P. (2007). *Management Consultancy*. London: Kogan Page.

References

Adams, S., and Zanzi, A. (2005). The Consulting Career in Transition: From Partnership to Corporate. *Career Development International*, 10 (4): 325–38.

Aneesh, A. (2006). *Virtual Migration*. Durham, NC: Duke University Press.

Armbrüster, T. (2006). *The Economics and Sociology of Management Consulting*. Cambridge: Cambridge University Press.

Biswas, S., and Twitchell, D. (2002). *Management Consulting: A Complete Guide to the Industry*. New York: John Wiley & Sons.

Brett Howell Associates (2007). *Financial Benchmarks: Management Consultants Survey*. BHA.

Coombs, R., and Hull, R. (2007). BPR as "IT-Enabled Organizational Change": An Assessment. *New Technology, Work and Employment*, 10 (2).

Craig, D., and Brooks, R. (2006). *Plundering the Public Sector*. London: Constable.

Datamonitor (2008). Global Management and Marketing Consultancy. October.

David, R., and Strang, D. (2008). When Fashion is Fleeting: Transitory Collective Beliefs and the Dynamics of TQM Consulting. *Academy of Management Journal*, 49 (2): 215–33.

Delbridge, R., and Turnbull, P. (1992). "Human Resource Maximisation: The Management of Labour under Just In Time Manufacturing Systems". In P. Blyton and P. Turnbull (eds), *Reassessing Human Resource Management*. London: Sage, 56–73.

FEACO (2006). *Survey of the European Management Consultancy Market*. www.feaco.org.

Fortune Magazine (2003). The Incredible Shrinking Consultant. 26 May.

Gershon, P. (2004). *Releasing Resources to the Front Line: Independent Review of Public Sector Efficiency*. HM Treasury, July.

Grint, K., and Case, P. (2002). The Violent Rhetoric of Re-engineering: Management Consultancy on the Offensive. *Journal of Management Studies*, 35 (5).

Gross, A., and Poor, J. (2008). The Global Management Consultancy Sector. *Business Economics*. October.

Hammer, M., and Champy, J. (1993). *Reengineering the Corporation: A Manifesto for Business Revolution*. London: Nicolas Brealey.

IBIS (2009). *Management Consulting in the US*. Report no. 54161.

IOIM (2009). Introduction to Interim Management. *Institute of Interim Managers*. www.ioim.org.uk.

IPSOS/MORI (2008). *Interim Management Association: Market Audit*. www.interimmanagement.uk.com.

Kennedy Information (2008). *The Global Consulting Marketplace: Key Data, Forecasts and Trends*. Fitzwilliam, NH: Kennedy Information Inc.

——(2009). The Reign of Business Advisory Firms. Webcast, 12 August.

Knights, D., and McCabe, D. (1998). Dreams and Designs on Strategy: A Critical Analysis of TQM and Management Control. *Work, Employment and Society*, 12 (3): 443–56.

Kumar, V., Maheshwari, B., and Kumar, U. (2002). An Investigation of Critical Management Issues in ERP Implementation: Empirical Evidence from Canadian Organizations. *Technovation*, 23 (10).

Lerner, M. (2003). *The Vault Guide to the 50 Top Consulting Firms*. Vault Inc.

——(2008). *The Vault Guide to the 50 Top Consulting Firms*. Vault Inc.

McCabe, D., and Wilkinson, A. (1998). The Rise and Fall of TQM: The Vision, Meaning and Operations of Change. *Industrial Relations Journal*, 29 (1): 18–29.

McKenna, C. (2006). *The World's Newest Profession*. Oxford: Oxford University Press.

MCA (2006). *The UK Consulting Industry*. PMP.

——(2007). *The UK Consulting Industry*. PMP.

——(2008). *The UK Consulting Industry*. PMP.

National Audit Office (2006). *Central Government's Use of Consultants*. 13 December.

Neal, M., and Lloyd, C. (2007). The Role of the Internal Consultant. In P. Sadler, *Management Consultancy*. London: Kogan Page.

Office for National Statistics (2005). *UK Business: Activity, Size and Location*. www.statistics.gov.uk.

O'Mahoney, J., Adams, R., Antonocoupoulu, E., and Neeley, A. (2008). *Contemporary and Future Challenges in the UK Management Consulting Industry*. ESRC/AIM.

PAC (Public Accounts Committee) (2007). *Central Government's Use of Consultants*. 31st Report of the Session 2006–7. House of Commons.

Peters, T. (1988). *Thriving on Chaos*. London: Harper Collins.

Saint-Martin, D. (2004). *Building the New Managerialist State*. Oxford: Oxford University Press.

Schein, E. (2004). *Organizational Culture and Leadership*. Hoboken, NJ: Jossey-Bass.

Sewell, G., and Wilkinson, B. (1992). "Someone to Watch over Me": Surveillance, Discipline and the Just-in-Time Labour Process. *Sociology*, 26 (2): 271–89.

Smith, P. (2002). The Generalist Approach to Consulting: The Strategic Value of Breaking Industry Barriers. In S. Biswas and D. Twitchell (eds), *Management Consulting: A Complete Guide to the Industry*. New York: John Wiley & Sons.

Sturdy, A. (2008). *Internal Consultants as Agents of Change*. ESRC Small Grant Award: RES-000-22-1980.

Tuckman A. (1994). The Yellow Brick Road: Total Quality Management and the Restructuring of Organizational Culture. *Organization Studies*, 15 (5): 727–51.

van den Broek, D. (2004). "We Have the Values": Customers, Control and Corporate Ideology in Call Centre Operations. *New Technology, Work and Employment*, 19 (1).

Xiang, B. (2006). *Global Body Shopping: An Indian International Labor System in the Information Technology Industry*. Princeton, NJ: Princeton University Press.

Internal Consulting

Alan Warr, Management Consultant and Chair of
the UK Institute of Business Consulting (IBC)
Expert Group on Internal Consulting

■ What is an Internal Consultant?

A large number of organisations now have internal consultants. These are employees of the organisation who provide consultancy to line managers and to internal projects. Most organisations in OECD countries will have at least some roles that carry the title of consultant or may carry a management title but where the role is substantially to act as an internal management consultant. Around 30 per cent of large UK organisations have internal consultants organised into internal consulting functions or practices. Internal consulting practices appear to be as common in the public sector as in the private and this is a growing area of consultancy.

The most common format is for internal consulting practices to comprise a mix of former external consultants and talented individuals with management or technical backgrounds from across the organisation. The leadership of internal practices is often from a former external consulting leader, but is also sometimes provided by a general manager with little formal consultancy experience. Both of these leadership formats can be successful. At its core, what makes an internal consultant different is that their relationship to the organisation is that of a long-term employee. And it is this relationship that determines the nature of the consulting interventions and which influences the style of consulting that is successful.

In the UK around 10 per cent of management consultants are internal consultants. There is evidence that this number is rising and also that the underlying needs and plans from senior executives and boards are for more internal consulting capacities in their organisations. Most internal consulting practices seem to be started by a top executive sponsor, then grow rapidly for three to five years, and then decline, often falling victim to downsizing or restructuring or decentralisation. However, in these circumstances it is nevertheless rare for the internal consultants themselves to be made redundant; they are almost always viewed as too valuable to lose and find themselves continuing to contribute but from within a new role or function. It is common for organisations to later re-establish their internal consulting practice under a new sponsor and in a different format but with substantially the same objectives. This relatively short life-cycle and the ways to avoid this problem are poorly understood but very common, almost universal, and have become the focus for investigations by both the UK's Institute of Business Consulting (IBC) and academics.

For individuals, internal consulting is often a fast track onto a senior management role. Indeed some internal consultancy practices have as one of their goals to be an "incubator" for talented junior and middle managers to broaden their understanding of the organisation and deepen their change management skills in preparation for senior management. This can be challenging for the internal consulting practice as a constant turnover of its most talented consultants can be disruptive. However, for the internal consultants, they know that their successful efforts as an internal consultant will lead into senior management and this can be a strong draw towards this work. An internal consultancy practice can also be an attractive way of enticing senior, external management consultants into the organisation and provide an opportunity to continue to be consultants whilst learning about the organisation and demonstrating their potential for top management.

■ The History of Internal Consulting

There is a general myth that management consultancy started with the early external consultants like McKinsey & Co. However, a cursory review of business history reveals a different story with internal consultants being the source of large parts of external consultancy. Frederic Winslow Taylor was acting as an internal consultant within the Bethlehem Steel Works when he developed the principles of work study and scientific management. Ernest Butten, who worked with Taylor, founded PA Consulting, the UK's largest indigenous management consultancy. Taylor's work fuelled the early consulting growth of the consulting industry. Ozzie Osborne was acting as an internal consultant when he led the deployment of the first general purpose business computer at GE's General Appliances Division in Ohio in early to mid 1950s. This successful deployment led on to the development of the IT consulting industry in the 1960s, 1970s, and 1980s. Today IT consulting accounts for around 70 per cent of all external consulting. Another example would be Six Sigma and Lean, which owe more to industrial engineers at Toyota and internal consultants at GE for their discovery and development than to external consultants, at least in their early stages. It is easy to argue that internal consulting is not only an important part of the consulting industry but has proven to be a continuous wellspring of techniques for external consultancies. This probably derives from their closeness to the emerging problems and challenges of organisations, which they experience first hand and close up and are heavily incentivised to try to address through innovation.

■ Why Do Firms Found Internal Consultancies

Almost every firm establishes its internal consulting function for its own unique reasons. But three common motivations seem to dominate:

1. **Replacing high-cost external consultants with lower-cost internal consultants.** In 2009 the Chief Executive of the National Health Service established an internal consultancy for that specific purpose to try to stem the rapidly growing costs of internal consultancy that had reached £600m per annum across the service, so significant it attracted an investigation by the UK Parliament's Health Select Committee. This is a common motivation for internal consulting practices and is underpinned by the different economics of internal and external consultancy. Internal consultants typically incur lower travel, training, and management costs, but more significantly internal practices do not have the management overheads and business development and sales costs of an external practice. Consequently internal consultancy is typically around half the economic cost of external consultancy.

2. **Providing a source of expertise to pursue continuous improvements in business operations and productivity gains.** Every organisation needs to improve its efficiency continuously over time and an internal consulting practice can apply standardised techniques like process improvement, Lean, etc. and build considerable expertise by working across the organisation and later pursuing further productivity improvements by leveraging the knowledge gained. The Nationwide Building Society founded such a team in the mid 1990s and it grew to over sixty internal consultants, a sizeable practice even by external consulting standards. It developed sophisticated techniques for productivity improvements, reported consistently impressive financial returns, and won national consulting industry awards, leading to widespread public recognition as a best-practice consultancy equal to any external consultancy. In such a model, an internal practice can develop expertise over time in both the tools and techniques of business improvement, change, and transformation and combine this with deeper and deeper expertise in the organisation's business model, processes, and culture, allowing it to outperform external consultancies in many situations.

3. **Creating a focus for innovation by providing a free pool of talented consultants to help senior executives get new ventures, innovative projects, and radical changes started.** This model recognises that innovation is often risky for general managers because of the inevitable risk associated with innovation that can dent an executive's reputation, even in organisations that advocate a tolerance for failure. An internal consultant can provide the initial work needed to investigate and trial an innovation using dedicated time and located in a special project outside normal business activities, thus providing a dedicated and flexible resource, and also by being able to position failures or difficulties as a valuable goal of the initiative. By making innovation easier, organisations can get more innovations under way and profit from their earlier exploitation. Bupa, an international healthcare organisation, created an

internal consultancy in 2003 for this purpose and in the three years that it worked to these objectives (which were later modified following corporate restructuring) its reputation for exceptional levels of innovation became recognised both across Bupa and within the wider consulting industry.

■ How Does Internal Consulting Differ from External Consulting?

There is undoubtedly some rivalry between internal and external consultants. Internal consultants are often frustrated that despite having equivalent consulting skills and superior understanding of the organisation, they find that external consultants get to handle some of the most sensitive changes and often remain the key advisers to the board on strategy. And the reason for this is typically that they bring an independence of mind and can be more dispassionate when hard decisions must be made affecting staff or cherished ways of working must be challenged. On the other hand, external consultants worry that internal consultants take work from them and see that they are sometimes used to help organisations drive down the price of external advice and expertise—especially where internal consultants have previously been external consultants. And the reason for this apparent competition is that organisations often find they cannot afford as much external consulting as can be justified by the savings available. Finite consulting budgets can therefore be stretched by using internal consultants wherever possible.

Increasingly, the very real differences are being recognised between internal and external consultants and also that these differences can be utilised positively. These two forms of consulting are typically best deployed in different situations. Increasingly organisations are beginning to combine internal and external consultants to good effect and try to get the best of both worlds—the independence and external expertise of external consultants with the lower cost and deeper understanding of the culture and politics that internal consultants can bring. Table 3.10 summarises some of the key differences.

■ The Future for Internal Consultants

There are good reasons to be very optimistic about the future of internal consulting. Top executives are continuing to sponsor internal consulting functions and the work by the professional bodies and business researchers is beginning to identify more clearly the approaches to internal consulting that are most successful and lead to longevity. The ambition of organisations for how to use internal consultants is rising, with organisations giving them major roles in large-scale transformation programmes that they would previously have reserved for branded external consultancies (e.g. British Telecom and the UK's Ministry of Defence) and also making them central to innovation and new ventures (e.g. GE and Shell). Salaries have narrowed dramatically between internal and external consultancy roles as external consulting day rates have come under pressure,

	Internal consultant	External consultant
Source of authority	Reputation of their consultancy	Internal sponsor and the relationship of their work to corporate strategies
Relationship with organisation	Typically short term	Long-term employee
Credibility	Brand and reputation of consultancy	Long-term personal reputation
Independence	Easy to be independent and frequently expected by senior executives	Independence compromised by need to fit in, conform, and be part of organisation. Enhanced by career dependence on clients
Consulting expertise	Common to all consultants	Increasingly comparable to external consultants
Business expertise	Broad and can bring new ideas	Deep understanding of the organisation and its history
Technical expertise	May be proprietary to consulting firm	Typically more limited to the knowledge gained within organisation
Sector expertise	Wider expertise of sector	Knows organisation intimately and competitors well
Knowledge of client organisation	Needs time to understand the people—may misinterpret culture initially. Typically needs a period of investigating the issue and the organisation which delays value add	Knows the people but may have preconceptions. Can often get going immediately as they know the organisation, its issues, and have relationships already formed
Investment in success of intervention	Low, can move onto next assignment	High, must live with consequences into next assignment and into future career
Ability to access	"On the clock"—availability is timed, expensive, and rationed by economics of charging	Typically free, accessible, and available at short notice and people are known
Agenda	Meets client's objectives	Follows corporate strategies and agendas

Table 3.10. Internal and external consultants

making this a much more attractive option for graduates and MBAs. In 2009 in the UK the salaries of internal and external healthcare consultants were almost at parity, allowing people to move between these two modes of consulting without significant loss of income. The distinction between the two forms has also begun to blur, with internal consulting practices like that of Schlumberger expanding to offer external consultancy services to their customers and firms like BT who need specialised internal consulting capacity achieving this by buying external consulting firms or targeting external consultants for recruitment. Ten years ago the internal consultant was a second-class citizen to the external consultant, but today the two modes are achieving closer and closer parity. There are undoubtedly many situations where external consultants are more effective, but there is an increasing realisation that there are also an increasing number of situations where internal consultants are a better choice. This complementing coexistence with client organisations utilising different types of consultants as appropriate and in increasingly sophisticated combinations seems the most likely future.

PART 2

The Practitioner Perspective

4

Clients

Chapter Objectives

The consultant–client relationship is central to both the theoretical understanding and the practical success of consultancy projects. In Chapters 5 and 6 we will examine consultancy work from the perspective of the consultant but this chapter focuses on the view of the client. Specifically, the chapter aims to:

■ Examine the processes underpinning the client–consultant relationship and the variety of roles this can mean for the consultant.

■ Detail the gradual shift from Personal to Procurement models of client engagement.

■ Outline the pros and cons of the procurement function for both consultants and clients.

■ Detail the procurement process: from finding and defining a project to recruiting consultants and negotiating fees.

■ Suggest methods for managing consultants once they have been recruited.

■ Introduction

As with most service industries, consultancy is a client-led business. Whilst consultancies can help direct demand, by creating new products, setting agendas, and publishing their ideas, clients have their own rhythms which live apart from, yet create, the world of consultancy. It is, therefore, surprising to see a number of otherwise excellent books on consulting giving only scant attention to the active role that clients play in informing the consultancy industry (e.g. Kipping and Engwall 2002; Clark and Fincham 2002; Sadler 2007; Biswas and Twitchell 2002). This is especially so as recent research has demonstrated that the relationship between consultants and clients is central to the outcomes of the project: not just in terms of success and failure but also in terms of the project content, its perception by stakeholders, and the outcomes for the individuals involved (Karantinou and Hogg 2001; Handley et al. 2007; Hislop 2002; Fincham 1999). For those entering the profession, understanding the client's perspective is also important from a career perspective: many consultants end up transferring to clients' companies to work on the procurement and management of consultants, so a better understanding of how clients work is essential to their career strategies.

Central to this chapter is the difference that the management of the consultancy relationship can make to the success of a project. The ability to be honest and fair, to build trust, and to communicate requirements, risks, and concerns cannot be done by one party alone. It was perhaps Machiavelli who put it best when he wrote:

> a prince who is not himself wise cannot be wisely advised . . . good advice, whoever it comes from, depends on the shrewdness of the prince who seeks it, and not the shrewdness of the prince on good advice. (1532/1998: 82)

This chapter first outlines the different roles that consultants perform in relation to their clients. It next describes the changing ways in which clients engage consultants, moving from personal relationship to more formal procurement processes, looks at the different types of relationships that exist, and goes on to examine how clients select and manage consultants. It then examines the ways in which clients find and recruit consultants, focusing on the Request for Quotation process and the steps this entails. Finally, it covers some recommendations for clients on the management of consultants once they have been recruited.

■ Client–Consultant Relationships

The Relationship

The relationship between the client and the consultant is incredibly important yet equally difficult to analyse, in part because it varies so much depending on time and place (Fincham 1999; Whittle 2006) but also because there are so many different perspectives on "how it works" and because the balance of power between consultants and clients constantly shifts. One perspective, for example, put forward by Clark (1995), is that consultants act as magicians or witch-doctors (Argyris 2000; Whittle 2005) pulling the wool over clients' eyes with clever rhetoric (Sorge and Van Witteloostuijn 2004) in order to sell their wares. Other writers, such as Kubr (1982), Armbrüster (2002), and McGonagle and Vella (2001), have inverted this statement and argued instead that it is clients who hold the upper hand through their ability to compare different offerings and terminate projects early.

In more recent years, however, more balanced analyses have emerged, arguing that consultant–client relationships are not predetermined and can result in a variety of outcomes (Fincham 1999) depending on a number of variables (Sturdy 2010). These include market conditions (Armbrüster 2006), the type of consultancy that is taking place, the agents involved, and the processes and procedures which govern the relationship (Werr 2005). It will partially depend on the type of work that is being done, but will also be influenced by culture and sector of the client and the consultancy, the individuals involved, and the economic and political environment at the time.

These empirically informed analyses often stress the importance of mutual trust in creating successful outcomes for both parties (Hislop 2002; Martin et al. 2001) and argue that clients must be proactive in shaping the projects that are implemented if both parties are to achieve buy-in and legitimacy (Clark 1998; Williams 2003). Below, the different types of relationships that consultants have with clients are considered along with the reasons why these approaches might be taken.

Consultancy Roles

Expert

The reason most clients cite for the use of consultants in their firms is to perform tasks in which the firm does not have expertise (Czerniawska 2002). This construction of the consultant as "expert" not only benefits managers who need to justify expenditure on additional resources but is also an image that has been highly cultivated by the top management firms (Alvesson and Robertson 2006). Interestingly, the earliest consultancies first took the medical doctors as their model of expertise as they felt the "diagnosis, treatment, and improvement model" was one that worked well for consultancy. However, as McKenna (2006) argues, this metaphor limited the use of consultants to times when the organisation was "sick". What consultancies actually wanted was to be used by healthy organisations to improve their existing performance. It is, after all, healthy, not failing, companies that have the money to spend on large consultancy projects.

Coach/Facilitator

In 1969 Edgar Schien wrote a seminal book for consultants entitled *Process Consultation: Its Role in Organisational Development*. Writing, he said, more in anger than with perspective, he argued that consultants should enable the client to understand the organisation better and allow them to take the lead in diagnosing and ameliorating organisational problems. The role of the consultant in this situation shifts from the expert to being a coach and facilitator. For Schein, process consultancy is:

> a set of activities on the part of the consultant that help the client to perceive, understand and act upon the process events that occur in the client's environment in order to improve the situation defined by the client. (Schein 1988: 11)

This emphasis gave consultancy an organisational development focus, which aimed to enrich the organisation through developing its people, their analytical skills, and understanding of their company.

Process consultancy is, of course, only suitable in some situations. Organisations may need a process consultant when there is uncertainty around what projects should be implemented. Once the implementation starts, especially in systems or outsourcing work, the client requires people who can simply get the work done effectively. It should be noted that process consultancy is very different from *business* process consultancy. The former is a style of consultancy which focuses on human development and understanding, whilst the latter is a method that focuses on restructuring what is done in a company.

Friend

At the senior end of consultancy engagements, especially in strategy firms, partners often develop strong friendships with CEOs and their board members. This relationship is established over years of interaction and is enhanced because many CEOs will often have once been consultants in the same firms and thus, in companies such as McKinsey, the alumni network becomes a rich source of engagement opportunities that consultants can draw on.

In an interesting article by an ex-McKinsey partner, Day (2004) argues that a value hierarchy of consulting interventions exists (Figure 4.1) in which there are peer relationships between senior clients and consultants where "there is true partnership, a degree of intimacy and mutual development . . . the consultants learn from the clients as much as the other way around" (p. 38).

These personal relationships may involve integrating personal life, playing sport together, and meeting up for updates on the industry and new ideas. In an interview, one partner told me, "I speak to several CEOs pretty much every day and we've known each other for years. We explore ideas and changes together and my time isn't charged for. However, they do know that, eventually, it would be good if they paid for one of the services that we discuss."

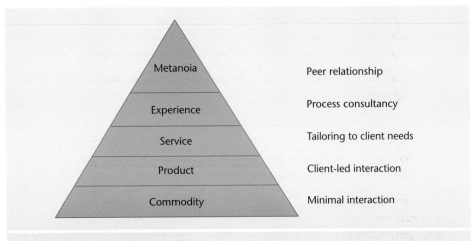

Figure 4.1. Value-add by consultants

Drones

From 2003 to 2006, Professors Andrew Sturdy and Tim Clark conducted a longitudinal study into consultant–client interactions. One of their central findings was that, contrary to popular belief, consultants only occasionally bring "expert" knowledge into an organisation. What they found was that it was much more common for consultants to undertake jobs that the firms were too understaffed to perform themselves and often required expertise that the firm already possessed (Sturdy et al. 2008). This phenomenon was demonstrated in a case cited by Werr (2005). In this case, named Alpha, consultants were explicitly prevented from making "expert" judgements because this was held to be "interpreted as a sign of managerial incompetence" (p. 104).

Werr (2005: 104) goes on to state that "this calls for an understanding of management consulting in relation to the managerial structures and processes in the buying organisation". This "functional incorporation" of consulting labour, termed "parallel management" by Fincham (1999: 347), stresses the way in which consultants can act in standard organisational roles rather than focusing on their external expert knowledge. This, Sturdy (2010) argues, emphasises the role of consultants less as outsiders and more as insiders, fulfilling standard on-going roles in organisational programmes. As Sturdy points out, this reflects a wider discourse by which the values and techniques of consultancy have increasingly become incorporated into internal mainstream organisational structures. Thus, it is increasingly common to hear of project groups, change champions, internal consultants, and business change/transformation managers as part of a normal organisational structure. It is not just that consultants are doing insiders' jobs, but equally that, as we shall see later in the book, insiders are becoming more like consultants.

Political Agents

When analysts and academics undertake qualitative studies into the use of consultants by clients they often find that, contrary to the formal, espoused aims of the project, which focus on enhancing organisational efficiency, consultants deploy themselves as political legitimisers of managerial action (Clark and Greatbach 2002). Such arguments are covered in more detail in Chapter 8; however, here we can summarise the main components of this perspective:

1. Consultants, both intentionally and otherwise, deploy themselves and the discourses around them as symbols of knowledge, power, and excellence (Alvesson and Robertson 2006).

2. In doing so, such symbols act as legitimisers of power, enabling and disabling the voices of different groups and their claims and rights to deploy managerial knowledge (Suddaby and Greenwood 2001).

3. In doing so, consultants not only position themselves as elite agents of legitimate knowledge but also those managers that align themselves with them. Managers draw upon this legitimacy to gain power in organisational struggles and justify their decision-making processes (Bloomfield and Ardha 1992).

Such an argument points to consultants less as valuable for what they know in terms of management expertise, and more for their ability to create and associate themselves with symbols of power and prestige and to signal these associations through performances by which meaning, and legitimacy, is transferred to agents and practices in the consultancy and the client.

I don't think either the client or the consultant often knows exactly what their roles are until the project is really under way.

(Consultant/academic, USA)

> ### CASE 4.1
>
> ## When Relationships Go Wrong
>
> Martin was a consultant for a niche consultancy, employing seven consultants that specialised in Organisational Change and Leadership Development. One of Martin's most fruitful contacts was an old school friend of his who was an HR director in a large organisation, Sarah. Sarah would frequently engage Martin for training courses and leadership development work and, even when Sarah had no budget for consultancy, she would recommend Martin to her colleagues. Over several years this relationship grew close and also accounted for Martin winning significant consulting work and rising up to director in his firm.
>
> As Martin progressed, so too did the work he undertook. One of his largest projects was working for the CEO undertaking an organisational redesign implementation. However, early on in the project, Martin realised that the project, which focused on outsourcing key functions such as HR and IT, might result in Sarah being made redundant.
>
> His first quandary was whether or not he should warn her of this. The project was meant to be confidential but he felt a loyalty to Sarah. Whilst he was considering this, the CEO asked Martin to generate a list of people he thought could be made redundant in the transformation and also asked if he would like to take on the, very profitable, project of implementing those redundancies. Whilst Martin realised that Sarah was dispensable, he hated the idea of making her redundant.
>
> • What would you have done if you were Martin?

■ From Personal Engagements to Procurement

The Personal Engagement Model

As spending on consultancy has grown over the last twenty years the systems that are designed to recruit consultants have also changed. When projects were smaller, the recruitment of consultants would often be done on a personal basis where the business owner (i.e. the client manager who wanted consultancy work done) would contact a consultancy (usually through personal contacts or recommendations) and then negotiate the work that was to be performed. As projects were typically smaller then, fees could often be paid out of discretionary or departmental budgets that did not need to be approved through finance or purchasing committees.

This personal approach to recruiting consultants has several benefits. The first is that, in the recruitment phase, the manager can meet the consultants face-to-face and assess the 'fit' between their personalities and the client team they will be working with. Second, as the business owner frequently turns to the same consultants for work, they can build up a strong level of trust between the two parties which means that contracts can be flexible and informal and working relationship more cohesive. Finally, personal recruitment is often faster, as it avoids bureaucratic channels, and arguably results in good communication between consultants and business owners because there are no intermediaries.

The standard steps in the Personal Engagement Model are:

1. The business owner recognises a need for consultancy work.
2. The business owner contacts the consultancy to discuss the project.
3. A "loose" contract is agreed which is flexible, informal, and based on previous models.
4. The work is performed by the consultant and managed by the business owner.
5. The work is paid for, often out of the business owner's discretionary, or departmental, budget.

However, whilst this relationship based engagement has some advantages, it also poses several problems that have exacerbated over the years:

- Quality Choice: the business owner may not know all the consultancies that could potentially perform the required work and therefore may not select the best consultancy for the job.

- Cost: business owners may not be the best people to negotiate the best-priced work, and without several consultancies competing for a contract, the client may not get the best price. Additionally, individual business owners may miss out on discounts for bulk or repeat business if others in their organisation are using the same consultants.

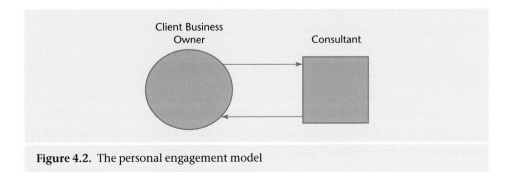

Figure 4.2. The personal engagement model

- Transparency: the personal relationship between business owner and consultant is potentially open to abuse. There are numerous instances of this relationship leading to bribery or "kick-backs" where the business owner is rewarded by the consultancy for passing business their way (see Chapter 9).

- Governance: in government departments it is especially important to be able to track and justify decisions for the public record and to be able to comply with laws that govern fairness, equality, and ethics. The personal model of engagement does not lend itself to such bureaucratic systems.

The Rise of Procurement

The limitations of the personal model of engagement pose significant problems for businesses that wish to demonstrate that they are getting the best consultants for the best money. This is especially true in the public sector where the use of taxpayers' money means that greater levels of accountability and transparency must be adhered to when dealing with the spiralling costs of consultants in government organisations.

Governmental leadership on the issue of procuring consultants was given impetus by a series of global and European laws which pushed the themes of equality, transparency, and globalisation of services along with that of free trade. These laws were initiated with the World Trade Organisation's Government Procurement Agreement (1979) which led to several EU Procurement Directives that developed from the mid 1980s onwards. These in turn have been translated into national laws in the USA and EU member states which govern the procurement processes in all public sector bodies.

As laws became more complex and spending became more scrutinised, responsibility for the engagement of consultants, especially in the public sector, was, in the 1990s, increasingly given to specialist procurement departments. Procurement departments, traditionally responsible for managing and purchasing supplies and equipment for large companies, provided a ready-made system of governance for companies seeking more formality in their engagement with consultants. However, as demand for procurement increased, specialist procurement organisations began to develop in the 1990s which promised to cut an organisation's spend on goods and services by up to 40 per cent.

In its standard format, the procurement function sits in between the business owner and the consultant ensuring that costs are driven down, that engagement is legal, transparent, and fair, and that there is a central point of coordination and management in engaging consultants. The resulting diagram looks something like Figure 4.3.

This diagram shows the central position of the procurement function between the business owner and the consultants they use. A key component of the process is Preferred Supplier Lists (PSL) which procurers turn to first when looking for a suitable consultancy. The PSL is a database of suppliers who meet a key number of minimum conditions. For example, they may be members of a consulting profession, have reliable references, have demonstrated a strong financial footing, or worked successfully with the client before. Acceptance on the PSL is also usually dependent on the consultancy accepting a set of standard terms and conditions which will include everything from daily rates to liability

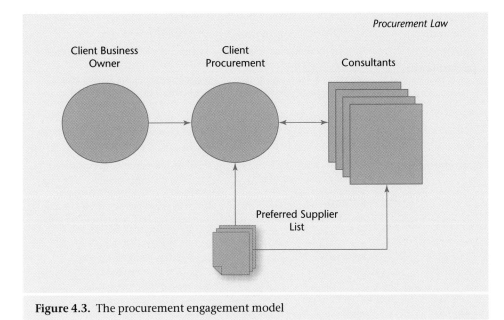

Figure 4.3. The procurement engagement model

	Strengths	**Weaknesses**
Cost	As most purchasing is centralised in the procurement department, they can achieve economies of scale when buying consultancy services. Thus, in a large organisation, procurement can often negotiate rates up to 40% lower than if directors contracted individually.	Procurement functions are not cheap and often employ upwards of twenty people. Moreover, my own interviews with consultants found that many increased their prices by 10–15% when dealing with procurers in the expectation that this would later be negotiated down. This finding is echoed by Lindberg and Furusten (2006).
Speed	Preferred Supplier Lists with pre-agreed terms and conditions means that significant time can be saved in negotiating terms and drawing up contracts.	In order to ensure due process when engaging consultants, procurement departments often follow bureaucratic and time-consuming paper-trails. In some cases, procured projects can take up to a year just to recruit the right consultants.
Choice	A procurement department will ensure that tenders for work go out to a number of consultancies and the selection is made consistently on clear, fair, and consistent criteria.	Lindberg and Furusten (2005) found that their client interviewees felt that the personality match between consultants and business owners was an important factor in their future success but something that procurement systems didn't and couldn't take into account.

Table 4.1. Strengths and weaknesses of the procurement function for consultancy services

	Strengths	**Weaknesses**
Quality performance	By increasing the number of consultancies that tenders are sent to, procurers argue that they are more likely to find consultants with the right competences.	As procurers are commonly measured on the cost reductions they make, they often go for the lowest-cost consultancy (Kambil and Sparks 2001). This invites the problem of the winner's curse, where the lowest bidder cannot afford to do a good job for the price they specified.
Communication	Procurers tend to ensure that all consultants get the same, consistent information from the client about the project. This helps avoid accusations of plagiarism or unfair influence.	When projects get communicated from the business owner to the procurer to the client, a game of Chinese whispers can be set in play in which project requirements get lost or misunderstood (Kadefors 2003). O'Mahoney et al. (2008) argued that procurement is unpopular with many business owners for this very reason.
Legality	The procurement function helps prevent collusion between business owners and consultants by preventing them communicating directly during the engagement process (Svensson 2003). As discussed in Chapter 9 this helps prevent illegal activity such as bribery or kick-backs.	As we will discuss in Chapter 9, the procurement function has not prevented high-profile cases of bribery, even in the public sector. The complicity, when it happens, tends now to be between procurers and consultants, rather than business owners and consultants.

Table 4.1. Continued

clauses (called a 'Framework Agreement'). The process for using the procurement function varies from company to company, and is defined in the next section.

As with the Personal Model of Engagement, the procurement model has a number of strengths and weaknesses. These are summarised in Table 4.1.

As procurement has become more important to businesses and the public sector, a number of institutions have emerged which attempt to prescribe best practice in the area. In the USA this is the Office of Federal Procurement Policy (OFPP), whilst UK, for example, the Office of Government Commerce (OGC) was created in 2000 to help public sector organisations develop procurement expertise. The effectiveness of such institutions in achieving cost reductions is a moot point (Public Accounts Committee 2007; Craig 2006) but there is no doubt that there are increasing efforts by procurers to control and commodify the recruitment of consultancies, and equal efforts by consultants to resist such pressures.

CASE 4.2

Johnson and Johnson

With sales of $53bn in 2006 J&J faced massive procurement costs in both materials and services. In their procurement of consultants there was little central visibility of spend, especially with regard to small projects. More importantly, the differing descriptions of consultant levels meant that advice was not given to managers on rates that they should be paying, projects were often badly managed, and the wrong consultants were often selected. Seventy-five per cent of reported spend for consultants was for vaguely defined "management services".

After a review of best practice and a gap analysis, J&J created three teams to organise the new system:

- "Find it" analysed past projects and developed a series of categories for consultants, projects, and consultancies so conformity to common standards could be achieved. The team improved spend visibility by 50%.

- "Get it" were responsible for developing a consulting sourcing strategy. They standardised the bid processes and developed common guides and policies on RFPs, NDAs, and contracts. Their clients, the business owners, reported a 100% increase in "benefits realised" after using their tools.

- "Keep it" sustained and improved relationships and delivery from existing suppliers. They developed a "Supplier Relationship Manager" role and a scorecard for managing delivery of projects. The amount of consulting spend that was managed proactively increased from 27% to 60%.

Johnson and Johnson believe that the success of their programme was down to senior buy-in for the changes, collaboration across the company and with suppliers, and a focus on common standards with reliable spend data.

Sources: Grable (2007) and Siegfried (2007).

■ Recruiting Consultants

The Procurement Process

There are few consultancies, large or small, that have not been subject to a formal procurement process. As this can be an extremely complex and laborious process for clients to manage, this section takes the process and explains it in four key steps: defining projects, finding consultants, selecting consultants, and negotiating the contract. These are the main steps of any procurement process, although, as we will see later, the steps can be much more fragmented and complex.

Below, the main steps the client takes in the procurement process are outlined. In the next chapter, we delve into more detail regarding the role and work of the consultant in this process; however, the focus here is primarily on the client and their perspective.

Defining Projects

What's the Problem?

Most project failures involving consultants are in trouble even before the consultants arrive. The issue is usually one where the client has failed to sufficiently define the problem, failed to assess the resources that they have to cope with the problem, or not understood why they need consultants at all. Too often, especially where there are large discretionary budgets, consultants are turned to automatically without careful considerations of why a project is necessary, what its objectives are, and how it is best achieved. This then results in consultants being unclear of their scope and managers unsure about their goals, leading to requirements changing, projects overrunning, and costs spiralling.

To avoid this situation, it is important that projects are linked to the organisational strategy. There are, then, two key questions which need to be asked:

- **What outcomes will help our company achieve its strategy?**
  It is essential to link all projects (consultancy or otherwise) to the organisational strategy. Porsche might make a lot of money launching a low-cost, budget car, but unless this fits with their long-term brand strategy, it should not be attempted. Note that this question focuses on outcomes rather than projects: often clients charge into specifying a project without knowing exactly what they want it to achieve.

- **What projects could enable these outcomes?**
  Now the client knows what outcomes are desirable, it can turn its attention to how best to achieve them. Some outcomes may simply require decisions on activities or resourcing, but others will require projects both to assess what exactly should be done and also to actually implement the work.

These questions are essential to the strategic planning of any company and especially important in understanding if consultancy work can be avoided. Consultancies are often very skilled at agenda setting, which often makes expensive consultancy interventions seem like the only solution for an organisation. Of course, some clients may turn to consultancies to help them answer these questions, which is fine if the skills are not available in-house. However, clients usually aim to separate the project which asks "what should we do?", from the actual project of "getting it done". Otherwise, the client puts themselves in the situation where the people responsible for deciding who gets paid to implement the project put themselves forward as the best contender. In Chapter 9 we discuss how this often blinds managers to potentially cheaper alternatives.

Creating the Business Case

Once it seems apparent that something *could* be done to improve the company's strategic position or profitability, clients will need to understand whether that thing *should* be done. This, in some companies, will lead to the definition of a business case for the project. As with any other business case, this document will focus on defining the *business* need for a project and might include:

- The specific business need that is driving the project.
- The strategic fit of the project with the company's overall strategic plan.
- Key benefits to be generated from the project and estimated financial benefits.
- The potential costs of the project—both financial and other costs.
- Funding options.
- High-level plan including major tasks and timelines.

In order to gauge what kind of budget might be made available for the project, the client should have an idea of what the "problem" is costing or will cost the organisation over a period of time. In some cases this may be difficult to ascertain; however, estimates based on solid assumptions should be made by the client so that their senior management can at least trace why the decision to move forward with the project has been taken or not.

The extent of the business case produced by the client will depend on the size of the project and the nature of the company. Some buyers choose to skip this part all together, whilst others, especially in the public sector, will break the business case down into several significant sub-documents, each requiring authorisation. The business case is a good opportunity for clients to gauge sponsorship for the project before, for example, realising that, whilst it is a useful project, nobody really wants to take responsibility for it.

Skills Assessment

As part of the business case, or as an activity following the business case, the client will often perform a skills analysis to assess the expertise required for project completion and the available human resources. This will usually involve considering the following questions:

- What skills/methods are required for the project?
- What time period are these skills likely to be needed for?
- Are the skills/methods available in-house and can they be reallocated?
- What support/expertise is available externally?
- What other requirements exist and how are these best met?

The answers to these questions will determine whether the work should be performed by the client's own workforce or whether they need to look externally. It is important to stress that "looking externally" need not be consultants, but might include: student placements, academics, or businesses that have solved a similar problem. In deciding who is best placed to perform the work, it is important to consider whether the skills are better developed in-house or sourced externally. If it is agreed that consultants are necessary, the business case and the skills assessment will often feed into, or become, the Request for Information (RFI) document discussed below. If it is decided that the relevant skills can be sourced internally, these documents will feed into the project definition for internal teams.

At this early stage, the client will usually focus on defining the problem with the stakeholders, the outcomes required, any outstanding questions that need to be answered, and gaining as much background information as possible. During this period, it is important for the client to include cross-company communication, especially with procurement and programme management, to ensure that similar, connected, or impacted projects are considered. For example, the client's payroll department may be considering introducing procurement software at the same time as HR is considering payroll software. Overlaps and conflicts with other projects need to be identified early on to avoid replication and maximise efficiency.

Involving Consultancies in Project Definition

After the business case has been defined, the client will start putting some "meat on the bones" of a potential solution. Again, this is something that may often be done in conjunction with a consultancy, but it is essential that a senior client employee, usually known as the Project Champion, takes a stake in driving the project forward and a business owner is assigned responsibility for the project. A senior Project Champion in the client team is important, not just to give the project credibility, but also to ensure there is someone associated with the project who the consultancies cannot afford to alienate. Later on, the Champion, even if they take a hands-off role, can prove decisive when requirements change.

It is common for consultancies to play a significant part not only in defining the future direction of a company but also in defining the projects which are required to facilitate organisational change. Even aside from strategic work, consultancies are often brought in at an early stage when project definition requires expert knowledge. However, there is an obvious danger here that the consultancy will create a requirement that makes them, rather than their competitors, more likely to win the work. In many countries' public sectors, legislation actively prevents the consultants who define the work from bidding to perform the work. However, in the private sector, there are many examples which attest to the proclivity of consultancies to write tendering documents that maximise their own chances of winning the work.

The Request for Information (RFI)

The Request for Information (RFI) document is a document that the client produces in order to see how consultants might, at a general level, approach the solution to their problem. Many clients use an RFI to obtain feedback on their initial proposal from several consultancies. Whilst this is useful in providing the client with ideas of how the project should be defined, it is important here that the client does not lose sight of their core business objectives: some clients fall into the trap of simply incorporating all the ideas from the consultancies, which typically results in a loss of project direction, unnecessary complexity, and increased expense.

The RFI, sometimes called a specification, provides a general overview of the problem the client is facing and asks a wide range of consultancies what approach they would take to solve the problem. It is intended to be quite high level so as to provide the buyer with useful information about what the best direction for the project should be. An RFI will usually provide:

- **An Introduction**: who the RFI comes from and what they do.
- **Scope**: what the project includes and does not include.
- **Terminology**: a detailing of all abbreviations and clarifications required in the document.

- **Procedure**: the format responses should take and who to contact.
- **Timetable**: the key milestones in selecting consultants and running the project.
- **Background**: a high level overview of what needs to be done. Scenarios are often useful here.
- **Requirements**: any business requirements that have already been specified.
- **Criteria**: the selection criteria for consultancies (optional).

At this stage, the client would also have given some thought to the assessment criteria by which the consultancies will be judged when they return their responses. The skills assessment, business case, and the RFI will all feed into this consideration. The RFI should be focused on outputs (i.e. what business objectives are achieved) rather than inputs (what the consultancy will do in order to achieve this) and should have some prescription for how these outputs are measured. Measures should be clear, linked to important outcomes, and agreed with the consultancy. A sample RFI is provided in the Online Resource Centre.

The Request for Proposal (RFP)

A few weeks after sending out the RFI, the client should begin receiving responses. These can often be quite varied. The responses to an RFI will usually enable the client to draw up a shortlist of consultancies and to clarify the details of the project. Usually, this will lead to the shortlist being sent a Request for Proposal, a more precise document which specifies the detail, structure, and methods that the project will use. This document may include the sections detailed in the RFI but might also include requests for much more detail in the consultancy's proposal such as:

- **Consultancy details**: a request for references, cases, and history for the consultancy.
- **Staff**: the CVs, training, certificates, and experience of all those to be involved in the project.
- **Method details**: a breakdown of any methods, software, or formats the consultancy intends to employ.
- **Plans**: a detailed breakdown of activities, milestones, review dates, and resources required in the project.
- **Costs**: a breakdown of costs, payment options, and schedule.
- **Terms and conditions**: usually standard terms for the buyer/client.

The RFP is essential to get right as this will form the basis of the contract and will, in turn, form the basis of the consultants' work. It will also specify how the work is communicated and tracked. The details of the plan and method can be elaborated in the response to the RFP and in the negotiations once the right consultant has been selected. However, at this stage, it is important to set expectations as to what work will be performed and at what pace. Many consultancies, at this stage, ask the consultancies to make a presentation. This should involve the sales team, a few choice senior stakeholders, and should also include any specific staff that are expected to work on the project.

It is quite important for the client to demand the response in a standardized format together with a standardized use of terms, especially in reference to skills and staff. It is incredibly difficult to compare different proposals, but this is especially so when a "project manager" can range from a secretary with no experience to a director-level consultant charged at £2,000 per day.

Levels of Detail

A final issue concerning the project specification/RFI is the ambiguity of the project definition. On the one hand an overly specified project means that some consultancies may find they cannot apply for the work, despite having a potentially strong solution, because a software, resource or reporting requirement precludes their application. It could also mean that when requirements change, which they undoubtedly will when consultants come onboard, the costs may spiral, and, at worst, the project may need to be put out to tender again. However, a vaguely defined document makes it difficult for consultancies to specify and price their potential solutions.

Ironically, many academics have specified that ambiguity in consultancy offerings is key to the successful diffusion of those products (Benders and van Veen 2001; Giroux 2006). However, as Lindberg and Furusten note, "a widespread notion among consultants is that, in procurements where the problem has been defined without the involvement of consultants, the specifications are often vague and problems ill-defined or even misinterpreted" (2005: 173): the assumption being that the ambiguity is often down to the incompetence of the procurement department rather than a strategic decision on the buyer's behalf. As a consequence, RFIs and contracts routinely include a clause that new requirements may be incorporated into the document at a later date if they are unforeseen.

Finding Consultants

There are many different routes to finding consultants, some more popular than others (see Figure 4.4.).

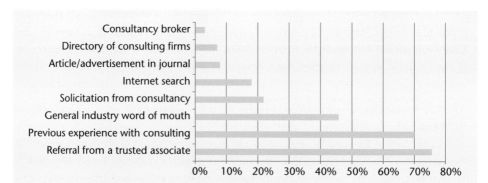

Figure 4.4. How consultancy firms are identified by clients
Source: Consulting Intelligence (2007).

The RFI/RFP approach can work with anything from two to a hundred different consultancies, but the ways in which these are sourced deserve individual attention. Below, types of recruitment processes that clients use are outlined and the strengths and weaknesses of each are provided.

Starting from Scratch

If the client's organisation is an SME or one which rarely uses consultants it may be that they will be starting from a blank sheet when seeking suitable consultants. There are several routes to ensuring that this does not place the client at a significant disadvantage when seeking the right people. These include:

- **Word of mouth**
  Recommendations from friends and similar companies should not be underestimated and are the most common source of referral for consultants. The best measure of the quality of a consultant is their recommendation from previous clients and businesses. Businesses are often willing to share the names of good consultants they have used.

- **Bidding websites**
  In the last ten years a number of websites have emerged which bring together clients with consultants. These range from large e-procurement systems in the public sector to e-bidding microsites for small projects. These sites are most useful for simple commodified projects.

- **Conferences**
  There are hundreds of business conferences each year on specific business topics such as outsourcing, systems development, or strategy. If a client has a problem in one of the areas covered by a conference it is often worth attending for two reasons. First, presenters and attendees will be interested in the topic so it presents a good chance to learn about the issue. Second, consultants often present their approaches and success stories, which give the client good leads to consultants that they think might be useful.

- **Assured lists**
  There are a number of lists of consultants that are worth reviewing that have some quality assurance (i.e. are better than opening the Yellow Pages). One in the UK, for example, is provided by the Institute of Business Consulting whose members all, as a minimum, have Professional Indemnity Insurance, recent relevant experience, and membership of the Institute. A more detailed list is hosted by www.sourceforconsulting.com along with cases they have implemented and recommendations from clients. Management consultancy associations also often provide a searchable database of their members.

- **Direct contact**
  If the client has a reasonably large or specialised project, there are probably less than twenty firms that can undertake it for them (many of these can be found in Chapter 2). For example, if the client requires a consultant to carry out a large outsourcing or systems development project, then it would be foolish not to at least communicate with Accenture. Most of the large firms have a Request for Services email on their website which allows clients to send them RFIs or even general business enquiries.

- **Do-it-yourself**

  A couple of years ago I was seeking some design consultancy work for a company I ran, but had little personal experience in design at all. I first trawled the internet and any directories I could find to find suitable firms and simply listed all 195 of them in Excel. I then visited their websites to see which could provide all the services I wanted, had a good website (who would employ a design consultancy with a badly designed website?), and had some experience with similar products to my own. I then removed all of those that were located too far away to visit regularly. This left twelve companies which I visited and scored on a number of factors that seemed essential to the project, which narrowed it down to the three to whom I sent an RFI. Maybe not the most scientific method of selection, but the consultancy I was left with did a fantastic job.

Starting from scratch is a difficult business and requires a lot of time and effort to ensure that the client is at least selecting from a relatively wide pool of good consultants. It is for this reason that many companies who use consultancies frequently have either a formalised procurement process and/or a list of preferred consultancy suppliers. It is these that are discussed next.

Preferred Supplier Lists

Preferred Supplier Lists (PSLs) are used by clients to specify a select group of consultants that managers can chose from when considering consultancy contracts. The reasons for wanting to set up a PSL are varied, but can include:

- To prevent managers dealing with consultancies that have a poor track record.
- To ensure that consultancies meet minimum standards (e.g. in ethics or insurance).
- To save the time of managers in the selection of consultancies.
- To prevent managers recruiting consultancies they have a personal interest in.
- To ensure a clear and consistent message in the form of standard contracts, terms, and conditions.
- To ensure that rates, fees, and contracts are relatively standardised.

Often PSLs have been drawn up in advance by the company's procurement team and are relatively open to consultancies that wish to apply for listing. Of course, being on the PSL does not mean that the consultancy will actually be employed, simply that it may be taken into account by a business manager when seeking a consultancy. When assessing a consultancy for inclusion on a PSL, a procurement department may consider:

- Adherence to professional ethical policies.
- Public Liability Insurance.
- The use of specific communication channels and forms.
- Rules on expenses, invoicing and payments, cancellations, and confidentiality.
- Specific fees for specific grades/qualifications/experience.

If considering the use of PSLs it is important that the client is clear on the reasons for doing so. Some of the reasons listed above, such as preventing managers dealing with consultancies with a poor track record, are completely valid, whereas others, such as standardising rates, may be counterproductive. PSLs also have drawbacks. The first is that the client may be missing out on some good consultants by not simply advertising the project in the local paper and seeing who applies. The second is that these relatively standardised processes work well for fairly standard projects, but not for one-off or niche projects, which may require non-standard suppliers. The third is that removing discretion from managers may be counterproductive. Managers may be able to negotiate better rates based on tacit knowledge or repeat business that the PSL rules don't take into account. In short, PSLs are not necessarily a bad idea, but should be used as a guide with exceptions not imposed as a rule.

I would say that 90% of engagements are either through personal contacts or pre-existing relationships.

(Sales director, niche consultancy)

Selecting Consultants

The selection of consultants will depend upon criteria that will have been defined early on. The selection criteria will evolve as it becomes clearer what the project comprises. It will have been influenced by the skills analysis, the business case, and the writing of the RFI and RFP, but is likely to include the:

- Quality of the proposal.
- Capabilities of the consultancy.
- Experience and qualifications of key staff.
- Financial stability.
- Estimated project cost.
- Staff size and location.
- Quality of presentation.

These categories may well be sub-divided and entered into a spreadsheet so they can be weighted and scored according to the client's preferences. Once a consultancy has been selected the client will then need to enter what is often termed "post-tender negotiations" where the final details and payment structures are hammered out. The client will also need to debrief the unsuccessful consultants as to why their bids failed. This should be handled honestly but delicately as the client may need to work with them in the future.

Only 1 per cent of clients say that they recruit their consultants primarily on price (Bryson 1997) and this is not surprising. In markets such as consultancy, where there is considerable ambiguity regarding the quality of the product, price tends not to be a major differentiator (Akerlof 1970). However, as procurement has become more dominant in organisations and large projects are increasingly commodified, price is still a significant component of the decision-making process, especially in companies with limited budgets.

Negotiating

From Specification to Contract

Due to the length of the RFI process the specification document should be seen as a work in progress that will change as the project becomes better defined and the capabilities of the remaining consultancies are better understood. It is important to remember that this document will, however, form the basis of a contract which will be legally binding on both sides. This transition will involve a detailed conversation with the selected consultancy to confirm exactly what is going to be delivered and when.

Consultancies will often try to get their "standard" contract to clients first to use as the basis of the agreement. The client manager will often try to avoid this situation as it places the onus on them and their legal team to understand, check, and modify their work. Instead, the client should get all consultancies to sign up to a standard contract which sets out the client's standard terms on expenses, working hours, liability, intellectual property, and other issues. Getting the consultancy to sign up to the client's terms rather than their own is sometimes difficult, especially if the client lacks buying power. Consultancies will often take their time on this, which they can afford to do if they have already been selected. This requires careful management by the negotiator; once a consultancy is certain that all other bidders have been eliminated and the client cannot reasonably go elsewhere, they can take the upper hand. For this reason it is important to get the most controversial and difficult negotiations out the way as early as possible, preferably agreed in principle before the final selection is confirmed.

For the client, if possible, it is essential to involve procurement in the negotiation phase. Procurement may not know the business as well as the buyer but they can usually negotiate better than most business owners, especially if they have been involved in the project definition. Even if the client has skipped procurement during the entire engagement process, it is still a good idea to use their negotiators' advice and skills where possible. Of course, every contract is going to be different and will depend on the company, its environment, and culture as well as the consultancy they are dealing with. However, there are some key issues that every client should be aware of:

- **Measure the business outcomes**
  The business outcomes are central to the success of the project and the consultancy should see the achievement of these as their primary purpose. The outcomes should be specific, measurable, attainable, relevant, and time-bound (SMART).

- **Move to framework agreements**
  These are agreements with named suppliers which usually specify a fixed price for on-going contractual relationships. In effect, the practice of framework agreements means that a buyer can continue to use a supplier, or suppliers, for on-going work without having to go out to tender or through procurement every time a new project comes up.

Framework agreements save the client a lot of time as they do not have to renegotiate every consultancy contract and can often achieve economies of scale by indicating the need for on-going work with a consultancy. For these reasons, larger clients would be well advised to avoid single-engagement contracts and instead move to framework agreements where terms are standardised.

- **Intellectual property (IP)**
  This is often a tricky subject for negotiations and one that is best dealt with early. If a client is paying a consultant to develop intellectual property for them—for example a training package or a software development method—the client will not want the consultant to turn this into a product which is then sold to the client's competitors at half the price. The consultancy, however, will want to retain as much as they can of their own development work. As a middle way, it may be possible to license the IP to the consultancy, so they get a cut every time it is sold on.

Agreeing Fees

Whilst it is common to get a breakdown of costs in a response to an RFP, exact fees are not usually finalised until the post-tender negotiation. Consultancies usually state that their fees are fixed and that any reduction is achievable only through a lessening of the workload. However, fees can often be reduced if:

- The consultancy is expecting more work to follow on from the existing project.
- The project is large enough to enable the client to force a discounted rate.
- The consultancy is working in competition with a rival on the same project.
- The project enables the consultancy to develop a new competence or some IP.

Payment Structures

There are several different ways to pay consultants which emphasise different aspects of the work, and getting this wrong can make the difference between success and disaster. In Chapter 6 we outline the different types of payment that suit different projects. From a client's perspective, the following should be remembered:

- Most consultancy projects are costed at an hourly or daily rate. This is suitable for consultancies that the client has not worked with regularly. For most projects, the hourly/daily rate should be multiplied by the project resourcing to give an overall cost for the project.

- Clients should ensure that payment is triggered by the achievement of specific business deliverables, for example the training programme is delivered within three months to 120 employees with feedback exceeding 70 per cent. Success is easier to quantify with some projects rather than others; however, it is important that the question of what success entails is agreed with the consultancy so that both parties are clear what is being paid for.

• Clients should ensure that the contract specifies what happens if the business deliverables are not achieved. Sometimes this can include penalty clauses, partial payment, or, conversely, the lack of a bonus payment.

• Payments which add in bonuses or penalties for early/late completion or under-/over-achievement should only be undertaken with consultancies that you know and trust. Otherwise the possibility for opportunism may damage the project.

• Penalty clauses should be used with care. One of the key reasons Accenture withdrew from a multi-million pound UK health project was down to it facing excessive penalties for its failure to deliver. This withdrawal arguably cost the client more than the penalty fees would have brought in.

Putting the Pieces Together

When the steps detailed above are put together, they form a coherent process by which a client goes from identifying a potential project, all the way through to the signing of a contract. This "procurement process" is done in many different ways in different organisations: some deal with the process in an highly informal and flexible way, whilst others, especially in the public sector, are more bureaucratic and procedural. Figure 4.5 shows a simplified version of a procurement process that I put together for a company.

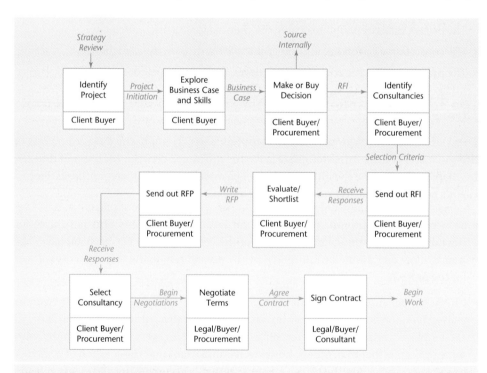

Figure 4.5. A typical procurement process

Does Procurement Work?

The comparison and selection of consultants is incredibly difficult to get right, especially if the client has not worked with the consultants previously and has little feel for their capabilities, personalities, and processes. The key factor for successful business change is the ability to change mindsets and attitudes (IBM 2008) but the ability of consultants to achieve this is hard to assess without actually meeting and interacting with the team that will be working on the project. This places the realist business manager in a difficult position. On the one hand, the best-practice advice and, in the public sector, legislation specify that the selection process be transparent, fair, and equitable. On the other hand, if the business owner is focused on what is most likely to ensure success, he or she may well consider that a consultancy that they have worked successfully with in the past is more promising than leaving the process to the procurement department's scoring system.

Whilst many business owners are aware that this is not best practice and potentially illegal, it is, as Lindberg and Furusten (2005) point out, relatively common. In fact, in their survey of such quandaries, the authors found a number of business owners that "quite frequently make illusive procurements for the sake of appearance only. In practice they have already decided whom they want to work with . . . the buyer then tailors the evaluation criteria so as to fit the preferred supplier perfectly" (p. 180). Even in the public sector, where there are usually rules to prevent business owners recruiting whoever they wish, the authors found a number of methods used by business owners to get around these restrictions. These included the following.

Ignoring the Law There is growing evidence that not only do some public sector organisations fail to engage with best practice procurement recommendations but a few simply ignore the relevant procurement laws regarding consultant engagement (Craig 2006). This is often less the fault of the organisation and more down to the individual managers who bypass procurement. In the case study conducted by Lindberg and Furusten (2005) managers who did this felt that the procurement law was an unnecessary burden and, whilst useful for goods, was less suited to consultancy.

Splitting up Projects Many countries specify a threshold spend on professional services, under which buyers are not required to abide by procurement law and can therefore contact and recruit buyers directly. To get below this threshold, projects are sometimes cut up into smaller deals so that the buyer can avoid going through procurement at all.

■ Managing Consultants

Preparing the Organisation

Whilst clients often recognise the need to manage consultants tightly and communicate with them effectively, many forget to prepare their own organisations for the experience.

When asked what would have had the biggest impact on the success of the project, 45 per cent of buyers said both "being clearer to our own people why we were using consultants" and " better internal sponsorship and commitment in our own team" (Czerniawska 2006). For this reason, it is important for the client to prepare the client organisation to receive consultants.

Good practice for preparing the organisation might include:

- Explaining to staff why consultants rather than internal resources are being used.
- Communicating exactly what the consultants are doing and when they will be leaving.
- Providing guidance on communication with consultants.
- Communicating the project management structure and the appropriate access points for any queries.

One of the key points raised by Czerniawska (2006) is the importance of securing a senior sponsor for the project. This is fairly standard advice for all projects; however, it is especially important when dealing with consultancies. This is not simply down to the usual messages of having someone senior drive the changes in the organisation but also to have a stakeholder that the incoming consultancy cannot afford to annoy. If a consultancy thinks they might lose their entire income from an organisation they are much more likely to go the extra mile to ensure the project is a success.

It is important also to recognise that the further down the organisational hierarchy the less enamoured with consultants employees become (Figure 4.6). The only group who scored lower with their satisfaction levels were those people seconded to the project from elsewhere in the client organisation, only a third of whom reported that consultants were honest and only 11 per cent of whom were satisfied with the project (Czerniawska 2006). This indicates that both end users and those seconded to projects involving consultants have a pretty poor experience of the consulting profession. Given it is these very people who can best sabotage a project through withholding

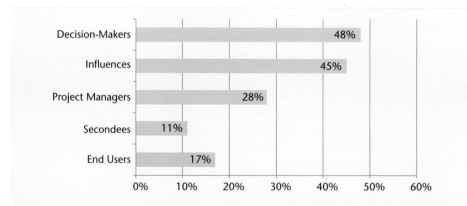

Figure 4.6. Satisfaction levels with consultancy projects
Source: Czerniawska (2006).

information or playing politics, it is important for a client organisation to get their own employees on side before introducing the potential disruption that consultants can bring.

Reporting and Managing

The management of consultants once recruited should not be left to the consultants, or to any other consultancy. This is not because they cannot be trusted but because it is only the business owner who really knows what the business wants and the communication and clarification of these requirements on a daily basis. However, the reporting and management structure will very much depend on the project, the culture of the client, and the amount of trust that has developed between the client and the consultant.

Client Roles

The client will usually have someone (or several people) fulfilling specific roles in relation to the consultancy and the project. It is important for the consultancy not simply to know who they are but also to understand their impact on the project and their potential for enabling future projects. The names of the roles will vary from company to company and one person may perform multiple roles. Despite this, the positions will remain relatively stable throughout the project. It should also be noted that other than the budget holder and the project owner, the rest of the roles are sometimes performed by consultancies, especially in large projects. In Table 4.2 a breakdown of these roles is provided together with their main contact person from the consultancy.

Communication and Reporting

The biggest problem clients report of consultancies is their failure to understand the business problem (58 per cent). The next most significant problems are consultants going over budget (56 per cent) and over time (56 per cent) (Czerniawska 2006). For these reasons, it is essential that the reporting of progress and the establishment of clear communication are not neglected. Specifically, there should be clear processes to ensure that:

- Progress is tracked.
- Issues are raised.
- Changes to the work schedule are processed.
- Clarification and direction is set.

The reporting and communication should be clearly tied to the plan or methodology agreed in the contract.

How this is achieved, however, is very much dependent on the project. In a large systems integration or outsourcing project, clear processes will need to be mapped out,

Client role	Activity	Must be ...	Consultancy contact
Budget holder	Their budget will fund the consultancy work.	Informed	Partner
Governors	Senior people who, for political reasons, must be communicated with about the project.	Informed	Partner
Business owner	Accountable and responsible for the outcomes of the project.	Accountable	Partner/principal consultant
Programme manager	Coordinates the project with all the other projects in programme.	Consulted	Principal consultant
Project manager	Responsible for planning the project.	Informed	Senior consultant/ consultant
Team leader	Responsible for managing the work of the team.	Responsible	Senior consultant/ consultant
Supports	Responsible for working with the consultants to get the work done.	Responsible	Consultant

Table 4.2. Client roles in a consulting project

communicated, and built into the bureaucracy of the project management. However, if the consultant is an individual who is coaching an executive, for example, such processes can be made informal—though not neglected. It is often a difficult conversation for managers to have if something goes wrong, and too many leave it to recrimination at the end of a project. Having a clear opportunity and a process for managing concerns and issues is central to project success.

On the client side, it is also important to document as much as possible and to enlist the consultant's help in achieving this. The client should not want all the information to be held in the consultant's head because at some point, they will leave the project—sometimes unexpectedly—and if this happens, the more that is written down, the better. In addition, it is important that a senior client manager has a day-to-day overview of what is going on in the project. A former colleague of mine who started a small consultancy several years ago found himself responsible for the client's decision-making which kept his consultancy in work. Needless to say, three years later, the consultants are still there and the client appears blissfully unaware.

General Management

In addition to the usual processes, reporting structures, and meetings that scaffold a consultancy project, there are several additional tips that clients should be aware of when managing consultants:

- Don't rely on the contract. By all means make it as strong as possible, but a contract will not stop a project failing. Especially with big projects, both sides need to be flexible and forgiving if a project is to work. When a dispute ends up in court, both sides will lose out to the lawyers.

- Have a Plan B. Consultancies occasionally go bankrupt. Data sometimes get stolen. Budgets are often unexpectedly cut. When setting up your contract and your project ask yourself, what would happen if a major problem occurred?

- Have a project grievance procedure for all parties. Ill feeling is often bottled up, especially by team members who are working with consultants. It is much healthier to get things out in the open and to resolve problems quickly. The Principal Consultant will help you do this and will appreciate the process.

- If you are working with a new consultancy, assign a mentor to the project early on. The mentor, preferably a senior manager, should shadow the project and provide an independent view on how it is progressing, flagging any issues that occur.

- Ensure that you get the people you asked for. One of the major criticisms of consultancies from clients is that "the last time you see the people that convinced you to hire them is when you sign the contract" (McGonagle and Vella 2001: 178). "Bungee consultants" that drop in to make a splash at the beginning of the project and then disappear are not useful to the client.

Building the Relationship

When workers want to bring a company to its knees without a formal strike, they engage in a practice called "working to rule". This highly effective form of resistance is based on the workers only doing what they are contracted to do. As good work depends so much on activities that are not contracted, working to rule is feared by most directors. Similarly, a consultancy engagement which relies purely on a formal contractual relationship is the worst type of engagement. For this reason it is important to build trust and familiarity quickly so that the work goes "beyond contract".

In *The Trusted Firm* Fiona Czerniawska (2007: 42) argues that it is generally not the individual consultants that the client has difficulty trusting but the consultancy itself: "clients like and respect the individual consultants they work with but are suspicious of the motives of the firm". However, whilst Czerniawska's study focuses on what the consultancy can do to repair this relationship, it is equally important for the client to focus on building this relationship to ensure project success.

Unfortunately, there are no easy answers to the problem of creating good relationships other than being open, honest, and equitable in the treatment of consultants. I have worked on several consulting projects where the consultants were treated like second-class citizens by the client. Of course, there are often understandable reasons for this, such as fear, envy, and suspicion, but the end result is that the consultants become less committed to the project and more interested in getting out of there as quickly as possible. A chapter I wrote a few years ago (O'Mahoney 2007) describes how this cycle of distrust between consultants and clients can spiral into a mutually damaging relationship which harms both the project and the individuals involved:

> Low trust relationships were exacerbated with client employees who were suspicious (often rightly so) that consultants were being brought in to downsize the operation. There was also inevitably a certain amount of jealousy of people "doing the same work for double the money" as one client employee told me. This, more often than not, meant that employees treated consultants badly. In one company, a re-engineering exercise I was involved with suffered badly from all the usual forms of sabotage from client employees towards consultants: information was withheld, software and hardware was lost or damaged, confidential documents were leaked and relevant meetings weren't communicated. Whilst this behaviour was entirely understandable, the instinctual reaction of many consultants, including myself, was to react in kind. Trouble makers were identified and briefed against and processes were designed to minimize the power of awkward managers. (2007: 216)

As we discover in Chapter 8, the inherent ambiguity of the consultant–client relationship means that the development of trust acts as a safety net where processes and procedures cannot. Ensuring that both parties are treated with dignity and respect goes a long way to helping achieve project success.

Handover and Exit

In the excellent Dilbert cartoons consultants are often called "consul-ticks" on account of the difficulty in removing them. This is usually blamed on the consultancy's desire to make themselves indispensable to the organisation and to build strong relationships with key decision-makers. However, whilst this is a fact of life, from the client's perspective it is entirely understandable to want to keep hold of a group of highly motivated, well-trained workers who arrive before, and leave after, everyone else. In order to guard against these tendencies, remember:

- **Keep the end in mind, from the beginning**
  Too many consultancy contracts start without a clear vision of what the organisation will look like when they leave. This vision should be built into all the documents and meetings that communicate the clients' intentions to the consultants.

- **Build knowledge transfer into the contract**
  The last thing a client wants to be left with is a perfectly working system but with no idea how to manage it. It is important, then, to identify and specify the knowledge transfer that will enable the client to continue working effectively when the consultancy has left. This will usually involve training and what is termed "man matching": getting an employee to understand and take over the support roles that the consultants were performing.

- **Set headcount milestones**

  The client's contract and plan will have various milestones which mark the progress of the project towards completion. If possible they should tie these to headcount reductions. For example, through controlling badges and passes, the client should automatically default to removing the access consultants on the day they are due to leave. Any exceptions should go through change management.

- **Have a clear handover plan**

  Once the project milestones have been hit, there should be a clear plan of what documents, resources, and processes will be handed over, where they will reside, and how they will be managed on an on-going basis and by whom. It should also be specified in the contract how follow-up or remedial work will be performed and if it will be charged for.

Evaluating Consultancy

As consultancy has taken up a bigger slice of client spending over the years, it has become increasingly important for consultants to demonstrate value for money and for buyers to be able to demonstrate to their bosses that an investment is worthwhile. However, only 25 per cent of projects attempt to measure the return on investment on their projects, and only 3 per cent specifically measured the Return on Investment (ROI) on the use of consultants (Czerniawska 2006). In addition a third of the managers surveyed stated they wished they had done more to measure the contribution of consultants.

To some extent, the lack of measurement is understandable. Imagine a car manufacturer which, as part of a larger project, is changing its design software. Consultancy X has successfully bid for and delivered some training in operating that software. How would the client go about measuring the return on investment of that training? The short answer is that they probably couldn't. They could perhaps measure the effectiveness of the training or benchmark the feedback from the attendees. However, tracing the impact of the training through the new software, its contribution to enhanced design, and the knock-on effect to higher sales or prices is unlikely to be convincing even if the client were inclined to attempt it. The push, then, to quantify the contribution of consultancy engagement in terms of return on investment, whilst possible in some cases, is perhaps ambitious in most situations. However, this does not mean that *qualitative* assessment and evaluation should not be attempted.

Central to both the client's and the consultant's management processes should be a commitment to continuous improvement. By examining the project and learning lessons from what could be improved on both sides, the processes by which the consultant and the client manage consulting engagements can be improved in subsequent projects.

The qualitative review should not happen right at the end of the project when both sides are often exhausted, but should usually wait for three or four months after project completion so that changes have had a chance to settle in and both parties have had a chance to reflect upon their working relationships.

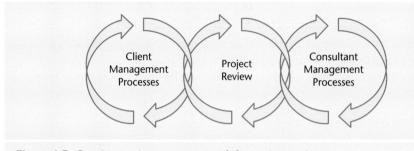

Figure 4.7. Continuous improvement and the project review

The only way the client or the consultant learns how to do things better next time is through a project review. But so few places do this properly.

(Procurers, public sector company)

The primary feedback should focus on the stated objectives, plan, and timelines specified in the contract. Were these met, and if not, why not? However, feedback should also be sought and supplied on both sides as to the working relationship: communication, management, issue escalation, the change management process, and the individuals in each team. This, in turn, should feed into the performance and project management systems on both sides. It is essential that feedback is not only provided at a senior level. All surveys of consultancy work show that the more senior a stakeholder the more satisfied they are likely to be with the project. The real criticisms often come from those who worked closest with the consultancy team and these should be embraced, not feared, by both groups.

■ Chapter Summary

This chapter has provided a detailed description of the client's perspective of the consulting relationship. In particular, it has:

• Explained why clients use consultants.

• Described the procurement process.

• Explained how clients find, select, recruit, and negotiate with consultants.

• Demonstrated how consultants are managed by clients.

Student Exercise

In 2004, Crouch and O'Mahoney did a comparative study of the ways in which companies in Italy and the UK employed outside advice. They found that Italians were much more likely to turn to friends, family, and even competitor firms before going to a consultant, whereas in the UK consultants were often chosen as the first option. When one examines the statistics the UK accounts for 24 per cent of the European consulting market, whereas Italy accounts for only 3 per cent, despite having similar sized economies.

1. Why do you think this is?

2. How would you test your hypotheses by doing further research?

Discussion Questions

• Explain the RFI/RFP Process.

• What are the pros and cons of the procurement function? Why has it become more dominant in recent years?

• What are the costs considered when weighing up whether to use external or internal management consultants? Are there any others that should be added?

• Why do public sector clients have much more stringent procurement rules than the private sector?

Case-Study Exercise: StayMobile Technology

Your Tasks

Split into two groups of roughly equal sizes (2–3 in each). One group will represent the directors of StayMobile Technology. One group will represent the consultants of ConsultCo, a generalist consultancy.

• You will first meet to exchange information, discuss the requirements of the business, and decide which single consultancy project will most benefit the company (15 minutes).

• Each group will then create a one-page document. The consultancy will produce an abbreviated draft proposal (one page) and the directors will produce a one-page assessment document which will be used to weigh, score, and assess the proposal, and other proposals, they might receive (15 minutes).

• The two groups will then meet and agree a high-level project (activities, resources, and costs). You will then exchange documents and, after reading them, discuss how each group could have improved their work (15 minutes).

You may then be asked by the tutor about the key learnings that the exercise taught you and anything that you would do differently next time.

Common Information

StayMobile Technology has a patent on, and manufactures, lockers that recharge mobile phones. The locker is called the BuzzBox. The basic scenario is that the BuzzBox is leased (free of charge) to a venue (e.g. hotel, airport, train station). Customers pay £1 to recharge their phone. Their phone is locked securely, by the customer, in one of eight compartments, each dedicated to a different phone manufacturer. The charge takes 20 minutes. Revenue is also generated through advertising on the front of the lockers. Usually, revenue is shared 50/50 with the venue.

StayMobile is a start-up company. The ten shareholders each invested £10,000 to get to the prototype stage. The company employs two full-time people:

- The MD/manufacturing director: he designed and ordered the parts for the prototype BuzzBox and puts them together in his attic. He is also responsible for all MD activities and much of the decision-making. He is an engineer by trade.

- The marketing director: she is responsible for getting publicity for the product, finding venues to install it, visiting these venues, and agreeing on high-profile locations. She is also responsible for finding advertising for the machines. She is also responsible for producing business plans and giving venture capital presentations. She was previously a management consultant.

In addition, the company draws on the part-time services of:

- An electrician. Whilst the MD can do the physical engineering required, there is relatively complex circuitry involved in the machine. The electrician designs and manufactures the circuit boards.

- A finance director. He provides advice on the finances of the company, checks business plans, submits tax and company returns.

Further Reading

There are surprisingly few good texts that examine the relationship between clients and consultants. From the academic side, one of the most influential articles was written by Fincham (1999), which highlighted the contingent and influential nature of the interactions between the client and the consultant. A strong but under-cited study is to be found in *Dealing with Confidence*, a deeply analytical collection of essays on the interactions between clients and various management advisory companies by Furusten and Werr. As ever, in this area, it is worth keeping an eye open for work by Tim Clark, Andrew Sturdy, and Andrea Whittle, all insightful commentators in this area.

Outside academia, the best work in the area is by Fiona Czerniawska, who combines practitioner insights with strong analysis. Her book entitled *The Trusted Firm* offers a well-researched argument that "trusted advisers" are no longer enough: that consultancies need to be trusted as well.

If you are simply looking for a "how to get and manage clients" book, there are thousands of them on Amazon, all giving pretty much the same advice: know and define your product well, market and sell it intelligently, have a logical system for managing the "sales pipeline", and do good work. One of the more interesting texts is by Scott (2008), who recommends writing a short, engaging book in order to maximise client engagement and communication. Her argument is that publications, be they books or articles, are a good way of building credibility and developing an engagement with potential buyers in a different way.

Finally, in terms of blogs and online resources for clients, I would recommend the following:

www.davidmaister.com—excellent blog and articles on client–consultant relationships.

www.verasage.com—a strong think-tank for professional knowledge firms.

www.ogc.org—the Office of Government Commerce.

www.ibconsulting.org—the institution website with free resources for clients and consultants.

www.mca.org.uk—the Management Consultancy Association which also has free resources on client engagement.

www.trustedadvisor.com—a consultancy with some good free articles.

www.constellia.com—procurement professionals who help clients control consultants, and organise the Consultancy Sourcerers Group, a networking group for consultancy buyers.

All of these, and many more links, are listed in the Online Resource Centre.

References

Akerlof, George A. (1970). The Market for "Lemons": Quality Uncertainty and the Market Mechanism. *Quarterly Journal of Economics*, 84 (3): 488–500.

Alvesson, M., and Robertson, J. (2006). The Best and the Brightest: The Construction, Significance and Effects of Elite Identities in Consulting Firms. *Organization*, 13 (2): 195–224.

Antal, A. B., and Krebsbach-Gnath, C. (2001). Consultants as Agents of Organizational Learning. In M. Dierkes, A. Berthoin, J. Child, and I. Nonaka (eds), *Handbook of Organizational Learning and Knowledge*. Oxford: Oxford University Press.

Argyris, C. (2000). *Flawed Advice and the Management Trap*. New York: Oxford University Press.

Armbrüster, T. (2006). *The Economics and Sociology of Management Consulting*. Cambridge: Cambridge University Press.

Benders, J., and Van Veen, K. (2001). What's in a Fashion? Interpretative Viability and Management Fashions. *Organization*, 8 (1): 33–53.

Berger, P., and Luckmann, T. (1966). *The Social Construction of Reality*. New York: Doubleday.

Biswas, S., and Twitchell, D. (2002). *Management Consulting: A Complete Guide to the Industry*. New York: John Wiley & Sons.

Bloomfield, B., and Best, A. (1992). Management Consultants: Systems Development, Power and the Translation of Problems. *Sociological Review*, 40 (3): 533–60.

—— and Danieli, A. (2007). The Role of Management Consultants in the Development of Information Technology: The Indissoluble Nature of Socio-political and Technical Skills. *Journal of Management Studies*, 32 (1): 23–46.

Bowers, S. (2006). Accenture to Quit NHS Technology Overhaul. *The Guardian*, 26 September.

Bryson J. (1997). Business Service Firms, Service Space and the Management of Change. *Entrepreneurship and Regional Development*, 9: 93–111.

Clark, T. (1995). *Managing Consultants: Consultancy as the Management of Impressions*. Buckingham: Open University Press.

—— (1998). Telling Tales: Management Guru's Narratives and the Construction of Managerial Identity. *Journal of Management Studies*, 35 (2).

—— and Fincham, R. (2002). *Critical Consulting*. Oxford: Blackwell Publishing

—— and Greatbach, D. (2002). Knowledge Legitimation and Audience Affiliation through Storytelling: The Example of Management Gurus. In T. Clark and R. Fincham (eds), *Critical Consulting*. Oxford: Blackwell.

Consulting Intelligence (2007). *Consulting Survey*. Consulting Intelligence LLC.

Craig, D. (2005). *Rip Off: The Scandalous Story of the Management Consulting Money Machine*. London: Original Book Company.

Crouch, C., and O'Mahoney, J. (2004). Machine Tooling in the United Kingdom. In C. Crouch et al., *Changing Governance of Local Economies in Europe*. Oxford: Oxford University Press.

Czerniawska, F. (2002). *Value Based Consulting*. Basingstoke: Palgrave Macmillan.

—— (2006). *Ensuring Sustainable Value from Consultants*. MCA/PWC.

—— (2007). *The Trusted Firm*. Chichester: John Wiley.

Day, J. (2004). Dynamics of the Client–Consultant Relationship. In J. P. Thommen and A. Richter (eds), *Management Consulting Today: Strategies for a Challenging Environment*. Wiesbaden: Gabler.

Dougherty, D., and Heller, T. (1994). The Illegitimacy of Successful Product Innovation in Established Firms. *Organization Science*, 5 (2): 200–18.

Fincham, R. (1999). The Consultant–Client Relationship: Critical Perspectives on the Management of Organizational Change. *Journal of Management Studies*, 36 (3): 331–51.

Furusten, S., and Werr, A. (eds) (2005). *Dealing with Confidence*. Copenhagen: Copenhagen Business School Press.

Giroux, H. (2006). It Was Such a Handy Term: Management Fashions and Pragmatic Ambiguity. *Journal of Management Studies*, 43 (6).

Grable, A. (2007). Johnson and Johnson Consulting Category Management. Presentation at the 8th Annual Services Group Conference, Phoenix, AZ.

Handley, K., Clark, T., Fincham, R., and Sturdy, A. (2007). Researching Situated Learning: Participation, Identity and Practices in Client–Consultant Relationships. *Management Learning*, 38 (2): 173–91.

Heusinkveld, S., and Benders, J. (2005). Contested Commodification: Consultancies and their Struggle with New Concept Development. *Human Relations*, 58 (3): 283–310.

Hislop, D. (2002). The Client Role in Consultancy Relations during the Appropriation of Technological Innovations. *Research Policy*, 31: 657–71.

IBM (2009). *Making Change Work*. IBM Global Business Services.

IPSOS/MORI (2007). *Paying More and Getting Less: What Clients Think about Consultancy*. Ernst and Young.

Kadefors, A. (2003). Trust in Project Relationships: Inside the Black Box. *International Journal of Project Management*, 22 (3): 175–82.

Kambil, A., and Sparks, M. (2001). *Seizing the Value of e-Procurement Auctions*. Research Report, Accenture Institute for Strategic Change, Cranfield University.

Karantinou, K., and Hogg, M. (2001). Exploring Relationship Management in Professional Services: A Study of Management Consultancy. *Journal of Marketing Management*, 17: 263–86.

Kellman, S. (2005). *Unleashing Change*. Washington, DC: Brookings Institution Press.

Kipping, M., and Engwall, L. (2002). *Management Consulting: Emergence and Dynamics of a Knowledge Industry*. Oxford: Oxford University Press.

Kitay, J., and Wright, C. (2007). From Prophets to Profits: The Occupational Rhetoric of Management Consultants. *Human Relations*, 60 (11): 1613–40.

Kubr, M. (1982). *Management Consulting: A Guide to the Profession*. International Labour Office.

Lindberg, K., and Furusten, S. (2005). Breaking Laws: Making Deals. In S. Furusten and A. Werr (eds), *Dealing with Confidence*. Copenhagen: Copenhagen Business School Press.

McGonagle, J., and Vella, M. (2001). *How to Use a Consultant in your Company: A Manager's and Executive's Guide*. New York: John Wiley & Sons.

Machiavelli, N. (1532/1998). *The Prince*. Cambridge: Cambridge University Press.

McKenna, C. (2006). *The World's Newest Profession*. Oxford: Oxford University Press.

Martin, C., Horne, D., and Chan, W. (2001). *A Perspective on Client Productivity in Business-to-Business Consulting Services*. *International Journal of Service Industry Management* (Bradford), 12 (2).

O'Mahoney, J. (2007). Disrupting Identity: Trust and Angst in Management Consulting. In S. Bolton (ed.), *Searching for the H in Human Resource Management*. Beverly Hills, CA: Sage.

—— Adams, R., Antonacopoulou, E., Neely, A. (2008). *A Scoping Study of Contemporary and Future Challenges in the UK Management Consulting Industry*. ESRC Business Engagement Project: AIM Research.

Public Accounts Committee (2007). *Assessing the Value for Money of OGCbuying.solutions*. June 2007, HC (2006–7) 275: 5–7.

Sadler, P. (2007). *Management Consulting*. London: Kogan Page.

Saint-Martin, D. (2004). *Building the New Managerialist State: Consultants and the Politics of Public Sector Reform in Comparative Perspective*. Oxford: Oxford University Press.

Schein (1988). *Process Consultation*. Boston, MA: Addison-Wesley.

Scott, S. (2008). *Doing Business by the Book*. Charleston, SC: Advantage Media Group.

Siegfried, M. (2007). Using Consultants Effectively. *Inside Supply Management*, 18 (6): 32.

Sorge, A., and Van Witteloostuijn, D. (2004). The (Non)sense of Organizational Change. *Organization Studies*, 25 (7): 1205–31.

Sturdy, A. (1997). The Consultancy Process: An Insecure Business? *Journal of Management Studies*, 34 (3): 389–413.

—— (2010). Management Consulting: A Future Research Agenda. In M. Kipping and T. Clark (eds), *Handbook of Management Consultancy*. Oxford: Oxford University Press.

—— Clark, T., Fincham, R., and Handley, K. (2008). Re-thinking the Role of Management Consultants as Disseminators of Business Knowledge: Knowledge Flows, Directions and Conditions in Consulting Projects. In H. Scarborough (ed.), *The Evolution of Business Knowledge*. Oxford: Oxford University Press.

Suddaby, R., and Greenwood, R. (2001). Colonizing Knowledge: Commodification as a Dynamic of

Jurisdictional Expansion in Professional Service Firms. *Human Relations*, 54 (7): 933–53.

Svensson, R. (2003). Visits to the Client when Competing for New Consulting Contracts: Sourcing Information or Influencing the Client? *Applied Economics*, 35 (14): 1531–41.

Werr, A. (2005). Taking Control of Need Construction. In S. Furusten and A. Werr (eds), *Dealing with Confidence: The Construction of Need and Trust in Management Advisory Services*. Copenhagen: Copenhagen Business School Press.

Whittle, A. (2005). Preaching and Practising Flexibility: Implications for Theories of Subjectivity at Work. *Human Relations*, 58 (10): 1301–22.

—— (2006). The Paradoxical Repertoires of Management Consultancy. *Journal of Organisational Change Management*, 19 (4): 424–35.

Williams R. (2003). "Consultobabble" and the Client–Consultant Relationship. *Managerial Auditing Journal*, 18 (2): 134–9.

Procurement's Role in Buying Consultancy

Alan Gotto, CEO, Constellia

The basic role of Procurement is to help clients buy well; this can be a significant challenge as consultancy is a very high-risk buy due to the multiplicity of often intangible variables which must be managed. Frequently a distress buy, consultancy is bought when clients know they have a problem which they can't resolve themselves, which often makes it hard for them to understand the solution/what they are buying.

It is no longer news to say that Procurement is now involved in many consultancy buys, as Procurement's role supporting, and acting as a key influencer to, client stakeholders is well established. Typically Procurement does this by appointing a "Category Manager" to manage this area of spend, who is then responsible for taking a holistic view of the consultancy requirements of a client, and developing a "Category Strategy" for securing the required services, as well as providing tactical sourcing support for individual projects.

And introducing some simple Procurement discipline can have significant benefits for a client, by applying levers such as:

- transparency: e.g. by asking consultants to rigorously detail in their proposals what they will do and deliver, the capabilities of their consultants, and to provide a full breakdown of their costs,

- competition: so that instead of handing projects to the same old supplier, the threat of introducing aggressive alternatives challenges them to improve their offering to win the work, and

- consolidation: by developing "Preferred Consultant Lists" fragmented spend can be channelled to a few key suppliers, enabling them to offer volume discounts and develop stronger relationships.

The challenge for Procurement has been to identify the right Procurement practices/tools to apply these levers to consultancy spend. For example:

- using tendering: an invaluable approach for introducing competitive pressure, but lengthy and bureaucratic tender processes should if possible be avoided, as they may cause delay where consultancy support is urgently required, create costs for all, and potentially restrict the consultant–client stakeholder interaction. Instead Procurement is learning to keep the process quick and encourage dialogue between the consultants and the client stakeholder—so that not only can the consultants understand what is required, but the client stakeholders can also understand the proposed solution,

- using reverse e-auctions: these have been very effective for driving down the pricing of highly commoditized products. But consultancy is a highly de-commoditised service, a key component of which is the people who will deliver it, making it impossible to precisely specify what you want to buy and make price the only variable. As such the cheapest supplier is likely to also be offering the lowest-quality solution, so Procurement needs to use this solution very cautiously in this space, and

- developing market and supplier knowledge: one of the key tasks of a Procurement professional is to know who the best suppliers are. But this is very difficult with consultancy as the market is very fluid, with individual consultants constantly moving between firms, and the value delivered by consultancy is very hard to measure. This is increasingly being countered by asking consultants to fully detail their experience, including at an individual consultant level, and then ensure that performance feedback is captured after projects.

Nevertheless the clichéd criticism of Procurement by consultants still persists that they are "cost focused" (i.e. just want the lowest price) when they should be "value focused" (i.e. they should recognise the return the consultant can give them for money). In fact it is day-one Procurement training to be "best value focused" (i.e. interested in which consultancy can give them the most for their money), but this is of course a challenge most consultants would rather avoid.

The consultants who are prepared to meet the challenge to offer best value, though, are able to benefit from treating Procurement not as a "barrier to sale" but instead as a "sales channel", as Procurement will promote their engagement instead of the lower-value alternatives. And as expert buyers Procurement can then ensure projects are set up for success, for example by ensuring that client stakeholders are fully aware of the support they must give the consultants to enable them to deliver.

Doing the above will de-risk the buy, and give client stakeholders who might have previously thought twice about spending a significant sum the confidence to do so. And clients can then avoid the cycle of spend freezes they often see as the only option when consultancy spend gets out of control.

An intelligent consultant will therefore recognise that, whilst Procurement may still be perfecting its approach to managing consultancy spend, it is in their interests that Procurement it is successful in doing so.

5

The Consulting Life-Cycle

Chapter Objectives

This chapter explains the consultancy life-cycle to the reader. It first introduces the concept, and goes on to detail the four stages it incorporates: sales, research, delivery, and exit. In doing so, this chapter aims at providing a realistic and practice-informed overview of consultancy work giving real insights into the day-to-day lives of consultants.

The chapter:

- Introduces the consulting life-cycle.

- Examines the different sales approaches that consultancies utilise.

- Explains how to write and manage proposals.

- Shows how negotiations are managed and contracts are drawn up.

- Introduces the main research skills used by consultants to find and analyse data.

- Details how consultancy projects are planned, controlled, and delivered.

- Explains how projects are wound up, handed over, and reviewed.

■ The Consulting Life-Cycle

Consultancy work is sometimes depicted as a "life-cycle": a process that traces the phases of work from beginning to end, and afterwards, to be in the position to begin again. The exact phases in the life-cycle vary from text to text (see Markham 2004: 158; Weiss 2003: 138; Holmes 2002: 65). However, they generally describe the processes which connect the initial approach made to a client by a consultant to the final project review and exit. The process described below is based on my own experience and attempts to incorporate the stages identified by other authors.

The steps depicted in Figure 5.1 form the basis of this chapter and are summarised in Table 5.1.

Before moving on, however, it is worth noting four caveats that should be considered when using the life-cycle model. The first is that especially in larger companies the steps are usually not all present in a single consulting project. If the client wants a strategy deliverable, for example, the consultant may undertake the research step but there may

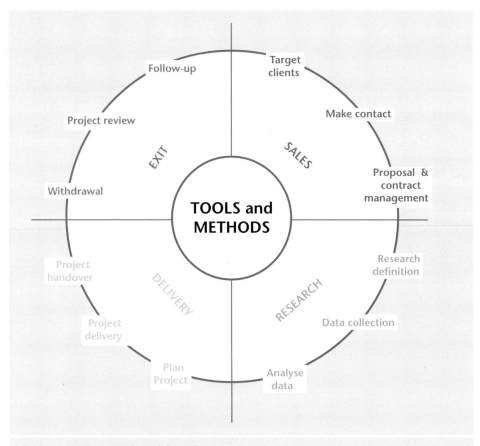

Figure 5.1. The consulting life-cycle

Phase	Step	Activity	Common deliverables
Sales	Target Clients	Finding the right clients to sell the consultancy products to.	Sales strategy and plan
	Making Contact	Establishing lines of communication and building trust.	Request for Information (RFI) or Request for Proposal (RFP)
	Proposal and Contract Management	Writing and developing proposals that form the basis of solid contracts.	Signed Contract
Research	Research Definition	Agreeing what the research will actually achieve.	Research Plan
	Data Collection	Using appropriate methods to collect the information that is needed.	Data Results
	Data Analysis	Structuring the collected data so find trends, patterns, and answers.	Report/ Recommendations
Delivery	Plan Project	Structuring the project to achieve delivery on time and budget.	Agreed project plan and deliverables
	Deliver Project	Ensuring all agreed objectives and deliverables are done on time.	Sign-off on individual deliverables
	Project Handover	Passing responsibility, training, and documentation to the client.	Project sign-off
Exit	Withdrawal	Leaving the project.	Payment
	Project Review	Learning improvement lessons for future projects.	Internal Improvement Plan
	Follow-up	Pursuing sales leads generated during the project.	Sales Leads

Table 5.1. The consultancy life-cycle

be no delivery other than the strategy document. Alternatively, there may be no research phase if, as is increasingly common, the client already knows what they want. The second caveat is that all of the phases and steps are rather idealised. In practice, some of the steps are not only missed out, but they can be ill defined, completed in a different order, or overlap to such an extent that their actual identification can be difficult.

Third, many representations of the life-cycle assume that consultants will use their research to recommend solutions which are most appropriate to the client. However, few, if any, consultants go into an organisation with a blank slate, defining their solution according to what would best suit the client. Instead, most consultancies are solution-led, offering clients a fixed number of standardised solutions or methodologies. Often, especially in smaller consultancies, only one or two products will be offered. A salesperson in a consultancy that specialised in BPR told me, "there are very few problems that I can't get a business process angle on. It's like the saying that, 'to a hammer everything is a nail'; to me, everything can have a process solution."

Finally, it should be noted that it is increasingly rare for consultancies to perform any project from beginning to end as is implied by the life-cycle diagram. Instead, projects are usually broken up into stages where two or more consultancies do the work. For a large project, such as a global ERP system, one may have up to ten consultancies involved in the implementation, with another handful looking at strategy, project, and programme management. These fragmented projects are often seen, especially by government procurers, as a good way of avoiding over-reliance on one team and also as a way of ensuring that no consultancy believes that it is irreplaceable.

I was taught about the consulting life-cycle in my MBA, but in reality you only ever see a small part of it—unless perhaps you're a partner or a director.

(Recent graduate, large audit-based consultancy)

Regardless of these caveats, the life-cycle is still a useful way of structuring consultancy work. The subsequent sections focus on the four phases of the life-cycle: sales, research, delivery, and exit. Within the description of each phase, the different steps are broken down so the reader can achieve a complete understanding of the work that consultants usually perform.

■ Sales

A Sales Overview

Consulting is a push rather than a pull industry. In other words, clients generally don't come running to consultancies with bundles of cash, asking for interventions. One of the reasons consultants have to charge upwards of £1,000 a day is to cover the huge effort and expense that goes into marketing and selling their products: writing white papers, drafting proposals, attending conferences, sponsoring events, and entertaining client contacts. As the sales process often involves free advice and up to a third of a consultant's time, this overhead needs to be costed into any work that is actually charged for in addition to the usual overheads of offices, support, personnel, and materials. A consultant with an eye on their career, therefore, will do well not to forget that consulting is about sales. You may be the best process engineer, project manager, and strategist in McKinsey but if you cannot sell, it is unlikely you will ever rise far above the Senior Consultant grade.

Poachers Turned Gamekeepers

In the "old days", let's say the 1980s, the sales effort was often characterised by heavy lunches, large expense accounts, and strong personal networks. However, as we discussed in Chapter 4, clients are increasingly limiting the access consultants have to key decision-makers and budget holders in their companies, making the sales effort much harder. The new world that consultants face is one where clients are more sophisticated and formal in their engagement with consultants and frequently employ ex-consultants who understand the "tricks of the trade" in order to keep down the consulting spend. As we saw in the last chapter, larger clients have increasingly turned to procurement departments to deal with the complex task of selecting the consultancy to perform the work. Of course, for consultancies, this is all very upsetting. Imagine selling your car to a young, naive, and inexperienced driver, only to find they turn up with their dad, who is a part-time mechanic, ex-car-salesman, and an experienced negotiator who knows plenty of other people selling cars like yours.

Procurers have attempted to standardise processes and projects to make consultancy proposals easier to compare. Procurement processes have, over the years, become more procedural, and attempted to turn consultancy services into commodified, easily comparable, products. This commodification pressure from the procurement system has resulted in the squeezing of consulting margins which in turn has hit consultancy profits and salaries. As a result, consultancies have had to up their game, recruiting professional sales teams and specialists to help deal with the procurement process.

Managing the Sales Pipeline

Regardless of the quality of the consultancy's sales team and consultants, it is important to understand sales as a process that needs to be managed rather than an event. The failure to do this can lead to several mistakes, the most obvious of which is selling too much. This happens when sales processes are not coordinated, and well-meaning consultants successfully achieve several contracts simultaneously, leading to a lack of resources to complete the work. Whilst such events can be managed by slowing the contracting process or taking on short-term hires, there is often a risk that projects become understaffed, or worse, staffed with weak consultants, or even worse, cancelled by the consultancy. These outcomes can easily lead to bad-will from clients and consultancies being taken off preferred supplier lists.

The way to avoid log-jamming the sales pipeline is for the sales director to manage contracting processes so that not too many leads are at the same stage. For example, sales directors will often map out the progress of all sales processes onto a chart, with each sale charted from the merest hint of an opportunity all the way through initial meetings, project formulation, proposals, and contract. Of course, these steps will vary, depending on the project, but the important point for the sales director is to have a relatively constant flow of opportunities at each stage so that over- and under-capacity can be avoided.

On Developing a Sales Strategy

In recent years I have had the opportunity to interview some of the partners responsible for sales and marketing at the top consultancies around the world. A common thread to many of the interviews was the response that the sales strategy of a consultancy should put consultants in a position where it is almost impossible *not* to sell. Central to achieving this aim is the production of a perfect fit between the products that the consultancy is selling, the market they are in, and the strategy of the consultancy itself.

The key questions consultancies should ask themselves reflect the concerns of these areas. The first concerns the core product of the consultancy:

- What is your core proposition?
- How is it unique? What competitors do you have offering it?
- How do you ensure your proposition or product is continuously improved?
- How do you know when it can be improved?

The second concerns the consultancy itself:

- What is your growth strategy?
- What is your delivery capability? How scalable is this?
- What types of projects do your sales and delivery capacity match?
- How can these be improved?

Finally, the consultancy should consider the types of clients that match both the product proposition and the capacity of the consultancy.

- What client segments are there in your market? Think vertically (industry types) and horizontally (size, tier, sector).
- What phase of growth does your proposition most favour?
- Based on the previous questions, which are your priority segments?
- Which clients within your priority segments are spending on your type of product?
- In which clients can you most readily access decision-makers?

Out of these three areas (Figure 5.2) a consultancy should be able to ensure that their strategy and their product are most appropriately aligned with the clients they wish to bring in. If these areas are unaligned, clients can receive confused signals and wasted work may be carried out.

Targeting Clients

In 2008 I interviewed the CEO of a successful and growing medium-sized consultancy who, amongst other things, told me:

> The best advice I was given when starting this practice was to find my clients strategically. If you chase after any consultancy work that comes your way or fail to plan your sales strategy, you will end up with no core proposition. Your knowledge will rarely improve because you will rarely repeat the same work twice . . . To succeed, and get known, you need to specialise, identify your clients, and perfect your art. If you don't do this, your company will never accumulate value.

Many consultants will do any work they can get their hands on, which is understandable in hard times. However, it is important, in the long term, for consultancies to develop and

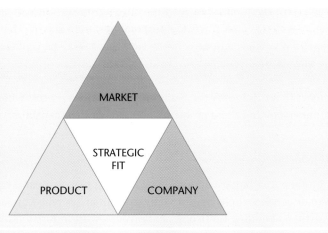

Figure 5.2. Strategic fit: product, company, and market

market their products in a strategic manner. Matching a core proposition, or a handful of key products, is essential if consultancies are to accumulate the expertise and experience necessary to really offer clients economies of scope and scale.

Once a key proposition has been developed by a consultancy, be it innovation training, call-centre outsourcing, or scenario planning, the consultancy is able to target potential clients who have not yet benefited from the product. More importantly, it allows the consultancy to target these clients strategically—to improve and tailor the product to different markets, to accumulate success stories and references, and to match the size of the project with the growth of the firm.

The strategic identification of client targets applies not simply to small firms but even to those large companies that one might think base all their sales on their existing contacts. This is Ken Taormina, the then Vice-President of KPMG Consulting, on the subject:

> For key targets, we look at the Global 2000 and the Fortune 1000 and we see how they match up with our lines of business and our expertise. Then we look at how big they are and their information spend . . . [and] where they are on their growth cycle.
>
> Based on that, we ask, "Who are the market leaders?" Then you go through those and determine which should be targeted and whether you can get the named account. When [the company reaches] named account status, we then determine whether it's a company that we're going to do a consistent amount of revenue with . . . we're going to be able to compete for that client because [it] believes we bring value. (Techrepublic 2001)

Even the most profitable and well-known names still need a strategic and consistent sales process to find new clients.

Making Contact

This section focuses on how consultancies get their foot in the door, how proposals are handled in the consulting world, and how good consultancies move to a contract as quickly as possible. Consultancies often put a significant amount of work into the analysis of potential clients and in writing proposals despite knowing that little may come of it. This speculative effort is done with the view that a small percentage may take off and fund future speculative proposals.

There are several ways of obtaining first contact with a client, but it is important to remember that this is only the first step of a laborious process which is aimed at building trust, understanding client problems, and assessing the capability of the consultancy.

Cold Calling

This is one of the hardest approaches to getting new work and equates to the tactics of door-to-door salespeople. Traditionally, consultancies relied upon their top consultants (i.e. partners) building up strong relationships with industry leaders and levering these contacts to return lucrative projects.

However, in recent years, some consultancies led by United Research (now Cap Gemini) have developed a specialist sales technique which used telemarketing professionals to arrange a one-hour presentation at different clients and then enlisted sales professionals who would use this hour to target the client's "red-spots"—e.g. worries regarding competition, suppliers, new products, markets, etc. (Pinault 2001). Unusually for the consulting industry, the consultant would not get involved until the work actually needed to be done.

However, whilst successful in that case, "cold calling is the least fruitful of hunting activities . . . calling out of the blue is least likely to work; warming up clients beforehand is essential" (Markham 2004: 43). Sadler (2002: 206) agrees: "do not cold call a prospect without first working out something you want to give them."

Thought Leadership and Research

A consultancy's main asset is its intellectual capital. What distinguishes it from a group of random contractors are the agreed methodologies, expertise, and insight that the consultancy accumulates after repeatedly working with clients with similar problems. One way of demonstrating the pedigree of intellectual capital is to create what is termed "thought-leadership" through research and publications.

Research is central to a consultancy's effort both to identify new trends in consulting markets and to create an image of knowledge expertise. Many consultancies, such as McKinsey and Accenture, possess research arms that provide detailed data and analysis on challenges for different sectors, services, and countries. Other consultancies commission joint research with institutes such as the Economist Intelligence Unit or elite business schools such as Harvard, Yale, and Stanford. McKinsey and Bain both make a consistent effort to publish with the Harvard Business Press. Other consultancies attempt to pursue a similar path through regular publication in magazines, white papers, case studies, and journal articles.

Such research ensures a consultancy stays abreast of new trends and developments in its clients' industries and may also create new sales leads. The idea is that managers and executives will read articles and books about the issues that affect them most and will notice who commissioned the work.

Schmoozing

Schmoozing, or exploiting the corporate entertainment budget, usually means having a corporate credit card to help get the client on side by socialising with them informally. However, it can also mean the consultant in question soon requires elasticated waistbands and a very understanding spouse, as the dinners, functions, and after-work drinks can eat into what little spare time a consultant has. Whilst formal procurement processes have cut down the effectiveness of schmoozing clients it can still be a highly profitable investment.

Schmoozing is not, of course, illegal. However, as discussed later in Chapter 9, there is a sliding scale, and at some point schmoozing can turn into corruption. Playing golf with the CEO of a target client, digging up your consultancy's alumni, or taking the business owner out to dinner are not illegal. However, offering a key decision-maker a job in return for a contract, paying bribes to procurers, or not declaring a directorship with a client or a consultancy obviously are. In recent years, rules have tightened up, especially in government projects. Procurers and key decision-makers are increasingly bound by rules which prevent direct exchanges between them and potential consultants prior to a project being tendered, but this does not stop consultancies seeking to use their influence to gain additional work, especially once they are inside a client organisation.

More often than not, all the dinners, corporate events, and rounds of golf are simply aimed at building trust and familiarity which helps give clients confidence in their decisions. For an interesting discussion of the use of dinners and "backstage" occasions, it is worth examining Sturdy et al.'s (2006) paper on "liminal", or in-between, spaces. Taking meals as an example, they argue that the spaces between work and home, such as client dinners, provide consultants with different opportunities to engage strategically with clients.

Using Insiders

Consultancies hate wasting time (and money) on lengthy procurement processes. If a consultancy already has consultants working with a client it is much easier to develop leads internally. Often a consultancy will identify a piece of work that is a natural extension to the work they are doing. They will suggest the work to the client and informally propose a plan, timescale, and cost for the work, which can then be added onto the existing project rather than being put out to tender again. If the client is happy and trusts the consultancy they will sometimes give the go-ahead without further ado. This is a common approach with smaller, niche consultancies who have developed a strong relationship with one client or with independent consultants who have built up a good rapport with the client. In the words of one consultant, "your best sales pitch is doing a good job".

This is a common approach with strategy work, where consultancies working at a senior level will identify work tasks and projects that happen to fall into their own areas of expertise. Once these needs have been identified, it is a fair bet that the consultancy will then take responsibility for a number of the identified projects, simply because they will often work the requirements or assessment criteria to match their own core competencies.

Upselling

There is significant pressure on consultants from their employers to "up sell" during the delivery phase of any project. This involves getting the client to sign up to work that they did not originally specify but may be related to the project in hand. This not only brings in additional sales for the consultancy but also, if presented as an extension to the current project, can avoid the necessity of going through procurement and the associated risk that another consultancy will win the contract.

When undertaken solely as a profit-seeking exercise, upselling can be unethical, counterproductive, can alienate clients, and lead to the loss of contracts. However, the problems that consultants work on for clients are often part of larger systemic issues. Late deliveries *may* be down to an inefficient stocking system, but they could also result from a badly evolved business with inconsistent data and laborious business processes. A good consultancy will spell out the options to a client and recommend an analysis phase to identify the best solution for the money available. As a new consultant, it is a good way to impress your line manager if you can identify potential follow-on work.

Referrals

Referrals are introductions and leads provided to the consultancy from their previous clients. Referrals are the most common method by which consultancies get recruited (Consulting Intelligence 2007). Referrals can take place between firms, but are also important within firms: clients are much more likely to use the same consultancy again if they have had a positive experience previously. However, there is little consultancies can do to encourage referrals other than simply asking clients to recommend them to their peers.

Managing the Proposal

Writing a proposal, either as a response to a Request for Information (RFI) or simply as a result of a successful sales pitch, is central to the sales processes of most consultancies. This is not only because it specifies how consultancies propose to run a project but because the quality of the proposal is itself a powerful sales tool. Moreover, a well-written proposal should be easily translated into the formal contract which binds the consultant and client before the project starts.

On Not Writing Proposals

Consultants frequently report their frustration at spending hours writing a proposal only to have the project handed to another consultancy. Later it often becomes clear that the proposal didn't have a chance in the first place and that the proposal was subsequently used by the client to help guide the work of the successful consultancy, or worse, batter prices down. This is understandably frustrating and it is often assumed by consultants that there is little that can be done to avoid this as sales directors are unlikely to smile upon those consultants who say, "thanks for the multi-million pound lead, Mark, but I decided not to put a proposal in because I didn't think we'd get it ...". However, there may be an alternative.

It is important to ensure that the client really wants the proposal in the first place. This means knowing when *not* to write a proposal. One good way to understand whether a client is asking for a proposal for nefarious purposes is to press them further when asked to write one. Instead of the post-presentation conversation going like this:

> Client: Well, that's great, Dave, why don't you get us a proposal?
> Consultant: Great! When do you want it?

there are a number of alternative questions that will allow you to explore whether you are really in with a chance or whether the client is simply wasting your time. These include:

- **Can you provide us with a stakeholder who we can liaise with when drafting our proposal?**
  This shows that the client is willing to spend some time with you in ensuring that you understand the problem and that the proposal will be useful to them. If they are not willing to do this, at the very least, then it's unlikely they are serious about your contribution.

- **What are the success criteria for the proposal? To what extent is the selection based on cost?**
  This question seeks to understand if there is a level playing field between you and the competitors or whether they already have a favourite in mind. More importantly, it gives you an idea whether the selection of the project will be on price alone—if so, you are usually best leaving these clients alone.

- **Where is the money coming from to fund the project?**
  Whilst your contact may well bluff on this question, their response should give you an idea whether or not there is a designated budget for this and, if so, why it has been generated.

- **What are the timelines for responses, feedback, and project kick-off?**
  This is aimed at getting reassurance that the proposal forms part of a planned project and is not simply being demanded on the whim of a manager who has no plans to implement any of the proposals.

A good consultant will be able to see if the client is hesitant, unsure, or confused in their responses and will seek to understand why. An interesting alternative by VeraSage, a think-tank for the professional services industry, is to charge for a proposal. After all, they reason, a good proposal is a lot of work and has significant value.

What is in a Proposal?

The proposal format suggested below can be expanded or contracted to fit the client:

- **Executive Summary (a summary of the report)**
  Keep this section simple—a few key points. Do not include costs here as they will distract the client.

- **Background to the Project (why the project is on the table)**
  This section should reiterate the key information that the client has already provided you with. It is sense-checking that what you understand to be the problem, is actually the problem. Don't state the obvious by telling them how big they are and what their turnover is. Focus on the problem.

- **Objectives/Deliverables (what the project will do and when)**
  Exactly what is the project attempting to do? Ensure that if what the client wants is unrealistic (and they know this) then you do not sign up to it. For example, if your client wants to decrease supplier costs by 20 per cent, state that you will introduce a tendering process with the *aim* of reducing costs by 20 per cent. In other words, never commit to something that you may not be able to do.

- **Scope/Dependencies (don't leave yourself open!)**
  One of the most important skills a consultant can learn is how to properly define the scope of the project (i.e. what the consultant will actually be responsible for). Clients often approach consultancies believing that they can simply offload their problems and return in six months when the solutions are up and running. In reality the consultancy has large dependencies on the client for information, resources, and skills. Defining these dependencies is essential, not simply for the successful completion of the project but also because, if the relationship breaks down and ends up in court, the failure of the client to provide these deliverables can result in them losing the case.

- **Outline Approach (high-level overview)**
  A quick summary of the work. What you will be doing and why. If you are using any key methodologies or tools, this is the time to mention it.

- **Success Measures (quantifying business results)**
  How will your success be measured? Ensure that these measures are realistic. You may well not be paid if the client can show you didn't fulfil these—even if, in every other respect, you did a good piece of work. Ensure you differentiate those which are central to the project and those which are aspirational.

- **Work Breakdown/Plan (how the consultancy will achieve success)**
  What are the key activities which will be taking place? When will they take place? Who will do the work? This should be a simple plan. Include key dates and review points. You may give the client different options which should be costed out separately.

- **Resources and Responsibilities (who will do what)**
  What roles are working on the project? What are they responsible for? Put CVs in an appendix. The consultancy should also include brief biographies of each consultant that will be involved with the project. It is common, though ethically dubious, practice for consultancies to focus on the highly experienced consultants, even if they only turn up once.

You should ensure that the client is very clear that they need to support the project in various ways—ideally getting some of their staff to do some of the work.

- **Costs (cost breakdown: person and activity)**

  Costing a project is a complex business and there is no substitute for experience. Each deliverable in the project should be broken out separately and the input of different roles identified and costed.

  For example, a software implementation might have four stages: analysis, design, development, testing and implementation. One stage of this will be the testing which might involve a business analyst, two testers, a project manager, and a PA. An approximate breakdown might be as follows:

	Cost per day	Workload	Total
Business Analyst	£750	3 days	£2,250
Project Manager	£650	3 days	£1,950
Testers (×2)	£650	10 days	£6,500
PA	£250	3 days	£750
			£11,450

When costing the project it is also important to be clear on who pays for expenses as the costs of housing, feeding, and transporting consultants can sometimes average out at over £500 a day each.

For clarity, it is also worth breaking down costs by separate activities. For example:

Item	Time	Cost
Project management	0.5 day	£300
On-going consultancy with client	1.5 days	£900
Workshop		
Preparation for workshop	1 day	£600
Workshop	2 days	£1,200
Market entry plan		
Define and develop market strategy	3 days	£1,800
Develop market entry plan	4 days	£2,400
Total	12 days	£7,200

- **Expenses (who will pay them and when)**

- **Processes (control, escalation, reviews)**
  What are the key processes and responsibility for dealing with problems? What happens if your client asks you to change the project somehow? Consultancies should build review points into the plan and ensure there are clear routes for the escalation of issues. Additionally, a perceptive client will ensure that there is a clear exit strategy for the work defining how specific knowledge is passed, deliverables handed over, and reviews undertaken.

- **Dependencies and Risks (cover yourself!)**
  Ensure that you are very, very clear about your dependencies on the client's workforce (information, labour, documents, communication).

- **Legal Disclaimer (Confidentiality)**
  This is a common feature of many engagements, especially with large firms. However, with smaller engagements, especially when you are unsure whether you will be getting the job, leave this out for the time being. It will only mean your proposal will be sent down to the legal monkeys, who will make hats out of it.

Proposal Style

The style of the proposal will very much depend on who it is being sent to and should suit the culture of the company and the expectations of the client. A large, bureaucratic organisation such as a government department will usually want a long, detailed, and thorough proposal. An innovative start-up may simply require a letter. I recently cemented a piece (short) consultancy work with an exchange of emails. It should also be noted that public sector proposals are usually more thorough and formulaic than private sector ones because of the rules and regulations the public sector is bound by.

Key pointers on the style of a proposal include:

- Avoid consultantese. There's nothing that will turn a client off quicker that a document that patronises and confuses them. Keep your language simple. Other times, nomenclature can be confusing as different terms means different things to the stakeholders. For this reason, consultants and clients should communicate frequently about confusing terms.

- Avoid filler. Whilst a client will want to know a bit about your company and what you will bring to the project, it's a big turnoff to get something that could be a photocopy of another client's proposal. Ensure that 90 per cent of what is in the proposal is geared to solving your client's problems.

- Be innovative. Don't be afraid of unusual propositions and methodologies. One of the big complaints clients have about consultants is that they are not innovative enough.

- Present well. When working for a client in 2001 a large golden box of chocolates arrived on my desk with the consultancy's name lavishly embossed on the front. Opening the box, half of it was filled with the finest Belgian truffles and the other half had an immaculately presented proposal ready for my perusal. The presentation, at the least, ensured that I was in a good mood when reading the proposal.

Moving to Contract

A well-drafted proposal will easily convert into a contract. Good sample contracts and advice for managing them can be found on the Office of Government Commerce website listed in the Online Resource Centre. It is likely that a typical contract will include the items listed in Table 5.2.

The negotiation of the contract is likely to involve a serious discussion with the client, not just on costs but also on timelines, responsibilities, and details such as intellectual property, expenses, and liability. In a large consultancy it is likely that experienced negotiators will be on hand with a significant legal department to assist in negotiations. Additionally, large clients will, via their procurement departments, usually have standard terms and conditions or "framework agreements". However, in a small consultancy or as a more senior consultant, it is likely that you will have to at least become involved in, if not lead, negotiations with clients.

The Balance of Power

Although every project and client is different, when it comes to hammering out the details of the contract it is important to bear in mind the main principles of negotiating a consultancy contract. The advice below comes from interviews with consultants who have experienced the process and from key texts that focus on the issues (Maister 2003; Kubr 2002; Cohen 2001).

Component	Description
Assignment agreement	The name of the parties involved in the contract. Clarification of nomenclature. The legal jurisdiction under which the contract is governed.
Obligations and deliverables	What the consultants will do and how they will do it. Reference can be made here to the project plan.
Reporting	Who shall be reported to, how, and when.
Fees and expenses	What will be paid, when, and how. What happens when payment is late.
Intellectual property	Who owns the work, methods, and materials developed by the project. Use of the project in publicity.
Liability	Who is, or is not, liable for what. Insurance required for the project.
Termination	Who may terminate the contract, with how much notice, and how this is done.
Breach of contract	What happens if the deliverables are not delivered? What compensation is payable?
Settlement of disputes	The process for settlement and arbitration if parties cannot agree within the project.
Standard terms and conditions	Use of sub-contractors, compliance with all laws, adherence to ethical codes of practice, day rates, confidentiality. The process for managing changes to the contract.

Table 5.2. Key components of a contract

A while ago, people thought that the negotiation was your chance to screw the other side. But that approach only works once. If you want a long-term relationship, you've got to go for what is fair, not what suits you best.

(Associate consultant, strategy consultancy)

First it is important to bear in mind that your ability to negotiate is limited by a number of factors that are beyond your control. As Armbrüster (2006) points out, there is a power relationship inherent in any negotiations and a number of factors will skew this for or against the consultant. These include:

- How far the client has progressed in the selection process. If they still have ten consultancies to choose from, you are not in a strong negotiating position.

- Whether procurement is involved with the negotiation. If your contract is small enough to fly under the procurement radar it is likely that you can avoid the stringent terms and conditions associated with standardised client contracts.

- How well the client knows you. If you have worked with the client before they are likely to seek to apply the same terms and conditions as they did previously. However, if you have built up a good relationship with the client and have specific issues, such as the use of intellectual property, they may be more inclined to trust your intentions. Even if the client has not worked with you, your reputation can help set expectations for fee rates.

Preparing for Negotiations

Preparing for the negotiation is crucial, especially if you work in a team. I have witnessed several negotiations turn sour because the three, or sometimes four, representatives of one side simply weren't clear what they were trying to do. Often consultancies will bring in a legal representative, the lead consultant, and a seasoned negotiator to deal with this phase. A preparatory meeting with your team should be absolutely clear on:

- What your goals are: this includes what you are aiming to achieve and what the minimum you will accept is. This needs to be broken down by every category in the proposal or contract and should also include anything that you think the client might bring up.

- What your strategy is: what is the structure of the negotiation to be? How should the meeting be structured? What are your contingency plans? How up front will you be in your negotiations? What are the ground rules for your team?

- What your team structure is: Who is in charge? Who can make offers or accept deals? What should you do if you disagree or are unclear on a point? A walkthrough of different negotiation scenarios is useful in discovering the flaws in the best-laid plans.

Doing the Deal

Every negotiation is different and it is hard to prescribe how they should be conducted at a generic level. Due to the positive influence of strong trust relations on any consultancy project it is of utmost importance that the contract negotiations do not become a zero-sum war of attrition. Instead, both parties should focus on creating a situation that both feel is fair. With this sentiment as a baseline, the following pointers may help improve the negotiating position of the consultancy:

- Try to understand and empathise with the other party. What are their fears, concerns, and desires? How do they see you and the negotiating team? What issues are likely to cause them most problems?

- Whilst there will be sticking points, especially around responsibilities, fees, and deliverables, it is important that the negotiations do not become conflictual. Taking a break, moving location, and socialising together may help ease an atmosphere that threatens to turn nasty.

- Avoid underhand tactics. Deception or intimidation may result in short-term victories, but in a long project, such methods destroy trust and reputations which are far more fundamental to success than any other factor. A client should never leave feeling that they have been cheated.

- In sticky positions, ensure that you acknowledge the client's concerns, keep talking, and ask for clarification. Spend a lot of time listening to the client as many projects have been lost due to poor communication.

- Lead by example: if you are honest, equitable, and focused on the project, it will not only set the client's mind at ease but also encourage them to treat you in a similar manner.

Types of Payment

In the contract, it is likely that payments will be specified. Below, different payment structures are outlined and linked to different types of projects.

Free Consultancy

Free consultancy usually comes under the heading of "spec", short for speculative, work. This is work that a consultancy will do in the hope of obtaining a contract. A consultancy might, for example, undertake an analysis of a potential client which suggests the need for some form of consulting services, which would then be presented to a senior director. Much of the work that consultancies perform for a proposal is spec work and obviously hits utilisation rates. This work will usually point to other projects that the client should complete; however, the drawback for the consultancy is that it may be their competitors that win the follow-on work.

Project Fee

This is a common form of payment involving a fixed fee for work undertaken, usually paid at milestones in the project. For the consultancy and the client this provides clarity and predictability. However, there is a danger that this form of payment provides little incentive for the consultancy to perform to a high standard. With this type of payment, the contract should be very clear about the standards required to trigger payments.

Increasingly, buyers are taking the approach of stating up front what the budget for any given project is. This saves consultancies from groping around in the dark trying to second guess what their project fee should be and also saves clients binning proposals from good consultancies that simply misinterpreted the scope.

Fixed Time Rates

This involves a fixed hourly, daily, or weekly fee for consultants' time, graded at different levels for different consultants. Naturally, this is usually calculated into other forms of project pricing, but this option bases fees solely on the time spent on the project. This is usually used for open-ended or ambiguous work projects. The obvious danger for the client is that the consultancy has an incentive to spin out the work to maximise their income or has little control over the final bill. Several commentators, such as the think-tank Verasage, believe the billable hour is a disincentive to both clients and consultants.

Risk/Reward

More popular in economic downturns, risk–reward payment models remunerate the consultant according to their performance. That is, if the project does badly, they get paid less, and if it does well, they get paid more. These models account for around 5 per cent of projects in the public sector and 10 per cent in the private arena (Maister 2003). For these to work, the client should not see the payment structure as an opportunity to cut costs or for the consultancy to inflate them; in other words, high-trust relationships and usually a history of working together are necessary for both sides to believe the other will not take advantage of the contract. Also key to success are the fairness and transparency of the measures by which the success will be gauged.

Risk/reward can seen as the carrot or stick approach: the former being incentives for good performance such as a bonus payment; the latter being penalties, such as reduced fees, for poor performance. Performance is commonly based on completing the project on time, but might also include efficiency savings, quality of work, or 360-degree feedback from the project team. Clients should be prepared to pay extra for excellent work and be prepared to put in extra work themselves to support the consultants.

Penalty Clauses

As projects get larger and more risky, some clients are insisting on penalty clauses with their contracts. In other words, if a consultancy fails to deliver on specified business objectives, they pay a penalty. Unfortunately, however, this can damage the client as well as the consultant if the consultant decides to withdraw from the project halfway through. Accenture's failure to deliver to an agreed timetable with a large health project meant it was facing so many penalties that it eventually withdrew from the project (Bowers 2006).

■ Research

Introducing Research

Consultants usually make their money solving problems that a client doesn't have the time or skills to do for themselves. Often, this involves collating, interpreting, and presenting data to answer business questions. The sections below describe the process of research that many consultants use to find and analyse their data. They can also be used as a guide for students undertaking research projects into business issues more generally. The research process, outlined in Figure 5.3, is the backbone of the consultant's research.

The process is a logical progression ensuring that for any given problem, the right questions are asked, the appropriate methods are chosen to answer those questions, and the analysis is capable of generating the correct answers. It should be noted that during the analysis stage, the researcher may find that their research questions need some adjustment to better define the problem. Each phase of this process is detailed in the following sections.

Planning Research

Problem Statement

Business problems are, by nature, complex, messy, and highly changeable. For this reason, issues that clients bring to consultants frequently require clarification and simplification by both parties. This step is important not only because it clarifies the work that the consultant will perform but because it also provides a consultant with an insight into how the client thinks about their own organisation and the challenges they are facing. Ensuring that the right problem is being focused on is an essential but often fraught process.

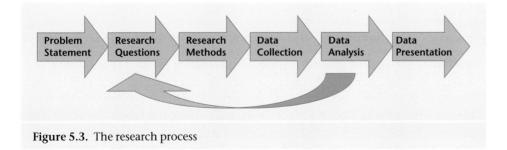

Figure 5.3. The research process

For example, this is an email from an MD of an anonymised company which we can call ClientCo to a new consultant:

> Bob,
>
> I trust you've had a chance to go through the production figures for ClientCo I've sent you and seen how poor our productivity per worker is compared to our competitors. This is obviously a contributing factor to the losses we made last year. I admit motivation isn't what it should be and the walk-out last week didn't help our figures. If you could put together the options for an employee survey to assess attitudes and perhaps find some benchmarks to compare our results against, I'd be grateful.
>
> See you next Tuesday,
>
> Mike.

The obvious temptation here for the consultant is to simply do the survey, find the benchmarks, produce a report, and send the invoice. However, note how Mike jumps from a problem (low productivity) to a diagnosis (poor morale) without any evidence. There could, of course, be any number of causes for reported levels of low productivity, including inefficient work processes, poor reporting, flawed measurements, unsuitable machinery, incorrect or unsuitable benchmarks, and bad management. None of these mean that poor morale does not exist, but there is a possibility that there are other issues that require further exploration. More importantly, Mike does not specify why addressing low productivity is such a priority for the business. It may be, for example, that productivity is the least of Mike's problems and that instead he should be focusing on increasing sales, changing the price of his products, or entering new markets.

The "problem statement" is a good way to focus entirely on the business issue rather than jumping to conclusions about what causes the problem. Sitting down in a meeting with the client to sort out exactly what the problem consists of is a good way of ensuring that both sides agree on what the issue is. It is also important for the consultant to know why this specific problem is being highlighted.

In the initial meeting, therefore, it is useful to ask the following questions:

- What does the client believe the problem to be?

- Why are they focusing on this problem?

The answers to these questions will help create a "problem statement". In the crafting of the statement, the consultant should focus on fact, rather than opinion. For example:

> Around 35 per cent of ClientCo's orders are produced on time compared to an average of 75 per cent for ClientCo's competitors. In customer surveys this was identified as the top reason for the 15 per cent decline in purchases over the last two years. Increasing productivity by 10 per cent would, it is estimated, enable 80 per cent of orders to be completed on time and thus improve customer retention.
>
> Reported production figures in the period Jan 2009–Jan 2010 indicate that productivity per worker in the gearbox assembly unity averages 7.3 completed units

a day. This compares unfavourably with benchmarks with similar companies of around 9.8 units.

 This research will seek to understand the causes for the reported low production figures.

Note that this problem statement does not identify the cause of the poor productivity but instead focuses on the known facts. It also includes the reasons why the problem is so important to the client.

Research Questions and Hypotheses

The central point for any research design are the research questions or hypotheses. These are the questions that must be answered, or ideas that must be tested, in order for the research to be successful.

 Research questions tend to be used in exploratory, inductive research that seeks to understand and explain a social phenomenon. They can be used for both qualitative and quantitative research. In the case of ClientCo, the research questions may be as follows:

- Do competitor benchmarks provide a fair comparison for order completion and labour productivity?
- Is the measurement and the reporting of productivity accurate in ClientCo?
- Which processes, people, and technology contribute to lower productivity figures?
- Which factors contribute most to lower productivity?
- How do the identified factors contribute to lower productivity?

Note that some research questions have sub-questions. Creswell (2003) suggests no more than ten questions in total in order to keep the project manageable.

 Hypotheses are often derived from or used instead of research questions. Hypotheses provide a testable, predictive statement which must be falsifiable (Popper 1959). Hypotheses are usually associated with deductive, statistical studies. For example:

- Motivation will have an impact on levels of productivity.
- Training will have no impact on levels of productivity.
- Higher levels of machine maintenance will increase levels of productivity.

Consultants will then collect statistical data that allow these hypotheses to be tested. Whilst the use of hypotheses is rarer in consulting research, it is still often seen, though not essential, in surveys, questionnaires, and studies which involve large amounts of quantitative data. However, it is not essential to use hypotheses in statistical studies. Consultancies frequently simply present the findings of their questionnaires and surveys in various charts without statistically *proving or disproving* a hypothesis. Whilst such an approach might not pass a scientist's standard for quality and reliability, clients are often in a hurry and are happy to have a quick indication of issues rather than a long, and expensive, social investigation. This is possibly one reason why consultants and academics treat each other's work with some scepticism.

Quantitative and Qualitative Research

Quantitative research is concerned with using statistics to answer research questions or prove hypotheses. It is, therefore, important to be precise in their formulation so the researcher knows exactly what they are looking for. For example:

- What percentage of Argentineans would buy our brand of washing-up liquid?
- What does it cost our company to answer an average sales enquiry?
- Will sales increase as a result of increased advertising spend?

The answers to these types of questions will usually be statistical or will prove, or disprove, a hypothesis. Both will often incur a level of confidence: a statistical statement of how certain the researcher is that their answer is right. Details on how to achieve this can be found in Rea and Parker (2005).

Qualitative research (usually interviews), on the other hand, is suitable for questions where the researcher needs to explore and interpret complex social issues that cannot be proven through statistical analysis. As such it is suitable for research questions which are less clearly defined, such as:

- What brand would best fit our marketing strategy in North America?
- What should we do about the emergence of a new competitor?
- Why has our investment in a new computer system not improved our production efficiency?

Note that these questions cannot have a clear statistical answer and will necessarily involve some opinion, interpretation, and exploration on behalf of the researcher. For this reasons, qualitative research is often said to be *interpretative*, which means that the data could be interpreted differently by different researchers. This inevitably can lead to disagreements on the perspective the researcher has taken, so it is important to gain as much evidence as possible for one's interpretation. More on how to deal with such issues can be found in Creswell (2007).

Often qualitative and quantitative approaches to research are perceived as antithetical. However, this is not the case. In practice, qualitative and quantitative research are highly complementary with the former often generating hypotheses that the latter can test, or the latter throwing up anomalies which require a qualitative explanation. In academic terms, many researchers incorrectly assume that qualitative data must be associated with an interpretative ontology and statistics with a realist ontology, when in practice they can be highly compatiable.

Research Methods/Data Collection

The way in which data are collected needs to be driven by the research questions or hypotheses. There is a variety of methods of data collection which consultants use to gather the information they need. These are described below.

Literature Reviews

Consultancies often have access to very large libraries of surveys, expert opinion, analysis, and data from previous clients. Thus, much of the information that consultants use for their deliverables to clients can be found in their existing sources, including the internet. Often, for example, a preliminary strategic analysis of a company will include data about its market, competitors, and financial position which are often available from the company's own accounts and from research companies such as Datamonitor, the Economist Intelligence Unit, or Forrester. Such reports can cost the consultancy between £700 and £10,000 depending on the depth and range of the research. However, most consultancies buy subscriptions to research services which enable them to have access to a whole range of reports.

In academic research, or MBA dissertations, a literature review is usually required by the university. It will usually focus on providing background to the topics and highlighting relevant themes that will come out of the research. In higher level academic work, a literature review will focus on highlighting a "gap" in the literature and, therefore, justifying the need for the research. For example, an academic study which examined whether the consulting industry would ever fully professionalise would, in its literature review, focus on providing the background to the debates in the professionalisation literature, but also try to show that the question had not been tackled adequately.

For dissertations which take the form of consulting reports, the literature review will mostly provide background and context to the topic and thus support the analysis of the business problem. There is usually no need to show a "gap" in the literature as the client will not be interested in furthering knowledge for academics but simply making their company more profitable. For example, a strategic analysis of a telecom client might use existing literature to provide an overview of the telecoms industry and ascertain key figures and trends concerning competitors, markets, and performance. It may also use literature to find a suitable strategic framework or tool to structure the analysis. It is unlikely, however, to delve deeply into academic or theoretical debates.

Interviews

Interviews are usually used by consultants for collecting qualitative data which will answer an exploratory research question such as "why does Company X have such high labour turnover?" or "how do users of product X feel about its phasing out?" The benefit of an interview compared, say, to a questionnaire is that it allows the interviewer to explore ideas with the interviewees, which often means the former learns a lot from the latter.

Interviews often allow researchers to gather information which then forms the basis of a questionnaire. For example, a CEO of a large company might wish to know the reasons for the low levels of motivation in their workforce. However, it is unlikely that they, or the consultant, would know enough about the situation to put accurate options into a questionnaire. They might, for example, start off by asking a cross-section of employees, and recent leavers, their thoughts on the low levels of motivation. This, in turn, might generate twenty different reasons, which could be put into a questionnaire which would then be distributed amongst the whole workforce to get an idea of the weight that should be attributed to each reason and the effect each might have.

However, interviewing is a difficult and complex skill to acquire and there are several issues that should be considered before conducting this kind of research.

What Can Interviews Tell You?   It is important to note the limits of one's research method. Interviews are often expected to be representative of a larger population. For example, if you were asked to find out the reasons for levels of low motivation in IBM, are you likely to get any useful information by asking twenty people in the sales department of the New York office? The answer is probably no, because you could have little confidence that they are representative of the entire firm. Instead, you would be expected to interview a representative sample: not simply different locations, but differing functions, grades, races, sexes, and levels of experience.

Interviews are generally designed to be exploratory. Unless you are interviewing a large sample of a small population, the findings are unlikely to be generalisable to the wider population. For example, you obviously would not be able to generalise about the attitudes of the Russian people to a new brand of ice cream by asking ten Russians. Your interviews may, however, be able to generate hypotheses that you may feel are worthy of further study.

Who Should Be Asked?   Students often ask me how many people, and which people, they should interview for their research project. The answer to this question depends entirely upon the research questions and the confidence that the researcher wishes to have in the answers.

If the question is "why do some production workers in our factory stay late without being paid overtime?" then you might start with a few in-depth interviews with relevant workers to elicit a variety of reasons. You may not actually know how many you need to ask until you start getting the same responses and thus get diminishing returns. You may wish to follow this up by using the responses in a questionnaire that would be distributed to all relevant workers. If, on the other hand, the question is "what is it like being the CEO of Google?" then one interview, if you can get it, would obviously suffice.

When you do not know if different responses may be made by different groups (e.g. men vs. women; older vs. younger) then it is often wise to ask a cross-section of the groups, a technique known as "stratified sampling". However, if such categories are irrelevant to your research then it is more important that the interviewees are chosen completely randomly. For more on different ways to select participants for different types of research questions, see Corbin and Strauss (2007).

CASE 5.1

Dignity and Respect at Food Company X

One of my first consultancy assignments as an independent consultant was with a company who discovered through their corporate survey that their female staff felt they received significantly less "Dignity and Respect" at work that their male counterparts. I was asked to discover why this was.

To achieve this, I agreed a number of exploratory research questions with the client that led me to take interviews as a good starting point. The questions included:

- Did men and women expect different levels of dignity or respect at work? I asked this question to see if women in the company expected more dignity and respect than the men and were, therefore, less satisfied.

- What other variations in dignity and respect are found (e.g. at different levels, in different departments, or according to age)? I asked this question to understand whether the gender gap might be linked to different issues.

- Is the perceived difference reflective of a wider trend? Are there other surveys in other companies which have asked the same questions and come up with a similar finding?

I first examined the surveys originally conducted by the client and found that the levels of "dignity and respect" were different between men and women only in Production, where women were outnumbered by men three to one. In the rest of the company, reported levels were quite balanced. At this stage I also did a search of surveys that had been conducted in other companies but found nothing that appeared relevant to this case.

Next, I undertook interviews with several workers to understand what they felt might be the causes of the difference. It became clear amongst the interviewees that expectations between the sexes were very similar but that it was the working conditions that were central to the feelings of dissatisfaction. The women tended to work in roles, in packing, which had little autonomy and were tightly controlled. The men, by contrast, worked in roles in mixing which had greater autonomy with considerable freedom. This appeared to be an explicit HR policy so my next step was to interview HR. Sure enough, the key person who decided who would work where in production told me:

> I put women in packing because their fingers are smaller and they're much more nimble when it comes to dealing with details. Men tend to get surly if you don't give them enough space. I tend to put them in mixing where they can put their muscles to good use.

To explore this further, I spent a day working in mixing and another in packing and, unsurprisingly, found the latter very repetitive, controlled, and monotonous, with little comradeship and workers tied to the production line. In mixing, however, the design of the work gave workers much freedom and autonomy.

My subsequent report to the senior management outlined the reasons for the difference in reported levels of dignity and respect was primarily due to a sexist, and probably illegal, form of job selection. To their credit, the offending HR manager was sent on training, the gendered selection practice was abandoned, and the different groups were, after some training, given the opportunity for job rotation. When I checked back a year later, the reported levels of dignity and respect in production were virtually identical between the different sexes.

- Can you think of anything else I should have done in this case?

Questionnaires/Surveys

A survey or a questionnaire is suitable for research questions (RQ) or hypotheses (H) which concern an aggregate population. For example:

(RQ) How do adults aged between 21 and 35 perceive the Apple brand?

(RQ) What would the average male pay for a new brand of chocolate bar?

(H) Productivity in manufacturing plants is positively associated with job satisfaction.

(H) French people are more likely to buy mobile phones than English people.

However, it should be noted that survey responses are rarely provided by an entire population. Instead, analysts seek a representative sample which then gives them some confidence that their results can be extrapolated to the whole population. The level of confidence in the survey results will increase by the response rate and the similarity of the answers provided ("variance"). Many consultancies don't bother with analysing levels of confidence, especially if the population is a relatively small one. Instead, they will simply present the results of everyone who responded to their survey.

The design of questionnaires is important in achieving representative answers. Issues such as avoiding ambiguity, bias, and leading questions are essential in achieving independent answers. Guidelines on achieving this can be found in Brace (2008) or Larossi (2006).

Other Research Methods

There are several other research methods consultants can use. These include:

- Ethnography: working alongside the people you wish to study, usually in the same kind of role. By immersing oneself deeply in the cultural practices of the organisation, it is possible to get a much deeper understanding of the values, assumptions, and attitudes of the workforce.

- Action research: this integrates research with active and reflexive problem solving in a work situation. Action research is a common form of research for part-time students who perhaps wish to complete a dissertation whilst at the same time undertaking a project in their own organisation.

- Work shadowing: in order to better understand the roles of senior executives. For example, in succession planning or training requirements, consultants will sometimes "work shadow" an individual, noting their activities, skill requirements, and competences.

- Work observation: work observation usually involves a consultant following a process of work and measuring the time taken for each stage, the inputs and outputs of each activity, and the data flows to and from the tasks. Such work was the basis of early time-motion studies and is now frequently used in process re-engineering work.

Data Analysis

Data without analysis are worthless. Analysis gives data a purpose by making them useful to someone or something. The usefulness of data in research is created through their sifting,

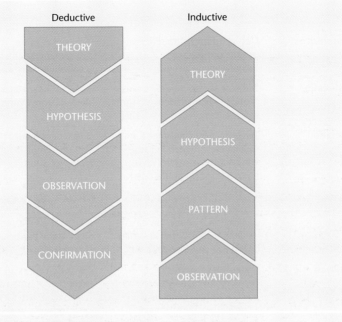

Figure 5.4. Deductive and inductive analysis

structuring, and modelling, so that they answer research questions, prove hypotheses, or lead to conclusions.

The analysis of data mediates the relationship between theory and data. Generally speaking, though not always, quantitative analysis uses a top-down deductive analysis which starts with hypotheses which can be deduced from a theory or framework. Through an analysis of the data, these hypotheses can be confirmed or rejected. Qualitative analysis, on the other hand, usually starts with the data which are sifted through to find patterns or themes, often through coding. These are then used to generate hypotheses which, in turn, can support a theory of how the system "works" (Figure 5.4). Typically, deductive research in consultancy starts with hypotheses and ends with confirmation or refutation, whilst the inductive work starts with observation and ends with a hypothesis.

In analysing the data, Excel or PowerPoint are often used to turn numerical data into simple charts or graphs and expertise with these software packages should be the aim of any aspiring consultant.

Often a client will require two data sets to be linked in some way. For example:

- Do the client's products sell best amongst young females?
- How is employee motivation related to performance?
- Does smoking cause cancer?

In these cases, the consultant needs to have some idea of the strength of a relationship between two, or more, data sets. These are depicted in Table 5.3.

	Description	Example
Categorisation	Data are sorted into different groups using internal definitions.	Types of religion. The categories are self-generated and not derived from a coherent external theory.
Classification	Data are sorted into different groups which are derived from external definitions.	Species. The categories have been derived from evolutionary taxonomy.
Association	Two or more phenomena are qualitatively related in some way, but the relationship is not necessarily correlated or causal.	Some people associate higher taxes with increased public spending. However, this may not always be the case.
Correlation	A more precise form of association. Variation in one variable is statistically linked to changes in another variable.	The use of Bain & Co as consultants is correlated with superior share-price performance. Note that *causation* is not demonstrated.
Causation	Causation can explain correlation. There is a credible mechanism that explains a correlation. Difficult and complicated to "prove".	Smoking causes an increased likelihood of lung cancer. The mechanism for this is the carcinogenic substances in cigarettes which enter the lungs and damage a human's DNA causing cells to grow and mutate.

Table 5.3. Methods for data analysis

There is not enough space here to delve into the hundreds of different methods for analysing data. However, a number of common principles are consistent in all data analysis:

• The analysis should follow logically from the original purpose of the research, be it research questions or hypotheses. For example, if you start with a hypothesis that "fewer French people buy soap than German people", your analysis should not be based on interviews with twenty people.

• The data are usually analysed through the application of a framework. With interviews, this may require that answers are coded to certain themes, with survey data this may simply involve the use of structured statistical analysis.

• The data should be analysed honestly and transparently. Subjectivity on the part of the researcher easily confuses fact with opinion. Where subjectivity cannot be eliminated, it should be stated in the end report.

• The limitations and constraints of method or analysis should be highlighted to the reader.

Once an analysis has taken place, it should now be a matter of presenting your data. Advice on how to do this is given later in the chapter on Consulting Skills.

Research that consultants do isn't too different from any other research. I suppose the difference is that we don't stop at the findings. We go on and make recommendations.

(Sanjay, lead consultant, large audit-based consultancy)

■ Delivery

Given all that has been written about the value of the experience that consultants accumulate by completing project after project, one might think that delivery was one area where they might excel. However, this is not always the case. When asked about what impressed them most about working with consultants, only 4 per cent of clients specified the quality of the final output with over 55 per cent of clients complaining about the budget, timing, and solutions that consultancy work produced (IPSOS/MORI 2007). Below, a number of features of delivering a successful project are outlined. These have been split into "building a project partnership" which focuses on softer, more interpersonal themes, and "planning delivery" which emphasises more formal processes such as planning, control, and communication.

Building a Project Partnership

A survey by Czerniawska (2006) found that where clients reported a "genuine partnership" between themselves and their consultants, 81 per cent of projects were successful. Indeed, one of the rare occasions where academic and managerial writers agree is the extent to which trust and interpersonal relationships inform a well-delivered project (Glückler and Armbrüster 2003; Wickham and Wickham 2008; Czerniawska 2007).

Building a trusted partnership is always going to be compromised by the fact that the relationship is primarily a commercial one. Thus the structure of interests, be they of the owner or the shareholders, will be to maximise profits. As a result, there is a reasonable distrust of consultants from both clients, 40 per cent of whom would not describe their consultants as trustworthy (IPSOS/MORI 2007), and amongst the general public, who rate consultants as less trustworthy than accountants, teachers, and doctors (Consulting Intelligence 2007). Of course, as Furusten and Werr (2005) argue, it is entirely plausible to run a successful project without a trusting relationship, providing there are necessary legal sanctions and enough incentives for both parties to cooperate. However, most studies point to the intangible yet real rewards of building a trusting relationship.

The positive, and negative, aspect of trust, or distrust, is that it tends to self-reinforce. If one begins by believing that the other party is trustworthy, one is more likely to take a risk and give them an opportunity to demonstrate this. Considerable evidence supports the argument that the higher the levels of expectation one party has of another, the higher that party will perform. In psychology, this is known as the Pygmalion Effect (Rosenthal and Jacobson 1968).

The reciprocity of trust is also a well-reported phenomenon in the consulting literature:

In the collaboration between consultants and clients, trust is the basis that makes the joint thinking, learning and experience process possible . . . Every project fosters the trust of the company, common experience promotes mutual trust. Hence it is no coincidence that long-term client relationships are the rule . . . The client relationship rarely ends with the conclusion of the project. (Heuskel 2004: 24)

There is a more detailed theoretical discussion of trust in Chapter 8, where we consider the role of the consultancy's reputation and the client's previous experience in building institutional trust. However, below, a number of methods are outlined by which personal trust can be developed in a project.

- Being professional: being a professional consultant means being open, honest, and ethical in your relationship with the client. The institutions of consultancy, such as the MCA and the IBC, publish a code of ethics and, if the consultant is seen to be adhering to this, it associates them with a trustworthy profession (Weiss 2003).

- Cultural cohesion can be important for clients who wish their consultants to fit in with their company and set their employees at ease. In his book *The Chameleon Consultant*, Holmes (2002) argues that the consultant should be aware of the client's values, attitudes, language, and symbols. This "cultural intelligence", Holmes argues, allows the consultant to win the client's trust.

- Working on personal relationships is also crucial in building up personal credibility with the client. If a client can see you acting with integrity in different social settings, they will build up a trusting relationship that quickly becomes habitual.

Planning Delivery

The formal structure of any consultancy project should be familiar to those who have experience in project management. The basis of any project is to ensure that delivery of the project is adequately resourced, controlled, and communicated. Below, the three main components of any delivery are examined: planning and control, communication, and resources.

Planning and Control

The plan is the spine of any project. In most projects, it is likely that a plan will already have been agreed in the accepted proposal. The plan will outline a number of activities over a period of time that are linked to the deliverables of the project. This allows the Project Manager to update the plan with the progress of the project and to identify activities that are falling behind schedule. The plan will include the resources, deliverables, and timelines of the project and also include a number of project milestones such as formal reviews, invoice dates, or key meetings.

The project manager is responsible for ensuring that the three key factors of any project are balanced: project requirements, time, and resources. Where one of these is insufficient, the project manager will raise the issue with the management and request that requirements or deliverables are reduced, or time or resources are increased. It is for this reason that project managers often keep a risk register. The risk register (Table 5.4) scores

Risk	Probability (1–10)	Impact (1–10)	Score	Mitigation	Contingency	Action
Employee strike	2	8	16	Communication with union	Rapid diffusion by negotiation	JOM
Technical failure	4	5	20	Testing before deployment	Back-up system in place	EF
Overrun on testing	8	2	16	Greater resource allocated	Communication to board	CPM

Table 5.4. An example excerpt of a risk register for a consultancy project

the main risks according to the impact they might have on the project and the likelihood of them occurring. It also outlines what actions will be taken to minimise the risk and who is responsible for implementing the mitigation.

As the poet Robert Burns noted, however, it is a rare plan that is implemented as originally intended. For this reason, a key process in any project is that of change control (Figure 5.5).

To aid the control of the project, most contracts specify a change control process (CCP). The CCP not only ensures that all proposed changes to the project are assessed for their suitability before they are implemented, but also that the impact on the existing project and the associated increases in resources or time are accounted for. The control process should specify the routes and responsibilities for different forms of change requests. It is important that the client plays a central part in signing these off as they will frequently result in increases to the time, and therefore the budget, of the project.

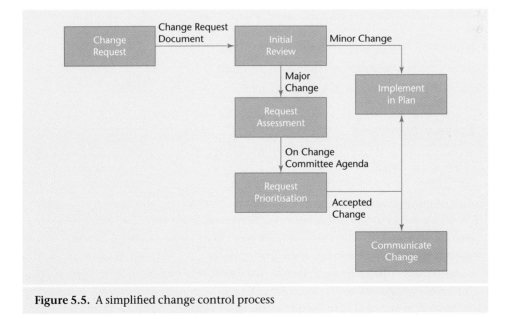

Figure 5.5. A simplified change control process

Well-run projects will have allocated sufficient time and resources to each activity in the plan and ensured that, where possible, independent activities are run simultaneously to ensure that the project completes as quickly as possible. Where activities are dependent upon each other, the project manager should have mapped out a "critical path" which represents the most amount of time the project should take and the critical activities that enable this to be achieved.

For the new consultant, much of this activity will be the responsibility of others. However, it is important that every consultant has a clear view of their deliverables, what work is required to achieve these, and what resources are required to support this work. For most consultants, a good way to organise this is to have a project folder (real or virtual) which includes:

- A detailed diary which outlines the activities the consultant will be performing to produce their deliverables on time.

- A table of dependencies so that the things which each activity relies upon can be identified.

- A personal risk register which outlines the risks that might affect the availability of resources, the activities of the consultant, or the deliverables. Important risks can then be raised with the project manager.

- A communication plan outlining the key stakeholders of the project and how they should be communicated with by the consultant.

- A reflexive diary outlining one's thoughts and comments on the project. Whilst this might not seem important at the time, many consultants find it an essential tool for reflecting on past projects and learning lessons for the future.

With these tools, a consultant should be able to avoid angry questions from project managers, business owners, or principal consultants such as:

- Why wasn't I told about this earlier?
- What exactly have you been doing with your time?
- Surely you knew this was going to happen?

CASE 5.2

The 99% Project

One of the first cases I took on as a management consultant was a project management role for an airline interested in implementing some e-training software. Each individual in the consulting team was allocated tasks in the meetings, progress was given as a percentage, and risks were managed.

As the weeks progressed, the major tasks were reported to be 20%, then 30%, then 50% completed. In the last few weeks, all tasks were either completed or at 90%, and the recorded risks were all in the "low" category. So far so good.

However, as the days passed, I noticed that one of the individuals began to constantly repeat that his progress was at 99%. At the same time, other team members, who were dependent on this consultant's work, had to stall their own work until it was completed. As I took a closer look at this individual's work, it was clear that he had badly underestimated how long the last part of his work would take. When I spoke to him about this, he told me that in meetings he felt that he needed to keep up with the others in terms of his own progress.

Fortunately, some other consultants had been freed up and were available to help him complete his tasks. According to his progress reviews, his last 1% took as many man-hours to complete as his first 20%. The lesson he learned was to be more honest and realistic with his reporting. The lesson I learned was to keep a closer eye on inexperienced consultants, especially those who felt pressure to conform.

- What systems might a project manager put in place to prevent this happening again?

Communication

Any consultancy plan should build in formal communication processes. This often involves a variety of different types of communication and formats, as depicted in Table 5.5.

With all client meetings there are a few key pointers that consultants should bear in mind. First, wherever possible, have a client manager chair the meeting. This instils a sense of ownership and makes clear that it is the client not the consultant that is primarily responsible for delivery. Second, prepare for the meeting effectively: communicate with all attendees beforehand so there are no surprises for you or them, ensure you have all the information you need to conduct a successful meeting, and consider the room, the seating, and the resources required. Finally, ensure the meeting is run effectively: an agenda, minutes, and actions with clear deliverables and named individuals should be obvious but are often absent.

Type	Format	Purpose	Frequency
Progress Report	Brief report (email/spreadsheet/database).	Updating the client programme manager on the progress of key deliverables.	Once or twice a week.
Progress Reviews	Detailed meeting between senior consultants and clients.	To perform a detailed review of the project against the original plan.	Between 3 and 5 reviews per project.
Decision Meetings	Short meetings to make project decisions.	To discuss options and make decisions on the project with client stakeholders.	Whenever required.
Issue Meetings	Communication between lead consultant and business owner.	To solve any issues that arise. Usually called by client concerned with individuals or activities.	Whenever required.

Table 5.5. Forms of formal client communication

In addition to the formal communication, there is of course, the informal communication and socialising that happens with every project. A word of warning on this. Whilst it is important to build trust and develop relationships, never make the mistake of giving the client something that they may hold against you. I often saw consultants removed from projects every year because they said the wrong thing to the wrong person after a few pints or mistook friendly office banter for real friendship.

Resourcing

Another responsibility of the project manager is to ensure that there are adequate resources to complete each project activity on time. Managing consultancy projects is particularly complex because of the number of different reporting lines that make up a team. As projects often cut across several departments and organisations, a typical fifteen-person team may consist of:

- Contractors: who report both to the project lead (who may be a consultant) and to a client manager.

- Consultants: often from several different consultancies. These may frequently report to their lead consultant, the project lead, and the client department. Furthermore, some consultants may be working on more than one project, in more than one company, each with its own demands on his or her time.

- Client employees: these will often work in a matrix structure and report to both their head of department and the project lead.

In addition, the project will be structured by seniority with some client employees reporting to consultants, and vice versa.

Insofar as is possible, the project manager needs to avoid upsetting the interests of other departments or organisations that his current team might report to. It is easy especially when different departments are working on the same project for "silo warfare" to emerge where different teams bond within those from their own department instead of focusing on the project. One of the best project managers I worked with, Mike Sturrock, managed to avoid this by working on two things. First, he built the team up so that their main loyalty was to the project. By treating them fairly, sticking up for them against senior management, and investing time and effort in social events, he developed considerable loyalty from the various people on the project. Second, he communicated well with the various departments and organisations that had a vested interest in the project. By regularly updating interested parties on the project's progress and challenges he managed to avoid the split loyalties that plague so many similar projects.

■ Exit

Project Handover

The project handover is often presented as part of the exit phase of the consultancy life-cycle. However, in doing so, this means the process is often done too quickly and not given the attention it deserves. The handover is a central part of any project and must be planned, resourced, and managed as well as any other deliverable.

The point at which the project is wound up is much clearer in some deliveries than others. A training course or a strategy report have very clear endings. With the training, it is when the agreed courses have finished, whilst with the strategy report, it is when the document has been completed and signed off. However, a change management, or a software development project, do not have clear end points. With the former, the success of the change, and how embedded it is, will often be a moot point. With the latter, there are always bugs that need fixing or errors that need correcting. For this reason, the contract and proposal of these more ambiguous projects will usually have devoted considerable space to defining project completion, tying it to specific rather than ephemeral measures (Kubr 1993).

For handover purposes, it is useful to classify consultancy projects into three sequential types (Table 5.6): advisory, implementation, and support. The delivery of one type of project should naturally lead to the following type; an advisory project will set up an implementation, an implementation project will set up project support.

Whilst it is understandable that a consultancy, once it believes the job has been completed, and it has been paid, will seek to minimise its involvement, actually the opposite should happen. The handover phase is the ideal time to develop the sale of follow-up work.

A typical handover will involve the following stages:

- The creation and implementation of a handover plan, agreed with the client. Usually, handover will be phased with the withdrawal of the consultancy team over a number of weeks.

- The plan should include activities to develop client capabilities to the point where they can easily take over any outstanding work. Usually, a high-level handover plan will have been drafted at the beginning of the project.

- The identification of key client individuals that will take over any on-going processes, work, or activities that were previously the responsibility of consultants.

- The physical and electronic handover of all formal documentation, software, and material.

- The handover of all security passes and a request to security to change access passwords and codes or terminate the consultancy user accounts.

- Providing the client with a key contact within the consultancy should they have follow-up questions or need clarification.

Project type	Example project	Handover effort	Next phase
Advisory	Strategic analysis	Low	Implementation
Implementation	Process re-engineering	High	Support/further implementation
Support	Maintenance of software	Medium	Further support/ none

Table 5.6. Types of project

Withdrawal

We are told (Headey et al. 2004) that events such as moving house, losing one's job, and workplace stress are heavy contributors to individual stress. At the end of a project, a typical consultant goes from working incredibly hard to meet a deadline to being removed from the social and physical norms that have surrounded them for the last few months. It is worth acknowledging the complex emotional effect that the sudden withdrawal from a project can have on a consultant.

For this reason, the lead consultant, and the consultancy firm, should do their best to support individuals, especially if the project has been long and stressful. Key tips include:

- Ensuring frequent contact with the consultancy throughout the project to avoid consultants going "native".

- Acknowledging that withdrawal can be a stressful time and asking individuals to be aware of how they react to moving on.

- Providing consultants with time "on the bench" so they can spend a decent amount of time with their friends and families before moving on to the next project.

- Bringing the consultancy team together after the project is completed to socialise informally.

The project review, described below, can also help with the process of closure.

Project Review

Project reviews do not always happen as often as they should. However, they are increasingly common, as clients, especially during a recession, frequently tie payment to the evaluation of a project. If the project has been based on payment by results then the project review can take a number of days of data collection, negotiation, and settlement as the consultant aims to maximise the return on their own investment in the project. However, in a well-managed project, success measures, such as hitting milestones, will be produced throughout the delivery process. If there is divergence between the client and the consultant as to the extent to which the project targets have been hit, it is a good idea to go to arbitration before ending up in the courts, which can be exceedingly expensive for both parties.

For projects which are not based on payment by results, the project review should not simply be a chat about what went well or badly. The review should feed into a formal process of improvement by which recommendations for future projects, for both the consultancy and the client, can be implemented. These can concern any aspect of the project, from negotiation through to handover, but the focus should be on constructive criticism and praise, where it is due.

The review should also be a chance to get feedback on individual consultants and, if they desire, client employees. Where possible, a consultancy should have a system by which consultants can get 360-degree feedback from the client and consultant team members.

Finally, the consultancy, and the client team, should have their own reviews where they can meet privately and discuss the project amongst themselves. This step is ignored by many consultancies but is crucial in enabling the team to discuss frankly what went right and what went wrong. This review is also a chance for the consultancy to improve its tools, techniques, and methods. This step is essential in ensuring that the key asset of the consultancy, its knowledge, is continuously improved.

Follow-Up

Consultancies will often be examining opportunities for follow-up work as soon as they have entered the client organisation. However, this should not be a distraction but be part of recognizing the wider issues of the project. By the time the handover is on the horizon, the lead consultant will usually already have identified, prioritised, and planned potential solutions for further client issues. It is important for the lead consultant to begin discussions on follow-up work before the handover. However, it is unseemly and unprofessional to be seen to be looking for work when the client is already paying for your time on an existing project.

By the time the handover occurs, the follow-on work, if there is any, should already be at a stage which can lead to a contract being signed. Ideally, the work will move from a single project to on-going work. In the words of Holmes (2002), from "hunting to farming". An example of this is when a colleague of mine won a piece of work training the senior team of a cosmetics company in the principles of "lean work". Whilst they got their internal team to cascade training down throughout the organisation, the consultant was made responsible for the "train the trainer" work and also was able to produce and sell a "licensed" toolkit for every employee.

A Final Note

A final, but important, word about consultancy work needs to be made here. Many young consultants believe it is their responsibility to get projects delivered and become stressed when things are going wrong. Consultancies and clients will frequently place a lot of psychological pressure on new recruits to work harder, and when the individual fails to deliver quality work on time, the employer often places the blame squarely on the shoulders of that individual. This pressure leads to some consultants suffering from stress and eventually having nervous breakdowns or suffering from panic attacks, depression, and anxiety.

The most important lesson one needs to learn as a consultant, and one that most senior consultants have mastered, is to realise that it is not the consultant's responsibility to deliver on time. This slightly counter-intuitive comment needs some unpacking: an individual can only succeed if given the necessary time and resources. Even then, a lot of luck is required for things to run smoothly.

Frequently, employers, especially in high-pressure jobs, try to make additional profits by making young consultants work excessive hours knowing full well that they can be replaced easily should the stress get too much for them. Whilst this is rarely an explicit strategy it often becomes an emergent strategy as pressures to maximise profits are passed down through the organisational hierarchy. From a legal, moral, and sustainable perspective, individuals can only perform if they are given enough time to do the job well.

The new consultant, therefore, should, above all, learn to proactively manage their workload and be able to raise risks of under-staffing or lack of resources without feeling it reflects a weakness of their own. After all, if the work was that important, they would double the resources on it, or extend the deadline.

This approach requires an honesty and confidence that is actually respected by most senior managers as it indicates a willingness to tackle difficult issues and also ensures that projects are not jeopardised by consultants that keep quiet and pretend everything is fine.

■ Chapter Summary

The life-cycle is a way of describing most of the work that consultants perform. However, as with any models, it is a simplification and should be treated as a guide rather than a rule. This chapter has:

- Introduced and explained the consulting life-cycle.
- Described the importance of sales to successful consultancy practices.
- Shown how to write successful proposals.
- Explained the types of research that consultancies perform.
- Described how consultancies deliver their work and exit projects successfully.

Student Exercise

A client that owns a chain of supermarkets has called you in to investigate what he calls "theft from my stores". It appears that each month, the client loses around £120,000 from the chain of fifty-two stores. The client has asked you to do some empirical research on where and why the "thefts" occur.

In pairs, produce a one-page summary which details your research strategy for the project:

1   What would your research questions be?

2   What research methods would you use?

3   How would you analyse and present your results?

Once you have completed this, get together with another pair and discuss why you might have approached things differently. Try to agree on the best route for the research project to take.

Discussion Questions

- What are the steps in the consulting life-cycle?
- How do consultancies sell to potential clients?
- What forms of data collection might a consultant use?

- What is the difference between inductive and deductive research?
- What components should a delivery plan include?

Case-Study Exercise: Gekko

Part 1

History

In 1677, one year after the Great Fire of London, the first mention of Gekko can be evidenced. Thomas Gekko established the company in order to supply the army of Charles II with brass buttons for their uniforms. On the back of British Imperial expansion as well as the First and Second World Wars, Gekko grew. However, after 1950, the inaction and reduction in the British military meant that Gekko's problems began to emerge.

Gekko's products are very high quality. The breastplates, for example, which are made for the Queen's Cavalry, can only be made by four people in the UK, and three of them work at Gekko. On some of the lines it can take up to ten years to learn sufficient skills; on others, a production line produces hand-painted work to customer requirements. The issue of quality is what most of the Gekko employees believe makes them special. The managers maintain that many bulk orders for plastic or printed objects can be done more cheaply elsewhere.

Work Practices

The importance of tradition in the company has meant that most of the work in the shop has not been modernised for tens, if not hundreds, of years. The factory still operates a bureaucratic piece-rate, time-motion attitude towards work. "We have a strict hierarchy here," one production manager pointed out; "the offices and factory are separate and we have the production manager, superintendent, supervisors, charge hands and then the workers". Change, innovation, and democracy were not seen as good things.

Up until the 1980s the workforce was strongly unionised and at one point the factory was closed down for nine weeks concerning a redundancy dispute. Health and Safety was such a low priority in the factory that two Improvement Notices were placed on it by the Health and Safety Inspectorate. Few of the stampers that have been at Gekko for a while have all their own fingers. Despite this, the workers are generally loyal to the company and are proud of their reputation for quality.

The lack of formal procedures has led to a reliance upon the intrinsic knowledge of many of the workers. The know-how to manufacture breastplates or cavalry helmets is not written anywhere within the company. Even the old quality manager (appointed three years ago) pointed out that "if you stuck to the rule book, you'd never get anything done".

Gekko had strong ties with its suppliers and had been using some of them for over a hundred years. Material comes into the workshop regularly and is processed by several (manual) production lines. There are no information systems and all jobs are organised by "old hands": experienced production managers who know where the relevant casts are kept and how to set up the ancient machinery.

The Forces for Change

After 1980 several market factors combined to necessitate changes within Gekko:

- The cutting back of military expenditure meant that there were fewer orders for the buttons and badges which had been the staple product of the company. The decline in orders has caused the workforce to fall to a third in the last thirty years.

- The movement towards competitive tendering in the MoD meant that Gekko now had to compete with other companies in India and China who were catching up with Gekko quality but at a much lower price.

Internally, a number of issues began to develop:

- Gekko's processes had not modernised. Orders often arrived late and it was virtually impossible to let customers know when their deliveries would arrive. Although training was allocated an increased budget, there was no system to identify training needs, nor the effectiveness of training. Whilst the quality inspector received no training, people were allowed to train on computers who did not use them in the workplace.

- Administration (there was no marketing department) would create deadlines for production which production could rarely meet. The adherence to quality, of which production was so proud, meant that set-up and turnaround times were very slow and quality control very stringent.

- Due to the increase in labour, insurance, and material costs overheads were increasing and consequently profits were diminishing, whilst during the 1980s and 1990s the turnover at Gekko remained a constant at around £2m.

- The machinery and procedures at Gekko were ancient and the lack of investment in the company worsened the situation—quality was only being produced at a high premium. The decision taken in 1993 by the MoD to deal only with firms who possessed ISO 9000 meant that the company needed to modernise quickly.

- The ancient production systems within Gekko meant that work was often retracing the same steps and that as a consequence delivery times were rarely met. This state of affairs was known by management as "the Gekko shuffle" and was a constant source of conflict between management and workers.

The culture of the company was very traditional and neither workers nor managers liked the idea of change. Workers saw themselves as highly skilled artisans who should not be directed. Distinctions between levels and roles were closely guarded with a long apprenticeship needed for any newcomers.

As administration generally dealt with customer complaints, they increasingly became dissatisfied with the performance of production. The bad feeling was made worse by the differentiation between administration and production on working times and pay. Production would start half an hour earlier than administration on weekdays, but would leave at 1.30 pm on Fridays, which appeared unfair to many of those working in administration, especially when customer complaints came in on a Friday and could not be responded to by production. Conversely, production disliked working on a piece-rate system when most of the administration department were being paid a salary. This was, they maintained, symbolic of the differential esteem bestowed upon offices, as opposed to the shopfloor.

- What are the main problems at Gekko?

- What frameworks might you use to analyse their problems?

- What solutions might you recommend?

Part 2

In 1993, Gekko was bought by a Taiwanese billionaire, who gave the company to his son. Tim, a marketing executive, was determined to modernise Gekko but his impulsive decision-making made him few friends.

Tim's aim when he joined the company was to change the culture from what he called a "backwards, traditional and confrontational attitude" to a modern, cohesive, Japanese style of working. Tim's effort's to transform Gekko involved:

Architecture

Tim brought in a more open-plan workplace which enabled customers to come and tour the factory, although many workers objected to this. He also brought in lockers so that workers didn't keep their jackets and food where they were working. However, his style of implementation was not always welcome—when he saw a jacket in the wrong place, he would lay it out on the floor. He also brought cameras into the workplace which he hoped would encourage workers to work harder; but these were resented by many and often vandalised.

New Products

Tim began a policy of buying in pens, sweaters, baseball caps, and other goods which could be labelled, and then simply added the Gekko name to them. Thus, a cheap baseball cap could be imported and a company logo added to it, but because it was "manufactured" in Gekko it could be sold on for a much higher price. The immediate effect of this was to cause the traditional workforce to become worried about the security of their own jobs. As they were paid on a piece-rate system, any lessening of their output would mean a lower wage.

In 2000, Gekko took over a company called Piney which produced up-market accessories such as cuff-links, handbags, and compacts. The intention was to use this company to cross-sell into other markets. Gekko also outsourced much of its mass production to China.

New Technology

A consultancy, Systems magic, was brought in to improve efficiency through the introduction of modern manufacturing systems. They introduced a measurement system by which each shopfloor worker was to measure their work schedule and the time it took. Each job that was completed was to be written down, so that the "progress chaser" knew where it was, and the time it took was to be recorded so that productivity improvements could be quantified. The reactions to the system have not been welcoming:

- "I can't see how we have changed in the last few months … it has increased rather than decreased the amount of paperwork,"

- "I can't see the point in me doing graphs," or

- "it cost £80,000 to teach us how to do our jobs."

The introduction of computers was hoped to make the planning, ordering, and accounting easier, but workers were highly resistant to any changes in their work because they distrusted managerial motives. As a result there was little evidence that the system produced improvements in communication.

Policies

In an attempt to have a more cohesive attitude between the workforce and managers, Tim got rid of the managers' canteen in the hope of encouraging the two groups to mix. Whilst this had some effect, it also meant that the managers resented his style and could often be seen joining in the criticisms of his style. However, he did not attempt to change the working hours or the pay structure of the shopfloor.

Attitudes

Tim attempted to bring in teamworking but the type of work (piece-rate) didn't lend itself to this. Moreover, the suggestion box only ever had one suggestion in it, which was for Tim to leave the company. Contrary to what he was trying to do, the relations between Tim and the rest of the company worsened, with several walk-outs taking place.

Redundancies

When Tim took over the factory, he assured workers three times that they would not lose their jobs. Two days later, following advice from Systems magic, Tim made fifteen workers redundant. One team leader captured the resulting emotion best:

> It was very bad actually. Morale was very, very low and it was a complete shock to everybody—there's a lot of bad feeling . . .

The lack of communication not only served to make the shock bigger, but also made the transition period more difficult:

> none of the supervisors knew anything about it—how it was going to affect their department. It just hap pened . . . supervisors seem like they've had their heads cut off.
>
> They'd get rid of someone and not discuss people who were doing that person's job. People were saying "it's not my job". So there's buttons being made wrong and being scrapped.

The bitter reaction from the workforce was much worse because there was a genuine belief that the wrong people had been made redundant. This belief proved well founded when Tim was forced to get some key workers back as consultants. It was, in the words of one manager, "a balls up". Regardless, the factory continued to make redundancies over the next few years and by 2005, the number of employees had fallen from 135 to 65.

Postscript

Despite a 20 per cent reduction in costs, 20 per cent improvement in sales, a new five-year contract with the MoD, and increasing exports, Gekko was hit by the rising cost of exports, the £1m cost of modernisation, and, most importantly, a £2m pension deficit. The law meant that any deficit needed filling before the company could be sold which Gekko did not have the resources to do.

Gekko was put into administration and the administrator wound the final pension scheme up and sacked eleven more employees. Once the pension obligations had been offloaded, Gekko was bought by a quality clothing manufacturer, Bingo, who safeguarded the remaining sixty-one jobs.

- What would you have done differently from Tim?

- What difficulties might Systems magic have faced in working with Tim? How would you have dealt with these difficulties?

Further Reading

There are a number of good books which describe the work of consultants in detail. The best two are listed below. The former is more thorough and academic, whilst the latter is a brief guide for the busy practitioner:

- Kubr, M. (2002). *Management Consulting: A Guide to the Profession*. London: International Labour Office.

- Markham, C. (2004). *The Top Consultant*. London: Kogan Page.

There are also a number of populist "kiss-and-tell" books which provide an alternative, if anecdotal, view of the dark side of consultancy work. With the caveat that these books are often out to shock the reader, they can be an interesting read. The two I would recommend are:

- Craig, D. (2005). *Rip Off: The Scandalous Story of the Management Consulting Money Machine*. London: Original Book Company.

- Craig, D., and Brooks, R. (2006). *Plundering the Public Sector*. London: Constable.

References

Alvesson, M., and Robertson, M. (2006). The Brightest and the Best: The Role of Elite Identity in Knowledge Intensive Companies. *Organization*, 13 (2): 195–224.

Armbrüster, T. (2006). *The Economics and Sociology of Management Consulting*. Cambridge: Cambridge University Press.

Bowers, S. (2006). Accenture to Quit NHS Technology Overhaul. *The Guardian*, 26 September.

Brace, I. (2008). *Questionnaire Design*. London: Kogan Page.

Cohen, W. (2001). *How to Make it Big as a Consultant*. AMACOM.

Consulting Intelligence (2007). *Consulting Survey*. Consulting Intelligence LLC.

Corbin, J., and Strauss, A. (2007). *Basics of Qualitative Research*. Beverly Hills, CA: Sage.

Cresswell, J. (2003). *Research Design*. Beverly Hills, CA: Sage.

—— (2007): *Qualitative Inquiry & Research Design*. Beverly Hills, CA: Sage.

Czerniawska, F. (2002). *The Intelligent Client: Managing your Management Consultant*. London: Hodder Arnold.

—— (2006). *Ensuring Sustainable Value from Consultants*. MCA/PWC

—— (2007). *The Trusted Firm*. Chichester: John Wiley.

Freedman, R. (2001). Exec Explains KPMG's Consulting Lifecycle. *Tech Republic*, 11 June.

Furusten, S., and Werr, A. (eds) (2005). *Dealing with Confidence*. Copenhagen: Copenhagen Business School Press.

Glückler J., and Armbrüster, T. (2003). Bridging Uncertainty in Management Consultancy: The Mechanisms of Trust and Networked Reputation. *Organization Studies*, 24: 269–97.

Headey, B., Holmström, E., and Wearing, A. (2004). The Impact of Life Events and Changes in Domain Satisfactions on Well-Being. *Social Indicators Research*, 15 (3).

Heuskel, D. (2004). The Truth Seekers. In J. P. Thommen and A. Richter (eds), *Management Consulting Today*. Bornhofen: Gabler Verlag.

Holmes, A. (2002). *The Chameleon Consultant: Culturally Intelligent Consultancy*. London: Gower Publishing Ltd.

IPSOS/MORI (2007). *Paying More and Getting Less*. Report for Ernst and Young.

Kubr, M. (1993). *How to Select and Use Consultants*. London: International Labour Office.

—— (2002). *Management Consulting: A Guide to the Profession*. London: International Labour Office.

Maister, D. (2003). *Managing the Professional Service Firm*. Free Press Business.

Markham, C. (2004). *The Top Consultant*. London: Kogan Page.

Pinault, L. (2001). *Consulting Demons: Inside the Unscrupulous World of Global Corporate Consulting*. New York: Harper Business.

Popper, K. (1957). The Logic of Scientific Discovery. New York: Basic Books.

Rea, L., and Parker, R. (2005). Designing and Conducting Survey Research: A Comprehensive Guide. San Francisco, CA: Jossey-Bass.

Rosenthal, R., and Jacobson, L. (1968). *Pygmalion in the Classroom: Teacher Expectation and Pupils' Intellectual Development*. New York: Rinehart and Winston.

Sadler, P. (2002). *Management Consultancy*, 2nd edn. London: Kogan Page.

Schein, E. H. (1988). *Process Consultation*. Reading, MA: Addison-Wesley.

Sturdy, A., Schwartz, M., and Spicer, A. (2006). Guess Who's Coming to Dinner? Structures and Uses of Liminality in Strategic Management Consultancy. *Human Relations*, 59 (7): 929–60.

Weiss, A. (2003). *Getting Started in Consulting*. New York: John Wiley and Sons.

Wickham, P., and Wickham, L. (2008). *Management Consulting*. Englewood Cliffs, NJ: Prentice Hall.

Client Interventions

Beverley Brookes, Partner, Advisory, KPMG

Performing management consultancy for clients is initially a case of understanding and managing expectations. The reasons behind a client seeking to engage a management consulting firm are varied but broadly fall into three main areas:

- "Help me understand and fix my problem."
- "Help me make the best decision on the way forward."
- "Help me execute effectively."

■ The Big Issue: What Do They Really Want?

The key challenge is in understanding where the client is with respect to what they've asked for—indeed, whether what they've asked for is what they really need. Management consultants are often accused of the classic client intervention "lend me your watch and I'll tell you the time". In reality, this first intervention is far more subtle and its aim is to work closely with the client and his or her team to bring them to a common understanding of what their real goals are and how they might approach achieving them. A recurring mistake of consultants at this stage is to engage in a way which "tells" the client what they should be doing—the results of this often materialise as consultant-led initiatives and projects where the client and their team feels no ownership or accountability for the outcome. I am a firm believer that the success of a client engagement, whether it lasts weeks, months, or years, is the moment that your client becomes fully independent and confident of moving forward without you.

An illustration of this came quite early in my management consulting career when I was asked to meet with the CIO of a multinational travel organisation to discuss his clearly stated requirement for a five-year IT strategy. As the conversation progressed, it became clear that he had reached the conclusion that laying out his vision of IT strategy would resolve a number of the issues he was facing—within both his company and the travel market overall. This was that a huge shift in the way people buy and take their holidays was happening—they didn't want to buy the classic "package holiday" any more, wanted more freedom of choice in terms of configuring their own components (travel dates, flights, accommodation, hire cars, golf, and other activities) in a way which suited them not the tour operator.

For his organisation, this represented a big change not only in the technology required to deliver this, including what we all take for granted in 2009, the "online booking" experience, but also for the business model overall, from contracting airline seats and hotel rooms through to actual travel agency and tour operations. I worked with this client for a year, with a small team—carefully blended from a mix of business and IT consultants—to engage with the broader organisation and make sure that the CIO could define and implement his IT strategy and be confident that it supported the underlying business model changes and that his fellow executives perceived the real value that IT was delivering in moving the business forward through technology innovation. The CIO was able to articulate the strategy in business terms and execute with his own team over three years (rather than his original five) to keep this travel organisation at the head of the field.

■ The Consulting Conundrum—Do I Stay or Do I Go?

Client expectations of a management consultant range quite broadly from seeking a "trusted adviser" to someone who will do everything for them. The former is an extremely privileged position to be in as a consultant and is often independent of whether you're actively engaged with them on project work. In its most elemental terms, it means that the client will instinctively pick up the phone or ask to have a drink with you as their first response to any number of situations they need to handle and seek your honest advice. This often results in "chargeable" work but by no means in all cases. I have a US-based, very senior client with whom I eat dinner every few weeks, and exchange email and phone calls in between—I have delivered a couple of key projects for him successfully and as a result have become his sounding board. He often points other colleagues in my direction on specific issues and has become one of KPMG's valued references.

The latter is a much rougher ride from the management consultant's standpoint. I have ended up in a situation on at least two client engagements where our team was literally doing all of the "heavy lift" work on the project and the client team saw their only responsibility as turning up to meetings and reviewing outputs. This is always a difficult situation to handle—on the one hand, the fees generated as a result tend to be higher and longer term. On the other hand, if the situation is allowed to continue the client sooner or later resents what they're paying you and wonders how they will ever get rid of you. Many consultancy firms "talk the talk" on client responsibility, challenge, and knowledge transfer but rarely "walk the walk". In particular, when the engagement is fixed fee or outcome based it is often necessary (not to mention easier) to do it all yourself rather than persuade your client of their accountabilities.

My personal experience (both good and bad) has taught me a hard lesson—you have to be very clear with the client up front about what you will and will not do. By default, that gives them a good understanding of what's expected of their team and helps them bring the best talent into the project at an early stage. When working with a global telecommunications client on a back-office transformation (organisation, processes, and systems), we helped them develop a clear strategy for building their own teams, enhancing skills in the organisation, and providing career development via the project for talented individuals.

That was done by helping them decide which elements of the project they needed to own and execute and which elements could be farmed out for delivery to a systems integrator or other third party. The decisions were based on long-term value to the organisation—what needed to be retained as an in-house capability versus what was really commodity delivery. That KPMG did much of the "heavy lift" work in the early stages whilst that was developing coupled with helping them set up governance and organisation to manage multiple third party providers effectively resulted in a successful transformation and business benefits being delivered ahead of plan.

■ Conversations with Clients: Lose the Jargon, Please!

If I had a pound for every time I've been in a meeting and a client staff member has listened attentively to what I or a consulting colleague has said, then walked away and told someone else they have no idea what we're on about, I would be a very rich woman.

In common with all industries, we've developed our own language and way of speaking which is so familiar to us that we don't realise how impenetrable it can seem to people who aren't management consultants.

When working on a project for a high-technology organisation (no strangers to jargon themselves!) a workshop was in progress, discussing essentially what activities in their IT function should be stopped, what should continue, and what should be modified. One of my colleagues explained this as "your IT heat map demonstrates a high tendency towards project overload". Having subsequently overheard this repeated in the coffee shop, punctuated by laughter on more than one occasion, I promised myself that I would always speak in plain English (or on occasion, French or German). This for the simple reason that *every* conversation must be clear, simple, and understood by everyone participating . . . otherwise, how will your client ever trust you to deliver anything!

6

Consulting Tools, Skills, and Techniques

Chapter Objectives

This chapter covers the key tools, skills, and techniques that the consultant can draw upon in order to help their clients. Specifically, the chapter:

■ Discusses the limitations of the tools and techniques of consultancy.

■ Provides an overview of the main analytical frameworks in consultancy.

■ Explains how consultancies develop their own tools and products.

■ Illustrates the soft skills that consultants develop in the course of their work.

■ Introduction: The Art of Consultancy

Anyone who has worked in a company knows that organisations are complex, messy, and open-ended systems riddled with informal rules, political infighting, and sometimes conflicting sub-cultures (Tsoukas 2001). For this reason those who try to effect organisational change are not practising a science, but an art. Science uses the experimental method where experiments can be isolated and undertaken in a sterile environment which is "closed" to outside influences and can, therefore, be repeated over and over again with predictable results. Organisations, as with any social systems, cannot be isolated from their environments, and changes resulting from interventions cannot be tested, predicted, or scientifically validated (Popper 1957).

The unpredictable nature of consultancy interventions means that, unlike scientists, there are few prescribed methods for organisational interventions. This statement might come as a shock to many students who believe they have spent years learning prescribed methods for exactly this purpose, but, on closer examination, the statement holds true. Compared to other "expert" professions, such as law, accountancy, or medicine, the consultant's, or even the manager's, toolbox remains a vague, contested, and ever-changing place. Even if one examines very specific forms of intervention, such as BPR or outsourcing, there are hundreds of different variants of each, and they will produce different results depending on the people who implement them, the organisation they are implemented in, and the environment that exists at the time. Thus, whilst there may be many routes to failure in organisational interventions, there are also as many routes to success. The consequence of this argument is that, in organisational terms, there is no such thing as "best practice", as such a concept cannot be demonstrated or proved.

Consultancy tools and techniques, therefore, are not scientific instruments and are closer to the instruments of art: they can be used in many different ways, their use is highly subjective, they are interpreted differently by varying groups, and they can be used to produce an infinite number of different outcomes. Moreover, as with artists, the hundreds of thousands of tools, techniques, and frameworks that consultants use are less important than the consultant that uses them. For this reason, when consultancies recruit, they generally do not look for someone who has passed exams in consulting, but instead seek people who can adapt, think on their feet, and build confidence in any given approach.

Consulting work concerns both the content (what the consultant knows) and the process (how the consultant works). The former may involve using a method such as BPR, a tool such as Excel, or technique such as financial forecasting. The latter may involve softer interpersonal or presentation skills or include the innovation by which consultants change their methods to suit the client. The process of consultancy incorporates the way in which the consultant seeks to use the tools they have. This means many things but includes:

- Engaging the client and seeking to understand their needs rather than insisting on a standardised, one-size-fits-all solution.
- Ensuring that the method is consistent with the client organisation and is agreed with the client.

- Making sure the method is reflected upon and improved upon every time it is used.

- Ensuring that the use of the tool or method never gets in the way of your integrity as a professional consultant.

This chapter, therefore, does not seek to suggest the tools and skills it describes are "best practice", for such a concept is ill suited to a world in which frameworks change every few years. Nor does it suggest that these tools will always effect successful change in organisations. Instead it seeks to provide readers with the knowledge and vocabulary they need to understand how tools and techniques can be used to understand and tackle complex organisational problems.

The tool is less important than the box you put around it. You need to be able to intuitively understand the client, to identify their needs and refocus the work you are doing. The box for the tool is at least, if not more, important than the tool itself.

(Claire, CEO, small consultancy)

The chapter first examines the different types of tools and techniques consultants have developed and attempts to provide some classification to them. It then outlines some of the main analytical frameworks that are associated with consultancy. As part of this section, the chapter discusses how consultancies and consultants create "bespoke" tools which can then be used for marketing purposes. The frameworks described in this section will be useful, not just in organisational analysis, but also in tackling cases such as those outlined in Chapter 11. The chapter then moves on to provide an overview of the softer process skills that consultants deploy in their day-to-day work such as presentation, interpersonal, and political skills.

■ Frameworks for Business Analysis

Introducing Methods and Tools

There are hundreds of thousands of tools, techniques, and methods that consultants have developed in order to help transform businesses. In addition to the famous generic approaches such as Business Process Re-engineering or Total Quality Management, there are a myriad of virtually unknown methods and tools which small consultancies have developed to better sell to their clients. In effect, these are products that consultancies develop and own the intellectual property rights to.

Each aim of business change is associated with a number of different approaches. For example, the aim of quality improvement is associated with human relations, quality management, and Japanese management techniques. In turn, these approaches have led to a number of proprietary methods, including global brands such as ISO 9001 or EFQM, and also small company products such as QRUP©. Each of these proprietary methods draws on a number of tools or techniques, which, in this case, might include quality circles, suggestion schemes, quality training, and delayering. Another example, of business efficiency, is outlined in Figure 6.1.

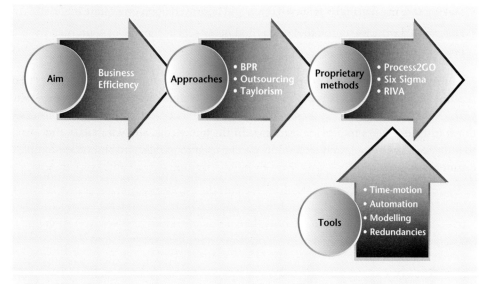

Figure 6.1. The aims, approaches, methods and tools of business efficiency

The Basic Tools of Business

Not long ago, a recruitment consultant for an American consultancy told me:

> it's amazing, absolutely amazing, how many business graduates who we get in front of us who have no idea at all about the basics of business. Sure, they can tell me all about Maslow or Ford, but have no idea how to handle questions about how businesses work ... questions like, should we sell this product in Russia? How much should we sell it for? Who should we sell it to?

It's important to remember here that the recruiter was not looking for the right answer—in fact, she went on to state:

> you definitely don't want someone who just shouts out an answer, "YES! ... FIFTEEN DOLLARS! ... WOMEN! ... EXPAND IN CHICAGO! Instead, we look for people who can think—who can apply a logic or a method in order to get an answer. For us, the method is more important than the answer—at least when we're recruiting.

What the interviewer was looking for from graduates was not an immediate answer to business problems but a method, or a framework, for approaching common questions that clients ask. Below, five of these basic questions are provided and possible frameworks for analysis are given. These questions are also the basis for tackling most case interviews given in consultancy interviews so will be useful to you generating questions and undertaking analyses in Chapter 11. These questions are:

- What should our strategy be?
- How can we improve our operations?

- How can we maximise our profits?

- How should we price our products?

- What markets should we enter?

The sections below take each one of these questions and provide some frameworks that should be useful in tackling them. I hope the reader will forgive me for leaving out a few quite well-known frameworks. I have done so either because they state the obvious, for example cost–benefit analysis, or because I have never heard of them actually being used for problem solving. An example of the latter is the BCG matrix which, despite its common presence in business books, has not been used seriously by any consultancy for thirty years or more.

What Should our Strategy Be?

The Four Cs

The Four Cs are used to assess a new course of strategic action, especially when launching a new product or service.

	Questions
Customers	Will they pay for the service? How much? Are there enough of them? What trends are discerniable? What do they think of the company?
Competition	What market share do they have? Where is the client in relation to them? Can they copy the service? What differences and strengths do they possess?
Cost	How much will the course of action cost? Where will the funding come from? When will the project break-even? What will the cost of the service be?
Company	What strengths does the client have? What are their people, processes, and technology like? What trends can be discerned?

Table 6.1. The Four Cs

Porter's Five Forces

Porter's Model is often taught on MBA programmes as a way of assessing the strength of a company's or industry's strategic position. The five factors that Porter outlined were:

1. The Threat of Substitute Products: which concerns the ease with which a company's product might be dropped by customers. Such a calculation includes the buyer's propensity to substitute, the costs to the buyer of switching products, and the difference in price and performance of the products. This is often a difficult calculation to make as psychology is often a key factor. Google, for example, is, in theory, easily replaceable, but still retains a powerful strategic position.

2. Threat of Entry of New Competitors: how easy it is for new companies to enter the market. This involves an assessment of factors such as barriers to entry, for example

costs or intellectual property, the power of the brand, economies of scale, advantages of time (e.g. a long learning curve), and legal issues, such as government legislation.

3. Buyer Power: which concerns the ability of customers to drive prices down. Factors that are often considered include: switching costs, buyer: firm ratios, price sensitivity, volume of purchasing, availability of similar products, and availability of information to the customer.

4. Power of Suppliers: which concerns the ability of suppliers to drive prices up or disrupt operations. Things that are often considered here are: supplier switching costs, the numbers of suppliers to chose from, and the ease with which supplies might be switched. As suppliers also include employees (who supply labour) the analysis should also include the solidarity and unionisation of the labour force.

5. Competitive Rivalry: which concerns how competitors in the industry compete. This is focused on: the number of competitors, the similarity of their strategies, the barriers for exit in the industry and the market growth rate, and the way information is available in the market.

Figure 6.2. Six forces model

However, several academics have made criticisms of Porter's analysis, arguing that it lacks empirical verification, that it is not suited to dynamic market conditions, and that it ignores the cooperation between buyers, suppliers, and competitors (Coyne and Subramaniam 1996; Shapiro and Varian 1998). It also needs to include "complementors", which combine the efforts of different companies to produce value. For example, the mobile phone manufacturer and the network provider, or the PC maker, the chip manufacturer, and the writer of the operating system (Brandenburger and Nalebuff 1997). This produces a six forces model, as depicted in Figure 6.2.

McKinsey's 7-S Framework

The McKinsey 7-S Model was developed by Tom Peters and Robert Waterman while working for McKinsey & Company, and by Richard Pascale and Anthony Athos (Pascale and Athos 1981; Peters and Waterman 1982). Its aim is to show the holistic integration of a company's strategy, structure, systems, style, skills, and staff with the company's shared values. It emphasises how each factor is interrelated and integrated with other parts.

The framework, along with any other holistic representation of an organisation, is useful in ensuring that all aspects of a company are considered when undergoing organisational change. However, I have never seen it used in a sophisticated way and it appears to be more common in textbooks than it is in actual business practice.

A lot of the more famous frameworks that are taught in MBAs aren't really used in consultancies any more. I think the idea is to get used to thinking in terms of simple models that are quite marketable.

(Recent graduate, large outsourcing consultancy)

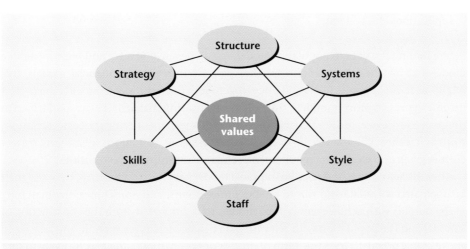

Figure 6.3. The McKinsey 7-S Framework

How Can We Improve our Operations?

Modelling

Modelling involves the production of an abstracted representation of reality to solve a problem or predict an outcome. Most models include mapping both entities (things) and relationships between those entities. The types of modelling involved will depend on the problem that is being tackled and the method that is used. Examples of models include:

- Financial Models: most financial models produce predictions about the future financial state of a company, market, or other economic system. Financial models are incredibly varied and include everything from spreadsheet models which predict profit and loss accounts for venture capitalists to massively complex banking models which calculate derivative risks for billion dollar transactions.

- Process Models: process models, for consultants at least, tend to focus on business or systems process and are used to represent the different activities and relationships of any end-to-end process. Process modelling is used to map both the current and future states of any business or system process and can be extended to incorporate information about costs, labour, speed, and data management.

- System Modelling: systems modelling can, again, be used for any number of purposes, but will tend to focus on the relationships between entities in an entire system. Examples include soft systems methodology (SSM) and System Dynamics which are used to model complex systems and how they change over time.

- IT Modelling: there are a number of methods of modelling IT systems, many of which include variants of process or systems modelling, or both. Structured Systems Analysis and Design Method (SSADM) and Unified Modelling Language both provide methods for modelling systems which specify relationships and entities for the creation of new applications and systems.

Before finding the data to populate a model, researchers will first try and build a credible model that matches the relationships they perceive in reality. In financial models, this might mean linking sales items and prices together in the right way to provide the correct income figures; in process models, this will mean ensuring that activities are performed in the correct sequence; in Systems Dynamics, this will mean identifying the correct relationships and feedback loops. Finally in IT systems modelling, this means identifying correct entities (such as classes), data requirements, and relationships between entities.

After the key entities and relationships in a model have been established, they can then be populated with data and run to predict future events, and, sometimes, the matching of the outputs with actual events allows models to be improved. Both the construction of a model and the population with relevant data can be seen as research. In the case listed above of low productivity, some form of process or system modelling may be likely to spot the causes of the problem better than interviews or questionnaires.

Value Chain Analysis

Value Chain Analysis was invented by Michael Porter (1985) in his book *Competitive Advantage: Creating and Sustaining Superior Performance*. Businesses, he noticed, often make profit by adding value to a product. The process by which this happens is the value chain: a series of events, or *primary activities*, which make an item more valuable than it was previously. The more value that can be added during each primary activity, the better for the business. In addition to these *primary activities*, Porter detailed a number of *support activities* which are supporting activity that do not directly add value to the product and can sometimes be outsourced to specialists.

The *Primary activities*, i.e. those that usually add most value, are listed by Porter as:

• Inbound logistics (receiving materials from suppliers).
• Operations (the production of products or services).
• Outbound logistics (distributing or providing a service).
• Marketing and sales (e.g. promotions, communications, and advertising).
• Service (such as after-sales or pre-installation).

Support activities include procurement, HRM, technology, and infrastructure.

The value chain analysis has three steps. The first is to break down the activities of the company to each mentioned in the framework. The second step is to assess the potential for adding value with each activity, either by cutting costs, differentiating, or improving quality. The third step is to find strategies to add sustainable competitive advantage. The value chain analysis is more complicated than it sounds and a good analysis can take some months. However, the framework is suited primarily to manufacturing companies and is less suitable for service companies, especially those which are network or knowledge based.

Business Process Re-engineering

Business Process Re-engineering (BPR) is the radical restructuring and redesigning of organisational processes to be cheaper, more efficient, and quicker. Introduced by Hammer and Champy (1992), BPR aimed to cut the waste out of organisations through the radical use of IT technology and the elimination of waste. Instead of focusing on traditional vertical departments, such as HR, Production, or Marketing, the re-engineering effort concentrates on horizontal processes such as "Manage Order", "Handle Complaint", or "Recruit Employee".

Despite early efforts having very high failure rates (Valentine and Knights 1996), BPR has been a popular tool for enhancing efficiency in many sectors. The standard method for implementing BPR is first to map the business processes in the organisation, second, to identify areas where redesign or IT might improve the processes, and subsequently to estimate the cost savings that might occur and prioritise the most efficient areas. The final, and trickiest, part of the redesign is implementing the new processes and technologies to achieve the savings. BPR is a complicated and risky form of change and it is often associated with cost cutting and redundancies.

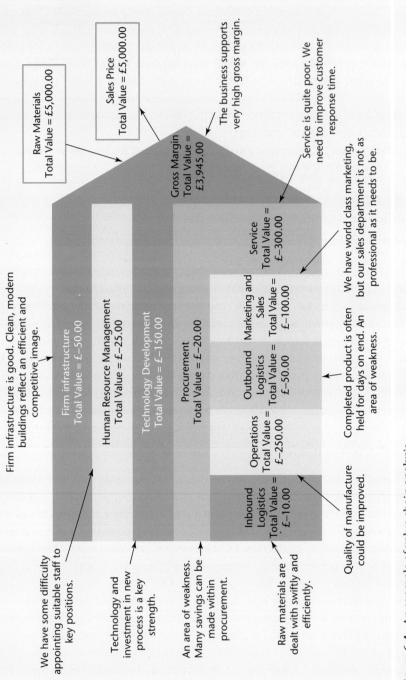

Figure 6.4. An example of value chain analysis

Source: Market Modelling Ltd.

---

you've got to be careful when using some terms. Phrases like "efficiency savings", "process re-engineering", and "restructuring" can terrify a workforce into being very uncooperative with consultancy. You've got to plan your message.

(Academic/consultant, USA)

Total Quality Management

Total quality management was introduced by Peters and Waterman (1982) after studying the practices of high-performing companies around the world. In the 1970s many Western companies possessed poorly performing manufacturing companies that were being overtaken by competitors in Japan and other Asian countries. A key reason for this, Peters and Waterman argued, was that Western companies relied on old Taylorist, time-motion ways of management where workers were treated as robots and quality inspectors were relied on to ensure products were good enough to leave the factory.

At the heart of TQM is a commitment to bringing quality into all aspects of the organisation. Thus, workers are not simply seen as the doers of managerial bidding, but take responsibility for identifying improvements, producing quality goods or services, and implementing changes in the workspace. Compared to BPR, TQM brings in a much more incremental, "bottom-up" form of change where themes such as "continuous improvement", "right first time", and the "internal customer" dominate.

Balanced Scorecard

The balanced scorecard is a method of performance management which links operational activity to the organisational strategy and seeks to improve the company performance on many measures, not just the usual financial ones. Based on a book by Kaplan and Norton (1996), the concept has evolved and improved considerably in both the measures it uses and the processes for its implementation. A typical scorecard framework is outlined in Figure 6.5; however, the categories can, and often do, include many more areas, such as the environment, people, or communities.

The method for implementing the scorecard is based on the following: first, the organisation defines their strategy and vision and communicates this to all stakeholders. Second, the vision is translated into objectives, and then measures, in different areas. Third, these measures are linked to day-to-day performance measures in the company. Finally, a process of feedback and continuous improvement is implemented to constantly adjust the measures.

The Four Ps

The Four Ps are used help with new product development and marketing. In case interviews, they should be used to understand the costs and benefits of launching new products or explore ways of assessing the effectiveness of existing ones.

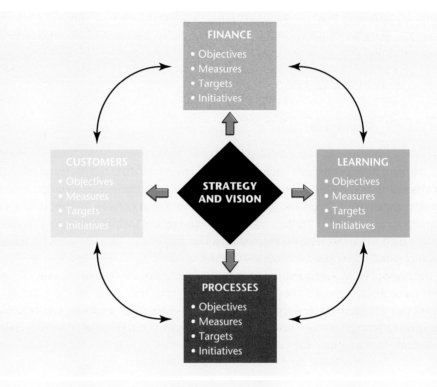

Figure 6.5. A typical balanced scorecard framework

- **Product:** What is unique about the product?
- **Price:** What will it sell for? Is this competitive? What about discounts? How will prices be charged? Can it be leased? Should it be a loss leader?
- **Promotion:** How will customers be made aware of this product? How will the product be advertised? What marketing and branding will be used?
- **Place:** this is actually "Distribution" and means things such as: how will the product be distributed? How will it be sold? How will it be controlled?

How Can We Maximise Profits?

In order to be able to help your clients, you need to know what is most important to them. In a word, this is profit: the money the company has left over after its expenses (costs) have been deducted from its revenues (income). Generally speaking, and there are some exceptions, the higher a company's profit, the more valuable it is. This is the extra money that has been generated that can be used to invest in the company or to return dividends to shareholders.

The basic profit calculation is: Profit = Revenue – Costs

If you are given a case or a client whose profits are sagging, you will obviously need to examine either rising costs or shrinking revenues (or both). Costs can be broken into fixed costs (large up-front costs, e.g. rent, rates, salaries) and variable costs (which increase with every product sale and therefore increase with the numbers of products). This provides you with a more detailed equation of:

$$\text{Revenues} - \text{Costs} = [(\text{price} - \text{variable cost}) \times \text{quantity}] - \text{Fixed Costs}$$

Costs

When breaking down a client's costs there are two factors that should be considered. First, the cost of goods sold (COGS): the expenses associated with producing each item, such as labour, raw material, delivery, and packaging. These costs increase with every product sold, although it is expected that there will be economies of scale to be achieved as the number of products increases. Second, operating costs: these are fixed and variable costs of operating the business, and include items such as insurance, rent, depreciation, administration, and R&D.

Cutting these costs may mean leaning on suppliers, sourcing cheaper materials, introducing new technology, cutting back on staffing levels, re-engineering processes for greater efficiency, or outsourcing some areas.

Revenues

Revenues can be increased by:

- **Increasing prices:** this cannot simply be done offhand but needs supporting reasons. For example, the client could attempt to increase quality, corner the markets, or change pricing structures.
- **Increasing volumes sold:** the reasons associated with this may be: an expanding market, increased market share, increased customer loyalty, increased sales effort, different sales structures, or discounts for larger orders.

Maximising Profits

When asked for solutions to a profit problem, there are a number of areas a consultant should automatically consider and several of these are outlined in Table 6.2. However, each of these also has drawbacks which can hit the client in different ways. Working out which is the best solution will depend on a careful consideration of the client's needs. Clients tend to cut costs in recessions and tend to invest in methods to increase income in times of prosperity.

Financial Tools

When discussing profits, there are a number of terms a consultancy graduate should be aware of, even if they are not specialists in finance. Some of these are provided below.

Cutting costs	Increasing income
Reducing waste	Introducing new products
Pressuring suppliers	Taking over/merging with a company
Increasing efficiency	Improving quality
Economies of scale	Starting a new company
Specialising (focusing on key products)	Increasing sales
Divesting (selling off parts)	Entering new markets
Budget cuts (e.g. HRM, marketing)	Increasing prices
Pay cuts (e.g. bonuses, pay, redundancies)	Improving brand/marketing
Centralising operations	Creative accounting

Table 6.2. Methods of increasing profits

Cash Flow Cash flow is the amount of money flowing through a business. It is an essential concept and the fundamental requirement of all good businesses. Even highly profitable businesses can have cash-flow problems and go bankrupt. Cash flow is usually measured over a fixed period of time, for example, a year.

To avoid cash flow issues, companies can think about the following:

• Paying bills later: creditors will often be happy to provide short-term credit if it means on-going business. Employees can be paid at the end of the month, or even better, be paid in stock options, or, in extreme situations, be paid "in kind': often the products that the company is making. Spreading payments over several months, even if there is a charge, can help.

• Receiving payments earlier: companies should arrange their sales income as early as possible. Sometimes, it makes financial sense to discount for earlier payments. Penalising late payers is one route to ensuring prompt payments.

• Selling off under-utilised assets is a good way to free up cash. Often, property or equipment can be sold off and leased back. Whilst this may not make financial sense in the long term, it can free up short-term cash to ensure the business remains solvent.

• Factoring is a term used by which outstanding invoices are sold, usually at a slight loss, to a third party, often a bank. This frees up cash earlier on in exchange for a third party taking on the risk of non-payment or late payment.

• Purchase-order funding: if you have a number of orders you can often use these to secure a short-term loan from a bank. This only works if the customer is credit-worthy.

Net Present Value/Cost of Capital Due to inflation, risk, and other factors, money today is usually worth more than money tomorrow. For this reason, it is important to be able to calculate the value of future spending or income at the present moment by discounting it at a certain rate. This calculation generates the Net Present Value of future returns, and the rate at which future spending or income is discounted is known as the cost of capital.

The NPV equation is:

$$NPV = C_0 + \sum_{t=1}^{T} \frac{C_t}{(1+r)^t}$$

Where C = Cashflow, T = Time Period, and R = Discount Rate.

The present value of future income or expenditure is necessarily linked to what your money could be doing if it was elsewhere. For example, if that bank was paying you 10 per cent interest on your money, then any alternative investments would have to be compared to this to see if they were worthwhile. The rate that your potential investment is compared against is the cost of capital.

The cost of capital may be the rate of inflation, interest rates, or any other return on investment that one wishes to use as a point of comparison. However, the cost of capital calculation necessarily includes the risk that the rate will not be achieved. In other words, if one is going to compare the utility of a future investment to, say, stock returns from the banking industry, then one needs to take into account the risk that those returns may not appear. Failure to do so can lead to unrealistic expectations of future returns, as happened with the recent banking crisis.

Return on Investment/Rate of Return The return on investment (ROI) or the rate of return (ROR) is the ratio of returns, or losses, from an investment, to the amount of money invested. It is usually shown as a percentage. The equation for the ROI is:

$$\text{ROI (\%)} = \frac{\text{Net Program Benefits}}{\text{Program Costs}} \times 100$$

How Should We Price our Products?

The Price Trap

Pricing is central to business. Low prices can mean popular products, but costs need to be covered. High prices can lead to increased profitability, but may also result in declining sales. The examples below give an idea of the challenges of setting prices:

- New 3G telecoms operators have spent around £10bn developing systems to send multimedia to mobile phones. What should the cost of a video of a football goal be?

- Governments redesign traffic blackspots to save lives. How many lives need to be lost before the government should spend £1.5m on a new roundabout system?

- What discount should a PC manufacturer offer if customers buy online?

Many businesses would like to increase the prices of their products. This strategy is difficult, however, because the customers will usually respond by shopping elsewhere. For many consultants working in this area, this requires a vast amount of statistical modelling in order to work out the optimal pricing structure. Often price increases need to reflect some "added value" that will enhance a client's product. For example, if the product improves in quality, image, or what it offers the customer, then it may be possible to charge higher prices for it. In the 1990s, for example, Skoda improved both the quality of its product and the perception of its brand so it could charge higher prices for its cars and thus generate higher profit margins.

Alternative Pricing Structures

If adding value is not an option, there are other ways of introducing higher prices to customers through different means usually by charging customers in different ways for the product. For example:

- Many computing outlets make significant profits on the extended warranties that they sell their customers. The true cost of these warranties is often hidden because the customer pays monthly.

- Mobile phone companies often tie customers into complex tariffs so that customers don't always know what their costs are going to be. My own tariff provides 400 minutes and texts a month, but as I have no easy way of checking what I have used I frequently exceed this limit, thus incurring significant costs.

- Razor, printer, and water-filter manufacturers often provide the basic product at a low cost and charge the customer for the perishable parts (i.e. the razor blades and the filters).

- Many supermarkets use "loss leaders". These are cheap products which are sold at a loss to encourage customers to come in and purchase other, more expensive items. Charity mailings often give away pens in the hope that this will "guilt" customers into sending them money.

Pricing New Products

Many assignments ask you to price a new product. A computer game, an everlasting light bulb, or in one case, a life. When approaching this question it is important to start with a structure. There are two main routes to determining a price:

- Cost-based pricing: How much does it cost to develop the product? What "reasonable" margin can be added to sell on to the consumer.

- Market-based pricing: What are competitors selling similar products for? What value does this product add and how can this be quantified? What are people prepared to pay?

When examining questions of pricing, consultants need to take the following into account:

- Market conditions: What competition exists? Is the market likely to grow? If, so, how fast? Is the competition rational or based on personal factors? How will the competition respond?

- Customers: What will customers pay? What do they pay for similar products? What types of customer do you have? Which are the most profitable and loyal? How sensitive are customers to price changes?

- Company: Will pricing decisions affect the company's brand? Does the company have the resources to withstand low prices longer than their competitors? Does the marketing strategy match your pricing decision?

Whilst it is simple enough to plug market data, forecasts, and pricing options into a spreadsheet to work out "optimum" pricing, many of the factors involve the analyst's perception, interpretation, and judgement which, in an open system, mean that even the most sophisticated models can be wrong. For a great example of this, read *When Genius Failed*, by Roger Lowenstein.

What Markets Should We Enter?

For most companies, a clear understanding of the marketplace is essential in developing competitive products. This isn't simply understanding the market as it is now, but trends that may affect the company in future.

Market Challenges

The difficulties companies face in markets are usually associated with a declining market share. However, the reasons for such a decline can be attributed to several different phenomena and selecting the correct combination is the analytical task of the consultant. Root problems may include:

- Changes in customer preferences.
- Shifts in segmentation.
- Encroachment of (new) competition.
- Merger and acquisition activity.
- Shifts in routes to market (e.g. distribution costs or new outlets).
- Introduction of new/replacement products.
- Shrinking/expansion of overall market.
- Changes to market competition structures, e.g. monopolies.
- Barriers to market entry (e.g. R&D, patents, excessive costs).

Analysing Markets

In order to understand which of these challenges is affecting the client, the consultant will need to undertake a market analysis which models the changes in market patterns. This will involve getting figures (or making assumptions) for:

- **Market Segmentation**

  How big is the market? What market segmentations are there? Do different segments buy differently? Which are the most profitable segments? Are markets segmented by income, age, gender, location, or another variable? Should you have different products for different markets?

- **Consumer Purchasing**

  What is customer loyalty like? What purchasing patterns do customers have? What similar products do they buy? What else do they buy when purchasing the specified goods?

- **Competitor Analysis**

  Who are the competition? What is their market share? Is this growing or falling? How do their products differ from your clients? Is competition intensive or weak? Is this changing? Are the competition's customers different from your clients? If so, how?

- **Advertising and Branding**

  What is the brand awareness? Do your marketing messages reach the right people? How does their advertising compare to that of the competition? How successful is the marketing? What are the conversion rates?

In dealing with the problems that are consequentially identified in the markets, consultants might consider applying the following strategies:

- Increasing sales by selling more or introducing new products (though this may increase the client's expenses).

- Building brand awareness and messages through targeted marketing and branding campaigns.

- Tying in customers to the product through loyalty schemes such as loyalty cards, tokens, discounts, or stamps. It should be noted that these schemes can often backfire by rewarding customers for behaviour that they would have undertaken anyway.

- Strategic alignment with other companies. For example running cross-company discounts or promotions.

- Specialisation or diversification. Companies which are small or fighting a losing battle on market share may find that specialisation enables them to use flexibility and specialist knowledge to their advantage. Larger companies may (or may not) use diversification to maximise economies of scale and apply their expertise to new markets.

- Introducing new products. New products can open up new market segments and introduce new customers to your other products. However, there is considerable overhead with new products, and market analysis needs to be undertaken before any decisions are reached. Clients should also beware of cannibalising their existing products.

These guidelines should not be used as a rule, but more as a guide to how one *can* think about organisations by applying different perspectives. They can be used to quickly provide potential solutions to organisational problems and, therefore, are equally suitable to a case-study question in an interview or an exam as they are to real life organisations.

Bespoke Frameworks

As tools and frameworks are a central asset of the consultancy business, it is unsurprising that consultancies themselves take it upon themselves to develop their own bespoke frameworks and methodologies to better market to potential clients. Any bespoke tool is useful for three main reasons. First it is a learning artefact. Most tools or methodologies are the result of years of individual or group experiences at solving complex organisational problems. Once created, they are constantly fine-tuned as they are used in different settings. Some tools, such as the Structured Systems Analysis and Design Method (SSADM), have been through several different revisions and taken over twenty years to develop. As such, they represent an accumulation of experience and knowledge.

The second reason for the use of bespoke tools is that they are excellent for marketing a firm. A tool or method provides an excellent way to communicate a successful change in an organisation. They are especially useful in press releases, conference presentations, or journal articles as a way of communicating the essence of what a consulting firm does. A friend of mine in Los Angeles developed a tool for organisational change which he now licenses out to consultancies in developing countries to use on their clients. This income stream is so significant that he no longer has to do any of his own consultancy work.

Finally, and more philosophically, the diagrams which accompany most tools and frameworks provide clients with a reassurance and security of a fixed and understandable reality which belies the reality of a complex, messy, and often unmanageable organisation. If you type "Organisational Change Framework", "Process Tool", or "Leadership Diagram" into Google images, you will be returned thousands of frameworks which show only what the consultancy feels they can control.

As with modern art, such pictures often leave enough room for the client to make their own interpretations, making sense of what is often an ambiguous set of relationships. The diagrams in Figure 6.6, for example, at first glance, look insightful and meaningful. However, once one begins to ask exactly why those titles, relationships, and shapes were chosen, and not others, one might realise the picture means nothing at all and was created by playing with PowerPoint and a few choice buzz-words. This is not to say that most tools do not provide a useful service, simply that their visual nature lends the tools an ambiguity that favours easy marketing.

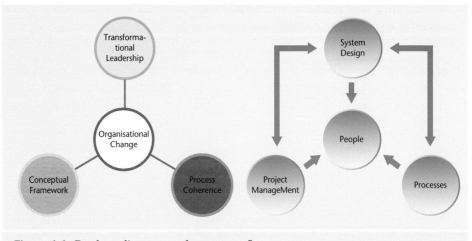

Figure 6.6. Do these diagrams make any sense?

CASE 6.1

Intellectual Property Problems

An SME client that developed and sold computer games wanted a faster way to design and build their products. They turned to a niche project management consultancy to build a bespoke development toolkit that would enable them to achieve this aim. The consultancy spent a long time working with the client's workforce, examining what they did and looking for ways to cut waste, time, and expense.

In the end the collaboration produced a bespoke development method that was based in part on the client's existing processes and in part on new ideas generated by the joint team. The method enabled considerable savings for the client and the project ended.

However, a few months later, an employee of the client noticed that the consultancy was selling the methodology as a product on their website. Concerned that this might be sold to the client's competitors, the employee notified the CEO of the company who complained to the consultancy.

The consultancy pointed to a sub-clause in the contract the client had signed that stated "all intellectual property developed shall remain in the ownership of [The Consultancy] unless otherwise agreed with the client". The client CEO said that he had not noticed this clause and had assumed that the methodology which had been developed would be the property of the client.

• What would you do if you were running the consultancy?

■ Soft Skills

As discussed earlier, one's effectiveness as a consultant, whether in business development, implementation, or analysis, is, to a large part, dependent on the skills one might develop. For this reason, consultancies are very keen to recruit individuals who not only have a highly developed set of interpersonal and functional skills but also fit with the style and culture of the firm.

The skills one develops as a consultant are very different from those used in a standard day-to-day job. The consultant tends to see their work as a series of projects which have their own life-cycle and, therefore, focuses on progressing the project from initiation to completion as quickly and effectively as possible. This approach to work is incredibly valuable and effective for companies that have a focus on change. It is for this reason that many firms have begun to train their employees in "consulting skills". Below, a number of skills are outlined that are important to becoming a competent consultant.

Personal Skills

A consultant's personal skills are the most important they can develop because these provide them with a reflexive ability to understand what skills they need to develop. For example, you may not be the best communicator, team-player, or negotiator in the world, but if you are aware of your weaknesses and can develop a plan to address them, this will enable you to continuously develop your abilities. Some consultants may well start off with strong communication or sales skills, but if they are not reflexive enough, they may never improve them.

Figure 6.7 illustrates the steps a consultant or student can take to develop their skill-set. Seeking honest feedback from people who have a strong set of skills should be essential after any presentation, delivery, or engagement. This in turn should lead to individuals and their managers seeking to improve their skills through practice, training, or watching others, which should then lead to their skills improving. This cycle should continue until the individual becomes an expert in any given skill-set. Whilst this cycle should form the basis of any organisational appraisal or training system, it is often lacking and the individuals themselves often have to take responsibility for ensuring that it happens.

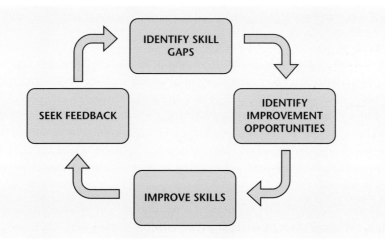

Figure 6.7. Continuous skills development

Communication and Presentation Skills

The Invisible Communicator

Consultants tend to have better presentation and communication skills than any other professional group. The primary reason for this is not only that they have to constantly sell, but also that they have to present ideas, plans, and progress to senior, and often sceptical, managers. However, it is often an area that students misunderstand. Having perhaps watched too many episodes of *Dragon's Den* or *The Apprentice* many students believe that an arrogant, combative, and "in your face" style of presentation is likely to elicit admiration. This is, fortunately, very far from the truth. In reality, most clients want the presenter to be an invisible conduit to the message, argument, or data which is being communicated. This should be a reassuring message for those students who get nerves before a presentation: most audiences are not interested in the presenter in the slightest and, ideally, would wish their presence to be completely unobtrusive. In the words of Hans-Paul Bürkner, the boss of BCG, "my choice of ties is not necessarily the best, but most of the people I work with wouldn't notice" (*Financial Times* 2008).

There are, of course, some exceptions to this rule. Management gurus, such as Michael Hammer, cultivate a highly personal, flamboyant, and egocentric style where the presenter almost *becomes* the presentation (Huczynski 1993). However, such characters, at least in their role as gurus, cannot seriously be called management consultants in the traditional sense.

The focus on the presenter's invisibility also implies that the focus is on the message the consultant is trying to get across. This means that their entire focus should be helping the client, whether it is trying to convince them of the benefits of a course of action or simply updating them on the progress of a project. All the advice below, therefore, focuses on making the consultant, their ego, style, and technologies, as invisible as possible and on making the message central to the presentation.

Preparing your Presentation

Below is an excerpt from a blogger known as The Whisperer (2008):

> A couple of consultants, retained by a colleague and me, were floundering their way through a positively dreadful presentation. Picture 25 senior and mid-level executives, watching a very smart, but poorly prepared, dude waving his hands about, knocking over water bottles, and putting the crowd through a mix of boredom and confusion. The poor guy didn't know how to use the slide changer remote . . . and didn't realize that he was flipping through a million slides a minute as he spoke. When he somehow managed to open his email application for the audience, one of my colleagues denounced loudly, "You have to stop doing that right now. Give me the remote."

Such an eye-wateringly bad presentation is not uncommon in the consulting world and points to the importance of solid preparation. Below, the key steps to producing an effective presentation are outlined.

What Is your Key Message? Even if you have several messages to put across to an audience, there is often one underlying theme that you want to get into their heads. Often, the key message is left unarticulated, especially if the project involves stakeholders with conflicting interests or if decision-making is highly political. Occasionally, the key message is one that you don't want to give or that you might think is impossible to achieve. Typical key messages that I have had to give include:

- This project is going badly because the client team is uncooperative. I would like a senior manager to intervene to improve the situation.
- The best way to create this venture is to start with a market and competitor analysis. Our team is best placed to achieve this effectively.
- Due to cost cutting in production you are at risk of redundancy. However, we would like you to remain cooperative and motivated until we have decided who will be made redundant.
- Your investment in this business is a good opportunity for you even though I cannot guarantee you any returns.

The key message is the underlying information that you wish the audience to have in their heads when they leave. You will need to ensure that the message is either one that you repeat frequently or one which your presentation leads to as a consequence of its logic. Some suggest that presentations distinguish between an "act now" message to clients should make their point early on, and a "balanced" message which first presents the evidence and then leads the client to make up their own minds based on the evidence in front of them.

Who Is your Stakeholder? You may have one or several stakeholders or, alternatively, your key stakeholder may not be present. It is this person, often the key decision-maker, or the project sponsor, to whom your central message should be addressed. When I started consulting, the preparation for any presentation would include a list of key stakeholders and a brief analysis of what they expected and what message would win their cooperation. Where appropriate, key stakeholders should be communicated with prior to the presentation so that their support can be developed and so that there are no surprises for them when you finally present.

There will probably be an audience in addition to your stakeholder(s). It is important, of course, to understand why they are there and what their needs are too. However, you should not forget who is paying your fees and what they have asked you to do.

What Is your Medium? Most consultants, and students, revert automatically to PowerPoint when they are presenting. The ubiquitous "stack" of slides almost defines consultants more than their Airmiles accounts or their expenses forms. However, PowerPoint should not be the default position for presentations. Focusing again on the "invisible" presenter, you should select the medium that gets your message across with minimum interference.

If, for example, you have been invited into a meeting that will already have started, the last thing the audience will want to do is to watch you scrabble round on the floor, loading your presentation and trying to get the projector working. It may be simpler to walk into the room, introduce yourself and start speaking. In addition, you may wish to consider:

- Hand-outs: unless you are referring to them during the presentation, it is best to give these out as the end as they can often distract the audience from your presentation.
- Digital storage: if you have a number of files, promotional material, or audio/video that you think the audience may be interested in, you can buy personalised, branded, and pre-loaded CDs or USB sticks for under £5.
- Flip-charts are useful to capture points that you may wish to return to or take away and write up after the presentation.
- Changing speakers: if your presentation is long, or not likely to be inspiring or exciting, it is best to introduce some variation in speakers or to get audience members involved by asking them questions.

Using PowerPoint If you do decide that PowerPoint is the most suitable format, do ensure you know how to use it well. Often, younger students and new consultants are so spellbound with the possibilities of the software that the presentation turns into a circus of sounds, animations, and avatars. A team I was working on once almost lost multi-million pound backing because we didn't realise the Hong Kong billionaire we were presenting to despised clip-art. I would urge presenters to keep the technology invisible but focusing only on animations that will reinforce their message.

Styles will vary incredibly according to the stakeholders and the audience. A marketing presentation that wants to elicit an emotional response will often be heavy on pictures and light on text. A presentation which communicates project progress, a business architecture, or an organisational structure will be entirely different. As a rule:

- Keep sentences short, readable (minimum 30 pt), and punchy. Talk around key ideas.
- Only use sounds, clip-art, or fancy animations if they help explain your concepts better. Keep it simple.
- Use images, graphs, tables, or models only if they are central to your message.

PowerPoint is incredibly feature rich. I once saw an excellent presentation by a consultant who used PowerPoint as a mock-up for a gaming website. However, this doesn't mean that all the features *should* be used in any presentation.

Preparing and Practising Your presentation should be planned in the same way as any other deliverable. Its style, length, methods, and objectives can all be specified and tailored to the stakeholder requirements. Once it has been created, practise it and time it, preferably several times and preferably to a small audience.

Part of preparing is also to make sure the room, technology, and back-ups are prepared. How the room is structured is dependent on the message and the audience, but it is usually appropriate that the attention of the room is on the presenter rather than their slides. Ensure there is enough space for the audience, that there is ventilation and refreshments if the presentation is a long one, and that latecomers don't disrupt the entire session. Ensure that the technology has been tested, is ready to go, and that you know where the technician is if you need one. Finally, should things not work at all, ensure you have good back-up—hand-outs, laminate slides, even an alternative room if necessary.

Delivering your Presentation

When it is actually time to deliver the presentation, your preparation should have helped both ensure its success and that your nerves are at a minimum. In delivering a presentation there are a few key pointers that all guides recommend:

- Do not read from the screen, especially if this places your back to the audience. Have notes in front of you if necessary.
- Check the tone, variation, and speed in your voice. At some point record a presentation and see how your style can be improved.
- If there are team members with you, ensure their attention is always on you. If they aren't interested how can the audience expect to be captivated?
- Keep ticks, scratches, key-jangling, and other distractions to a minimum.
- Never read from a script, it has a magical ability to deaden an audience. Use notes if you have to.

Dealing with Questions

One of the big changes in graduates I notice when they become more experienced is their ability to deal with questions. Often, new MBA students or consultants become very defensive when asked a question or challenged. For a client, a consultant who cannot accept criticism or change their approach based upon feedback is someone best avoided.

If you know the answer to a question, provide it. If you do not know, say so, and say you will get them the information after the meeting. If the questioner criticises, seek to understand their concerns and consider how they can be dealt with. Remember, if your focus is on making the presenter invisible and the message visible, then you must not take criticism as a challenge to your ego. Becoming an "invisible" presenter relies on shifting the focus of attention from your own insecurities, ego, and identity to the problems of the organisation, and honesty is one of the best methods to achieve this.

CASE 6.2

The Evolution of Management Ideas

A few years ago (O'Mahoney 2007) I authored a paper in the *Journal of Management Studies* which argued that management products such as TQM and BPR actually evolve over time. Using BPR as an example, I showed how, in two cases, the idea evolved through the processes of selection, variation, and reproduction.

This "memetic" perspective shows how ideas can sometimes act like viruses, infecting organisations and spreading through "carriers" like consultancies, guru books, and executive education. This view emphasises the longevity of an idea and argues that to understand an idea, it may be necessary to trace it over several organisations to see how it was spread, how it altered, and when it dies. Consultancies are central to this view as they make the "virus" more potent by commodifying it and making it more infectious.

1 What conditions are necessary for a management idea to successfully spread and evolve?

2 What are the limitations of the virus metaphor?

3 What other examples of evolving ideas can you think of?

Team Skills

Team skills are central to being an effective consultant whether your team is a group of fellow consultants or composed of client employees, contractors, or consultants from another company. When asked whether it was the consultancy's reputation or the team of consultants that made the most difference to a project, 92 per cent of clients opted for the latter (Consulting Intelligence 2007). However, these softer skills which enhance the project so much are very often neglected by consultancies:

> Many of the consultants I knew were eager to apply standard MBA frameworks like Five Forces, statistical regression, and the marketing 3Cs/STP/4Ps, but few talked about client facilitation in explicit terms. (Shu 2008)

The actual mechanisms for running a team-based project were covered in Chapter 5. Here, we will examine some of the main skills that are required to be an effective team member.

Communication

When I asked senior consultants and partners what is was that made an excellent consultant, most of them put communication skills at the top of their list. Similarly, when clients are asked what qualities they evaluate consultants on, effective communication comes second only to competence (Consulting Intelligence 2007). The ability to communicate clearly, openly, and in a timely manner to the team is essential to producing a good working relationship with the client.

As a consultant, you are in a privileged position to be able to bring independent, honest, and objective advice to client teams and enhance the working relationships of the team you are assigned to clients, and clients value this when it is done appropriately. One of the biggest mistakes new consultants make in their communication is an over-reliance on email. The written word is so open to interpretation and the email mechanism so abstract that misunderstandings are common and overly aggressive messages are easily written. If a message is tricky, go and see the person. If this is not possible, get on the phone. This is difficult for some people but so important in learning to focus on the project instead of the personality of the person you are working with. If an email does have to be sent, never send one while you are still angry or hurt. Go for a walk, talk with someone, and write when you are objective again.

Team Building

As a consultant you cannot simply afford to be a passive member of the team as it is part of your job to make sure the project, and therefore the team, works. You should not simply act as another team member, but be actively involved in facilitating the team, ensuring it works effectively, and supporting other team members. This will involve taking the initiative with things that you formally don't have to do, such as:

- Ensuring the team, and individual, goals are clear, cohesive, and achievable in the time and with the resources available, and communicating upwards if this is not the case.

- Providing feedback and recommendations on how the team works, how decisions are taken, and whether its skills are appropriate for the tasks it has.

- Building the team up by encouraging honest, face-to-face communication, praising people for good work, instilling confidence, and providing constructive criticism when people aren't performing.

- Building momentum for the team by generating short-term goals, encouraging leadership in the team, and ensuring the overarching purpose is remembered.

- Recognising and tackling interpersonal issues early on before they hamper the project. This will also involve you remaining objective and professional and not joining any cliques or factions.

- Ensuring that the informal, cultural, or political rules of the group are not getting in the way of achieving its objectives.

- Ensuring that socialising, good humour, and informal gatherings are present throughout the project to help bond the informal side of group work.

■ Chapter Summary

This chapter has covered the hard tools and soft skills that enable effective consulting work. In doing so, the chapter has shown that:

- Tools and techniques do not solve organisational problems by themselves. The ways in which they are used, interpreted, and communicated are more important in effecting successful change.

- Questions regarding strategy, operations, pricing, and markets can all be helped through the use of common consultancy frameworks.

- Consultancies use bespoke frameworks and tools to help market their work and demonstrate their experience.
- Soft skills are the most important skills to develop and hone as a consultant, especially with regard to communication, presentation, and teamwork.

Student Exercise

Think about a business challenge that your company, university, or organisation faces. Prepare a ten-minute presentation on how you would research the problem and what frameworks you would use to generate a recommendation. Do not talk about the solution itself. In small groups, do the presentations in front of each other. Give each other constructive feedback according to the following criteria.

On the research problem:

1   Is the problem definition clear and coherent?

2   Are the research questions/hypotheses defined? If not, is there a clear method for generating them?

3   Are the research methods appropriate to answering the research questions/hypotheses?

4   Are the analysis techniques and frameworks appropriate?

5   Are the outputs of the research clearly defined?

6   Will the outputs answer the research questions/hypotheses?

7   Are the limits of the research defined?

8   Will the findings be generalisable to other companies? Why?

On the presentation:

1   Is the purpose/message of the presentation made clear?

2   Is the structure of the presentation clear? i.e. do listeners know where the presentation is going?

3   Is the speaker's voice clear? Do they hesitate or use "fillers" such as "um" or "er"? Is their tone interesting?

4   Is their body language confident? Do they have habits that distract the audience?

5   If they use slides/hand-outs are these appropriate and easily understood? Do they distract from the talk?

Discussion Questions

- Is consultancy an art or a science?
- What is the difference between a research question and a hypothesis?

- What different types of analysis are there?

- What are the main questions a client could ask you about their company? How might you address these?

- Why do consultancies develop bespoke frameworks and tools?

- What different types of consultancy skills are there?

Case-Study Exercise: Mobile Music

Introduction to Mobile Music

During the period 1999–2006 a number of governments sold licences for mobile companies to operate on the 3G bandwidth. In effect, this mean that, for the first time, mobile phone companies could distribute multimedia to their customers via their mobile phones.

This enabled mobile phone companies to create a number of new products to sell to their customers including sports clips, digital radio, maps, and music. However, as this had not been done before, many companies were unsure how best to go about achieving a successful product and so turned to consultancies to help them.

Tele-case

Tele-case, a company in South America, bought 3G licences from five South American countries. Tele-case was a new company and had no existing mobile customers. Therefore, it intended to build the company from scratch, with a view to floating it on the NYSE five years after it became operational.

Tele-case split the company into three main parts:

- Products, who dealt with developing new products to sell to the customers.

- Networks, who were responsible for physically rolling out the new 3G network.

- Business Services, who provided the back-office support for products to work effectively: for example, billing, customer relationship management, and content management.

The Music Product

One of the product teams was the music product (MP) who were responsible for making money out of selling music to customers over their phones. However, the team were relatively new and, whilst they knew a considerable amount about music, knew little about business strategy, models, or markets. The team comprised:

- The Product Manager, who led the team and was responsible for the success of the music product(s).

- Two Music Executives, who had joined the team from the music industry. They had strong connections with music rights holders such as Sony and BMI. They were responsible for providing expert knowledge and doing music deals.

- A business analyst, who was responsible for communicating the Music Team's requirements to other teams that integrated with them and for assessing the business deals that they conducted.

- A financial analyst, who was responsible for putting together the team's business plans and keeping track of their expenditure.

Although the actual product had not been designed or delivered, the music companies that owned the rights to artist's music charged the team a small fee ($0.50) for every download. In addition, the team incurred a charge from head office ($0.50) for incidental costs such as the use of the network every time a customer downloaded a song. The Product Manager had to deal with key questions that she did not know the answer to. These were as follows:

1   How should the MP have sold music? There were a number of options including:

   (a) Pay per play: where customers pay every time they play a song.

   (b) Pay per download: where customers pay for every download they make but, once downloaded, can play a song as much as they wish.

   (c) Monthly subscription: where customers pay each month to download a, yet to be specified, number of songs.

2   Technology, called DRM, was available to restrict or prevent customers from sharing their music. Should the MP have allowed customers to share music with their friends? If so, should the MP have charged the customer or the friend for use of the music track? The music companies who owned the rights to artists' music charged the MP treble if a music track was unprotected and thus freely available.

3   Should the MP have allowed customers to put their own music on their mobiles? If this happened, the manager was worried that the customers would not use the MP. However, if this did not happen, it may have made other mobile operators that offered the service more attractive to the customer.

The Product Manager knew that further research was required in order to be able to answer these questions and asked you to write a proposal summarising the research project needed. You need to make some assumptions in the proposal where relevant information is not available.

The proposal should be around three pages long and take the format below. For more information on how to write a proposal, see Chapter 5:

- Executive Summary (a few lines).

- Background to the project (a paragraph).

- Objectives/deliverables (a few lines).

- In Scope/Out of Scope (a few lines).

- Outline Approach (a few lines).

- Success measures (a few lines).

- Work breakdown/plan (a Gantt chart or a table).

- Resources and Responsibilities (a table).

- Costs (a table/chart).

- Expenses (you may leave this section out).

- Processes (you may leave this section out).

- Dependencies and Risks (a small table).

You should do this exercise in teams of two and assume that you are both researchers/analysts for a niche consultancy. There will be two of you working part time on the project and you may make up the skills you possess to enable you to complete the project effectively.

Further Reading

There are, perhaps, too many sources of information on consultancy skills, frameworks, and methods. Both the web and bookstores are brimming with advice from consultants, teachers, clients, and armchair gurus on how work should be done. The reason for this, of course, is that so many projects go wrong, when it seems so simple to get right. My advice on this plethora of information is to ignore most of it. Once you have understood the basics of consultancy skills, the only method to become an expert is to practise them, to seek feedback, and to improve next time you try them. In the meantime, a few outstanding texts, which develop some of the themes introduced here, are mentioned below.

With regard to research methods, Robson (2002) provides a good overview of what he calls "real world research". It is, perhaps, a bit too detailed for the consultant in a hurry, but it has a couple of useful appendices from practitioners. Similarly, Lancaster (2005) is a detailed account of research for managers. It devotes a whole chapter to management consultancy research; however, in the rest of the book, overly complex terms and unnecessary concepts creep in. Finally, in the research category is Saunders et al. (2007) which, whilst not aimed at the consultant, probably provides the most comprehensive and easily understood guide to research for business students. By far the most interesting, and useful, book ever written for consultancy researchers is over fifty years old and entitled *How to Lie with Statistics* (Huff 1957/1991). It is not as cynical as it sounds, and teaches, with humour, the dangers of relying on statistics. It is a thin paperback and can be read in an afternoon.

I would not recommend reading any more on frameworks, tools, and methods for consultants. These change far too frequently to keep up to date with and, if you understand the basics, only practice will make you more adept. For those of you who wish to have a relatively comprehensive database, just in case you need to swot up for a client, Aku Kwapong (2005) will provide this. Alternatively, use www.valuebasedmanagement.net or search Google.

Similarly, it is difficult to recommend more texts on consultancy skills. First because there are so many, and second because only reflexive practice will improve your skills. However, a good all-round guide can be found in Markham's (2004) book *Top Consultant*. For presentations, which often scare inexperienced students, there are numerous online aids and examples. Websites such as www.slideshare.net have many examples of powerful presentations. However, do not slip into thinking that their "visual" style is appropriate for all audiences. Most clients will want more for their money than a picture of a cute kitten, no matter how good the photo. For examples of excellent speakers in action (and for excellent ideas in general) it is worth visiting www.ted.com which has presentations from some of the leading speakers in the world.

References

Aku Kwapong, O. (2005). *MBA Concepts and Frameworks: Tools for Working Professionals.* Songhai Empire.

Boal, K., Hunt, J., and Jaros, S. (2003). Order is Free: On the Ontological Status of Organisations. In R. Westwood and S. Clegg (eds), *Debating Organisation.* New York: Wiley-Blackwell.

Brace, I. (2008). *Questionnaire Design.* London: Kogan Page.

Brandenburger, A., and Nalebuff, B. (1997). Co-opetition. *Broadway Business.*

Burrell, G., and Morgan, G. (1979). *Sociological Paradigms and Organizational Analysis.* London: Heinemann.

Cohen, W. (2001). *How to Make it Big as a Consultant.* AMACOM.

Consulting Intelligence (2007). *Consulting Survey.* Consulting Intelligence LLC.

Corbin, J., and Strauss, A. (2007). *Basics of Qualitative Research.* Beverly Hills, CA: Sage.

Coyne, K., and Subramaniam, S. (1996). Bringing Discipline to Strategy. *McKinsey Quarterly*, 4: 14–25.

Cresswell, J. (2003). *Research Design.* Beverly Hills, CA: Sage.

—— (2007). *Qualitative Inquiry & Research Design.* Beverly Hills, CA: Sage.

Financial Times (2008). We Want to Change the World. 15 September.

Hammer, M., and Champy, J. (1992). *Re-engineering the Corporation.* London: Nicolas Brealey.

Huczynski, A. (1993). *Management Gurus.* London: Taylor & Francis.

Huff, D. (1957/1997). *How to Lie with Statistics.* London: Penguin.

Johnson, P., and Duberley, J. (2000). *Understanding Management Research: An Introduction to Epistemology.* Beverly Hills, CA: Sage.

Kaplan, R. S., and Norton, D. P. (1996). *Balanced Scorecard: Translating Strategy into Action.* Cambridge, MA: Harvard Business School Press.

Kubr, M. (2002). *Management Consulting: A Guide to the Profession.* London: International Labour Office.

Lancaster, G. (2005). *Research Methods in Management.* London: Butterworth-Heinemann.

Larossi, G. (2006). *The Power of Survey Design: A User's Guide for Managing Surveys, Interpreting Results, and Influencing Respondents.* Washington, DC: World Bank Publications.

Maister, D. (2003). *Managing the Professional Service Firm.* London: Free Press Business.

Markham, C. (2004). *The Top Consultant: Developing your Skills for Greater Effectiveness.* London: Kogan Page.

Market Modelling Ltd (2009). www.market-modelling.co.uk/.

Okasha, S. (2002). *Philosophy of Science: A Very Short Introduction.* Oxford: Oxford University Press.

O'Mahoney, J. (2007). The Diffusion of Management Innovations: The Possibilities and Limitations of Memetics. *Journal of Management Studies*, (43) 8.

Pascale, R., and Athos, A. (1981). *The Art of Japanese Management.* London: Penguin Books.

Peters, T., and Waterman, R. (1982). *In Search of Excellence.* New York: Harper & Row.

Popper, K. (1957). *The Poverty of Historicism.* London: Routledge.

—— (1957b). *The Logic of Scientific Discovery.* New York: Basic Books.

Porter, M. (1985). *Competitive Advantage: Creating and Sustaining Superior Performance.* New York: Free Press.

Rea, L., and Parker, R. (2005). *Designing and Conducting Survey Research: A Comprehensive Guide*. Hoboken, NJ: Jossey-Bass.

Robson, C. (2002). *Real World Research*. New York: Wiley-Blackwell.

Saunders, M., Lewis, P., and Thornhill, A. (2007). *Research Methods for Business Students*. Upper Saddle River, NJ: Pearson Education.

Shapiro, C., and Varian, H. (1998). *Information Rules: A Strategic Guide to the Network Economy*. Cambridge, MA: Harvard Business Press.

Shu, S. (2008). *A Perspective on Client Facilitation Skills*. http://steveshu.typepad.com. 10 January.

Tsoukas, H. (2001). What is Management: An Outline of Meta-theory. In S. Ackroyd and S. Fleetwood (eds), *Realist Perspectives on Management and Organisations*. London: Routledge.

Valentine, R., and Knights, D. (1996). TQM and BPR: Can You Spot the Difference? *Personnel Review*, 27 (1): 78–85.

Whisperer, The (2008). *Presentation Glitches*. http://tamarapaton.blogspot.com/. 29 February.

Buying Consultancy Services

Peter Walmsley, Head of Supplier Relationship Management, The Home Office

■ The Challenges of Procurement

The old jokes about how many consultants it takes to change a light bulb (don't know, they never get past the feasibility study) might as well be complemented by how many procurement staff it takes (no idea but they'll get you 10 per cent off). And so the convergence between procurement and consultants continues!

At the heart of the interaction between consultants and procurement are some fundamentally different drivers. Consultant marketability (and personal worth) is reflected in the day rate and career progression on the ability to win and grow business. Procurement success is measured in demonstrating value for money and control of risk. Added to that are a number of market inefficiencies: solution knowledge (and therefore power) tends to lie with the consultant; differentiation between firms is weak; and quality and pricing are opaque. As a result buyers tend to rely on proven relationships or known brand names which by default become the principal marketing tools of the consultancy.

The buying of consultancy services therefore remains fraught with traps for the unwary. Consultants often feel that procurement just focuses on day rate and prevents a relationship with the real customer whilst procurement struggles with the complexity of the consultancy offer. Yet with a few relatively simple rules of engagement, it can be a win-win situation.

■ Procurement Tools

The principal tool in the procurement kitbag is the business case which should state the nature of the requirement. Not the project requirement, the *resource* requirement. It is reasonably well accepted that consultancy services are concerned with providing advice. Contractors, at a very different price point, offer skills. And interim managers and specialist contractors fill permanent (or semi-permanent) roles temporarily, again at a different price point. But don't be fooled: consultants will happily fill both contractor and interim roles if allowed and contractors and interim managers will happily provide advice. The consequences can be significant overpayments or poor advice respectively and it is often very difficult to tell which hat the person across the table is wearing unless procurement is clear from the outset.

The second tool is output. What needs to be delivered and by when? Again, delivered not by the project but by the temporary resource being bought. Far too much consultancy is bought on the basis of project roles being filled rather than outputs delivered. Where the early stages of a project are to specify the outputs, this can look like a chicken-and-egg situation, but with a little thought it is usually possible to identify a clear deliverable and a timescale.

The third tool is governance. It can be so tempting to abdicate responsibility for the deliverable to the temporary resource carrying out the delivery, particularly in cases where the solution is technically complex. But resist. The senior project roles *must* be filled by permanent (or authorised interim) members of the customer organisation. Project and contract review meetings *must* also be carried out by permanent (or authorised interim) members of the customer organisation. And under no circumstances give hiring or expenditure authority to temporary members of the project team without appropriate business case and authorisation processes in place.

The fourth and fifth tools are skills transfer and exit strategy. Identify at the outset what happens when the work finishes. Where will the knowledge and dependencies lie, how will the knowledge gained during the project be transferred to or captured by the organisation, and who will carry on the follow-on (implementation) work of the project? Not only is the result then more effective but suppliers also appreciate and respond to the more professional engagement.

■ Understanding the Game

Application of the tools above will result in a better informed and professionally managed engagement which all but the most dubious of consultancy firms will welcome. In addition to these tools, however, there is a further body of knowledge which the procurement professional can acquire to improve the quality of the buying process.

Understand the market. Consultancy firms are generally reluctant to give clear statements of what they do because that also rules out opportunities which they might attempt. The market does not therefore easily segment; however, there is a differentiation between the small number of larger generalists and the much larger number of smaller firms who, by virtue of limited capacity, have to state a specialism. There is also a segmentation between what might be called "cultural heritage" of the large firms: those with accountancy origins tend to have a different offering from those with construction and project management heritage or those with IT backgrounds. Identifying the differences in approach can be instructive when running procurement competitions.

Understand consultancy pricing. Although a market characteristic in itself, consultancy pricing really can be a minefield and deserves mention on its own. In accordance with the segmentation above, the pricing of larger firms tends to be higher than that of smaller firms and both industry and service offerings have a hierarchy. Consultancy services in the finance sector, for example, tend to be more expensive than consultancy services in the public sector; and strategy work tends to be more expensive than project management services. Many other factors including consultant grade, utilisation factor, expenses arrangements, and novelty of the assignment also influence the rates, together with different incentivisation options, so a solid understanding is essential in agreeing final prices.

Lastly, a good procurement professional will understand project and contract management; have at their fingertips accurate spend information against well-defined consultancy categories; and participate in a variety of communications activities to share the details of successful assignments. This requires significant experience and a broad skill-set together with a longer-term commitment from the consultancy firm. Once the rules of engagement are clear however, the relationship has a solid foundation and the outcome should be mutually beneficial.

Simple as these rules and this expertise sounds, their application can be difficult in practice, and large organisations in particular need to work at changing the appropriate processes and behaviours, as the Home Office is now undertaking.

7

Running a Consultancy

Chapter Objectives

This chapter outlines the challenges involved in running a consultancy. Specifically, it:

- Explains the concept of leverage.

- Examines the strategic options for different types of consultancy.

- Outlines the unique characteristics of people-management in consulting firms.

- Explains the difference between types of knowledge management in consulting firms.

- Outlines the operational challenges of consultancy with specific focus on innovation, growth, and internationalisation.

■ Introduction

Whilst there are thousands of courses, books, and websites which tell readers how to be consultants, there are only a handful which touch on the subject of actually managing a consultancy. This is unfortunate because consultancy is an unusual industry in many ways.

First, consultancy relies entirely on selling expertise, a highly intangible asset which, as we shall see, does not conform to the usual rules of production and sales found in other industries. Second, consultancies tend to rely on partnership models of ownership rather than the more common CEO and directorship approach found in private firms. This raises all kinds of awkward questions about how profits are reinvested, what different partners should be paid, and how decision-making should happen. Third, consulting has one of the highest labour turnover rates of any professional industry yet relies heavily upon the expertise of its staff. This challenges traditional people management strategies in terms of training, promotion, and pay. Finally, many consultancies and texts talk of the "professional values" of consulting practice which should be internalised in individuals through organisational cultures. Whilst this is easily achieved when there is external training and accreditation, as in accounting, law, and medicine, how this is to be achieved in a consultancy, where sales are the primary motivator, is difficult to prescribe.

The challenges involved in running a consultancy firm can also be evidenced from an examination of the market outputs. The relatively low entrance criteria for establishing consultancy firms can be seen from the fact that small firms comprise around 98 per cent of the sector (Brett Howell 2007). The vast majority of these are sole-trader firms with one person providing expertise to a loyal client base. However, despite such low barriers to entry, only a handful of firms have grown big enough to challenge the dominance of the old strategy firms and the large audit firms, the biggest 2 per cent of which bring in 50 per cent of the sector's revenue. Such a persistent dominance within an industry sector usually indicates that the strategic challenges firms face must be both unusual and complex.

In this chapter, we examine some of the challenges that owners face in managing their consultancies. First, we examine some of the key metrics in the industry, especially leverage, which is central to all aspects of consultancy organisation, and introduce the key concepts by which consultancy performance is measured. This is dealt with first as it introduces a number of key terms which are used throughout the chapter. We then run through the main dimensions of managing a firm: strategy, finance, people, and internationalisation, showing how these link together to produce consistent consulting strategies. Some aspects of running a consultancy have been treated lightly in this chapter because they are covered in more detail elsewhere. These include marketing and sales (Chapter 5), product development (Chapter 6), and recruitment and selection (Chapter 10).

■ Key Metrics

Calculating Profit Per Partner

In any sector, there are a number of key metrics which will tell you how financially healthy a company is. With a company that is floated on the NYSE, these may revolve around the share price, its profitability, and its cash flow. However, the archetype for a consultancy is a professional partnership, where the company is owned by the partners. As we will discuss later, this model is becoming increasingly rare but its centrality to the strategies deployed in the industry make it the most important model to discuss. In partnerships where the company is owned by the partners, profitability is only useful if it provides a substantial income for each partner: profits of £10m look less impressive in a company with 500 partners, as this provides them with an average annual income of only £20,000. Profit per partner (PPP) is, therefore, the consultancy equivalent of the return on equity, and key to understanding the health of a typical firm (Maister 2003).

For a moment, put yourself in the position of an average partner at AT Kearney. What factors decide how much profit you will take home in any one year? The three factors which are central to this figure are:

Margin: in the same way that the CEO of Toyota may boast that they make 30 per cent margin on each car, so too must the consultancy partner be concerned with the margin they make on their fees. High fees are not impressive if they do not make a profit. The margin is calculated as the total profit of the firm divided by the fees the firm brings in:

$$\text{Margin} = \frac{\text{Profits}}{\text{Fees}}$$

Productivity: of course, it is no use having large margins if the firm's consultants are not particularly productive. Consultants spend a significant amount of time preparing bids, reporting to their consultancy, taking holiday, and sitting on the bench. As none of this is billed time, the *productivity* of the consultant is another key contributor to profits. Productivity is calculated as the fees the firm brings in divided by the number of consultants:

$$\text{Productivity} = \frac{\text{Fees}}{\text{No. Staff}}$$

Related to this equation is the concept of utilisation. Utilisation is the percentage of a consultant's time that they are actually billed for (as opposed to on the bench, on holiday, or doing administration). Total fees charged obviously go up if consultant utilisation is high.

Leverage: if one multiplies margin by productivity per consultant, one gets the profits per consultant. However, profitable consultants have no effect on a partner's monthly cheque if each partner is only responsible for one or two consultants. The number of consultants per partner, therefore, is an essential component of calculating profit per partner. This ratio is known as "leverage" and is calculated as:

$$\text{Leverage} = \frac{\text{No. Staff}}{\text{No. Partners}}$$

This provides us with the overall equation:

$$\text{Profit Per Partner} = \text{Margin} \times \text{Productivity} \times \text{Leverage}$$

Or

$$\text{Profit Per Partner} = \frac{\text{Profits}}{\text{Fees}} \times \frac{\text{Fees}}{\text{No. Staff}} \times \frac{\text{No. Staff}}{\text{No. Partners}}$$

As Maister (2003) points out, whilst there are a number of variables that contribute to profit per partner, they are all difficult to improve without damaging the quality of delivery. For example, theoretically, profits can be increased by doing the same work with fewer people. In the long term, however, this will impact employee motivation, and thus staff turnover, and may hit the quality of the project. The holy grail of enhancing PPP without hitting the quality of delivery is to increase fees. However, in order to achieve this, the consultancy needs to demonstrate that the value of its products has increased: something particularly difficult in a competitive environment.

The Importance of Leverage

Leverage, the ratio of partners to consultants, is a disarmingly simple concept; however, it is central to most aspects of running a consultancy firm. "Leverage", in this sense, is a different animal from the "leverage" used in auditing (which concerns debt which is used to gain greater returns than the cost of interest). To illustrate the importance of leverage, consider two consultancies, both employing 100 consultants:

- AAA is a business process outsourcing consulting company. It specialises in large-scale call-centre outsourcing where it fits the client's requirements to its own templates and standards to minimise costs and outsources the work to its sister company in Mumbai.

- BBB is a high-end strategy company which provides bespoke solutions for clients. Its employees are a mix of ex-directors with strong industry relationships, and skilled consultants with experience of implementation. As with most strategy work, the projects BBB works on are generally small scale.

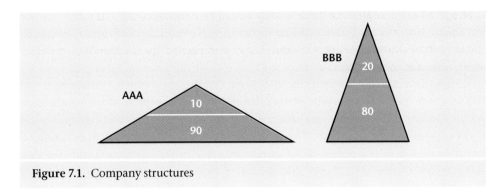

Figure 7.1. Company structures

Now, it should seem self-evident that the value of BBB's work will be greater than that of AAA. The salaries it will pay its staff will be higher and thus the daily fee rate will be higher. Additionally, the type of work means that AAA will require large numbers of relatively low-skilled graduates to make up the bulk of its project staff, whereas BBB will require more experienced and senior staff. This is likely to mean that the structure of AAA has a few partners overseeing fairly commodified junior work, whilst BBB has more partners managing relatively skilled senior work (Figure 7.1).

Given the type of work each company does, it is fair to make some assumptions about the finances of each company. Let us assume AAA charges its consultants out at an average of £400 per day and BBB charges its consultants out at an average of £1,200 a day and that the average wages are £40,000 and £90,000 p.a. respectively. We can also assume that both companies have an average consultant utilisation rate of 70 per cent. We can thus calculate income as the number of staff multiplied by the average utilisation, the days in a year, and the utilisation rate.

	AAA	BBB
Income (fees)	£10,200,000	£30,660,000
Costs (wages)	£3,600,000	£7,200,000
Profit	£6,620,000	£23,460,000
Margin	64.8%	76.5%
Productivity	£113,556	£383,250
Leverage	9	4
Profit per partner	£662,000	£1,173,000

Table 7.1. A comparison of ratios and profit between AAA and BBB

Now, these figures are simplified as they do not take into account office costs or any grading differences other than partner and consultant. However, despite this simplification, the table shows the differences that can occur in profit per partner in firms with different strategies but of the same size.

The impact of leverage does not stop at its impact on the finances of the company. It also has significant impact on the type of work that is done and how projects are organised. In AAA, for example, the leverage structure means that there are few experienced seniors and many inexperienced consultants. This structure effectively prevents AAA from taking on too many projects which require skill, experience, or judgement, as they will end up under-resourced with senior consultants, thus damaging quality, and under-utilised with junior consultants, thus paying salaries for people who are not being used. The converse is true of BBB. Should they happen to find themselves taking on too many procedural or implementation projects, they will find their income decreasing relative to their costs and, perhaps, a number of their senior staff leaving due to boredom. Careful planning and selection of projects is essential if consulting firms are to ensure they do not over-stretch or under-perform.

Leverage, as we shall later evidence, also has an impact on the people policies of the company. Firms such as Accenture have leverage ratios of up to 30, whereas companies such as McKinsey have ratios of around 7 (Hansen et al. 1999). Such ratios have an impact on the recruitment, training, and promotion policies of consultancies. Those with high ratios will require large numbers of consultants, promotion will be difficult, and mentoring by partners will be virtually non-existent (Maister 2003). However, in firms with more partners per consultant, there will be greater emphasis on developing and promoting talent, which may be one reason why strategy partnerships tend to have an "up or out" policy: they do not need large numbers of junior consultants blocking those who might make it further up the organisation.

Leverage is not just an outcome, it is a strategy, a performance indicator, and a design for the company.

(EO, medium-sized strategy consultancy)

As we explore the different aspects of consultancy practice we shall find further evidence of the importance of leverage.

■ Strategy

The Difficulty of Strategising

The peculiarities of the consulting sector offer several strategic challenges. One might assume, however, that, of all industries, consultancies were best placed to solve strategic problems. However, this is not always the case. Just as many business schools are run very inefficiently, many builders inhabit homes that are poorly maintained, and folklore has it that cobbler's children remain unshod, so it is arguable that even the best management consultancies are often poorly run, making unnecessary strategic errors and being run inefficiently. Examples include:

- In 2002, in the wake of the Enron debacle, PWC consulting spent around $110m rebranding its consulting service "Monday". The service was purchased by IBM a few days later who, removing the "Monday" name, incorporated the department into its Global Services Practice (BBC News 2003).

- After being spun out from KPMG, BearingPoint had a full order book and raised significant sums through an IPO in 2002. However, seven years later it filed for bankruptcy protection and was forced to sell off much of its company with critics arguing that it had mismanaged its own IT programme, taken on too much debt, and failed to reinvest enough of its IPO funding back into the company.

- In the midst of the dotcom boom, most large consultancies failed to realise the potential of IT consultancy until far too late. This enabled a number of niche IT consultancies to emerge and gain valuable market share at the expense of more established names.

There are several reasons why consultancies might have difficulties strategising. One factor may be the difficulty of getting in external consultants to assist them with the process. As this would be both a sign of weakness for a consultancy and provide a competitor with crucial insider information, few consultancies turn to others to provide an independent, objective perspective on strategic decision-making. The resulting difficulty, as consultancies often tell their clients, is that, no matter how bright they are, those working inside an organisation are rarely best placed to critique and advise it.

CASE 7.1

A Failed Take-over

The first large consultancy I joined was an IT and BPO consultancy, let's call it Young Process Consultants (YPC). As with many similar companies, YPC lacked the strategic offerings that would allow it to lever more business and win lucrative and influential mid-range consultancy projects such as programme management. The solution they chose to ameliorate this was to take over a smaller consultancy, Senior Experienced Consultants Ltd (SEC), which was populated with experienced strategy consultants, many of whom were ex-partners or ex-CEOs. This purchase cost YPC £56m. The senior partners of SEC made themselves very rich through the sale.

The difficulty was that YPC was, in comparison, a young, process-driven company with lots of procedures which were required to guide its relatively inexperienced staff. The SEC team were accustomed to a high degree of independence. When the SEC team were confronted with YPC procedures, forms, and processes for their work, many initially ignored them. YPC decided to force the issue and stated that they would withhold bonuses until the SEC team conformed.

Three months into the takeover, half the SEC team, the ones exempt from non-compete clauses, left, and started up a consultancy very similar to their old one, called Ex-SEC. Their experience and contacts meant they took away much of the

> value which YPC had originally purchased. As soon as the non-compete clauses had expired, much of the senior team also left to join their old colleagues. YPC had spent £56m for virtually no benefit and a considerable amount of management pain.
>
> * What might YPC have done to improve the outcome of this merger?

Another reason consultancies are not run as well as they might be is that most consultants want to consult rather than manage. Strategy formulation in management consultancies is, perhaps, not as exciting as many might think. The primary reason for this is that consultancy is primarily driven by what clients want. In an environment where client demands are highly variable it is difficult for consultancies to plan far ahead into the future beyond that of ensuring they make more profit than their competitors. David Maister, who wrote the "bible" on managing consultancies, had the good fortune to be able to review several strategic plans from leading consultancies, and had this to say:

> their strategic plans could have been reshuffled and redistributed, with firm names replaced, and no-one would have been the wiser ... every professional service firm in the world, regardless of size, specific profession, or country of operation, has the same mission statement: outstanding service to clients, satisfying careers for its people, and financial success for its owners. (Maister 2003: 223)

This is not entirely surprising as the financial success for consulting firms can only come through good people selling strong services that clients want.

The constraints to strategising have also been tightened by increasing attractiveness of the "middle market". As strategy work dries up and the margins on implementation work narrow, the lucrative middle ground, which incorporates areas such as programme and project management, is increasingly targeted by competing firms. The need to compete in this increasingly crowded area again ties the hands of corporate strategists.

All of the above makes consulting strategising problematic. What makes it more so is the inherent instability of the consulting market. As clients, regulators, and government policies change, so too must the consultancy strategies. This is not to say, of course, that consultancies do not strategise, but simply that long-term vision is difficult in a market that changes so frequently. It may be that tactics rather than strategies are the best way of dealing with an ever-shifting environment.

The Influence of Partnerships

Some consultancies are partnerships, whilst others are publicly floated on the stock exchange. This difference, however, is not simply one of ownership but pervades the entire strategic formation of the company. In an excellent article on strategy formation in professional partnerships, Greenwood et al. (1990) state: "The nature of the enterprise inevitably influences the strategic practices of any organization ... Partnerships differ from most other business firms because their form of ownership and governance is distinctive ... As a result, partnerships develop unusual structural frameworks within which strategic practices must evolve" (pp. 729–30).

The article goes on to argue that the forms of control in a partnership directly influence the types of strategy formation that the company practises. Greenwood et al. (1990) found that professional partnerships:

- tend to have decentralised control structures which provide local partners with considerable flexibility;
- emphasise "tolerant accountability" which enables long-term planning and the development of non-financial values;
- have less strategic analysis of threats, perform less forecasting, and give local partners more freedom and autonomy in their direction setting.

This form of organisation, termed the "P2 form", encourages a flexible, longer term, and less target-driven form of strategising than publicly listed companies:

> For the members of large, complex accounting firms, the idea of a directive, top-down approach to strategic management is not compelling. Equally unconvincing is the idea of clear internal controls circumscribing and channeling the behaviors of local professionals. Much more pertinent is the creation of representative structures that enable the outcomes of strategic processes to be negotiated and collectively agreed upon, combined with systems of market control that seem to confer corporate control but have more form than substance. (p. 750)

Such a flattering portrayal of the partnership system has prompted several commentators to suggest that partnerships "are the business model of the future" (Greenwood and Empson 2003; Empson 2006), though these analyses often ignore the structural and economic constraints that prevent simply any firm creating a partnership.

Over the last fifty years the proportion of the top consultancies which are privately owned partnerships has declined from around 85 per cent to around 40 per cent (Kennedy Information 2007; McKenna 2006): "by the start of the twenty-first century, 32 of the 50 largest consulting firms in the world were publicly quoted. Of the remainder, only eight remained partnerships, approximately half the number of ten years previously" (Empson 2006: 146). In an excellent, but rarely cited paper, Adams and Zanzi (2005) outline the effect of this transition on the career of consultants joining the firms. Central to their paper is the argument that publicly traded firms such as IBM and Accenture must focus more sharply on short-term returns to shareholders rather than sustainable, long-term growth. When they examine the levels of morale amongst employees of the different companies, and the reputation of firms amongst MBA students, they find that it is the privately owned partnerships rather than the publicly traded companies that have the highest morale and the best reputations.

Additionally, because public companies are floated on the stock exchange, their reporting requirements are much more stringent than for private companies. The difference in the cultures is so extreme that one commentator (Baseline 2006) argues that a key reason for the collapse of BearingPoint was that the majority of senior executives had come from KPMG, a private partnership, and were unprepared for the more pressurised and pressing demands of a company floated on the NYSE. Table 7.2 summarises the main differences between the two forms of ownership.

	Private partnership	Publicly floated companies
General HRM Principles	Linked to professional values and scope given to consultants to interpret the rules.	Detailed and formal prescriptions for each type of consultant.
Recruitment	Excellent general skills sought, often with MBA.	Excellent commercial and technical skills sought.
Selection	Based on personal interaction with senior consultants.	Formal selection (e.g. assessment centre) run by HRM function.
On-the-job	Based on observation of senior consultants.	Based on observation of peers.
Training	Focused on professional and interpersonal skills. Run by senior consultants.	Focused on technical and analytical skills. Run by HR trainers.
Feedback	Mostly on personal skills.	Mostly on technical and analytical performance.
Ownership	Owned by partners who buy into their share. Ownership bought back on retirement.	Widely distributed in publicly traded companies. Ownership maintained until sale of shares.
Exit	"Up or out" culture frequently forces exit.	Usually voluntary exit.
Support for Leavers	Excellent support through alumni network.	Limited support at all levels other than partner.

Table 7.2. The differences between private partnerships and public companies

---

A partnership is a legal entity. However, it is also a state of mind. Many organisations that have been publicly sold still try to retain the partnership mentality.

(Partner, large audit firm)

Strategic Directions

There are few writers that have actively promoted specific strategies for consultancies, but those who have tend to focus on maximising the value, rather than minimising the cost, of consultancies. This is primarily due to the fact that in a market which is based upon an ambiguous product, low prices are an unstable basis for competition (Armbrüster 2006). As Markham (2004) points out, a consultancy must provide value if it is going to be anything more than a conduit by which a client is connected to a consultant, otherwise the latter two parties may as well remove the "middleman". However, the form this value takes will depend on the type of consultancy and its clients.

Broadly speaking five strategic directions can be discerned in the provision of consultancy services. These are listed below. However, new firms don't simply get to choose what their strategy is. There is, as we shall see, a strong historical path dependence to most strategic positions (Garrouste and Ioannides 2000) by which the resources, reputation, and networks for firms institutionalise their market positions.

Growth

In his blog for Harvard Business Publishing, Professor Vermeulen urged firms to stop obsessing about size. Managers, he argues, are often taught to think that big is beautiful, without realising that "striving for size itself may be counterproductive for companies" (Vermeulen 2009). This is especially true of consultancies. Many consultancies believe that, in favourable market conditions, their strategy should be to grow as large as possible to maximise their revenue (see Schwenker 2004, for example). There are, of course, some advantages to growing a consultancy, primarily in the increased opportunities for promotion and enhancing morale. However, as labour is a consultancy's greatest cost, and there are no monopolies to be had, suppliers to be bartered with, and few economies of scale to be gained, the pursuit of size for its own sake suits consultancies less than it might other companies.

A key reason for this is that, in consultancies, increasing turnover by performing more of the same projects with the same leverage structure cannot increase a firm's profit margins. As Maister argues, "growing by 25 per cent and adding 25 per cent more partners is not a bad result but it does not further the goal of improving profit per partner. To do that, we must . . . either bring in work that has higher fee levels . . . or find ways to service the firm's work with higher leverage" (2003: 37). Changing the leverage structure, as we discussed earlier, is inherently risky because it means less senior time on each project.

Expansion through acquisition is especially dangerous if it is done simply to achieve growth for its own sake. Acquisitions of consulting firms are risky as they are often beset by complex cultural differences which frequently result in many staff leaving to set up, or move to, a rival consultancy. If acquisitions are ever to be seriously contemplated, they should be for strategic purposes such as leveraging higher level work or filling a gap in capability.

Quality

The pursuit of higher average fees per consultant is one of the only ways for consultancies to push up profit per partner without changing the leverage structure. This can usually

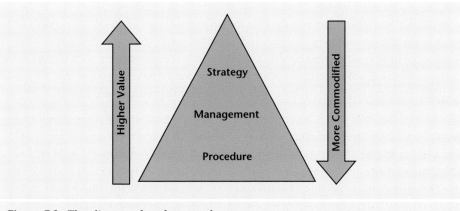

Figure 7.2. The client markets for consultancy

only be achieved by demonstrating higher value work. The pursuit of higher fees through an enhanced value proposition is, however, a difficult path to take for three reasons.

First, the shift requires a change in the sales activity of the consultancy. This can be challenging because the more valuable and senior relationships, especially in large companies, have long been monopolised by the strategy consultancies through their alumni networks. A partner seeking to move upstream to more lucrative, strategic work would find it incredibly difficult to develop the same types of relationships that McKinsey, Bain, and AT Kearney possess. Second, the consultancy would need to signal its strategy by recruiting higher quality people. This means having a strong cash-flow position so that higher wages can be paid for a period until additional revenue is gained. Finally, as Armbrüster (2006) argues, the reputation of the firm may provide a sticking point in marketing as most clients would not, for example, associate EDS or Tata Consulting with high-value strategy work.

Those companies that have successfully built up a "quality" strategy pursued this aim from their inception, rather than moving into the area. They achieved this by building up networks with CEOs and senior alumni, and investing in a brand which relies on signals of quality, such as hiring from elite business schools. As with many elite brands, these companies rely less on their product and more on developing a loyal relationship with key customers. As an ex-McKinsey partner argues, "at this level there is true partnership, a degree of intimacy, and mutual development ... It feels like discovery, both on the client's part and on the consultant's. It is, as a result, typically far longer-lasting" (Day 2004: 38). Such loyal relationships, the power of the brand, and the self-reinforcing perception of able MBA recruits mean that the dominance of such firms is rarely shaken.

There are few companies which have successfully moved up market once they are established. However, there are alternative strategies that firms pursue which also offer routes to profitability. These are discussed below.

Cross-Selling

Another strategy that some companies have pursued is to combine consultancy with another business function, for example IT development, auditing, or outsourcing. Strictly speaking, these three activities do not amount to consultancy work as they are not concerned with advice. From a strategic perspective, however, the combination of consultancy with these functions allows the opportunity for cross-selling services either to or from the consultancy practice and provides some strategic advantages whereby knowledge from one business function enhances the other. However, such a practice can often raise ethical problems concerning independence. Some examples of this are provided below together with the ethical conflicts of interest they sometimes raise.

Outsourcing Consultancies Combining outsourcing and consultancy is a powerful strategy for three reasons. First, becoming experts in the actual practice of outsourcing enables a consultancy to provide expert advice on if, when, and how companies should outsource. Owning an actual outsourcing practice provides companies like IBM with an in-depth expertise that non-outsourcers do not have access to. Second, the consultancy arms provides a sales channel for the outsourcing arm which can be so effective that often consultancy is given away free of charge in exchange for a future outsourcing deal. Finally, the sheer size of many outsourcing projects means that the operation creates a barrier of entry for firms that do not have the financial or human resources to operate in this field.

In 2008, Accenture earned $3.6bn from consulting revenue and $2.4bn from outsourcing services. As with many consultancies, much of its consultancy work focuses on giving advice to clients that wish to outsource various business processes to a third party. On the one hand, engaging a firm like Accenture for outsourcing advice does ensure that the client is receiving advice from an expert firm that has implemented outsourcing solutions thousands of times. On the other hand, it does mean that the client is much more likely to be given advice which will recommend the use of Accenture's solution.

Audit Consultancies Companies such as Deloitte, PWC, KPMG, and E&Y have developed strong, trusted, and board-level relationships with their clients, which allows them to sell consultancy services at a senior level. The analysis required for audit and accounting services often easily transfers to consultancy. For example, it is a short step from measuring cash-flow in a business process to then bench-marking this and then, perhaps, providing recommendations for improvements. However, some argue that the ability of audit consultancies to view the details of a client's finances means that these companies are unfairly positioned to understand the weaknesses in the client's business and also their propensity to pay for consultancy services. More worrying is the type of relationship that developed between Arthur Andersen and Enron by which favourable audits were encouraged in exchange for sizeable consultancy contracts. As we will see in Chapter 9, concerns from the Securities and Exchange Commission persuaded most audit firms to spin off their consultancy arms around 2001, but all of them have now redeveloped these services. As we will discuss later, there have been efforts made to minimise conflicts of interest in these areas, but their success is highly debated.

IT Development Consultancies For companies such as EDS and IBM, the distinction between management consultancy and IT is a grey area. A company's IT strategy and implementation plan is driven by their business needs and their business architecture so it makes sense for them, they argue, to both give advice on what IT solutions are appropriate and implement those solutions. Critics argue that consultancies which are tied to specific vendors or solutions can never truly be independent. However, as Czerniawska argues, "every firm, large or small, independent or tied, has an agenda. A tied firm may want to encourage its clients to buy a particular software package or outsource a specific function, but an independent firm has just as much of a vested interest in getting clients to buy more of its services" (2009).

Pile 'Em High

A complementary strategy to that of cross-selling IT and outsourcing services is a highly commodified form of consultancy which relies more on process and procedure than innovation or customisation. In stark contrast to the work of many strategy consultancies, companies such as Accenture and IBM have been able to produce highly standardised methods and products to meet the more common client challenges. This in turn enables them to recruit mid-ranking graduates and still produce a reliable service at a much lower cost than more high-end consultancies.

The sheer size of the BPO and IT Development consultancies means that this creates a barrier to entry for competitors. One partner at an audit consultancy told me, "even if we wanted to do BPO, we couldn't. The costs of entry are simply too high." The margins with this more commodified form of consultancy are much lower than pure strategy consulting. However, the size of some of the projects (such as Nestlé's $2.4bn SAP implementation) means that these companies can still generate a significant profit.

Buy Me

A final form of strategy which is worth investigating in more detail is the drive to be bought. For a partnership, being bought means that the profits from the sale can be split amongst the owners of the firm: the partners. For this reason, many consultancies, especially medium-sized niche companies, pursue a strategy which aims to enable the consultancy to be purchased by a larger consultancy.

The art of getting bought is not as simple as demonstrating profitable growth. As we saw above, there are considerable dangers involved in expanding a service solely on the basis of turnover, though profits are obviously important. The preparation for sale usually involves driving towards several aims. In order of importance, these are:

- Possessing strategic expertise which other consultancies lack. Specialist boutique consultancies are frequently bought to fill gaps in other firm's services or to lever additional projects. For example, strategy boutiques may be bought by implementation consultancies to provide them with greater influence in the board room. Less frequently, consultancies are bought by competitors to maximise their scale.

- Creating a clear, predictable, and well-managed sales pipeline resulting in a steady growth in profits. Many consultancies have a "feast and famine" pipeline which is unpredictable and, therefore, scares buyers off.

- Having a strong management team that are committed to the company. Partners and directors are usually tied to the company for a period after it has been purchased.

- Having built a strong network amongst key clients. This will not simply involve projects with clients but should demonstrate deep relationships that can generate on-going sales.

- Possessing a powerful intellectual property portfolio. Propriety methods and products, which are increasingly popular, are a clear asset for investors who might seek to internationalise a tool or integrate it within their existing portfolio.

- Achieving clarity and transparency in reporting. Many successful companies have terrible accounting systems. Having clarity on what is being bought is essential for a buyer's peace of mind.

Being bought is the golden egg for a small consultancy. However, purchasing activity is very dependent on the economic cycle and still relatively unlikely for small firms.

(Academic/consultant, UK)

A Strategic Checklist

In addition to these common strategies there are, of course, a myriad of other strategies firms can consider, especially with a view to simply improving their existing operations. Maister (2003: 225–8) provides a number of questions which should be incorporated into any strategising process. These include asking whether the firm can:

• Hire or train people to provide higher value services to clients.

• Develop superior methods or products which will offer clients additional value or cut costs.

• Share knowledge and expertise more effectively within the firm.

• Organise consultants more effectively to specialise in market niches or segments.

• Find out better information about the clients' needs.

• Do any of this in a way that competitors cannot imitate.

• Ensure that the strategy is put into practice through clear planning.

This stated, consultancies often have little room for manoeuvre when it comes to strategic planning. As previously mentioned, one reason for this is that consultancy is primarily a market-driven industry and, regardless of good intentions, changes in the market can scupper the best laid plans. Another constraint to strategy formulation is the finance available to turn plans into reality. It is, then, to the financial aspect of consultancy that we now turn.

■ Finance

A Question of Balance

The financial aspect of running a consultancy, at first glance, appears quite simple. Consultants are paid a salary of X and sold to clients at Y. The difference between the two, after costs have been taken out, is profit that is distributed amongst partners or shareholders, depending on the ownership of the company. However, this simplicity belies a number of complex financial tensions which a consultancy must manage in order to keep up with the competition. These involve questions such as:

• How should wages and bonuses be calculated?

• When should low levels of utilisation trigger redundancies?

• How much profit should be reinvested into the company?

• When should projects be run at a loss?

• Can costs be reduced without hitting quality?

• Can income be increased without over-stretching the business?

• Should the company buy, merge, or grow in order to expand its business?

The answers to these types of questions are often impossible to make simply through the use of financial calculations and require some level of qualitative appreciation of the business. This means that some companies, such as BearingPoint, get their decisions wrong, whilst others, either through superior strategising or just plain luck, get them right. To illustrate the complexities of such decision-making, let us examine the finances of a fictional consultancy in more detail.

A Closer Look: Clever Consultancy Company

Clever Consultants Company (CCC) is an Organisational Development (OD) company, specialising in leadership training and coaching for top management teams of blue-chip companies. The company employs 5 Partners, 10 Senior Consultants and 30 Consultants. Additionally, the company employs 5 support staff. For year-end 2009, the different grades had different metrics associated with them:

	Daily rate	Salary	Target utilisation
Partner	£1,500	£90k	40%
Senior consultant	£1,000	£65k	70%
Consultant	£600	£35k	85%

Table 7.3. Financial metrics for CCC grades

Note that as one progresses up the ranks, one's salary and charge-out rate increases, but one's target utilisation decreases. This is primarily due to the increased amount of sales and management activity that occurs as one goes up the hierarchy. An example of this is illustrated in Table 7.4:

	Partner	Senior consultant	Consultant
TOTAL WEEK DAYS	260	260	260
Public holidays	8	8	8
TOTAL AVAILABLE DAYS	252	252	252
Less:			
Annual leave	28	21	21
Sickness	5	5	5
Training	3	5	12
Sales work	45	21	0
Mgmt & admin	40	25	0
Utilisation days available	131	175	214
Utilisation rate	52%	69%	85%

Table 7.4. Target utilisation calculations for CCC

The target utilisation rates are calculated by the total days that a consultant is available for chargeable work, divided by the total days in the working year (usually assumed to be 252). With the metrics outlined thus far a number of calculations become possible. For example, if the target utilisation is achieved, one can then examine the fees generated per consultant and the subsequent profit per partner.

GRADE	Daily rate	Target utilisation	Days	Annual revenue	% of total revenue
Partner	£1,500	52%	131	£982,500	14.9%
Senior consultant	£1,000	69%	175	£1,750,000	26.6%
Consultant	£600	85%	214	£3,852,000	58.5%
			Total revenue:	£6,584,500	

Table 7.5. Income generation by grade in CCC (£)

This income can now be used to calculate the profit per partner in the same way as we did above on p.219. Professional wages come to £2.15m and total administrative wages can be estimated at £125k. I have estimated running costs (e.g. rent, utilities, travel etc) at 40% of wages. In some books, they leave out the running costs which effectively makes the Profit per Partner a gross, rather than a net, calculation.

	CCC metrics
Income (fees)	£6,584,500
Cost of sales (wages)	£2,150,000
Costs (general)	£1,035,000
Net profit	£3,399,500
Margin	52%
Productivity	£146,322
Leverage	8
Profit per partner (pre-tax)	£679,900

Table 7.6. Profit per consultant calculation for CCC

There are two interesting features to note here which are representative of many consultancies. First, the Partners, whilst achieving the highest salaries and daily rates, actually only bring in just over 15% of the income for the firm. The other 85% of the Profit Per Partner is generated by those who do not have a share in the company. Of course, it should be noted that not all the PPP goes into the partners' pockets, but usually a sizeable proportion does end up there.

Second, it should be noted that PPP is highly sensitive to utilisation rates. The utilisation figures provided in Table 7.4 are only targets and represent the maximum that could be achieved. If these dropped by 10 percentage points (to around 42%, 59% and 75%) the resulting profit per partner would reduce to £496,300, a drop of around 27%.

Crucially, the calculation of an average utilisation rate (chargeable days divided by total available days × 100) and the identification of an average daily rate (appx. £789) enables the identification of a break-even point below which the consultancy will begin to make a loss:

Consultants	Total days	Utilisation	Actual days	Income	Costs	Profit
45	252	10%	25	£894,726	£3,185,000	−£2,290,274
45	252	20%	50	£1,789,452	£3,185,000	−£1,395,548
45	252	30%	76	£2,684,178	£3,185,000	−£500,822
45	252	40%	101	£3,578,904	£3,185,000	£393,904
45	252	50%	126	£4,473,630	£3,185,000	£1,288,630
45	252	60%	151	£5,368,356	£3,185,000	£2,183,356
45	252	70%	176	£6,263,082	£3,185,000	£3,078,082

Table 7.7. Calculating profit on CCC's utilisation rates

This can be presented in a graph where the break-even point for average utilisation is around 35.6%.

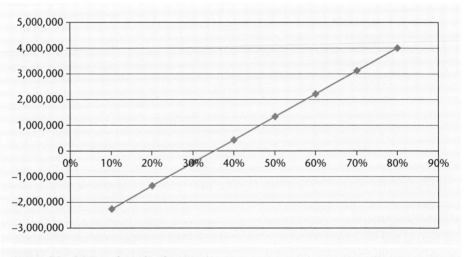

Figure 7.3. CCC profit and utilisation

These figures depend on the consultancy itself, its costs and the average daily rate it can charge. However, these basic calculations enable the partners to have a clear understanding of what the most sensitive variables are to the company profit and the ability to benchmark the business in a number of ways. These types of calculations also enable the partner to forecast what would happen if, for example, they promoted a senior consultant to a partner or reduced headcount by 10% in a recession. These figures also provide the basis for calculating costs and, therefore, understanding what fees should be charged to clients. It is to this that we now turn.

CASE 7.2

How Not to Run a Consultancy: BearingPoint

After pressure from the Securities and Exchange Commission KPMG spun off its consulting arm, in January 2000, raising over $2bn for the company. The company, the only audit spin-off to remain independent, began trading on the NYSE in 2002 as BearingPoint. Given the continuous growth of the consulting market between 2002 and 2008, many expected BearingPoint to rival the big players. Indeed, in 2006, Fortune has named it as one of the most admired companies, whilst Forrester Research ranked it as number one in client satisfaction surveys among IT service providers. As late as 2008, *Business Week* rated it as one of the top 75 places to launch a career.

Despite significant sales growth, which peaked at over $3bn, the company borrowed heavily in the 2001–2 period to expand its non-US operations through acquisitions, which landed it with debts of around $1bn. This surprised some analysts who pointed to other companies cutting back expenditure in a period of financial uncertainty.

As BearingPoint was a new company, it has no financial systems to keep track of its increasingly complex and internationalised client accounts and the myriad of companies it had acquired. As a result, it decided to build an IT infrastructure from scratch which would incorporate everything from IP telecoms, emails, and remote working to reporting, financials, and people management. The complexities of the new system, and the lack of training received by users, meant that the company mismanaged its 2004 and 2005 deadlines for filing its financial reports and also caused it to default on its Sarbanes–Oxley requirements.

The financial problems of BearingPoint prompted an SEC enquiry and a change of CEO and CFO in 2005, which further reduced the confidence of investors and creditors. The share price plummeted and valued consultants began to leave for competitors. To make things worse, it was discovered that previous financial reporting had been flawed for the previous two years and a director at the company was charged with falsifying accounts. The levels of debt dissuaded any potential buyers of the company and, increasingly unable to service its debts, BearingPoint filed for chapter 11 of the US Bankruptcy Code in February 2008. In the subsequent year, Bearing-Point's services and assets were sold to a number of buyers including PWC and Deloitte who could then cherry-pick relationships, contracts, and employees without the risk of taking on the company's debt.

The failure of BearingPoint was partially down to bad luck. A "perfect storm" of recession, increased reporting requirements, a terrible IT implementation, and a new company combined to generate an incredibly challenging environment. However, it must be noted that flawed strategic management turned this challenge into a disaster. The excessive borrowing, the over-ambitious IT programme, and a failure to deliver are problematic at the best of times, but when the company is a consultancy that prided itself on its strategy and IT services, the irony is more tragic than comic.

• Is it fair to judge the actions of BearingPoint as "strategic errors" in retrospect?

Sources: Echols (2009); Djurdjevic (2006); Baseline (2006).

■ People

Valuing the Key Assets

The phrase "Our people are our greatest assets" is one of the bigger lies of Western corporatism. Despite considerable evidence to the contrary, in the form of redundancies, union-busting, and work intensification, the phrase still persists in the PR literature of most organisations. The simple reason for the relatively low value of human resources is that people are replaceable and, compared to new products, new sales leads, or new financing, are relatively inexpensive to come by. However, if any industry can claim some credence to valuing their people, it is perhaps the consulting industry.

The reasons for this are threefold. First, as Armbrüster (2006) argues, the consultancy product is so ambiguous and indeterminate that clients have difficulty differentiating between high-value and low-value consultancies. One method of signalling quality to the market, he argues, is to recruit outstanding employees. Second, to a great extent, the consultancy product *is* its people. Whilst its products (such as methods or tools) may provide some value, these frequently change and, more to the point, are changed by the consultants themselves—there is rarely an external R&D department separate from those who are at the "coal-face" of knowledge generation. Consultants not only add value through their generation of innovative products but also through their networks and sales contacts which, at a senior level, are often tied to the individual rather than the firm.

The final reason for the value consultants place upon their employees is that good consultants are increasingly hard to recruit. Not only has the industry expanded to a point where hundreds of thousands of new recruits must be found each year, but pressure on fees and competition from banks increasingly means that high salaries can no longer be used to tempt talent (O'Mahoney 2008). To make things worse, many consultants, faced with stagnating income, longer hours, fewer promotion prospects, and lower training levels, are prepared to leave after only a few years in the industry, with top performers more than twice as likely to move elsewhere. This said, as we have seen in the last few years, consultancies are such a demand-led industry that they do not hesitate to make staff redundant in difficult times. This should not be a surprise, given that salary payments are the major cost of any professional service firm and cash flow in consultancies is often a fragile phenomenon.

Consultancy recruitment strategies, performance management, and promotion criteria are all covered later in Chapter 10 where we examine the consulting career in more detail. However, below, some of the strategic features of human resource management in a consultancy firm are examined. These are planning, culture management, training, and knowledge management.

Planning

Planning the people side of a consultancy business is crucial because, as we saw earlier, the leverage ratio in a consultancy is central to creating profits for the partners. It is also essential because consultants tend to be an ambitious group of people and a stagnant firm will often not be able to offer them the promotions they require whilst maintaining the existing leverage structure.

For example, if we take our fictitious company from earlier, CCC, we can see that they have five partners, ten senior consultants, and thirty consultants. If we assume that at least six of those consultants have at least five years' experience, then this is six people who will soon be looking for promotion and the associated pay rises. In addition, a few senior consultants will have their eye on a partnership. However, if a handful of consultants are promoted each year we can see that, within five or six years, there will be virtually no consultants to do the implementation work and too many partners sharing the spoils: the leverage of the company will have broken.

Such a scenario is only manageable if either the consultancy's market consistently moves to higher value work, which requires more senior people, or if the company expands so that there is enough room to promote experienced hires and recruit new consultants to replace them. As higher value work is, as we have discussed, very difficult to gain, then expansion, by default, is the option most expanding companies take. The usual method of achieving this is to ensure that one of the criteria for becoming partner is that the candidate brings in enough new business to stabilise the leverage ratio.

Consultancies need, therefore, to have a clear expansion and recruitment plan based upon the average tenure a grade should have before they get promoted and the turnover they expect though leavers, dismissals, and retirement. Whilst the exact numbers of leavers are not necessarily predictable, a consultancy that aims to maximise its profit per partner without damaging the quality of delivery will ensure that their leverage ratio is maintained.

This is an important point to remember for new recruits into consulting, or many other professions, where it is often incorrectly assumed that the lack of promotion is based upon a personal or professional weakness of the individual rather than a structural limitation of the company.

Culture Management

The cultural "fit" between a job applicant and a company is something we hear about more in consultancy work than most other businesses. Companies such as McKinsey, Bain, and BCG place so much emphasis on their culture that careers publishers such as Vault and Wetfeet annually issue detailed information about each firm's different cultures for aspiring applicants. There are three key reasons for the emphasis on culture in consultancy firms.

First, consultants rely on a professional work ethic. Issues such as confidentiality, trust, and integrity are important in building a reputation that clients can believe in. This is rarely about rules and regulations and more about how things are "done". Creating a professional culture provides consultancies with some form of control over what consultants do without needing to specify contingencies for every situation. Second, as consultants spend most of their time in client offices, a strong "one firm" culture provides them with an identity and a base that is separate from the client firm. As one consultant argued: "at any McKinsey office in the world the culture is very similar. A McKinsey person is a McKinsey person, no matter where they are" (Wetfeet 2005). Finally, having a strong culture provides a key differentiator for clients who may be trying to decide between companies or solutions that they know little about. Culture, in this case, enables clients to choose those companies they feel most comfortable working with.

Culture management in consultancies is inextricably bound up with the identities of consultants (Robertson and Swan 2003; Alvesson 2001) as the process by which culture is produced and reproduced depends heavily on the attitudes, assumptions, and beliefs which pass from the individual, to the team, to the organisation, and then back down again (Schein 1985). The "enculturation" (Kottak 2004) process happens in many different ways, such as procedures and rules, education, and symbols. Some examples of how this occurs in consultancy are provided in Table 7.8. This is discussed in more detail in chapter 8.

	Procedures and rules	Socialisation and education	Symbols and rituals
Individuals	Recruitment from top business schools; Up or out promotion criteria; Appraisals.	Induction programme; Professional associations; Partner mentoring.	Clothing; First in, last out; Professional conduct.
Teams	Teamworking rules; Knowledge management processes; Team targets.	Team review meetings; After-work drinks; Away days; Alumni networks.	Communal work space; Team branding.
Organisations	Organisational structure; Business processes; Partnership agreements; Legal reporting requirements.	Industry newsletters; Benchmarking reports; Market research; Corporate PR.	Myths and stories; Image of the CEO; Logos and name. Membership of professional associations.

Table 7.8. The management of consultancy culture in individuals, teams, and organisations

---
Culture is key to retaining consultants. As many companies find they cannot increase the pay of their hires, they have to look to intangible things to keep their recruits interested.

(Senior analyst, research firm)

Training

As consultancies have few assets other than their employees, one might expect formal and rigorous training programmes to feature heavily in the strategy of most firms. However, the pressures of the consultant's working life, the pressure to hit high utilisation figures, and the unpredictability of market demands often mean that training is a haphazard affair, especially in smaller and medium-sized consultancies (Kubr 2002). Training subjects can be categorised into four different types in consultancies:

1. Administration: this is the basic "hygiene" knowledge of working in a specific consultancy and will include an introduction to the company, the main HR and admin processes, reporting guidelines, and any software that is routinely used.

2. Corporate products: these are the proprietary tools, techniques, and methods that are used either in the consultancy firm or in the client organisation. These are usually provided by the consultancy but occasionally clients will include consultants on important training programmes.

3. Generalist skills: these are non-proprietary, generalist skills that consultants routinely draw upon such as negotiation, project management, and presentation skills.

4. Professional standards: these refer to the ethical and professional standards that are promoted by the various institutions of the industry.

There is a dearth of research on the training of management consultants; however, conversations with interviewees suggest that whilst many are trained in administration and corporate products, few are trained in generalist skills or professional standards. The exception is those few students or consultants who are undertaking a professional qualification with a consultancy institution such as the IBC, where such training is usually mandatory.

Two other pieces of research on consultancy may be relevant here. The first is a paper by Richter et al. (2008) which found a significant difference between private partnerships and publicly listed firms in their attitudes towards training. The former, they suggested, promoted (and sought out) generalist business skills, such as communication, presentation, and analytical thinking. The latter, they argued, preferred strong commercial and technical skills. Furthermore, partnerships training tended to be conducted by senior consultants and partners, whilst publicly listed firms tended to have specialist trainers and HR involved. Another survey, by the Institution of Management Consulting (1993), found that 45 per cent of consultants received no training in consultancy skills, 63 per cent received no training in management functions, and 60 per cent received no training in industry knowledge. Additionally, they found that consultants required training in sales more than any other competence (18 per cent), followed by IT skills (14 per cent).

Most of the large consultancies do invest in training, especially in the induction period. Accenture, for example, provides recruits with three weeks training at "consultancy school" in Chicago. However, the pressures outlined earlier mean that after this, training is often a sporadic affair. In contrast, the various professional institutes of consulting around the globe are placing increasing pressure on clients, governments, and consultancies to ensure that consultants have a minimum professional qualification. The exams that are associated with these qualifications tend to be focused on generalist skills and learning professional values.

As we discuss in the next chapter, the difficulty institutions such as the IBC and the ICMCI face is that the actual doing of consultancy is very difficult to commodify. The fact that the diagnosis of organisation ills and the implementation of tailored solutions is a highly interpretative, changing, and the subjective arena means that any prescription of "best practice" in an area soon becomes out of date or simply unfashionable. The UK Institute of Business Consulting is one of the most advanced professional institutes, but the final phase of Figure 7.4 points to the difficulties they face in creating standardised accreditation for advanced consulting practices.

Knowledge Management

What Does Knowledge Management Mean in Consultancies?

The central asset of a consultancy is its knowledge, which explains why "consultancies were among the first organisations to have knowledge management initiatives" (Kubr 2002: 751). Clients turn to consultants because they have, in their tools, methods, and products, accumulated years of experience in dealing with problems that many organisations will

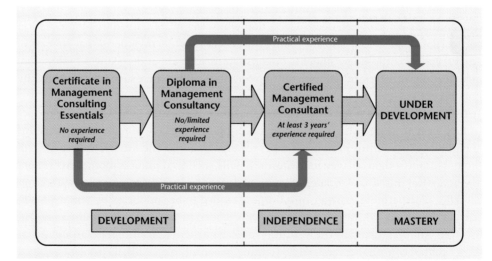

Figure 7.4. Institute of Business Consulting (UK) qualifications framework

only encounter once. However, the economies of scope and scale (Armbrüster 2006) that enable this value are only enacted if certain conditions are met:

1. That there is a mechanism for transforming experience into accumulated knowledge. This is the consultancy innovation process and is tantamount to a product development process. The tools, methods, and templates that the consultancy offers the client must be continuously improved and (re)created.

2. That there is a process for storing, finding, retrieving, and distributing accumulated knowledge when and where it is needed. In small firms, where everyone speaks together frequently, this may simply mean the storage is the consultants' brains and the retrieval and distribution is frequently conversation. However, in larger firms with thousands of employees scattered internationally, this may require detailed processes supported by an IT infrastructure.

3. That there is a mechanism for interpreting and applying knowledge in new circumstances. Werr and Stjernberg (2003) show that knowledge systems must be supplemented by experienced consultants who can translate, apply, and interpret the information within these systems. This, they argue, presupposes that those individuals have tacit knowledge of how to achieve this.

Knowledge Management Strategies

In an excellent article on Knowledge Management (KM) in consultancies, Hansen et al. (1999) outline two basic KM strategies that consultancies pursue: Codification and Personalisation. Codification involves capturing knowledge though IT systems and making it available across the consultancies for people to reuse. This tends to be used by the large, lower skill outsourcing and HR consultancies such as Accenture and IBM. Personalisation, on the other hand, is knowledge is created through personal interactions where IT is used to connect people. Hansen et al. (1999) argue that firms should not attempt to pursue both strategies equally, but that one should predominate and the other should be in a supporting role: 80 per cent of one and 20 per cent of another.

The differences, summarised in Table 7.9, create entirely different organisational strategies with very different implications for profitability, leverage, and recruitment.

Tackling Knowledge Management

The literature on knowledge management points to a number of practices through which knowledge is managed. These include:

- Case studies: written up after a project and used to inform similar cases.
- Libraries: research reports, books, and articles by experts in the field.
- Publications: in journals or books, written by consultants to engage with a wider audience.
- Talks: seminars, conferences, and meetings to discuss best practice and specific cases.
- Databases: to aid the storage, management, and retrieval of the material above.

	Codification	Personalisation
Strategy	Commodification and reuse using IT.	Creative people-based problem solving.
Economic Model	Invest once in knowledge asset and reuse many times. Generate large revenues.	Customised and personalised solutions though personal expertise. Generate high profit margins.
Knowledge Strategy	People → Documents. Use IT to codify, store and share knowledge assets.	People → People. Use personal interactions to create bespoke knowledge solutions.
IT Strategy	Invest heavily in IT. Focus on commodification and sharing.	Invest modestly in IT. Focus on connecting people.
HR Strategy	High leverage ratio. Recruit graduates who can store and reuse commodified solutions.	Low leverage ratio. Hire creative, expert problem-solvers who can tolerate ambiguity.
Examples	Accenture.	McKinsey.

Table 7.9. Commodification vs. personalisation strategies
Source: Hansen et al. (1999).

Much research, however, also shows how "best-practice" systems are often limited, constrained, and even contradictory. Werr (2002), for example, uses case studies of two consultancies to illustrate the incomplete nature of systems such as databases, case studies, and prescriptive tools. Whilst he accepts that "methods have a role as an organizational memory", he shows that "the method provided the basic structure and language which enabled an efficient interaction between consultants with different levels of experience ... consultants continuously managed the translation of the method to the specific case" (p. 107). Haas and Hansen (2005) found, for example, that highly experienced consultancy teams were actually more likely to lose bids if they "utilised electronic documents", suggesting, they argue, that "competitive performance depends not on how much firms know but on how they use what they know" (p. 1). A similar argument was made by McDonald (2005) when he finds that the lack of a tacit system of rules for engaging, valuing, and exchanging knowledge between consultant and client in new firms actually leads to a more efficient use of management consultancy services.

Others, such as Crucini (2003), show that knowledge is not an objective entity but a social artefact that is imbued with discourses, power relationships, and cultural interpretations. It is for this reason that knowledge cannot be treated as an asset like ball-bearings or pens. This observation prompted Maister (2003) to suggest that the biggest problem with sharing knowledge is not technical but due to the reluctance of partners to give away valuable information to other partners they may be competing with for bonuses.

From interviews and conversations with consultants in recent years I have noticed an increasing tendency for consultants to look to new forms of technology to support their knowledge management strategies. Networking sites such as Facebook, Linked-In, and Second Life provide new opportunities for informal groups to focus on areas of common interest, whilst other virtual sites provide structures for open innovation, anonymised discussion forums, and sales opportunities. The exploitation of such sites is still a source of experimentation amongst firms but appears to offer significant opportunities to bypass traditional hierarchies and capture inputs in dispersed communities. Studying the application of these emergent technologies may generate promising material for an MBA or PhD thesis.

More critical literature regarding both the generation of innovative products and the use of knowledge management systems is covered in Chapter 8. However, the key message for the partners of any consultancy is that no knowledge management system, especially an electronic one, is useful unless it has experienced and innovative consultants ready to translate and apply that knowledge.

■ Internationalisation

Managing the International

Examining the consulting industry from an international perspective highlights several interesting forces: different market requirements, the tension between the international ambitions of firms and the difficulties of achieving a global presence, the local "varieties" of consulting where practices are translated by regional customs and cultures, and the impact of shifts in power in the global economy. Below, we examine these, and other themes, and provide a brief overview of the different consultancy markets across the main global regions.

Drivers and Enablers of Internationalisation

The business model of consulting firms is, at its most basic, selling assets (expert labour) for a profit. The more expert labour available to sell and the more places to sell it, the better. Internationalisation, therefore, provides the consulting firm with opportunities to grow their business, reach new clients, and gain additional skilled resources, potentially at a lower cost. The two main drivers for this, unsurprisingly, come from the market: the internationalisation of client organisations and the growth of demand for local firms overseas.

One key enabler of internationalisation in the consulting world, as with their clients, has been the transformation in ICT, which has enabled a boom in the export of business services (UNCTAD 2002). For example, in 1996 the UK balance of trade in business services was £358m, yet ten years later had soared to £2.38bn (IFSL 2007), outstripping the trade balance of both law and accountancy. In recent years, this trade has been boosted by a number of Western consultancies licensing their products to the burgeoning Chinese and Indian markets. What this means for Western consultancies is that an increasing part of their business is based around the export of consulting advice and products. These figures do not just mean Western consultants travelling to foreign countries to perform consulting services, but also include:

• Foreign consultants coming to the West for training.

• Establishing overseas offices to sell services locally.

• Employing locals to perform consulting services for the Western company.

Selling Consulting Internationally

Differing international contexts offer different business development opportunities for consultancies seeking to sell internationally. In mature economies, consultancies generally sell the same types of services as they might in their home country. Thus, Accenture in the UK, France, or the USA offers the same types of services using the same methodologies. The people on the project, however, will be determined by a number of factors, including where the industry experts are based, if there is a relevant centre of excellence, who is currently on the bench, and whether there is a strategic need for overseas offices to develop their knowledge in a given area.

In a mature market, such as the USA or Western Europe, consumer markets are so large that businesses must make their money from economies of scale, new products, and tertiary businesses such as finance. Many consultancies focus on this mass market and focus on outsourcing and IT systems to cut labour costs for clients. Thus, consultancies such as IBM and Accenture increasingly base their businesses on massive outsourcing and ERP projects, where the advisory work is often undertaken at a loss and the operation of the project is where they make their margins.

With high-profile projects, international clients will often demand that they get the "experts" in from a given location if it will offer them a better service. On the other hand, often consultancies are happy to travel and discount their services if they are getting involved with a new, cutting-edge project. Thus, the battle for consulting work in new

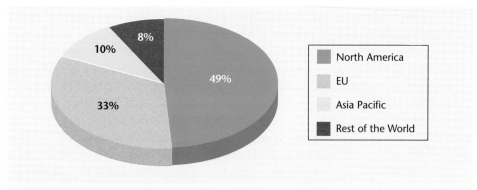

Figure 7.5. The global management consulting sector (2007)
Source: Gross and Poor (2008).

ventures such as dotcom or 3G is always very competitive because the winner can use the experience to secure future engagements based on their superior experience.

In less developed nations, the economies of scale in the consumer market are not always present and client firms are often not mature enough to invest billions of dollars in large ERP projects. Here, consultancy interventions focus on managing growth through strategic advice, reorganisation, IT implementation, and export support, and helping implement infrastructure projects such as telecoms, transport, and utilities to support and profit from the growing economy. Another key opportunity for consulting firms in developing markets is to follow their clients' international expansion. Thus, when clients expanded rapidly into Asia in the 1990s, it was no coincidence that many consulting firms followed suit.

When economies have been developing for some years, their increasingly prosperous middle class will send their children abroad to be educated to degree level in business and technical subjects. However, as with India, when this reaches a critical mass, centres of expertise can be developed in the home country enabling local consultancies to recruit local labour and undercut Western prices.

International consultancies tend to avoid working in undeveloped economies, as the risks are often high and there are rarely any strategic advantages such as follow-on business or development of expertise. Where they are present at all, consultancies in undeveloped economies tend to:

- Work with Western governments and banks to "restructure" (usually privatise) public utilities and improve local infrastructure.

- Work with Western companies to outsource their low-skill manufacturing operations to countries where labour is much cheaper.

- Work with large profitable local, usually Western-owned, businesses, such as mining, to lower costs and increase efficiency.

Shifting Strategies: From Imperialism to Localism

The changing size and types of economies across the globe provide different opportunities and models for consultancies to sell their labour. The traditional route for this has been for

	Undeveloped	Developing	Mature
Key local assets	Resources	Labour	Information
Typical consultancy	Privatisation and aid	Growth management	Knowledge management
Funding source	Overseas government and banks	Overseas and home businesses	Home businesses

Table 7.10. The development of consultancy markets

consultancies to move resources from their home location to anywhere where businesses can afford to buy it. Thus, it is not unusual, on a Sunday evening, to see at Heathrow, JFK, or Narita queues of well-groomed young consultants heading off for five days in whatever international destination the client happens to be in. This model, whilst still strong, is weakening, for three reasons.

The first is that Western consultants are growing more demanding in terms of their work–life balance and are more likely to say "no" when told they have to spend six months somewhere far from their friends and family. The second is that the sheer scale of business growth in developing countries such as India and China has far outstripped the supply capabilities of Western consultancies. As a result, local consultancies have grown to fill the gaps in demand.

Finally, the increasing education, training, and experience in developed economies has resulted in a highly educated and ambitious workforce which is well versed in the theory and practice of Western management techniques. Client organisations become less likely to accept a plane-load of expensive "outsiders" in five-star hotels when cheaper, local, native speakers exist who can do the job just as well. Indeed, seen like this, the traditional route of international consultancy can appear highly imperialist with the rich, white middle classes travelling to developing countries to tell them how to run their business.

These factors have combined to encourage local consultancies in developing countries to grow to the point where they have developed centres of expertise (even outside outsourcing and IT) and can begin to compete with Western consultancies in their own territory. In response to this threat, Western consultancies have moved to establish permanent footholds in countries such as India and China. In doing so, they have pursued differing strategies:

- Regional centres of excellence: some organisations have built offices that specialise in different geographical regions and which are often staffed by experts from those regions. However, ironically, they are often not located in that region. One large consultancy, for example, has its Knowledge Centre for China based in Germany. The reason for this is that these centres need to be on hand for clients interested in expanding to these regions and these tend to be from the USA or Europe.

- Joint ventures: joint ventures tend to be run by smaller consultancies pursuing business that is too large for their capacity in the foreign region. They are often project based and involve a handful of small consultancies working together on a large project. This arrangement usually throws up difficulties in matching standards, project governance, and political issues such as empire building. However, if the reward is great enough it will act as an incentive for cohesion.

- Transplantation: this involves setting up an office in a target country to act as a local consultancy. To ensure cultural fit and quality, this is often initially set up by senior members of the home consultancy who then recruit and train up local hires. This can take a while to establish but has the benefit of integrating local knowledge with central corporate standards.

- Acquisition: buying a local consulting firm is a quick way to add capacity in a foreign country and a common one in times of fast economic development. However, the drawback is that it is virtually impossible to ensure identical cultures, standards, and processes unless there is a heavy investment of people, time, and training from the consultancy that is doing the acquiring.

These can be used in conjunction with two final practices: sending home consultants abroad or using contractors (home or foreign) to supplement the arrangements.

Difficulties with Internationalisation

It is harder to export a service industry than, say, a manufacturing industry. With much manufacturing you can specify exactly what needs to be done to produce a standardised product. However, in the service sector, whilst standardisation is attempted, often skilled individuals are required to adapt standard processes for individual clients' needs. This is true, most of all, in the consulting world: even the most common problems require some form of tailoring and clients don't want to feel that they are receiving a standard or "boiler-plate" service.

This poses a difficulty for international consultancies in ensuring that the "local" office produces high-quality work to certain standards without imposing defined solutions. In an interesting chapter, Roberts (1998) outlines six methods that consultancies employ to transfer knowledge to international offices:

- Organisational culture: induction programmes and other methods provide consultants with a baseline to guide their actions and an informal network to look for advice.

- Global training: centralised training enables the dissemination of common standards and reinforces the communication of information between consultants.

- Centres of excellence: using these centres helps local staff bring in state-of-the-art knowledge and provides standardised benchmarks for local firms.

- Global databases: enables a common pool of resources for consultants and a repository for best-practice cases and success stories.

- Client relationships: global account managers for clients enable the cross-border exchange of knowledge through key individuals on specific projects.

- Boundary processes: a number of processes cross international and other boundaries to facilitate knowledge transfer. These include traded goods such as books and reports, promotional events and networking, research collaboration and intra-firm projects, and temporary secondments.

The extent to which these are imposed or simply offered to local firms will help define the balance between centralised and decentralised offices, which will vary by consultancy, location, and strategy.

This question of balance is central to a number of issues that firms face in establishing international offices. Take the issue of culture. A consultancy's culture is central to its operation, yet movement overseas can challenge this. On the one hand the consultancy will wish to maintain standards, have a consistent framework for dealing with issues, and try to develop a global culture. On the other hand, different international cultures require different approaches and attitudes. There is no golden rule to such dilemmas as each case needs to be tackled individually and follows its own trajectory.

Another issue is focused on establishing a foothold in the market. Often, especially in developing countries, business transactions are mediated through family or network contacts and it can be difficult to break such long-term ties. Additionally, much of the publicity material that consultancies generate, such as websites, white papers, presentations, and articles, is written in English. This is not always sympathetic to local sensitivities.

One final issue is that of talent. Often target countries, especially developing ones, do not have enough experienced consultants to satisfy demand, especially at senior levels. This is usually because there is such little consulting activity in that country. The result is that, initially, local firms are staffed by home resources. However, it is increasingly common for consultants to refuse to take on foreign assignments for long periods, especially in areas that can be dangerous for Western visitors.

■ Chapter Summary

This chapter has examined some of the challenges of running a consultancy. It has argued that:

- Leverage is a central concept in understanding the different strategies, structures, and operations of consultancy companies.

- Different strategies are available to consultancies, but that these must be consistent with the firm's leverage ratio, its structure, and its culture.

- The professional partnership is a different beast from the publicly listed company and, therefore, poses different challenges in everything from financing to people management.

- The finances of professional service firms are a complex but essential area to understand if long-term stability is to be achieved in a firm.

- People management and resourcing strategies are increasingly important in consultancy practice and must be aligned with the firm's financial and marketing strategy.

Overall, this chapter has shown that consistency and stability are great strengths in managing a consultancy firm. A steady hand may miss some short-term opportunities, but a greater risk to a firm's long-term interests is a speculative inconsistency which, as we will see in the case of BearingPoint, can lead the firm to a disastrous end.

Student Exercise

You are starting a firm with three other partners that will specialise in mid-tier programme management consultancy. This ranks somewhere between strategy work and implementation work in terms of fees. You are in a healthy, expanding market and have a number of sales leads, so you do not believe demand is going to be a problem. You have called a meeting to discuss how to structure the company and your initial recruitment drive. How would you tackle the following questions:

1 How would you set the rates for consultants, senior consultants, and partners?

2 What type of leverage ratio would you aim for?

3 What should your recruitment policies be for the next year? How will these change in years 2, 3, and 4?

4 What pressures might you expect in running the company?

Discussion Questions

- Why is it increasingly common for consultancies to pursue short-term financial revenues rather than focus on values and longer term planning?

- Why does growth for a consultancy business rarely mean increased profits per partner?

- What is the profit per partner equation?

- Why do consultancies place so much value on their people?

Case-Study Exercise: Dolphin Tankers—A Case Study in Managing Change

Dolphin Tankers was typical of owner-managed SMEs in the 1990s facing challenges from international competition, deregulation of government contracts, and changes in technology. This case study explores the nature of these challenges and details the response of this West Midlands manufacturing company. The case covers operational responses such as BPR and TQM as well as more ephemeral challenges such as HRM and culture change.

The Dolphin Way 1971–90

Dolphin was started in 1971 to produce road tankers. Their stated aim was less the pursuit of profit and more to provide a "pleasant place to work in". Dolphin expanded through the 1970s until the mid 1980s where sales reached a plateau. At this point Dolphin was supplying most local councils and contractors with tankage machines and employed over 150 people.

Under its eccentric managing director, Rob, who was one of three owners, Dolphin built up a strong reputation as a high-quality manufacturer, and exported its products internationally. In the 1980s Dolphin was a wealthy company with high pay and bonuses. Any excuse for a party, outing, or celebration would be taken up with as much energy by managers as by workers. The company's twentieth anniversary witnessed Rob spending £100,000 on fireworks alone.

Whilst being strongly respected by his workforce, Rob was a dictatorial manager. His "regime", variously described as "autocratic", "table-bashing", and "single-minded", paradoxically earned him the reputation of "a star" and "a friendly dictator" amongst the workforce. Accordingly, Dolphin developed through Rob's own interventionist and personal style. Rob's managers were not managers in any meaningful sense, in that they did not manage: they followed Rob's orders.

Those recruited by Rob followed his example. His Production Director, Aidan, was nicknamed "Bulldog" by the shopfloor. This top-down style of prescriptive management was called the "Dolphin Way". This emphasised conformity: "everything had to be done the 'Dolphin Way'—you always did it the Dolphin Way, even if the other way was quicker". This lack of autonomy and lack of investment in training meant that innovation was stifled and decisions were over-regulated. Dolphin's inventory was high, its deliveries often late, and the competition were improving all the time. Additionally, little was spent on R&D or technology.

The lack of representative procedures for the workforce (e.g. unions) did little to aid the situation. Rob hated the idea of unions at Dolphin: "never have been, never will be". However, the workers were very loyal to Rob. Rob's philosophy was not based upon procedures but on personal ties, as his most memorable quote suggests: "Sod the view, the plant, and everything else; If you haven't got good people you're in trouble . . . They have to be trained, they have to be loved, talked to and known. You have to know and care about their family lives because that's part of it."

On being questioned about a claim for unfair dismissal some years previously Rob retorted angrily, "HR is rubbish. It's arse about face and the ones who win are the stirrers . . . You are being doubted by people who shouldn't have the power to do it. You get some little sod in a firm like this that could wreck a reputation of a man in my position."

By 1995 two trends were forcing down margins at Dolphin. First, the increasing trend of councils contracting their sewage work out meant that tankers were worked harder and maintenance and warranty work was higher as contractors were less likely to buy new vehicles than the councils had been. Second, during the recession, several companies diversified into tanker manufacturing, putting pressure upon Dolphin in terms of price. Although the quality (and reputation) of Dolphin initially outstripped that of its competitors, the accumulation of experience and profits in other companies was increasing the quality of their products. On both counts Dolphin was finding itself increasingly exposed to, but less able to deal with, the competitive pressures of the 1980s.

Exercises

- What social, political, and economic factors can you see influencing the operations at Dolphin?
- What are the strengths and weaknesses of Dolphin's position?
- What would you do in Rob's position?

See Table 7.11.

	Turnover (000s)	Sales (trucks)	Profit (000s)
1975–80	6,000	2,100	228
1980–5	8,400	2,760	322
1985–90	4,800	1,040	184
1990–5	3,300	992	126
2000–5	3,180	788	120
2005–8	3,040	744	118

Table 7.11. Dolphin profit and turnover per year (averaged and weighted)

All Change 1990–9

The competitiveness in the market and the declining profitability of Dolphin suggested to the owners that Dolphin required "a more professional style of management" which Rob found difficult to provide. In 1993 Rob approached Colin, a director at Rover, to see if he would be interested in the post of MD and buying up part of the company. Colin accepted.

Aidan ("Bulldog") was in many senses the apprentice of Rob and resented being passed over for the Managing Director post. Aidan was also almost universally disliked as a manager within Dolphin as possessing all of the negative and few of the positive mannerisms of Rob. He was criticised by management and the workforce alike for having had preferential treatment from Rob and for his ignorance concerning manufacturing or production.

The Philosophy of Colin

Colin and Rob's approaches to management could not be further apart. Colin followed the TQM school of management and argued the need to improve efficiency for the company to remain competitive. The impediments to applying this perspective were considerable. The "Dolphin Way" represented an understanding or a set of assumptions concerning the nature of work, the relationship with management, and the boundaries of the informal contract. "Keep your head down, follow orders and don't think for yourself", one worker said, "but at least you knew that they'd take care of you." The attempt to change this mindset involved changes to a number of procedures and processes.

Changing the Culture

Colin focused on the idea of workers being the experts in their jobs. He got in a consultancy (Sid Joynson Training) to train the workers to come up with improvements to the way they worked. The training at Dolphin was aimed at encouraging workers to come up with ideas, problem solving, and Quality Circles. Colin also tried to standardise construction techniques on the shopfloor which has allowed multi-skilling (teams can interchange members) and a quickening of warranty work (any team member can safely repair another team's work).

However, some workers complained that managers were not listening to their ideas and refused to take them seriously when they suggested things. Other workers felt unable or unwilling to make the change to a more responsible and participative style of working, even to the point of refusing to go on training days. "The TQM course was crap," one worker complained, "I want a leader." The history of autocratic and high involvement leadership and the training through the "Dolphin Way" left a culture of employees who know how to think for themselves.

Aidan ("Bulldog") found this especially difficult to adjust to and continued in his usual approach of shouting at managers, telling workers what to do, and ignoring what workers were suggesting. When the new suggestion scheme got going, the most common suggestion was for Colin to sack Aidan.

Process Conformity

In order to improve the efficiency of the organisation, Rob bought in another consultancy (BallCo) to examine Dolphin's processes and see if any could be helped by new technology. They identified a number of areas that could be redesigned and suggested that a new paintshop be built closer to the factory. This would mean that the traditional route where tankers were driven, half-assembled, to a paintshop forty miles away, was to be abolished. This would mean that workers would not have to drive the three tankers produced each day for three hours and that the old site could be sold for around £70,000.

New Technology

BallCo also suggested that new technology be brought in and a specialist department be set up to deal with design. Colin invested in 3D Computer Aided Design (CAD) technology in the period 1995–9 and brought in design consultants and engineering specialists from outside Dolphin.

This would allow experimentation with infra-red, remote control, hydraulics, and electrical technology instead of relying solely upon the generally static skills and knowledge of the shopfloor.

However, workers noticed that the re-engineered design of the company and the new technology would mean that some of them might lose their jobs. Several of them began to send out their CVs to competitors and increasing numbers of workers were found to be going off sick with stress-related illnesses.

Exercises

- Look at the costs below: would you have approached things the same way as Colin? What would you have done differently?

- What are the biggest challenges to the successful transformation of Dolphin? How would you overcome them?

Costs

Computer Aided Design

Hardware	£7,000
Software	£6,000 a year
Training	£12,000
	£25,000

BallCo Consultancy

2 Consultants for 15 days @ £1,000/day each	**£30,000**

Sid Joynson Training

2 Trainers for 15 days @ £1,000/day each	£30,000
Preparation and administration	£10,000
	£40,000

Moving the Paintshop

Cost of new building	£70,000
Cost of new machinery	£190,000
Cost of disruption (est.)	£40,000
	£300,000

Further Reading

The bible of managing a successful professional service firm is to be found in David Maister's aptly named *Managing the Professional Service Firm*. This provides a detailed description of most aspects of professional management. However, it is also written to incorporate accountancies, law firms, and medical practitioners. Additionally, it does not describe all those consultancies that are publicly listed and run as "normal" businesses. Another useful resource for those charged with the management of professional service firms is the book *When Professionals Have to Lead* by DeLong et al. (2007).

Finally, two less standard resources are the AMCF Ratios report (2009), a useful resource for benchmarking the key financial figures for consultancies, and also the blog that David Maister writes, which can be found at www.davidmaister.com/blog. You may also wish to look at the website of the Advanced Institute of Management www.aimresearch.org for recent research in this area.

References

Adams, S., and Zanzi, A. (2005). The Consulting Career in Transition: From Partnership to Corporate. *Career Development International*, 10 (4): 325–38.

Alvesson, M. (2001). Knowledge Work: Ambiguity, Image and Identity. *Human Relations*, 54 (7): 863–86.

AMCF (2009). *Operating Ratios for Management Consultancy Firms*. www.amcf.org.

Armbrüster, T. (2006). *The Economics and Sociology of Management Consulting*. Cambridge: Cambridge University Press.

Baseline (2006). Compliance: How BearingPoint Lost Its Way. 2 July. www.baselinemag.com.

BBC News (2003). Monday Name Change for PWC. 10 June. www.bbc.com.

Brett Howell Associates (2009). *Financial Benchmarks: Management Consultants Survey*. BHA.

Consulting Magazine (2009). Retention Survey. October.

Crucini, C. (2003). Knowledge Management at Country Level: A Large Consulting Firm in Italy. In M. Kipping and L. Engwall (eds), *Management Consulting: Emergence and Dynamics of a Knowledge Industry*. Oxford: Oxford University Press.

Czerniawska, F. (2009). Is There Such a Thing as Independence? *Arkimeda*. www.arkimeda.com.

Day, J. (2004). Dynamics of the Consultant–Client Relationship. In J. P. Thommen and A. Richter (eds), *Management Consulting Today*. Bornhofen: Gabler Verlag.

Delong, T., Gabarro, J., and Lees, R. (2004). *When Professionals Have to Lead*. Boston, MA: Harvard Business School Press.

Djurdjevic, B. (2006). Where You-Turn Means Upturn. *Annex Bulletin*, 22. Annex Newsflash. 17 May. www.djurdjevic.com.

Echols, T. (2009). BearingPoint Declares Chapter 11 Bankruptcy. *Washington Business Journal*, 18 February.

Empson, L. (2006). Professionals in Partnership. In J. Craig (ed.), *Futures for Professionalism*. Demos Pamphlet.

Garrouste, P., and Ioannides, S. (2000). *Evolution and Path Dependence in Economic Ideas: Past and Present*. Cheltenham: Edward Elgar Publishing.

Greenwood, R., and Empson, L. (2003). The Professional Partnership: Relic or Exemplary Form of Governance? *Organization Studies*, 24 (6): 909–33.

——Hinings, C. R., and Brown, J. (1990). "P2-Form" Strategic Management: Corporate Practices in Professional Partnerships. *Academy of Management Journal*, 33 (4): 725–55.

Gross, A., and Poor, J. (2008). The Global Management Consultancy Sector. *Business Economics*. October.

Haas, M., and Hansen, M. (2005). When Using Knowledge Can Hurt Performance: The Value of Organizational Capabilities in a Management Consulting Company. *Strategic Management Journal*, 26: 1–24.

Hansen, M. T., Nohria, N., and Tierney, T. (1999). What's your Strategy for Managing Knowledge? *Harvard Business Review*, 77 (2): 106–16.

IFSL (2007). UK *Financial Sector Net Exports 2007*. London: International Financial Services. July.

Kennedy Information (2007). *Global Consulting Marketplace*. Kennedy Information.

Kottak, C. (2004). *Window on Humanity: A Concise Introduction to Anthropology*. Boston, MA: McGraw-Hill.

Kubr, M. (2002). *Management Consulting*. London: International Labour Office.

McDonald, S. (2005). Inexperience and Inefficiency in Information Transactions: Making the Most of Management Consultants. In D. Rooney, G. Hearn, and A. Ninan (eds), *The Knowledge Economy Handbook*. Cheltenham: Edward Elgar.

McKenna, C. (2006). *The World's Newest Profession*. Oxford: Oxford University Press.

Maister, D. (2003). *Managing the Professional Service Firm*. London: Free Press Business.

Markham, C. (2004). *The Top Consultant: Developing your Skills for Greater Effectiveness*. London: Kogan Page.

O'Mahoney, J., et al. (2008). *Contemporary and Future Challenges in the UK Management Consulting Industry*. London: ESRC/AIM.

Richter, A., Dickmann, M., and Graubner, M. (2008). Patterns of Human Resource Management in Consulting Firms. *Personnel Review*, 37 (2): 184–202.

Roberts, J. (1998). *The Internationalisation of Business Service Firms*. Aldershot: Ashgate.

Robertson, M., and Swan, J. (2003). Control—What Control . . .: Culture and Ambiguity within a Knowledge Intensive Firm. *Journal of Management Studies*, 40 (4): 831–58.

Schein, E. (1985). *Organizational Culture and Leadership*. Hoboken, NJ: Jossey-Bass.

Schwenker, B. (2004). The Challenge of Growth: How to Manage a Management Consultancy. In J. P. Thommen and A. Richter (eds), *Management Consulting Today*. Bornhofen: Gabler Verlag.

UNCTAD (2002). *The Tradability of Consulting Services and its Implications for Developing Countries*. New York: United Nations.

US News & World Report (2008). *Business School Rankings*.

Vermeulen, F. (2009). Stop Obsessing about Size. *Harvard Business Publishing Blog*, 1 June. http://blogs.harvardbusiness.org/vermeulen/2009/06/stop-obsessing-about-size.html.

Werr, A. (2006). The Internal Creation of Consulting Knowledge: A Question of Structuring Experience. In M. Kipping and L. Engwall (eds), *Management Consulting: Emergence and Dynamics of a Knowledge Industry*. Oxford: Oxford University Press.

——and Stjernberg, T. (2003). Exploring Management Consulting Firms as Knowledge Systems, *Organization Studies*, 24 (6): 881–908.

Wetfeet (2005). *McKinsey and Company, Insider Guide*. Wetfeet.

The Story of a Chameleon

Deborah Fleming, Director, Chameleon Works

Chameleon Works was established by Deborah Fleming in 2006 having personally experienced how self-awareness really works to support change on a variety of scales. Deborah, the owner and founder of Chameleon Works, has over ten years of experience as an internal and external Change and Organisational Development Consultant in a range of public and private sector organisations. Deborah also has extensive international experience delivering assignments in Colombia, Poland, Spain, France, the Netherlands, and Brussels.

■ Context

In 2005, frustrated with my current consulting job, I bought myself a ticket to Guatemala. I had no plan other than a return ticket three months later—all I wanted to do was find time to think and explore! I knew that I needed a change, but I didn't know what sort of change. I knew I had ideas, but I didn't know the best one … so I put a journal in my rucksack on and just went!

On a "rest day" in Colombia, I started to think about who I was, what I wanted to be, and more importantly what my uniqueness for business was. Consultancy businesses (especially small ones) are a highly competitive place to be. If I was to sell consultancy services on my own I had to know the "product" extremely well. My "product" was the knowledge I had gained from ten years in Change Management and Organisational Development (OD).

Kicking back in my hammock that day I scribbled these words about my current situation in my journal:

- I was in the process of reinventing my life.
- I was an expert at doing it for other people.
- I had a qualification and background expertise in supporting people through change.
- I was self-aware and afraid of going into debt to start a business.
- I was frustrated at not being appreciated for my skills in my current organisation.

Not many people did what I did well—in fact, change often failed because the "humanistic" aspects were misunderstood.

At this point in the "thinking time" I got distracted by a tiny gecko running across the ceiling. It suddenly lost its grip on the tile and fell right onto the hammock and into my lap. Now, I am not a believer in fate *per se*, but the timing of the little fella falling gave me the inspiration for my company's name: "Chameleon Works". I realised the name positively branded who I was and what I wanted the company to do. I was forever changing my environment and adapting to whatever happened around me so it seemed a turning point in making things happen towards starting the business.

■ Knowing Yourself and the Product

A third of the way around Central America, in the middle of a coup, I got stuck for a week without access to credit, debit, cash, or transfer! I was mobile phone-free and away from all my family. However, I managed to eat, sleep, and get to where I needed to be. I learned first that I was very resourceful, and second, that I could survive on virtually nothing.

The idea of starting a consultancy when you have £1,700 in the bank and an £800 a month mortgage is not for the faint hearted. In starting a consultancy of your own, it is important to recognise the risk and still take it! I would never have started a consultancy business if I had been scared of risk (or scared of not having any money). Shortly after, I got my flight home, got a lodger to help pay the mortgage, registered the name *Chameleon Works*, and handed in my notice to start my own consultancy.

■ A New Beginning

The early months were an exciting challenge with a very steep learning curve. I bought a PC, wifi'd my house, decorated my office, and bought a shiny new filing cabinet. Within two weeks I got my first piece of paid work with a major blue-chip company and earned my previous organisation's monthly salary in four days. Tapping into your existing contacts and network is vital to establish the brand early on. I gained references through this piece of work, designed a seminar based on the success, and won another piece of work.

Weaknesses are exposed very early on in a new business and I felt tired from learning about too many new things at once: accounts, technology, law, etc.: areas I had not had to think about before. I had a new respect for anyone administrative and, when I could afford it, I got help with these areas as a priority.

My business plan became a "living" document which I have added to and tweaked. It helps to focus your mind in the first few years, and once the ideas and words were committed to paper it made them real. I also had figures to work with which helped to remind me that I had targets to achieve. My website looked great but I learned later on that it dates quickly and works mostly as a "window" in my profession. It doesn't bring leads in like face-to-face networking does. It is important to invest in it and keep it alive but it does not always work well for selling OD and Change.

■ Year Three

At the end of year two I had stayed out of debt, managed to pay my monthly mortgage, I had completed some of my best, most rewarding work ever, and made twice my old salary in profit! It came at a high cost in sleep deprivation, hard networking, no holidays, and living from month to month. However, I kept remembering the experiences I had had during my travels and this grounded me. I won work by providing free reviews with clients and strong account management.

■ What Makes It Work?

I made a helpful decision to outsource things I was weaker on (like bookkeeping) in order to spend more time doing what I was good at (building relationships). I learnt early on that networking was important, very time consuming, and expensive. I also learned that it needed to be planned carefully to avoid time wasters. I managed to plan back-to-back meetings with my network and then plan "admin" days to follow up on the contacts. I got help with bookkeeping and also outsourced the cheaper domestic chores to keep me focused and productive.

One of the drawbacks is that you live in a constant state of ambiguity about whether you can win work. I remember feeling constantly tired from working both "in" and "on" the business. It is important to get comfortable with this level of ambiguity early on. What helps is to remember that working within an organisation can be just as ambiguous. The difference is that working for yourself can give you a higher level of commitment and control towards your own strategy and direction (more than any performance management process had given me in the past).

■ Looking Forward

Recently, I revisited my crumpled travel journal from the trip I did three years ago and realised how far I had come and how much running a business had change me. I also realised that one particular personal objective had been neglected since starting the business: "to continue my need to explore new things and new places in the world". Realising this, I booked a ticket to complete a long train journey in Panama—there is nothing like a good train journey to watch the world go by, forget about the recession, and have more "thinking time" to brew the next idea . . .

PART 3

The Critical Perspective

Critical Themes
in Consulting

Chapter Objectives

The chapter provides an overview of the critical themes which provide a deeper understanding and analysis of consultancy as a political and sociological phenomenon. The chapter:

- Explains the history and importance of critical thinking.

- Outlines the role of consultants in developing the knowledge economy.

- Assesses the extent to which consultants can be described as innovators.

- Explains the professionalisation of the consulting industry.

- Outlines the relationship between consultancy and the risks inherent in modern capitalism.

- Describes the approaches academics have taken to explain consulting identities.

- Examines consultancy as a contributor to the spread of neo-liberal forms of capitalism.

■ Introduction

Lecturers frequently urge their students to be more "critical" when studying management subjects. To be critical is to move away from the conception of consultancy as a money-making entity and to focus instead on its wider social and political role in constraining, enabling, and reproducing discourse, action, and identities. Such a perspective seeks to locate consultancy within a wider historical analysis which seeks to understand, and critique, the role of consultancy as a socially embedded institution.

This may sound like academic hyperbole, but to some extent, a shift in language is important in drawing the emphasis away from traditional business discourse. However, being critical is not simply about academic word-games. A social critique of the impact of society and capitalism on the individual is crucial in ensuring that ethical and moral concerns are not driven out by the current focus on growth, wealth, and efficiency. It is for this reason that many academic courses encourage students, especially MBA students, to be more reflexive in understanding consultancy from a multitude of different perspectives, not just that which focuses on improving efficiency or maximising profits.

From the consultancy perspective, the industry is interesting primarily as a way of making money or advancing one's career. From the perspective of the client, the purpose of consultancy is to improve organisational performance. This focus on enhancing business is often termed the "managerialist" or "unitarist" perspective by academics and assumes first that everyone is, and should be, concerned with what is beneficial to the shareholders and second that everyone will work together to achieve this goal (Fox 1974). This managerialist perspective is the primary drive of most business education, especially MBAs.

However, the perspective of the consultant or the client is not the only one that is important in studying the industry. Understanding consulting as a *social* phenomenon can also tell us a huge amount about society and the processes which link ideas, people, and organisations. This involves looking at consultancy, not in terms of improving its performance or maximising its income, but as a way to understand the social, political, and cultural phenomena that influence, and are influenced by, consulting practices. This "sociological perspective" does not focus on questions about income or profit but instead seeks to appreciate how work organisations are produced by society and vice versa. Typical issues that are tackled are not based, therefore, on "How can consultancies make more profit?" but instead:

• How is knowledge created in society? How does knowledge pass from one group to another?

• How are institutions, such as the consultancy profession, created? How are they different from other forms of working?

• How is capitalism sustained and spread by consultants?

• How does being a consultant impact the identity of the individual? How are these identities created and sustained?

• Why do consultancies behave in the way they do and not other ways?

Some academics take this further and argue that the starting point for social analysis studies should not be profit or efficiency, but "human emancipation". This perspective, commonly known as "Critical Theory", stretches back over a century and is based upon the radical premise that society can, and should, be changed for the better (Alvesson and Willmott 2003). Critical theory incorporates a number of different and overlapping traditions and approaches which include environmentalism, feminism, labour process theory, ethics, and post-structuralism (Casey 1995). These perspectives prompt critical management theorists to ask questions which aim to understand the ways in which management and organisations control, exploit, limit, and restrain the liberty of the minds, bodies, and language of those humans which inhabit their systems. In the consultancy world, such questions might include:

- To what extent does consultancy encourage conflicts of interest in both institutions and individuals?

- How are the work, motivation, and identities of consultants controlled?

- What forms of power in consultancies exist to enable such control?

- What forms of exploitation, stress, and anxiety do consultants experience? How do they resist these?

- How do consultants seek to control clients? What impact does this have on client managers?

- How and why do these things happen?

Answering such questions involves assuming a wider, historical perspective and using social and organisational theories to help expound the processes, structures, and actions which enable the consultancy world. This chapter, then, seeks to explain several critical approaches to management consultancy. It does not seek to translate every critique that has been made of capitalism into a corresponding analysis of the consulting profession but rather highlights a number of themes which are dominant in current critical analyses of the field.

It first examines the extent to which consultants have contributed to, and been shaped by, the shifts in knowledge which enveloped organisations in the twentieth century. It then looks at professionalisation literature and considers whether consultancy can now, or one day, be described as a profession. Next, the chapter examines recent analyses of modernity, and suggests that consultancies epitomise the transformation in risk and new forms of trust that global capitalism has produced. Finally, the chapter shows how consultancies can be seen as missionaries for capitalism, spreading neo-liberal policies and practice in both the developing and developed world.

■ Knowledge and Innovation in the Consulting World

The Growth of Information and the Specialisation of Work

The management of knowledge has always been crucial to the functioning of society, as without it, the skills, techniques, and information accumulated over time would be lost.

After the industrial revolution, the advent of mass production and mass consumerism led to the expansion not just of the factory system, but also of the information supporting this system (Myers 1996). As the numbers of workers and products grew, so did the systems that were required to monitor and control these resources and the data generated by these systems. The development of tools, techniques, and methods to support the industrialisation of society was embodied in a burgeoning literature of books, journals, and manuals which instructed workers, managers, and organizational scientists on how best to meet consumer demand and improve efficiency. As both factories and the knowledge required to support them became increasingly complex, economies of scale enabled the employment of specialist experts dedicated to maintaining and improving these systems (Clegg and Dunkerley 1980).

Thus, the model of the "renaissance man", who is adept in all areas, was gradually usurped by the "expert" who had a single specialism. Thus, general areas such as alchemy gave way, not just to chemists, but to biochemistry, analytical chemistry, organic chemistry, and physical chemistry. Similarly, in management, the cottage-industry model succumbed to a multi-tier system of supervisors, managers, and directors supported by a number of specialists in payroll, operations, sales, and recruitment. In larger companies, this gave way to further specialisms such as management accounting, product development, strategic planning, and e-marketing. By the second half of the twentieth century the growth of knowledge and the increasing specialisation of the business world had engendered and expanded a number of professions whose primary role was the production, management, commodification, and accumulation of knowledge. Solicitors, accountants, researchers, academics, marketing agencies, administrators, and technicians all developed, specialised, and, to varying degrees, professionalised, and, in doing so, created an expanded class of "knowledge workers" to both manage and lead the increasingly complex realm of ideas, information, and knowledge (Cortada 1998). The organisations which exploited capitalism's growing need for knowledge management have been termed "Knowledge Intensive Firms" (KIFs) (Alvesson 2004).

One area of "expertise" that was useful to the operation of larger businesses was that of management. By turning to "management engineers" company owners would receive expert advice on how best to organise their factories to maximise efficiency. By the end of the nineteenth century this function had transformed into a sustainable industry based on the production and dissemination of knowledge about management. Business schools began to specialise in the education of management experts, while several firms offered "professional management counsel" on a company's strategy, operations, and management (McKenna 1995). In 1893, for example, Frederick Taylor opened a consulting practice which proclaimed "Systematizing Shop Management and Manufacturing Costs a Specialty" (*Wall Street Journal* 1997). By the end of the twentieth century, this fledgling industry had developed through commodification and the sale of specialist knowledge products, from scientific management to Business Process Re-engineering, to become one of the most influential forces in modern capitalism (Kipping and Engwall 2002).

The classification of consultancies as Knowledge Intensive Firms places them alongside architects, doctors, and research companies as companies whose main asset lies, not in products, but in knowledge. To be more precise (see Figure 8.1) consultancy is also placed within the business services category of KIFs, a sub-category which includes accounts and lawyers.

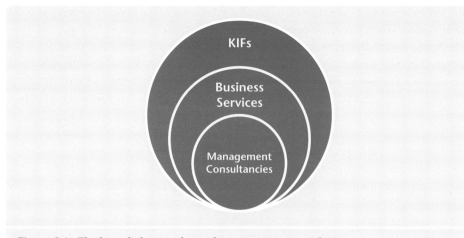

Figure 8.1. The knowledge typology of management consultancy

Given that consultancies have been one of the fastest growing and most influential professions in modern times, it is unsurprising that their creation, commodification, and dissemination of knowledge has been of great interest to critical academics and sociologists. Some of the studies conducted by these groups are outlined below.

Consultancies as Innovators

The creation and dissemination of management innovations such as Total Quality Management (TQM), Business Process Re-engineering (BPR), and Supply-Chain Management (SCM) is widely believed to have a significant and positive impact on economic productivity and efficiency (Hamel 2007; Birkinshaw et al. 2008) and management consultants are routinely portrayed as central to these processes (Haas 2006; Clegg et al. 2004; Suddaby and Greenwood 2001; Engwall and Kipping 2002). Consultancies, termed "innovation factories" by Hargadon and Sutton (2000: 161), possess, as their central business model, a remit to create, find, improve, and commodify management innovations and embed them through active intervention in client organisations. As a result, all of the prolific management innovations of the last fifty years have been strongly influenced, if not created, through partnerships with consultancies (Wood 2002).

So how does this process of knowledge innovation work? Literature indicates several factors that contribute to consultancy's ability to generate and exploit knowledge.

The Market

Without a market for their knowledge "products", management consultancies would not exist at all. It is, therefore, essential to understand the market mechanisms that have driven demand ever upwards over the last fifty years. The rise of the knowledge economy, mentioned earlier in this chapter, has played a central part in enabling consultancies to sell ideas, as products, to the managerial market (Heusinkveld and Benders 2003). The rise of globalisation, the neo-liberal economy, and IT systems have also helped stimulate demand by ensuring that expertise in, say, privatisation, systems development, and risk management has evolved unimpeded since the Second World War.

It should also be noted that consultancies have played a growing role in creating the market that they serve. This occurs both through the generation of "discourse" which emphasises the allure of the new, especially with regard to the importance of change to organisations (Grey 2002; Faust, 2002) and the process of agenda setting, particularly in the public sector (Craig 2005; Craig and Brooks 2006; Kipping 1999) where, as we discuss in the next chapter, consultancies seek to generate demand for their products by emphasising the inadequacy of existing systems and the allure of the new.

As Armbrüster (2006) argues, consultancies are often more able to meet this market demand than clients because they possess economies of scope and scale which allow them to develop and offer innovative products at a lower price. However, it should also be noted that consulting markets do not simply function on the basis of demand and supply. As Armbrüster (2006) and Kipping (1999) show, the market depends greatly on institutions that foster trust, which we examine later in this chapter.

Fads and Fashions

Academics studying management innovations in the consultancy world have emphasised the role of "fads and fashions" in enticing decision-makers into adopting management innovations (Abrahamson 1996; Grint and Case 2000; Jones and Thwaites 2000; Coulson-Thomas 1994; Knights and Willmott 2000). These writers hold that "change resembles the adoption of fashionable clothing—that, for example, BPR or TQM or MBO are implemented by clients, not because they are 'good' ideas but because they are fashionable" (Grint and Case 2000: 36). The market demand, from a fashion perspective, comes in part from the rhetoric which consultants employ to make their products more attractive (Alvesson 1994) but also from the insecurity of managers who seek certainty in the "expert" knowledge of various gurus and "trend-setters" (Sturdy 1997).

This emphasis on both markets and fashions helps situate consultancy within the wider capitalist processes which underpin the commodification of goods and the reproduction of market demands. As Marx realised, central to the generation of both the production and desire for new forms of produce is the constant negation of earlier incarnations:

> Constant revolutionising of production, uninterrupted disturbance of all social conditions, everlasting uncertainty and agitation distinguish the bourgeois epoch from all earlier ones. All fixed, fast frozen relations, with their train of ancient and venerable prejudices and opinions, are swept away, all new-formed ones become antiquated before they can ossify. All that is solid melts into air, all that is holy is profaned, and man is at last compelled to face with sober senses his real condition of life and his relations with his kind. (Marx and Engels 1848)

Thus, it is only the sweeping away and discrediting of previous management innovations that enables the fetishization and production of the new (Grey 2002). It is here, perhaps more than anywhere, that consultancies excel at both creating and riding the waves which managers fear most.

Networks

A key mechanism which facilitates the diffusion of management knowledge is the positioning of the consultancy within a number of networks that enable both the discovery of new ideas and their rapid dissemination. Academics who research this area focus on the channels by which innovations are spread (Tagliaventi and Mattarelli 2006). Sociologists such as Coleman et al. (1966) have analysed the significance of social networks in spreading medical innovations, whilst others such as Tolbert and Zucker (1983) have examined the role of institutional networks in influencing reform in the Civil Service. Analyses have investigated personal networks (Rogers 1983), corporate networks (Moxton et al. 1988; Mowery 1988), and research networks (Swan and Newell 1995; Newell et al. 2001) in dispersing ideas and innovations across intra-organizational boundaries.

The networking literature is very much focused upon the social processes and methods of information communication by which organizations learn of innovations. Consultancies are predominant in exploiting networks to sell and implement their work. Not only can consultants access and codify the expertise and best practice they find in their client organisations, but they can also build strong relationships with management gurus, academics, government think-tanks, and research institutions to help satisfy market demands (Wood 2002).

Evolving Knowledge

In a paper in 2007, I argued that the processes by which management fashions are selected by organisations can cause them to evolve in the same way as viruses or DNA. This occurs though the algorithmic processes of variation, selection, and replication (O'Mahoney 2007). The paper traced the evolution of BPR as it "infected" one organisation after another, spreading through academic studies, ex-employees, and management consultants. This theory suggests that consultancies are, perhaps, not as innovative as many think: that instead of "creating" innovations they simply translate existing ideas into new environments (Czarniawska and Sevon 1996) where popular ideas are selected and modified and unpopular ones die out. Such an evolutionary view emphasises the innovation itself, rather than the organisation or the managers, as the central point of analysis and shows how the "DNA" of management innovations is both carried and spread by consultancies into fertile client environments.

Not So Innovative After All?

Whilst the last six years have evidenced a 50 per cent increase in consulting revenues, analysts have noticed that both profit margins (Brett Howell 2007) and productivity (Sako 2006) have fallen. Recent research suggests that this decline may be due to the low levels of innovation in the industry. Three recent studies published in the last twenty-four months help illustrate this argument.

The first indication of issues with innovation surfaced in the 2007 Management Consultancy Association's (MCA) Annual Survey. It was noted here that only 59 per cent of clients were satisfied with their consultancy's innovation and creativity. This confirmed anecdotal evidence from MCA interviews, in which senior consultants urged the industry to become more innovative with the products offered to clients. A timely analysis by *The Economist* in September 2008 noted that: "the industry badly needs a 'New Big Idea' … Previous consulting booms were built on ideas such as TQM and BPR. But, at the moment, consultants have no successor to such money-spinners."

In the same year, working on an ESRC programme, Andrew Sturdy led a thirty-month empirical study of consultants in action. One of his key findings was the "that the conventional view of consultants as disseminators of new management ideas to clients is, at best, exaggerated" (Sturdy 2006). Such a depiction runs contrary to traditional representations which assume "that because consultants actively promote new management approaches and appear to be widely used, they do indeed perform this role" (Sturdy et al. 2008). Instead, Sturdy's study showed that consulting work was typically project based and not too dissimilar to their own clients' activities. One reason for this lack of innovation, he suggests, is that "clients were unlikely to welcome consultants if their knowledge was 'too new'" (Sturdy 2006: 42).

Finally, I recently headed a project examining the challenges facing the consulting industry in the UK (O'Mahoney et al. 2008). The study, based on interviews with sixteen senior stake-holders in the industry, found that both consultants and clients were concerned about *declining* levels of innovation in the industry. These interviews suggested not just that innovation levels might be lower than many believe, but that this had got worse over the last decade. The study elicited plausible reasons for such a decline but did not have the scope to further explore these potential influences. It did, however, suggest that future research should focus on understanding the potential decline of management innovation in consulting interventions and exploring the processes which underpin innovative practice in consultant–client relationships.

Knowledge Managers

If we move away from the image of consultants as originators or creators of knowledge, we need to ask what consultants "do" to knowledge in order to justify their fees. After all, if knowledge is already "out there", why do clients need consultants at all? Addressing this question, academics have developed different approaches to describe and evaluate the value consultants add to knowledge. Below, some of these approaches are outlined.

Applying Knowledge

Some academics argue that Knowledge Intensive Firms apply knowledge to solve problems (Starbuck 1976, 1992). Consultancies, for example, often utilise a pre-existing method, such as Soft Systems Methodology or time-motion studies, to solve a client's specific problems. However, as Starbuck points out, when workers adopt existing frameworks they often, intentionally or otherwise, end up modifying that framework or creating new knowledge as a result of that application:

> The distinction between creating knowledge and applying it is often hard to make … The [case study] engineers were applying known techniques, but they were applying them to products no one else had imagined … When it comes to systems as complex as a human body or an economy, people may only be able to create

valid knowledge by trying to apply it ... To my surprise, several experts described themselves as memory cells. They said their jobs are to preserve information that their clients have difficulty preserving. (1992: 722)

This sentiment is echoed by the work of Sahlin-Andersson and Engwall (2002) and Czarniawska and Sevon (1996), who argue that any form of implementation contains a translation into practice by which models of the world are altered. Clegg et al. (2004) make a similar point to this when they liken management consulting interventions to the disruption of a system made by noise or parasites, suggesting that instead of implementing a clear plan, consultants tend to open opportunities for transformation.

Commodifying Knowledge

A common process by which companies elicit value from anything is to commodify it. The process of commodification is based upon turning something into a product that can be controlled and sold (or exchanged). For example, a digital video clip today can be turned into a highly commodified asset through its processing, storage, and tagging. This enables it to be recorded, stored, searched, and distributed through television, the internet, and mobile phones. This can happen in international markets through many different media. In addition, sponsorship and advertising add yet more value, turning a clip of a drunk film star or an amusing kitten into a valuable asset that can be exploited. Prior to the advent of television, digital encoding, or metadata, the clip would have been less commodified and, therefore, less valuable.

In the consulting industry, the things that consultants most want to commodify are management ideas and expertise:

Consultancies are the main producers of management concepts, striving to "commodify" them. Concepts that are commodified have a better chance of attracting clients. Commodification means that consultants transform unstructured problems and problems solutions into standardised problems and solutions. (Kipping and Engwall 2002: 168)

Commodification is not simply the transmutation of knowledge into marketable products, but also the processes that underpin the consultancy's ability to achieve this goal: codification, abstraction, and translation (Suddaby and Greenwood 2002). Thus, all the larger consultancies have processes, formalised or otherwise, by which ideas are researched, experience is accumulated, and business trends are spotted (Sahlin-Andersson and Engwall 2002: 54). It is also vital, as we discuss later, to establish who is selling the commodity, as some brands are associated with higher value returns than others:

When the quality or value of a commodity is difficult to assess, the perception of who is offering it becomes important. (Alvesson 2004: 98)

However, whilst the commodification process yields products which are more marketable, buyers have become increasingly sophisticated and alert to the techniques used by consultants to seduce clients:

In large measure, the scepticism associated with the remedies promoted by [consultants] arises from an awareness ... that [consultants], like themselves, are operating in a competitive labour market where the pressure is to produce sellable commodities. ... Users are not dopes. By reflecting critically upon their work situation, users routinely suspect that [consultants'] claims to offer (neutral) expertise are conditioned by a "self-interested" concern to secure and advance their position in a competitive market place. As it becomes a commodity, knowledge enters a realm of political economy in which any claim to universal utility is subverted by its perceived value to parties ... who do not, in practice, routinely assume or accept a shared sense of their respective interests. (Elkjær et al. 1991)

It should also be noted that, as Marx pointed out, there is an inherent instability in the fetishism which accompanies any form of commodification. The value of any commodity, such as BPR, is only sustainable as long as the buyers believe in the mirage that has been created by the seller. Once this has gone, as the finance industry discovered in 2009, the value of any rhetoricised commodity vanishes (Marx 1992).

Legitimising Knowledge

Related to the commodification of management knowledge is what Suddaby and Greenwood (2001: 935) term the colonisation and legitimisation of knowledge: "Colonization involves the legitimation of specific social actors as the appropriate sources of management knowledge and the de-legitimation of others." The process of legitimisation involves, they argue, a number of interrelated actors, such as business schools, management gurus, consultants, and clients. These actors generate a discourse which normalises both the language and relations for management knowledge.

As with commodification, legitimisation takes place, not simply at the level of the method or tool that is being sold, but also within the processes which underpin the legitimisation itself. In an interesting paper by Clark and Greatbach (2002), they show how the rhetoric of consultancy gurus legitimises the gurus themselves more than the messages which they attempt to sell. It is this demonstration of authority that consultancies try and cultivate which provides *sustainable* legitimisation for their products.

In my own research, it is noticeable how different consultancies require different types of legitimisation. In larger consultancies, much legitimisation is provided by recruiting the "best and the brightest" from top business schools. As Armbrüster argues (2006), this provides a signal to the market of the quality of their products. However, in smaller or owner-manager consultancies, the expense of these individuals makes their recruitment prohibitive. Instead, such consultancies turn to professionalisation to provide them with a badge of legitimacy that few find elsewhere. It is to this issue that we now turn.

■ Professions

What is a Profession?

Looking up the word "profession" in dictionaries and encyclopaedias can produce substantially varying definitions. However, most agree that, at a minimum, a profession is an occupation that requires specialised training (OED 1989). Behind this basic unanimity, however, it is possible to discern a scale of professionalism, ranging from the strongly professionalised to the weakly professionalised occupations. A strong profession, such as law, medicine, or accountancy, is one where a number of criteria are fulfilled:

- To be a member of the occupation, one requires a licence to practise, thus creating a labour market monopoly.
- The state provides legal sanction for this licence. If one practises without the licence, one is breaking the law.
- There is a core codified body of knowledge which, whilst contested, provides the basis for practice.
- There are exams, often based on the body of knowledge, which practitioners must pass.
- There is a professional body which regulates the profession and its membership.
- There is usually a code of ethics associated with the profession which should guide members' practices.

Weaker professions, on the other hand, may only have some of these characteristics or may have all of these, but be voluntary rather than compulsory. Human Resource managers, for example, are not required to possess a licence to practise. However, in the UK, many of them choose to join their national professional institute, because it increases their employability and provides access to a codified body of knowledge and training.

Why Are Professions Interesting?

The academic focus on professions is in part kindled by the significant changes that have occurred over the last hundred years:

> Traditionally, society deemed only lawyers, doctors and clergy to be professionals... The skill and knowledge possessed by the professionals amazed the masses... with complete customer respect and no competition, professionals commanded virtual monopolies in their respective areas of expertise... those days are gone. (Ciccotello et al. 2003: 906)

Part of this change has been the sheer growth in the number of professions. In the article above, the authors report that in 1950 there were only 70 licensed professions in the USA, but by 2003, this figure had grown to over 500, employing 18 per cent of the work-force. Professions, then, play an increasingly dominant role in regulating labour markets and work in developed economies. Furthermore, they are significant actors in other operational aspects of society: mediating the relationship between the state and businesses, commodifying knowledge, and acting as lobbyists for their members. For academics, then, the increasing professionalisation of occupations is a powerful phenomenon worthy of investigation. However, analysts are unclear why change is occurring so rapidly and unsure whether the professions are a cause or an effect of social change.

This leaves a number of questions regarding professionalisation that would, if answered, help academics better understand the relationships between society, the state, and business. These include:

- Is professionalisation a cause or an effect of institutional change?
- How is professionalisation related to ethical practice? Are "professionals" more ethical?
- How is professionalisation achieved, or resisted, by organisations and their stakeholders?
- Can any industry professionalise?
- Should industries be encouraged to professionalise?
- How does professionalisation support the modern state?

Some academics argue that the creation of professional status enhances trust and accountability (Alvesson and Johansson 2002) whilst reducing ambiguity (Glückler and Armbrüster 2003). Others maintain that professionalisation provides labour market control and thus protects the income and status of individual members (Kipping et al. 2006) or that it helps prevent unethical behaviour (McKenna 2006). However, each profession offers its own answers and challenges in seeking to understand this complex phenomenon.

The consulting industry offers an interesting test case for those academics interested in professionalisation. After the Enron scandal, many commentators believed that some form of compulsory professionalisation was likely, yet, despite its strong similarities to accounting and law which have strong, compulsory professional representation, consultancy has not professionalised; however, in some respects, its traditional partnership structure has modelled itself on other professions. The question of why this is affords academics an opportunity to better understand the intermediary role of professions and their relationship to the state, individuals, and big business.

Is Consultancy a Profession?

The outward appearance of professionalism was, according to McKenna (2006), integral to consultancy's efforts to define their identity in the early twentieth century. Initially tempted to model themselves on doctors, consultants abandoned this metaphor because they did not want to simply service "sick" companies. Eventually, led by McKinsey in the 1940s, consultancies increasingly styled themselves on law firms in both their marketing literature and their corporate structure. However, as McKenna notes,

> consultants ultimately failed to professionalise because their use of strong professional metaphors could not fully compensate for consultants' weak professional credentials ... the leading consulting firms chose not to require that their staff obtain the Certified Management Consultant designation, because the certification of independent consultants would have weakened a management consulting firm's implicit certification of its own staff. (p. 203)

Consultancy became, therefore, what is known as a "weak profession" (Muzio et al. 2010). There are professional associations, such as the Institute of Business Consulting, that consultants can join, which publish best-practice advice, ethical guidelines, provide a register of members, and set exams for aspiring and existing consultants. However, associations such as the IBC are still voluntary and represent only 2 per cent of all management consultants, though this is a growing proportion. Furthermore, as consultancy is such a varied and changing industry, there is no codified body of knowledge even approaching what might be termed best practice.

Some academics contend that the "professionalisation" of the consulting industry is represented less by the formal professional association for consultants and more by the partnership practices of the large consultancy firms themselves in a form of "corporate professionalism" (Kipping et al. 2006). As the top ten consultancy firms employ around 20 per cent of all management consultants (Gross and Poor 2008), the practices and policies of these firms have a significant impact on the image of consultants as a whole. As all the major consulting firms possess training schemes, a knowledge management system, and a code of ethics, many of them argue that it is they, rather than an external association, that provide professional status for their consultants. As McKenna argues, the MBA became the *de facto* qualification for entry into the consulting industry from the 1950s onwards. However, this is a far cry from the consensus definition of "profession", which emphasizes the role of a state-sanctioned central body in setting standards, managing membership, and defining best practice.

Our brand is our professional status ... our consultants don't need to be part of a profession as clients never ask for it.

(Director, business advisory, audit consultancy)

The debate on professionalisation in the consulting industry is by no means over. In the 1990s the press and several academics claimed that consultancies' lack of professional ethics was central to both the dotcom crash and the Enron scandal (Cassidy 2002). In 1997, for example, the German institute of management consultants, the BDU, pushed for a law to force consultants to have minimum standards of education and experience. Whilst the proposal was rejected, appeals of a similar nature are predictably reiterated in the wake of any economic upset.

The current vogue amongst academics is not only to suggest that professionalism is an achievable goal for the industry but, further, to argue that this would be a positive thing for both consultants and their clients. Whilst I accept that "strong" professionalism is a possibility, albeit a remote one, much more evidence needs to be marshalled to prove the case that achieving this would result in positive outcomes for consultants, clients, and the wider society. The arguments for and against the professionalisation of consultants are outlined, briefly, below.

Whither Professionalisation?

Academics often imply that professionalisation would benefit consultants, clients, and society in general by improving ethical standards, quality standards, and by reducing uncertainty (Crucini 1999; McKenna 2007; Kipping et al. 2006; Groß and Kieser 2006; Kyro and Enqvist 1997). The arguments that these, and other, authors, have made for professionalisation can be grouped into three main areas:

1. It would help reduce ethical problems in the industry by:

    (a) Enabling the "striking off" of "bad" consultants.

(b) Ensuring that consultants are liable for any poor advice that they provide.

(c) Making consultants more committed to ethical standards.

2. It would help clients by:

    (a) Reducing risk and ambiguity for clients by providing common "best-practice" tools and methods.

    (b) Ensuring consultants have a minimum level of qualifications and experience.

3. It would help consultants by:

    (a) Improving their status and reputation.

    (b) Providing them with a library of best-practice knowledge.

However, each of these points has a reasonable counter:

- **Ethics**

  There is no evidence that "strong" professionalisation produces better ethics. Accountants and lawyers, for example, are rigorously professionalised but have an equally poor reputation, being commonly associated with client lawsuits, critical commentaries, and criticisms in the press. As we argue in the next chapter, ethical issues are rarely caused by "rogue" individuals but instead are generated by institutional conflicts of interest.

  It is for this reason, also, that the idea of striking off individuals from a register of consultants is only partially workable. If a consultant is in a large firm or team of consultants, it is virtually impossible for a client, let alone an independent profession, to prove unethical behaviour or incompetence. Indeed, the current situation is arguably significantly better: the consultant's employer can track their performance over a number of projects and take remedial action if necessary. A reputation for quality is so valuable to consultancy firms that incompetent employees are unlikely to be tolerated for long, though admittedly this stands in stark contrast to other "professions" in which individuals are rarely removed from the registers.

  Additionally, McKenna's (2006, 2007) argument that professionalisation would make consultants liable for the advice they provide is simply mistaken. If a KPMG consultant does poor work for a client, then KPMG is liable, not the individual consultant. This is the case with or without professional membership. Of course, if the consultant is negligent, it is possible for their employer to pursue them through the courts, but, again, professionalisation would have no impact on this.

  The argument that professionalisation would better commit consultants to ethical standards is a non-starter. Not only is there minimal evidence that ethical codes make any difference to ethical decision-making (Delaney and Sockell 1992), but in any case, all the major consultancies possess codes of ethics. Enron itself had a 36-page code of ethics.

- **Helping clients**

  Kipping et al. (2006) suggest that establishment of "best-practice" codes, such as those produced by the Office of Government Commerce (OGC) or the Institute of Business Consulting (IBC), encourage a more consistent quality of service. However, this argument ignores a crucial point about the difference between consulting knowledge, which is fragmented, mutable, and varies considerably by implementation (Alvesson 1994; Fincham 2006; Reed 1996), and the knowledge of medicine, auditing, or even law, where, whilst knowledge may be changeable, it is changed with reference to agreed principles. The variable nature of consulting knowledge accounts for why the "best-practice" guides of the IBC and the OGC refer to the engagement and management of consultants, and yet find it difficult to prescribe guidelines for the substantive work of consultants.

The argument that clients would prefer consultants to have a minimum level of qualification and experience may well be true, but determining what those levels should be is highly problematic. A "consultant" can be anything from a personal development coach or a systems development expert to a strategy analyst or a supply-chain expert. As such, a universal system of qualification or experience may well be counterproductive. Equally, a system in which each type of consulting work had its own unique set of standards and exams would be so impractical as to be unworkable. Unfortunately, the standards that most "professional" consulting qualifications tend to focus on are so low that few large consultancies or clients appear to value them. Indeed, in my own research, when I asked both clients and consultants about professionalisation, neither, with the exception of some very small consultancies, felt any desire to make them mandatory.

- **Helping Consultants**

Some academics believe that professionalisation is "central for [the] status, recognition, and legitimacy and, to some extent, the market value of consultants" (Alvesson and Johansson 2002: 233). To a certain degree, this is true. In my interviews with consultants (O'Mahoney et al. 2008) I found that some smaller consultancies appreciated both the information and status that a professional association offered. However, even amongst smaller consultancies, membership of the IBC is still a relatively rare occurrence.

Amongst the large consultancies, I found only one consultant, a partner at Accenture, who believed that professionalisation was a worthwhile investment. Interestingly he framed his argument neither in terms of knowledge nor credibility, feeling instead that his company, Accenture, comfortably provided such validation. Instead, he argued that the representation brought about by the professionalisation of consultants would be beneficial to the industry.

With regard to a codified library of best practice, it could be argued that this, even if possible, would be less useful to consultants than other professions. Not only is the knowledge associated with consultancy highly varied, fragmented, and changeable, but, in some respects, knowledge is not even the main part of a consultant's job. Consultants, unlike doctors, engineers, lawyers, and auditors, can often get by with simply a quick brain, a capacity to learn, and a confident style of presentation. Indeed, it is these attributes, rather than specific "business knowledge", that are identified and tested by the case-method interview used by most consultancies to recruit graduates. This is because, as argued in the introduction, consultancy is more of an art than a science, generating problems that are open ended and solutions which are always compromised. As such, consultancy stands in opposition to medicine, engineering, or audit, where problems are more often (though not always) closed: books can be balanced perfectly, coughs can be cured completely, and equations can be solved through the application of existing knowledge.

■ Trust, Risk, and Ambiguity

Conditions of Modernity

Three related sociological concepts cut to the heart of consultancy as both an epiphenomenon and a generator of modernity: trust, risk, and ambiguity. "Modernity" here means more than simply the modern industrial society; it also incorporates a form of engagement between society and citizens which prioritises reflexivity at a social, as well as an individual level. In addition, this definition also encompasses the disembeddedness inherent in the particular form of consumerist capitalism that typifies the early twenty-first century (Giddens 1990; Bauman 2001).

This form of modernity has "disembbeded" the familiar, local, and face-to-face trust that characterised previous modes of production and more sedentary communities. Concurrently, increased technology and globalisation has produced an escalation of both the scale and awareness of risk (Beck 1992). The solutions to such problems are, in contrast to those of scientism and Victorian teleologies, uncertain and ambiguous:

> Ambivalence is a consequence of modernity, a condition of our modern being.... there is security and danger, trust and risk. Social relations are abstracted from their local setting, lifted out or "disembedded". (Smart 1999: 6)

However, this is not all. If the world remained in ambivalence, unable to trust, it would not be able to act, for fear of both uncertainty and betrayal by the new faces of modern exchanges. Instead, as Smart argues, modern capitalism also offers opportunities to create new forms of (re-embedded) trust, particularly in expert systems and professionals:

> Individuals have become more and more reliant on experts and professionals, have been increasingly constituted as clients or consumers of professionally organised and produced systems, services and commodities . . . the systems of professional expertise on which we rely . . . occasions doubt and uncertainty. (Smart 1999: 6)

Seen through a historical lens, management consultancy, therefore, typifies and reinforces the "disembedded" forms of capitalism which characterise modernity. To some extent, consultants have always existed: biblical prophets, Mafioso *consigliere*, the Oracle at Delphi. All these, and other advisers, have provided the powerful and rich throughout history with ostensibly independent and often strategic advice. Yet under conditions of modernity, the powerful and rich are primarily found, not in the centres of government or the criminal underworld, but in corporations. The change in "consulting" is not, however, simply a transfer of location and focus, but also in the very relationships in which practice is embedded. As Giddens points out, these relationships in professional, expert systems develop and re-embed a form of trust which is different from that experienced in previous times. It is to this that we now turn.

Sources of Uncertainty

Giddens's analysis of professions and other sources of expertise indicates that they have become necessary due to the complexity of modern capitalism, as "large parts of our social life are organised by professional experts who possess technical accomplishments that we ourselves do not have" (Craib 1992: 99). As such, the lay person's lack of expertise in any area means that they cannot ever fully know, or adequately assess, the competence or ability of the expert:

> The pervasiveness of expert systems, therefore, gives rise to social relations that are founded on a faith in technical and professional expertise which, in general, cannot be fully justified . . . As the systems of expert knowledge which control our social and material environments become more complex we are all put in the position of having to trust. (Abbinnett 2003: 169)

Thus, the use of experts such as consultants is occasioned by conditions of modernity. Ironically, however, the shift away from the personal, face-to-face trust that characterised pre-modern relationships, and towards the "expert" systems that typify capitalism, means that risk and ambiguity are necessary features of business relationships. As McKinsey themselves stated: "Eliminate uncertainty and one eliminates risk. But we cannot eliminate uncertainty without eliminating capitalism" (McKinsey 2004: 6).

The sources of uncertainty in the consulting relationship are threefold. The first is found in the *type* of knowledge that consultants apply: as discussed earlier, consulting knowledge is often open-ended and involves considerable creativity and innovation, ensuring that neither consultant nor client knows exactly what they will actually be getting: "tensions derive from their contested and ambiguous knowledge base . . . consultancy work lacks the status and authority of other professional knowledge . . . management consultants have been unable to secure control over a distinctive domain of knowledge" (Ram 1999: 878).

The second source of uncertainty is located in what Glückler and Armbrüster term "formal institutional uncertainty" (2003). This uncertainty is associated with "the lack of formal institutional standards such as professionalization, industry boundaries, and product standards" (2003: 71). This "weak professionalism" means that clients find it virtually impossible to claim malpractice against consultants (Brockhaus 1977).

Finally, Glückler and Armbrüster (2003) outline what they term "transactional uncertainty". This describes the way in which consultants' work is unpredictable by the client. Several features of consulting work make it very difficult for clients to control: quality of service is difficult to measure (Clark 1993), the client is partially responsible for the work involved in the project (Sturdy 1997), and consulting firms are highly skilled at their own PR (Fincham 1999). However, as Glückler and Armbrüster (2003) point out, these ambiguities don't simply mean that the client may not get their "money's worth" of work, but, as consultants usually have access to their confidential information and will work with their competitors, there is also considerable risk to the competitive position of the client.

Of course, some uncertainty may be of benefit to consultancies. Uncertainty can provide consultancies with an opportunity to broaden scope and exploit their "expert" image, cultivating an image of certainty in uncertain times (Pinault 2001). Studies tend to find that institutions which might generate more certainty, such as interventions by professional institutes or the state, are resisted by large consultancies who wish to avoid standardisation and commodification (O'Mahoney et al. 2008; Amoore 2004). However, too much uncertainty would result in clients abandoning external consultants altogether. Given, then, the inherent instability and ambiguity of consulting operations, and the risks that these entail for clients, how does the system provide any basis for transactions at all? Below, some of the processes which underpin and ensure the continuing operations of consultant–client operations are examined.

Dealing with Ambiguity

Legitimising Institutions

In his analysis of the spread of Taylorism in the UK, France, and Germany in the early twentieth century, Kipping (2002) emphasises the role of "intermediary" organisations in enabling and constraining the growth of consultancy in different contexts. Germany, for example, possessed a number of existing government-backed institutions that "provided an alternative to consultancies ... As a conduit, these institutions have two potential advantages when compared to consultancies. First of all, they benefit from what could be called 'instant trust' ... Secondly, unlike consultancies which ... try to keep their proprietary approaches relatively secret, a single and strong institution ensures the adoption of uniform solutions throughout a country's industries" (p. 150).

Thus unlike Germany, where a number of institutions emerged to provide training and advice on the implementation of Taylorism, British corporations, having fewer options, tended to turn to management consultancies. In Britain, institutions avoided offering "best-practice" advice and instead provided an intermediary role between clients and consultants which aided both communication and exchange. By the 1950s, therefore, British use of consultancies was far ahead of that of Germany.

Today, as we witnessed in Chapter 2, there exist a number of institutions, such as the OGC, the MCA, and the IBC, which supply clients with advice on how to work with consultancies. In addition, a number of institutions provide training, advice, and consultancy to procurement departments in their quest to obtain the best consultancy for the most appropriate fee. These types of institutions are usually in constant contact with each other and share a common language and architecture for ensuring that the ambiguity of the client–consultant relationship does not get in the way of actually using consultants.

As Glückler (2005: 1731) states:

> The major problem for clients rests on the uncertainty of investing money, time, and effort in a consultant who lacks competence or acts opportunistically in the project. Because price obviously fails to be a sufficient condition for the consulting market to work, complementary mechanisms are required to reduce uncertainty and enable sustained transaction between consultants and clients. (Glückler 2005: 1731)

It should also be noted that consultancies use institutional relationships to help build credibility and legitimacy in the eyes of clients. Thus, the McKinsey imitation of established professions such as law and accountancy firms was specifically aimed at producing the confidence and familiarity that clients had already established with other groups (McKenna 2006). The same process applies to the frequent engagement between consultancies and high-profile universities such as Harvard, Yale, and Oxford. The connection to universities, whether it be sponsoring and running electives, conducting joint research, or co-authoring guru texts, provides consultancies with an aura of stability and legitimacy which they might otherwise be lacking. The close relationship with many MBA programmes also provides a ready cohort of future managers that will be familiar with both the existence and language of consulting engagements (Huczynski 1993).

Trust

A key component in reducing ambiguity is trust. Trust creates benefits for both the buyer and supplier of relationships; it reduces the need for monitoring and supervision, produces more positive working relationships, and aids communication by creating shared values and expectations (Von Krogh et al. 1998). Below we examine three forms of trust, all of which help reduce the ambiguity involved in consulting engagements: experience-based trust, reputation-based trust, and personal trust.

Experience-Based Trust If a client has experienced, or reliably heard about, a successful consulting engagement with a specific consultancy, they are much more likely to use that firm again (Furusten and Werr 2005: 165). For many consultancies, up to two-thirds of their business is derived from previous customers (Rassam and Oates 1991). In fact, as Glückler (2005) points out, trusted consultancies are often awarded work which they are ill equipped to undertake, simply because they have succeeded at other projects for the client. Glückler terms this phenomenon "over-embeddedness".

Reputation-Based Trust Experience need not necessarily be direct but may also be based on the reputation of the firm within the industry or the broader media. "Reputation is the expectation of future performance based upon the perception of past behaviour" (Glückler 2005: 1732). The methods by which reputational quality is transmitted are very much dependent on a network which prizes quality above, say, family ties and a network that is capable of transmitting such information efficiently. Interestingly, however, reputation is only partly based upon performance. McKinsey consistently tops polls of the public as having the best reputation in consultancy amongst graduates (Universum 2007) but actually comes fourth in client ratings of leading consultancies (Kennedy Information 2003). Of course, strong marketing departments also cultivate the association between the consultancy and a "trusted", communal entity, an approach illustrated by Accenture's alliance with Tiger Woods. This example also demonstrates the potential for such investment to backfire, as after allegations in the press about his personal life, Accenture dropped Tiger Woods in December 2009 (BBC News 2009).

Personal Relationships Personal relationships are central to the operation of consultancy. Jonathan Day, an ex-partner at both McKinsey and Monitor, argues that the most valuable form of consultancy is something he terms *metanoia*, a deep peer relationship between client and consultant: "consulting for metanoia is focused on dialogue rather than buy-in. It therefore requires a peer relationship between client and consultant. At this level there is true partnership, a degree of intimacy and mutual development" (Day 2004).

These types of personal interaction tend to take place between partners and directors at client firms. Indeed, partners are generally appointed for their network of contacts rather than their ability to sell. A friend of mine, for example, had worked at director level for five of the major pharmaceutical companies and was recruited by a large consultancy wishing to strengthen their presence in that marketplace. His job as partner now:

> Involves daily chats to these contacts, networking, providing them with support and ensuring that our analysis of their potential and actual business issues remains relevant and engaging … it's less of a sales pitch and more of a conversation … much easier because I've known most of these people for twenty years.

However, as Armbrüster (2006: 95) points out, "even in so called trust relations poor performance soon results in the loss of follow up contracts and networked reputation". It is therefore the combination of performance, reputation, and relationships that enables a consultancy to take the lead in client engagement.

Distrust

Significantly, however, when commentators reflect on the issue of trust and consultants they usually highlight how little of the former anyone has in the latter (Craig 2005; Pinault 2000). Indeed, a recent survey of clients revealed that 40 per cent would not describe their consultants as trustworthy (IPSOS/MORI 2007). Such findings are unsurprising, given the ambiguity inherent in controlling consultants' work and the lack of standards in the profession.

However, it is possible to argue that the *certainty* of distrust generates disciplinary mechanisms which provide client managers with some safeguards and, therefore, certainties, which in turn facilitate realistic expectations and mutually coherent communication. As one client director reported in an interview to me, "consultants can't be trusted, no. They'd sell ice to the Eskimos if they could. But as long as I know this, and they know that I know, it puts us on a level playing field where nobody is trusted but the job gets done." Thus, whilst clients may not trust consultants not to sell them unnecessary labour or attempt to expand projects, distrust is preferable to uncertainty, even if it is not, perhaps, as desirable as trust. This is, of course, one reason why procurement departments now dominate the buying of consultancy services, as senior managers felt that neither the managers nor the consultants could be trusted to do what was best for the business. This sentiment seems to support Giddens's thesis that the opposite to trust is not distrust, which is itself a form of knowledge, but angst, which is a type of uncertainty (Giddens 1992).

Living in Liminality

Regardless of the social institutions, the personal relationships, and the different forms of trust (or distrust) which, in part, expiate the ambiguity of consultancy practices, there still remains a considerable amount of uncertainty involved. Recognising the limits of how this can be tackled, some academics illustrate the ways in which both clients and consultants manage the ambiguity of their situations.

One concept which has been used to help explain and extend our understanding of ambiguity in consulting relationships is "liminality". A liminal space is an "in-between" stage and is used in anthropology to describe, for example, rites of passage where a person moves from childhood to adulthood. In consulting literature the concept is used by both Czarniawska and Mazza (2003) and Sturdy et al. (2006) to highlight how consultants cross boundaries, for example as insiders and outsiders, from the formal to the informal and what they term "back-stage" and "front-stage" work. Both articles argue that these areas of transition are central to the operation of most consulting practices and, indeed, form the sites of many of the important decisions between consultants and clients.

Other writers use similar concepts to emphasise the ambiguity and instability of the consultant's role: Clegg et al. (2004) use the concept of noise to show how consultants disrupt organisations "by introducing interruptive action into the space between organisational order and chaos" (p. 31). Kitay and Wright (2004) argue that consultants blur the boundaries of organisations by developing "embedded" relations with clients that span and cross traditional conceptions of insiders and outsiders. Finally, Sturdy et al. (2008) point to the role of humour in helping both consultants and clients live with the tensions, contradictions, and ambiguities which permeate their relationships.

Charisma and the Leap of Faith

Finally, an emerging area which shows some promise in helping explain how ambiguity is minimised in consulting engagements is the idea of charisma. Charismatic authority was introduced by Weber as a form of legitimacy that was contrasted with rational authority (1970). The former concerns "resting on devotion to the exceptional sanctity, heroism or exemplary character of an individual person, and of the normative patterns or order revealed or ordained by him" (Weber 1968: 52). Charisma, for Weber, is not to be found in the realm of logic or rationality, but instead is:

> a certain quality of an individual personality, by virtue of which he is set apart from ordinary men and treated as endowed with supernatural, superhuman, or at least specifically exceptional powers or qualities. These are such as are not accessible to the ordinary person, but are regarded as of divine origin or as exemplary, and on the basis of them the individual concerned is treated as a leader. (Weber 1947: 89)

In an interesting chapter on guru consultants, Fincham (2002) contrasts the charisma used by gurus with the technique used by consultants. The chapter goes on to show the different structural positions and forms of legitimacy that the two forms of authority provide both parties. However, as others have noted, it is common for consultants to be labelled with charismatic and strictly irrational metaphors such as magicians, witch-doctors, and missionaries (O'Mahoney 2007). It should also be noted that as one goes higher up in the consulting hierarchy and is increasingly expected to sell, charisma becomes important in forging and sustaining relationships with clients (Day 2004). This should, perhaps, indicate that the development of charisma, in the everyday, rather than the "irrational" Weberian sense, is not simply the preserve of gurus and might be found in standard consulting roles as well.

A different interpretation for charisma might be sought in religious studies, where charisma is presented as congruent with a "leap of faith" which changes the individual and their world view (Neitz 1987). The parallel with religion has been made by others, and can be found in books which parallel the secrecy, culture, and devotees of companies like McKinsey with various cults (O'Shea 1998). This is perhaps an avenue that might be explored further in future research.

■ Consulting Identities

From Rationality to (Post)Modernism

After the European Enlightenment in the eighteenth century, accounts of the cosmos tended to prioritise both the human as the centre of the Universe and the mind as a seat of rationality, control, and will. The rationality of humanity was encapsulated by the drive of science to map, measure, and control. Central to this presentation was a distinction of mind, and therefore rationality, from the body, society, and everything else that was change-able, fallible, and transitory. The dominance and rhetoric of logic and progress came to influence not simply science, but also art, philosophy, and society in movements such as positivism, rationalism, and materialism. In organisations, rationality was promoted in the "scientific management" of Frederick Taylor which presented management as the logical, thinking part of the organisation. This anthropocentric and rationalistic view of the work dominated art, philosophy, and society from the 1800s until the mid-twentieth century. Then things started to change.

The discourse of progress in the applied sciences, reflected in the ideas of Freud and Darwin, began to put pressure on the idea that mankind was in control of either itself or its destiny. In society, the belief in rationalism was severely dented by the horrors of the First World War, the Great Depression, and the Holocaust. In philosophy, anti-rationalists such as Nietzsche and Kierkegaard attacked the rational dialectics of Hegel and Kant. Out of these successive shocks, new ways of thinking emerged which challenged our under-standing of who we are. In art, traditional portraiture and formulaic rules collapsed, to be replaced with the monstrous and fractured selves found, for example, in the work of Picasso. In literature, the formulaic nature of nineteenth-century writing was usurped by the Modernist stream of consciousness, a style that challenged our conceptions of self in novels such as Joyce's *Ulysses*.

One of the children of this modernist movement was Michel Foucault. Foucault, as with all great thinkers, has been significantly misinterpreted at times (Al-Amoudi 2007). However, the caricature which arises from these misreadings has had a considerably and enduring impact and it is this that we will focus on here. Foucauldian studies react against the "rational self" of earlier thinkers and seek to show how our ways of thinking and ways of being are influenced, or "constructed", by the texts, architectures, and talk of the social world. Such "discourses", as they are known, do not simply appear from anywhere, but are both constitutive and reflective of power relationships in society. To put it simply, cat-egories such as "prisoner", "lunatic", "worker", "quality", and "expert" are not objectively "real", they are constructed by the social power relations which permeate their usage.

The work of Foucault gets to the heart of the identity, or identities, of the modern self. If, after all, categorisations are merely social norms, then the category of the self is worthy of similar deconstruction. This central idea in the work of Foucault, Derrida, Lyotard, and others has given precedent to the social analysis of identities: how they are (de)constructed, interpreted, and fragmented in conditions of modernity. Identity is both reflective and constitutive of a society in which consumerism, culture, and the self have been self-reflexive, fetishised, and thus undermined. Any cursory examination of social science journals, therefore, from the 1980s onwards, reveals a burgeoning interesting in identity management, construction, and deconstruction. Thus, to better understand consultants as both socially constructed categories and reflexive selves, we need to better understand the identities that they, and others, construct for them and to "deconstruct" the discourses and power relations which underpin these identities.

Consulting Identities

A vast amount of critical consultancy literature explores the processes by which consultants' identities are constructed and the effects of these on clients, the public, and consultants themselves. The work tends to focus on the discourses and power relations which underpin the processes of identity construction but vary as to their views on whether such constructions are necessary or inevitable. There are several areas which academics have highlighted.

Consultants as the Elite

The cultivation of an image of elitism occurs in many ways: by aligning with "elite" institutions and individuals such as universities, gurus, and media stars, through recruiting young stars from the top business schools, and by having an "up or out" system which encourages competition and the appearance of a Darwinian form of evolution (Robertson and Swan 2003). Once recruited, the elitist image of star employees is reinforced to both the consultants themselves and to the general public. This is achieved by creating a powerful culture with a strong "team" focus (Robertson and Swan 2003), a uniformity of character, clothing, and activities (Alvesson 2001), and, sometimes, a disparagement of those outside the consultancy, such as clients (O'Mahoney 2007). In Alvesson and Robertson's (2006) study of the construction of elitism in consulting firms, they emphasise both the material definition of elitism, such as large pay packets, first-class travel, autonomous work, and generous expenses, as well as symbolic representations such as qualifications, educational background, and class.

Consultants as Scientists

As we have discussed, there is considerable pressure on consultancies to create client confidence in their products. This is partly achieved by presenting the consultant as a scientist. The traditional route into top consultancies favours those with a quantitative analysis background, an emphasis which benefits recruits with degrees such as engineering, mathematics, and physics. As Berglund and Werr point out, "this view of knowledge makes it legitimate for the manager to ask for help … [by] depicting management as knowledge based expert activity, which in turn creates the client's need for advice from global experts" (2001: 22).

This scientific identity emerges, in part, through the quantification of management problems into vast data sets, which, in turn, generate models for managers to use. "By disentangling the complex reality, they make it easier for managers to grasp their day-to-day situations, increase their status and provide a feeling of control" (Berglund and Werr 2000: 640). Of course, the representation of inherently messy and complex issues into logical problems that can be neatly contained and "solved" through the application of the scientific method makes the sale of these solutions so much easier (Bloomfield and Vurdubakis 1994).

Consultants as Magicians

Literature that addresses the identity of consultants often incorporates metaphorical language to describe the mystique or "magical" powers of the profession. Thus, consultants have been variously depicted in academic literature as:

- Magicians (Schuyt and Schuijt 1998).
- Shamans (Fincham 2003).
- Preachers (Whittle 2005).
- Witch-doctors (Clark and Salaman 1996).
- Missionaries (Wright and Kitay 2004).

These metaphors, which allude to the mystical powers of consultants, point to roles that provide security in times of uncertainty, and have a capability to transform people, are unsurprising. What is interesting about them is that these approaches tend to use the roles as metaphors rather than examining them as identity archetypes. In other words, they are presented as mere illusions rather than discourses that have real effects on the project.

Too Many Identities?

The construction of a consulting identity is not, as many academics have pointed out, a simple exercise. As Whittle (2006) argues, consultants are subject to a number of contra-dictory pressures: to make money for their consultancy, to do a good job, to be "trusted advisers", to adhere to a code of ethics, and to look out for their own career. They are both "insiders" and "outsiders" when they work in client organisations (Sturdy et al. 2008) and are expected to present themselves as experts when often they are generalists.

You've got to be everyman to everyone and you can't do that indefinitely without going mad. Long holidays are my way of getting away from it all.

(Consultant, SME)

It is not surprising then that consultants develop "dramaturgical" selves which can provide "front-stage" performances, acting out different roles for clients, employers, families, and colleagues (Whittle 2005). Unfortunately, for consultants "the construction of self-identity can be seen as a constant struggle against the experience of tension, fragmentation and discord arising from different subject positions offered within discourses" (Merilianen et al. 2004). Such contradictions and tensions do not come without effects: the stress, anxiety, and, often, depression experienced by consultants are at least one reason for their high levels of turnover (O'Mahoney 2007).

CASE 8.1

Controlling the Identity

As service, quality, and interpersonal relationships have become more important to customers, the control of employees' emotions, identities, and very selves have become more important to their employers. Foucault (1979, 1981) argued that technologies of surveillance were central to the ability of society and organisations to produce a "self-disciplined" individual: a person who would internalise the requirements of society and forge their identities.

Foucault showed that, in the eighteenth century, a type of prison was designed by Jeremy Bentham. This prison allowed one guard potentially to see any prisoner from a central position without the prisoner knowing whether or not they were actually being watched. The "not knowing" meant that prisoners disciplined themselves. Since then, organisational theorists have shown that factory designs, internet technology, and virtual worlds also use a panopticon design to ensure the compliance of individuals (Burrell and Dale 2003; Townley 1993).

- Can you think of any other examples?

■ The Global Perspective: Colonisation and Capitalism

The Neo-Liberal Agenda

Finally, and briefly, it is worth mentioning the role of consultants in spreading both the ideology and practice of neo-liberal, free market economics. Whilst this is a fledgling area, especially for those who study management consultants directly, it is increasingly noticeable that academics in the area of political relations and the sociology of globalisation consistently name management consultancies as one of the central institutions leading to the encroachment of capitalism in new areas. By "new areas" I do not simply mean developing countries that are being transformed to fully fledged neo-classical economies but also the privatisation, in some form, of those public companies that, in Western countries, are increasingly being opened up to competition and private investment.

For most commentators, the last fifty years have seen a rolling out of neo-classical economics from Western Europe and the USA to virtually every other country in the world. In part, this was prompted by an attempt in the Cold War to remove Socialist, or worse, Communist, governments from countries wherever possible, but in recent years it has formed part of a "development" agenda (Stiglitz 2002). This, more recent, agenda has focused on a liberalisation project spearheaded by the World Bank, the International Monetary Fund (IMF), the World Trade Organisation (WTO), and the governments of the USA and Western Europe.

Liberalisation works in many ways, but a key mechanism is to link aid or loans, from either Western governments or the World Bank, to economic reform in the beneficiary state. Economic reform might include privatisation of public utilities such as health, water, and electricity, the opening up of local firms to foreign ownership, free-trade agreements enabling Western countries to compete with local producers, or the deregulation of industrial and labour laws (Baffoe-Bonnie and Khayum 2003). The failures and successes of this approach have been discussed elsewhere (Stiglitz 2002) and will not be rehearsed here.

Closer to home, the rolling-out of the neo-liberal agenda has focused on the privatisation of public companies and, where this is not politically viable, the partnering with private industry in coalitions such as the public–private partnerships (PPP) and private finance initiatives (PFI). In addition to this has been a new philosophy and approach to public sector management termed New Public Management (NPM) which has focused on the introduction of private sector management techniques such as the introduction of performance management, targets, e-business systems, contracting out, fragmentation of bureaucracies, flatter hierarchies, and an orientation around profits (Lane 2000).

Missionaries for Capitalism

With regard to the development of neo-liberal policies in developing countries, consultants have played a key role in apportioning the loans and aid provided by the World Bank and Western governments. In addition, consultants have also been pivotal in realising the reforms that necessarily accompany such funds. The World Bank, for example, employs 80,000 consultants in Africa alone (Baffoe-Bonnie and Khayum 2003), and the biggest spender in the UK government on consultants is not the NHS or the Department of Defence but the Department for International Development (DfID) who spent £255m on consultants in 2008.

The work that consultancies perform for global financial institutions rarely involves ensuring that aid is spent correctly. More often it is linked to implementing the reforms of public utilities, law, and governments mandated by lending institutions. Many of the consultancies involved, such as Adam Smith International, actively proclaim their commitment to the vision of a free-market economy, despite the failure of World Bank-sponsored privatisation projects in Tanzania, Armenia, Zimbabwe, and India (WDM 2007).

Consultants, however, do not simply act as the implementers of privatisation and other policies but, as they have so much to gain from fees in supporting these projects, they actively promote and lobby for this kind of work: "Consultancy firms such as PWC and PMG have been active in promoting privatization efforts in [South Africa] often acting as consultants to local governments investigating their . . . options . . . These same firms are also part of large pro-privatisation consortia in Europe and the US, lobbying for the expansion and acceleration of [privatisation]" (McDonald and Ruiters 2005). This practice has been criticised not only by human rights organisations and various charities, but also by government watchdogs, such as the Environmental Audit Committee:

> We have a tendency to pay consultants. We are talking millions in the aid budget to advise developing countries on reforming their water sector and invariably these consultants are recommending privatization. That is what they do. We have DfiD paying for public relations exercises to convince unwilling populations that they should support privatization. (EAC 2006: 98)

Consultants also play a central role in the promotion and enablement of offshoring and outsourcing work from Western companies to developing countries where labour is considerably cheaper. Whilst such activities undoubtedly help employment and skills in the host country, they are a politically sensitive issue in the West (Peet and Born 2003). This form of work, together with the market growth in merging economies, has led to all the major consultancies setting up offices in developing nations.

CASE 8.2

The Trap

In 1997 Adam Curtis produced a three-part documentary called *The Trap* which is freely available on Google Videos. The film shows how consultancies, business schools, and corporations have increasingly dominated government decision-making, social culture, and education. This "businessification" of society, he argues, has increasingly taken the form of a competitive individualism which breaks the ties of love, trust, and emotion that hold society together.

Whilst terms such as "goals", "strategy", and "plans" have long been common in private sector management, they have gradually spread, not just to the public sector, but to the everyday lives of normal people. Students are encouraged to maintain "personal learning portfolios", teachers are expected to create "reflexive planning charts", and dustmen have transformed into "waste management solutions" (Collins 2000). As Collins argues, these phrases are not simply buzzwords, but instead actively legitimise and reinforce the image of management and consultancy as something complex, scientific, and out of reach for the general public.

- Should any part of society (e.g. the arts or academia) be kept separate from the profit motive? Why?

If the ideas in these documentaries interest you, you might also like *The Fog of War* (2004), *Enron: The Smartest Guys in the Room* (2005), and *The Corporation* (2004).

Aiding and Abetting the New Public Sector Management

In his excellent book *Building the New Managerialist State*, Dennis Saint-Martin (2000) shows how think-tanks, banks, international institutions, governments, but above all, management consultants, all aimed, from the 1980s onwards, to introduce private sector management techniques into the public sector. The political opportunity for reform was presented in the 1980s as a reaction against the high costs of the public sector, the strength of the trade union movement, and the declining manufacturing performance of Britain and the USA against countries like Germany and Japan. Consultancies, he suggests, not only provided a mechanism for implementing the neo-liberal agenda of the Conservative government, but also "the use of consultants and their ideas gave credibility to managerialist policies because they came from the private sector" (2000: 3).

Furthermore, as with international development, consultants did not simply act as implementers of government policy but actively campaigned for an acceleration of existing liberalisation and privatisation policies. As we show in Chapter 9, consultants lobbied ministers, undertook internships, and provided "agenda setting" talks and training free of charge for influential decision-makers in the public sector to encourage what they termed "modernisation" (Craig and Brooks 2006). The massive increase in public sector consultancy contracts was the inevitable prize that emerged from successful lobbying by consultancies in the 1980s and 1990s.

■ Chapter Summary

This chapter has outlined the main critical themes of academic literature, with the most salient points as follows:

- Consultants epitomise the rise of the "knowledge worker" in the modern economy.
- Consultants contribute to the creation and diffusion of management innovations, but are perhaps not as innovative as they purport.
- Consultants direct considerable efforts towards finding, applying, commodifying, and legitimising their knowledge.
- Whilst consultancy is not a "strong" profession and shows few signs of becoming one it does exhibits some characteristics of a profession.
- There are a number of sources of uncertainty in dealing with consultancies but, equally, a number of mechanisms for dealing with such ambiguity.
- Consulting identities are complex, fragmented, and contested. This creates difficulties for both consultants and those wishing to classify them.
- Consultants have been integral to the diffusion of neo-liberal capitalism by both selling and implementing vision, policies, and rhetoric.

Student Exercise

In small groups of two or three prepare a ten-minute PowerPoint presentation on one of the following topics, presenting an argument for one perspective:

1 Should consultants be forced to professionalise?

2 Should consultants actively promote privatisation?

3 Is consultancy a force for good, bad, or neither? Should it be?

4 What metaphor or identity best describes what consultants are?

Present your argument to the rest of the class.

Discussion Questions

• What is a critical perspective? How does it differ from a unitarist/managerialist perspective?

• What are the arguments for and against the compulsory professionalisation of the consulting industry?

• What is liminality? How can it help describe consulting interactions?

Further Reading

There are relatively few books that provide a good critique of the consulting industry. The vast majority simply adhere to the managerialist emphasis on "what works". Those that do provide a strong critical perspective include:

• Clark, T., and Fincham, R. (2002). *Critical Consulting*. Oxford: Blackwell Publishing.

• Furusten, S., and Werr, A. (eds) (2005). *Dealing with Confidence*. Copenhagen: Copenhagen Business School Press.

• Kipping, M., and Engwall, L. (2002). *Management Consulting: Emergence and Dynamics of a Knowledge Industry*. Oxford: Oxford University Press.

• Sturdy, A., Clark, T., Fincham, R., and Handley, K. (2009). *Management Consultancy: Boundaries and Knowledge in Action*. Oxford: Oxford University Press.

Additionally, the vast majority of authors referenced in this chapter tend to write from a critical perspective. It is especially worth keeping an eye out for the work of Anthony Buono, Mattais Kipping, Andreas Werr, Andrew Sturdy, Matts Alvesson, and Tim Clark.

References

Abbinnett, R. (2003). *Culture and Identity: Critical Theories*. Beverly Hills, CA: Sage.

Abrahamson, E. (1996). Management Fashion. *Academy of Management Review*, 21: 254–85.

Al-Amoudi, I. (2007). Redrawing Foucault's Social Ontology: Towards a Critical Realist Reading of Michel Foucault. *Organization*, 14 (4): 543–63.

Alvesson, M. (1994). Organizations as Rhetoric: Knowledge Intensive Firms and the Struggle with Ambiguity. *Journal of Management Studies*, 30 (5): 997–1015.

—— (2001). Knowledge Work: Ambiguity, Image and Identity. *Human Relations*, 54 (7): 863–86.

—— (2004). *Knowledge Work and Knowledge-Intensive Firms*. Oxford: Oxford University Press.

—— and Johansson, A. W. (2002). Professionalism and Politics in Management Consultancy Work. In T. Clark and R. Fincham (eds), *Critical Consulting*. Oxford: Blackwell, 228–46.

—— and Robertson, M. (2006). The Best and the Brightest: The Construction, Significance and Effects of Elite Identities in Consulting Firms. *Organization*, 13 (2).

—— and Willmott, H. (2003). *Studying Management Critically*. Beverly Hills, CA: Sage.

Amoore, L. (2004). The Risk Masters: Management Consulting and the Politics of Uncertainty, paper presented at Constructing World Orders Conference, 9–11 September, The Hague.

Argyris, C. (2000). *Flawed Advice and the Management Trap*. New York: Oxford University Press.

Armbrüster, T. (2006). *The Economics and Sociology of Management Consulting*. Cambridge: Cambridge University Press.

Baffoe-Bonnie, J., and Khayum, M. (2003). *Contemporary Economic Issues in Developing Countries*. Westport, CN: Greenwood Publishing Group.

Bauman, Z. (2001). *The Individualized Society*. Cambridge: Polity.

BBC News (2009). Accenture Ends Tiger Woods Sponsorship Deal. 14 December. www.bbc.co.uk

Beck, U. (1992). *Risk Society: Towards a New Modernity*, trans. Mark Ritter. London: Sage.

Berglund, J., and Werr, A. (2000). The Invincible Character of Management Consulting Rhetoric: How One Blends Incommensurates while Keeping them Apart. *Organization*, 7: 633–56.

Birkinshaw, J., Hamel, G., and Mol, M. (2008). Management Innovation. *Academy of Management Review*, 33 (4): 825–45.

Bloomfield, B. P., and Vurdubakis, T. (1994). Re-presenting Technology: IT Consultancy Reports as Textual Reality Constructions. *Sociology*, 28 (2): 455–78.

Brett Howell Associates (2007). *Financial Benchmarks: UK Management Consultants Survey*. BHA.

Brockhaus, W. (1977). Prospects for Malpractice Suits in the Business Consulting Profession. *Journal of Business*, 50 (1): 70–5.

Burrell, G., and Dale, K. (2003). Building Better Worlds? Architecture and Critical Management Studies. In M. Alvesson and H. Willmott (eds), *Studying Management Critically*. Beverly Hills, CA: Sage, 177–96.

Casey, C. (1995). *Work, Self and Society*. London: Routledge.

Cassidy, J. (2002). *Dot Con: The Greatest Story Ever Sold*. London: Harper Collins.

Ciccotello, C. S., Grant, C. T., and Dickie, M. (2003). Will Consult for Food! Rethinking Barriers to Professional Entry in the Information Age. *American Business Law Journal*, 40.

Clark, T. (1993). The Market Provision of Management Services, Information Asymmetries and Service Quality: Some Market Solutions: An Empirical Example. *British Journal of Management*, 4: 235–51.

—— and Greatbach, D. (2002). Knowledge Legitimation and Audience Affiliation through Storytelling: The Example of Management Gurus. In T. Clark and R. Fincham (eds), *Critical Consulting*. Oxford: Blackwell.

—— and Salaman, G. (1996). The Management Guru as Organizational Witchdoctor. *Organization*, 3 (1): 85–107.

Clegg, S., and Dunkerley, D. (1980). *Organization, Class and Control*. London: Taylor and Francis.

—— Kornberger, M., and Rhodes, C. (2004). Noise, Parasites and Translation: Theory and Practice in Management Consulting. *Management Learning*, 35 (1): 31–44.

Coleman, J., Katz, E., and Menzel, H. (1966). *Medical Innovations*. New York: Bobbs-Merrill.

Collins, D. (2000). *Management Fads and Buzzwords: Critical-Practical Perspectives*. London: Routledge.

Cortada, J. (1998). *The Rise of the Knowledge Worker*. Maryland Heights, MO: Elsevier.

Coulson-Thomas, C. (1994). Business Process Re-engineering: Nirvana or Nemesis for Europe? In C. Coulson-Thomas (ed.), *Business Process Re-engineering: Myth and Reality*. London: Kogan Page.

Craib, I. (1992). *Anthony Giddens*. London: Taylor and Francis.

Craig, D. (2005). *Rip Off: The Scandalous Story of the Management Consulting Money Machine*. London: Original Book Company.

—— and Brooks, R. (2006). *Plundering the Public Sector*. London: Constable.

Crucini, C. (1999). The Development and Professionalisation of the Italian Consulting Industry after WWII. *Business and Economic History*, 28 (2).

Curtis, A. (2007). *The Trap*. Television documentary, BBC2.

Czarniawska, B., and Mazza, C. (2003). Consulting as a Liminal Space. *Human Relations*, 56 (3): 267–90.

Czarniawska-Joerges, B., and Sevon, G. (1996). *Translating Organizational Change*. Berlin: Walter de Gruyter.

Day, J. (2004). Dynamics of the Client–Consultant Relationship. In J. P. Thommen and A. Richter (eds), *Management Consulting Today: Strategies for a Challenging Environment*. Bornhofen: Gabler.

Delaney, J. R., and Sockell, D. (1992). Do Company Ethics Training Programs Make a Difference? An Empirical Analysis. *Journal of Business Ethics*, 11: 719–27.

EAC (2006). Trade, Development and Environment: The Role of DFID. Tenth Report of Session 2005–6. Environmental Audit Committee, House of Commons.

Economist (2008). Giving Advice in Adversity. 25 September.

Elkjær, B., Flensburg, P., Mouritsen, J., and Willmott, H. (1991). The Commodification of Expertise: The Case of Systems Development Consulting. *Accounting, Management and Information Technologies*, 1 (2): 139–56.

Engwall, L., and Kipping, M. (2002). Introduction: Management Consulting as a Knowledge Industry. In M. Kipping and L. Engwall (eds), *Management Consulting: Emergence and Dynamics of a Knowledge Industry*. Oxford: Oxford University Press.

Faust, M. (2002). Consultancies as Actors in Knowledge Arena: Evidence from Germany. In M. Kipping and L. Engwall (eds), *Management Consulting*. Oxford: Oxford University Press.

Fincham, F. (1999). The Consultant–Client Relationship: Critical Perspectives on the Management of Organizational Change. *Journal of Management Studies*, 36 (3): 335–51.

Fincham, R. (2002). Charisma versus Technique: Differentiating the Expertise of Management Gurus and Management Consultants. In T. Clark and R. Fincham, *Critical Consulting*. Oxford: Blackwell.

—— (2003). The Agent's Agent. *International Studies of Management and Organisation*, 32 (4): 67–86.

—— (2006). Knowledge Work as Occupational Strategy: Comparing IT and Management Consulting. *New Technology, Work and Employment*, 21 (1): 16–28.

Foucault, M. (1979). *Discipline and Punish*. Harmondsworth: Penguin.

—— (1981). The History of Sexuality, vol. i. Harmondsworth: Penguin.

Fox, A. (1974). *Beyond Contract: Work, Power and Trust Relations*. London: Faber and Faber.

Furusten, S., and Werr, A. (eds) (2005). *Dealing with Confidence: The Construction of Need and Trust in Management Advisory Services*. Copenhagen: Copenhagen Business School Press.

Giddens, A. (1990). *The Consequences of Modernity*. Cambridge: Polity.

—— (1992). *The Transformation of Intimacy: Sexuality, Love and Eroticism in Modern Societies*. Cambridge: Polity.

Glückler, J. (2005). Making Embeddedness Work: Social Practice Institutions in Foreign Consulting Markets. *Environment and Planning A*, 37: 1727–50.

—— and Armbrüster, T. (2003). Bridging Uncertainty in Management Consulting: The Mechanisms of Trust and Networked Reputation. *Organization Studies*, 24 (2): 269–97.

Grey, C. (2002). The Fetish of Change. *Tamara: Journal of Critical Postmodern Science*, 2 (2): 1–19.

Grint, K., and Case, P. (2000). Now Where Are We? BPR Lotus-Eaters and Corporate Amnesia. In D. Knights and H. Willmott (eds), *The Reengineering Revolution: Critical Studies of Corporate Change*. London: Sage.

Gross, A., and Poor, J. (2008). The Global Management Consultancy Sector. *Business Economics*. October.

Groß, C., and Kieser, A. (2006). Are Consultants Moving towards Professionalisation? In R. Greenwood, R. Suddaby, and M. McDougald (eds), *Professional Service Firms*. Emerald Group Publishing.

Haas, M. (2006). Acquiring and Applying Knowledge in Transnational Teams: The Roles of Cosmopolitans and Locals. *Organization Science*, 17 (3): 367–84.

Hamel, G. (2007). *The Future of Management*. Cambridge, MA: Harvard Business School Press.

Hargadon, A., and Sutton, R. (1997). Technology Brokering and Innovation in a Product Development Firm. *Administrative Science Quarterly*, 42: 716–49.

Heusinkveld, S., and Benders, J. (2003). Between Professional Dedication and Corporate

Design: Exploring Forms of New Concept Development in Consultancies. *International Studies of Management and Organization*, 32 (4): 104–22.

Huczynski, A. (1993). *Management Gurus: What Makes Them and How to Become One*. London: Taylor and Francis.

IPSOS/MORI (2007). *Paying More and Getting Less: What Clients Think about Consultancy*. Report for Ernst and Young.

Johnson, T. (1995). Governmentality and the Institutionalization of Expertise. In T. Johnson, G. Larkin, and M. Saks (eds), *Health Professions and the State in Europe*. London: Routledge.

Jones, M., and Thwaites, R. (2000). Dedicated Followers of Fashion. In D. Knights and H. Willmott (eds), *The Reengineering Revolution: Critical Studies of Corporate Change*. London: Sage.

Kennedy Information (2003). *The Client-Side Intelligence Report: Purchasing Behaviour, Brand Awareness and Firm Perceptions*. Peterborough.

Kipping, M. (1999). American Management Consulting Companies in Western Europe, 1920 to 1990: Products, Reputation, and Relationships. *Business History Review*, 73 (2): 190–220.

—— (2002). Consultancies, Institutions and the Diffusion of Taylorism in Britain, Germany and France, 1920s–1950s. In Michael Wood (ed.), *F. W. Taylor*. London: Taylor and Francis.

—— and Engwall, L. (2002). *Management Consulting: Emergence and Dynamics of a Knowledge Industry*. Oxford: Oxford University Press.

—— Kirkpatrick, I., and Muzio, D. (2006). Overly Controlled or out of Control: Management Consultants and the New Corporate Professionalism. In J. Craig (ed.), *Production Values: Futures for Professionalism*. London: Demos.

Kitay, J., and Wright, C. (2004). Take the Money and Run? Boundaries and Consultants' Roles. *Service Industries Journal*, 24 (3): 1–19.

Knights, D., and Willmott, H. (2000). The Reengineering Revolution: An Introduction. In D. Knights and H. Willmott, *The Reengineering Revolution: Critical Studies of Corporate Change*. London: Sage.

Kyro, P., and Enqvist, R. (1997). *Management Consulting as a Developer of SMEs*. Helsinki: PKT Consulting Forum.

Lane, J. E. (2000). *New Public Management*. London: Routledge.

McDonald, D., and Ruiters, G. (2005). *The Age of Commodity*. London: Earthscan.

McKenna, C. (1995). The Origins of Modern Management Consulting. *Business and Economic History*, 24 (1): 51–8.

—— (2006). *The World's Newest Profession*. Oxford: Oxford University Press.

—— (2007). Give Professionalization a Chance! Why Management Consulting May Yet Become a Full Profession. In S. Ackroyd, D. Muzio, and J.-F. Chanlat (eds), *New Directions in the Study of Expert Labour: Medicine, Law and Management Consultancy*. London: Palgrave Macmillan.

McKinsey & Company (2004). *Risk, Control, and Performance*. New York: McKinsey & Co.

Marx, K. (1992). Capital, i: *A Critique of Political Economy*. London: Penguin.

—— and Engels, F. (1848). *The Communist Manifesto*. New York: Signet.

Merilianen, S., Tienari, J., Thomas, R., and Davies, A. (2004). Management Consultant Talk: A Cross-Cultural Comparison of Normalising Discourse and Resistance. *Organization*, 11 (2): 539–64.

Mowery, D. C. (1988). *International Collaborative Ventures in US Manufacturing*. Cambridge, MA: Ballinger.

Moxton, R., Roehl, T., and Truitt, J. (1988). International Cooperative Ventures in the Commercial Aircraft Industry: Gains, Sure but What's my Share? In F. Contractor and P. Lorange (eds), *Cooperative Strategies in International Business*. Lexington, MA: Lexington Books.

Muzio, D., Kirkpatrick, I., and Ackroyd, S. (2010). Professions and Professionalism in Management Consulting. In T. Clark and M. Kipping (eds), *The Oxford Handbook of Management Consulting*. Oxford: Oxford University Press.

Myers, Paul S. (1996). *Knowledge Management and Organizational Design*. London: Butterworth-Heinemann.

Neitz, M. J. (1987). *Charisma and Community: A Study of Religious Commitment within the Charismatic Renewal*. Englewood Cliffs, NJ: Transaction Publishers.

Newell, S., Swan, J., and Kautz, K. (2001). The Role of Funding Bodies in the Creation and Diffusion of Management Fads and Fashions. *Organization*, 8 (1): 97–120.

OED (1989). *Oxford English Dictionary*, 2nd edn. Oxford: Oxford University Press.

O'Mahoney, J. (2007). Disrupting Identity: Trust and Angst in Management Consulting. In S. Bolton (ed.), *Searching for the H in Human Resource Management*. London: Sage.

—— Adams, R., Antonocoupoulu, E., and Neeley, A. (2008). *Contemporary and Future Challenges in the UK Management Consulting Industry*. ESRC/AIM.

O'Shea, J. (1998). *Dangerous Company: Management Consultants and the Businesses They Save and Ruin*. London: Penguin.

Peet, R., and Born, B. (2003). *The Unholy Trinity: The IMF, World Bank and WTO*. New York: Zed Books.

Pinault, L. (2001). *Consulting Demons: Inside the Unscrupulous World of Global Corporate Consulting*. New York: Harper Business.

Ram, M. (1999). Managing Consultants in a Small Firm: A Case-Study. *Journal of Management Studies*, 36 (6).

Rassam, C., and Oates, D. (1991). *Management Consultancy: The Inside Story*. London: Mercury.

Reed, M. I. (1996). Expert Power and Control in Late Modernity: An Empirical Review and Theoretical Synthesis. *Organization Studies*, 17 (4): 573–97.

Robertson, M., and Swan, J. (2003). Control—What Control . . .: Culture and Ambiguity within a Knowledge Intensive Firm. *Journal of Management Studies*, 40 (4): 831–58.

Rogers, E. (1983). *Diffusion of Innovations*. New York: Free Press.

Sahlin-Andersson, K., and Engwall, L. (2002). Carriers, Flows and Sources of Management Knowledge. In K. Sahlin-Andersson and L. Engwall (eds), *The Expansion of Management Knowledge: Carriers, Ideas and Circulation*. Stanford, CA: Stanford University Press.

Saint-Martin, D. (2004). *Building the New Managerialist State*. Oxford: Oxford University Press.

Sako, M. (2006). Outsourcing and Offshoring: Implications for Productivity of Business Services. *Oxford Review of Economic Policy*, 22 (4).

Schuyt, T., and Schuijt, J. (1998). Rituals and Rules: About Magic in Consultancy. *Journal of Organizational Change Management*, 11 (5): 399–406.

Smart, B. (1999). *Facing Modernity*. London: Sage.

Starbuck, W. H. (1976). Organizations and their Environments. In M. D. Dunnette (ed.), *Handbook of Industrial and Organizational Psychology*. Chicago, IL: Rand McNally, 1069–123.

—— (1992). Learning by Knowledge-Intensive Firms. *Journal of Management Studies*, 29 (6): 713–40.

Stiglitz, J. (2002). *Globalization and its Discontents*. London: Penguin.

Sturdy, A. (1997a). The Consultancy Process: An Insecure Business. *Journal of Management Studies*, 34 (3): 389–413.

—— (1997b). The Adoption of Management Ideas and Practices. *Management Learning*, 35 (2): 155–79.

—— (2006). *Knowledge Evolution in Action: Consultancy–Client Relationships*. ESRC Research Report, RES-334-25-0004.

—— Schwarz, M., and Spicer, A. (2006). Guess Who's Coming to Dinner? Structures and Uses of Liminality in Strategic Management Consultancy. *Human Relations*, 59 (5): 929–60.

—— Clark, T., Fincham, R., and Handley, K. (2008a). Management Consultancy and Humor in Action and Context. In S. Fineman (ed.), *The Emotional Organization*. Oxford: Blackwell, 134–53.

—— Handley, K., Clark, T., and Fincham, R. (2008b). Rethinking the Role of Management Consultants as Disseminators of Business Knowledge. In H. Scarborough (ed.), *The Evolution of Business Knowledge*. Oxford: Oxford University Press.

Suddaby, R., and Greenwood, R. (2001). Colonizing Knowledge: Commodification as a Dynamic of Jurisdictional Expansion in Professional Service Firms. *Human Relations*, 54 (7): 933–53.

Swan, J., and Newell, S. (1995). The Role of Professional Associations in Technology Diffusion. *Organization Studies*, 16 (5): 847–74.

Tagliaventi, M. R., and Mattarelli, E. (2006). The Role of Networks of Practice, Value Sharing, and Operational Proximity in Knowledge Flows between Professional Groups. *Human Relations*, 59 (3): 291–319.

Tolbert, P., and Zucker, L. (1983). Institutional Sources of Change in the Formal Structure of Organizations: The Diffusion of Civil Service Reform. *Administrative Science Quarterly*, 28: 22–39.

Townley, B. (1993). Foucault, Power/Knowledge, and its Relevance for Human Resource Management. *Academy of Management Review*, 18 (3): 518–45.

Universum (2007). *The Universum IDEAL Employer Rankings*. Universumusa.com.

Von Krogh, G., Roos, J., and Kleine, D. (1998). *Knowing in Firms*. London: Sage.

Wall Street Journal (1997). Frederick Taylor, Early Century Management Consultant. 13 June.

WDM (2007). Down the Drain: How Aid is Being Wasted on Water Privatisation. World Development Movement, January. www.wdm.org.uk.

Weber, M. (1947). *Theory of Social and Economic Organization*, trans. A. R. Anderson and Talcott Parsons. New York: Free Press.

—— (1968). *Max Weber on Economy and Society*. Somerville, NJ: Bedminster Press.

—— (1970). *From Max Weber: Essays in Sociology*. London: Routledge.

Whittle, A. (2005). Preaching and Practising Flexibility: Implications for Theories of Subjectivity at Work. *Human Relations*, 58 (10): 1301–22.

—— (2006). The Paradoxical Repertoires of Management Consultancy. *Journal of Organizational Change Management*, 19 (4): 424–43.

Wood, P. (2002). *The Rise of Consultancy and the Prospect for Regions*. In T. Clark and R. Fincham (eds), *Critical Consulting: New Perspectives on the Management Advice Industry*. Oxford: Oxford University Press, 50–73.

Wright, C., and Kitay, J. (2004). Spreading the Word: Gurus, Consultants and the Diffusion of the Employee Relations Paradigm in Australia. *Management Learning*, 35: 271–86.

Studying Consulting Critically

Andrew Sturdy

■ Understanding Academic Critiques

I have been asked to write a few words on why theories are important in studying consultancy and, in particular, what the point is in being critical whilst doing consulting research. In other words perhaps, why be so academic and negative about consultancy?

First, theory (i.e. explanation) is always present in any description of a social system, whether we make it explicit or not. However, it is often invisible or implicit to those actors embedded within it. The absence of an explicit theory can hide the assumptions being made by different actors about how they see the world and what they are trying to achieve. This makes it more difficult to judge the value and independence of what is being said. Making a theory explicit, therefore, helps us make clear how and why different stakeholders and social systems interact in the way they do.

Secondly, and my main focus, critique is important as a catalyst for debate and change. It puts another point of view across which might not otherwise get heard. In other words, critique can be highly constructive and is not simply concerned with being negative—although it can sometimes seem that way to practitioners and students.

Critique can also seem negative because we often take for granted certain assumptions about the way things are or should be. For example, most mainstream research assumes that helping management do their jobs better is a good thing for everyone (i.e. that management and other employees share all the same interests). This is not always the case or, at least, is a matter of perspective. Asking the question of who gains and loses from consultancy might then point to a more pluralist and inclusive approach to organisational interventions.

■ Critiquing Consultancy

In the context of consultancy, critique is especially interesting as the industry and occupation have, in many contexts, become objects of popular critique. Criticisms of public sector use of consultants, for example, can be found in the business and news media, from both the left and right sides of the political spectrum.

Criticism of consultancy	Implied concern
Rationalisers	Employee job security. Do the ends justify the means?
Ideologues/neo-imperialists	Maintaining local cultures and conditions
Money wasters	Fairness of rewards/efficiency of work
Accountability	Lack of transparency of power/legitimate responsibility
Self-interested/parasitic	Lack of ethics, ownership or humanity

Table 8.1. Popular consulting critiques and implied values

As I have argued elsewhere (Sturdy 2009), these criticisms cannot be wholly accounted for as a form of defensiveness, scapegoating, or resentment. They suggest some implicit concerns and values which could inform a wider basis for critical perspectives on consulting (see Table 8.1).

In this sense, then, critique is the mainstream. Indeed, there is far more and far stronger criticism of consultancy in the popular press than in academic research. If this is the case, the question that is pertinent is why is there so little critique in academic accounts?

First, many management academics who write about consultancy are also consultants as well. This is both a strength and a weakness—they have direct and deep knowledge of their own consulting, but they are unlikely to take a position which fundamentally challenges the interests of consultants. They also cannot so easily take an outsider's view of consultants, in the way that external consultants sometimes do themselves of their client organisations.

Secondly, even if they are not consultants, most management academics' prime interest is a practical one of improving management techniques or organisational performance. This perspective often assumes incorrectly that all stakeholders share the same interests and rarely considers the wider consequences of consultancy interventions on employees, society, or taxpayers.

Thirdly, being critical of consultancy may endanger academics' own interests of gaining access to do research or to participate in broader industry communities and networks. This is a lesser concern given that many clients/managers, for example, are also critical of consultants. Additionally, it is fair to state that, outside of the academic community, very few people read academic accounts of consultants!

Fourthly, many academics are not especially interested in being critical of consultancy in a political or radical sense. They are interested in being different. Indeed, in terms of publications (and therefore their careers), they have to say something which is seen as adding to (i.e. is different from) existing literature. Reproducing or restating the above critiques would not be novel. Furthermore, publishing in top academic journals requires that contributions should say something theoretical in addition to the empirical. Indeed, many studies simply use consultancy as a context to say something of wider and theoretical significance (see Sturdy et al. 2006 for an example of this).

Finally, when academic work is critical, it is often in the sense of challenging taken-for-granted assumptions or common claims such as that of the concrete nature of consultants' expertise (Clark 1995), their outsider status, or their innovation (Sturdy et al. 2009). This *limited* sense of criticality is illustrated in the edited collection entitled *Critical Consulting* (Clark and Fincham 2002). This is important work because it enhances understanding and can offer up alternative approaches or have policy implications. It is not the same, however, as what has become known as Critical Management Studies (CMS) where there is an agenda towards some form of emancipation or revealing patterns of power and inequality—"speaking truth to power".

■ A Different Perspective?

It may seem bizarre that I have spent most of this piece setting out why there is so little critical work on consultancy as an argument for a critical approach. But if we were to accept the central consulting premiss that an alternative perspective can be helpful or, if not, at least prompt useful reflection, then different approaches are needed. Academics and universities can (and should) play a key role here.

Why is there such a concern about critical perspectives, when such work is relatively rare? Is it because none of us likes to think that what we are interested in or aspire to is in some way problematic? We also don't generally like outsiders telling us this—academic accounts of consultancy are about as welcome as consulting studies of academics in their different contexts. But we each have something to say and a theory and an agenda too, even if these are not always made clear!

In conclusion, if change really is of interest to industry stakeholders, then non-critical accounts of current arrangements don't help. Change comes from new ideas and critique. It is just that we don't always like what we hear. This makes things uncomfortable, not wrong.

References

Clark, T. (1995). *Managing Consultants: Consultancy as the Management of Impressions*. Buckingham: Open University Press.

——and Fincham, R. (2002). *Critical Consulting: New Perspectives on the Management Advice Industry*. Oxford: Blackwell.

Sturdy, A. J. (2009). Popular Consultancy Critiques and a Politics of Management Learning? *Management Learning*, forthcoming.

——Schwarz, M., and Spicer, A. (2006). Guess Who's Coming to Dinner? Structures and Uses of Liminality in Strategic Management Consultancy. *Human Relations*, 59 (7): 929–60.

——Handley, K., Clark, T., and Fincham, R. (2009). *Management Consultancy, Boundaries and Knowledge in Action*. Oxford: Oxford University Press.

9

The Ethics of Consultancy

Chapter Objectives

Most chapters and articles on consulting ethics do three things. First, they state that ethics is very important to being a consultant. Second, they provide a code of ethics to guide consulting practice. Finally, they provide "ethical dilemmas" for would-be consultants to discuss. This chapter critiques this approach arguing that, despite the burgeoning interest in corporate social resposibility, ethical codes, and other pursuits, ethical practice in consulting is not getting any better. The reason, this chapter suggests, is because consulting ethics are increasingly being made the responsibility of the individual consultant rather than the institutions and structures which envelop consulting practice. Such an emphasis, it is argued here, ignores the conflicts of interest which often lead to unethical practice. The chapter:

■ Outlines the historical and institutional forces that have led to unethical practice in the consulting industry.

■ Examines the regulatory and voluntary changes that have occurred in consulting in the last ten years.

■ Argues that the responsibility for ethics is increasingly being placed on the shoulders of the individual consultant.

■ Suggests that without efforts to reduce institutional conflicts of interest, ethical practice cannot and will not improve.

■ Considers specific charges that have been made against consultants by academics and the press.

■ The Growth of Ethics?

In recent years, the issue of ethics has become integral to both the theory and practice of consultancy. Textbooks aimed at both academic and practitioner readerships are incomplete without an obligatory chapter on ethical practice and how it can be achieved. The same is true of professional bodies, such as the International Council of Management Consultancy Institutes (ICMCI), and trade associations such as the Management Consultancy Association (MCA), and consultancies themselves, who customarily dedicate a corner of their online presence to an ethical guide, policy, or framework.

In a climate where Corporate Social Responsibility (CSR) has become a focal point for education, business, and the media, the justification for the inclusion of ethics in professional texts is often taken for granted. The current outlook, however, is far removed from that of even twenty years ago, when such policies would have seemed incongruous with the dog-eat-dog mentality of a resurgent capitalism. This relatively sudden shift in the *discourse* of society reflects a growth in public awareness of the impact of capitalism on considerations such as the environment, the poor, and the third world, and also a belief that "bad" capitalism is damaging to things that make a difference to the individual's job, pension, expenditure, and tax. Despite this discourse, however, there is little evidence to suggest that actual practice has become more ethical. Indeed there are a number of indications that consulting practice has developed more potential for harm since the end of the Second World War.

Similar to other advisory professions such as law, medicine, and audit, the consulting industry holds a position of responsibility, both to its clients and to society as a whole. When bad advice is given or projects are poorly implemented, the cost to the client can run into billions. Governments can incur the wrath of voters if taxpayers' money is wasted through badly implemented and poorly advised projects. Worse still, if a consultancy becomes involved in illegal activity such as paying bribes, accepting kick-backs, or accepting consulting payments in exchange for favourable auditing, the consequences of these activities can shake the public's confidence in the economic system.

The charge that consultancy, and, by association, consultants, are occasionally, or even institutionally, incompetent or unethical is therefore a serious one. This impacts not only the reputation of the industry, but also the confidence of the public, economic stability, and, potentially, the policies of the government. Recruiters are increasingly aware that prospective applicants are turned off companies with unethical reputations and are unwilling to work on projects they deem immoral. One recruiter at one of the largest consultancies told me: "recruits are no longer passive. They question what we do and are very proactive in pushing for ethical practices. To be honest, this has been a major driving force of many of the changes we've introduced in that area."

Due in part to its growing importance and influence and in part to the visibility of high-profile failures and scandals, the consulting industry has, in recent years, come under attack from politicians, the popular press, journalists, and critical academics for a number of alleged offences. These include wasting public money in government contracts, selling fads that don't work, taking advantage of managers to sell unnecessary interventions, and encouraging conflicts of interest in their dealings with clients (Craig and Brooks 2006; Kiln 2005). This chapter assesses the validity of these claims and assesses what can be done to improve the situation.

The chapter first outlines the growth of institutional relationships that have led to charges from the media and academics that there are conflicts of interest at the heart of consulting practice. Specifically, it focuses on the institutional relationships between consultants, governments, the IT industry, and audit houses. The chapter then gives an overview of the resulting "crisis of confidence" which some argue has afflicted the consulting industry since 2000. The chapter next considers the charges which academics, journalists, and authors have made against the industry and finds, that whilst some accusations have some validity, they are often prompted by a misunderstanding of the industry and how it operates. Finally, the chapter outlines the methods by which ethical practice is secured in the consulting industry, concentrating specifically on professionalisation and ethical guidelines. However, it also argues that, because these frameworks devolve ethical responsibility to the individual, and not the institution, they can only ever be part of the answer.

■ Institutional Relationships 1950–2000

The ascendancy of consulting ethics is undoubtedly related to the growth of the industry over the last thirty years. In the 1950s, the thousand or so consultants operating in the UK were restricted to relatively technical projects. The impact of a badly implemented project was, therefore, necessarily limited. Whilst early consultancies may have encouraged hard-sell techniques, their ability to damage a large company, let alone sway public confidence in the economic system, was virtually non-existent. However, year-on-year growth in the profitability of consultancies and the size of the projects with which they engaged meant that, from the 1970s onwards, the industry had the potential to cause significant damage to clients and to the wider economy. This was especially so during the period 1995–2007 when the consulting industry trebled in size, spurred by the growth in public sector consulting, IT projects, and outsourcing. For our purposes, this growth both encouraged, and was supported by, strengthening institutional relationships in three key areas: audit, IT, and the government. These are examined in more detail below.

Audit Companies

For professional business service companies with established relationships with blue-chip clients, the post-war boom in the consulting industry offered a strategically aligned market for expansion. Realising the potential for cross-selling consulting services to existing clients, large audit firms, from the 1960s onwards, began to move into the consulting industry. Whilst initially the additional profits were negligible, the growth in consultancy markets meant that by the 1990s, big audit companies such as KPMG, PWC, and Arthur Andersen dominated the consultancy market.

Unsurprisingly, however, concerns emerged regarding the partiality of companies practising both consultancy and auditing services for the same client. Regulators of financial institutions such as the SEC and the Financial Services Authority (FSA) became worried that firms receiving significant consulting fees from a client might be disincentivised to do a thorough job in auditing their accounts and, therefore, could be less likely to expose any malpractice that was found. Indeed, there was mounting evidence, leading up to the turn of the millennium, that such conflicts of interest were, indeed, taking place. In 1998, for example, a company called Waste Management was found to have exaggerated its earnings by $1.7bn with the help of Arthur Andersen, which was simultaneously receiving large consultancy fees from the company (SEC 2001).

Wise to the conflict of interest between audit and consulting functions, the SEC, at the end of the 1990s, advised audit houses to divest their consulting arms. All of these firms (apart from Deloitte) began the process of selling off these lucrative departments leaving the firms with audit, accountancy, and tax functions but with no management consultants in sight. The consulting division of the soon-to-be bankrupt Andersen became Accenture; KPMG's consulting arm became BearingPoint; Ernst & Young's consulting unit was sold to Cap Gemini; and PricewaterhouseCoopers sold its consultancy wing to IBM.

CASE 9.1

Enron, Arthur Andersen, and McKinsey

Established in 1931 as the Northern Natural Gas Company, Enron was the apparent triumph of market deregulation. Growing through acquisitions and aggressive strategies, it had become one of the highest-valued energy companies by 1999. Named as "America's Most Innovative Company" by *Fortune* magazine for six consecutive years, and on *Fortune*'s "100 Best Companies to Work for in America" list in 2000, the company was lauded as an inimitable success by consultants, analysts, and traders. However, in one of the biggest financial exposés of the modern age, it was later revealed that many of Enron's recorded assets and profits were either inflated or simply non-existent. Debts and losses were hidden within an arcane network of "offshore" entities created specifically for the purpose of boosting their own reported profits.

Critical to the fraud was the involvement of Arthur Andersen which provided both consulting and audit services to Enron. Enron was Andersen's second largest client, paying them a total of $52m in 2000, $27m of which was for consulting services. It was this incentive that caused Andersen to overlook several instances of fraud when auditing Enron's books (Frankel et al. 2002). Worse, when the fraud was discovered, Andersen instructed its employees to destroy virtually all the evidence relating to the case, a process which took several weeks (Elkind and McLean 2004).

Another firm fundamental to the practice of Enron was McKinsey, which received up to $10m in consulting fees from Enron. Whilst McKinsey was not implicated in any fraudulent behaviour, it was undoubtedly intrinsic to the culture, structure, and ideas that enveloped Enron at the time. McKinsey encouraged the type of "off-balance sheet" reporting that helped enable the company to hide its losses and exaggerate its income (McKinsey Quarterly 1997), and also introduced the "rank and yank" and "loose–tight" practices that some believe contributed to a culture of arrogance and hubris (Gladwell 2002). Enron used McKinsey for over twenty internal projects and a McKinsey partner, Richard Foster, attended over twenty board meetings at the company. McKinsey also produced two of the "bibles" in use at Enron, *The War for Talent* and *Creative Destruction.* Indeed, not only did McKinsey provide hundreds of consultants for Enron, but it also gave them its CEO, Jeff Skilling, a partner at McKinsey, who was later given a 24-year sentence for his role in the fraud.

- How can conflicts of interest between audit and consultancy services be prevented?
- Should consultancies be accountable for the success of their clients' implementations?
- "Rank and Yank" was an HRM system where employees were graded on their performance from 1 to 5. The bottom 10 per cent of performers each year were fired. What are the pros and cons of this system?

The Government

The relationship between government and the consultancy industry has flourished over the past four decades. In the UK, for example, government spending on consultants increased from £20,000 in 1964, to £830,000 in 1969, to £4.8m in 1972 (Saint-Martin 1998: 337) and then to around a billion pounds in 2006. Similar patterns emerged in most Western countries.

From 1979 onwards, these costs were primarily directed towards modernisation and privatisation projects, but in more recent years government consultancy spending has been targeted more at e-business and IT implementation. As this exponential growth in expenditure has taken place, the public sector market became a key battle ground for consultancies seeking to influence government decision-making through agenda setting. For companies such as Logica, EDS, Accenture, and PA Consulting, which derive over half of their income from public sector projects, building relationships with central government can make the difference of millions to the balance sheet.

These relationships are central to the power relations which govern, not only which consulting projects are initiated and managed, but also the discourse of modernisation which encourages work to be given to consultancies in the first place. These relationships not only involve consultants becoming close to ministers through the usual forms of entertainment budgets, but also consultants actually becoming ministers themselves. Whilst there is a strong reason for encouraging "experts" to join government, the placement of ex-consultants in key government positions allows their old employers preferential access to key decision-makers. Additionally, such placements add to the rhetoric of change and modernisation (Grey 2002) by which "management speak" spreads to colonise new areas.

Consultancy role	Government role
Former UK boss of Accenture, Ian Watmore	Head of the government's e-government project
Former senior executive with Accenture	Director-General of Personnel and Head of the Civil Service Capability Group
Former senior executive with Accenture	Change Director: Cabinet Office
Former managing director at Accenture	Chief Executive: Identity and Passport Service
Former head of a "procurement solutions unit" at Accenture	Commercial Director: Home Office
Former head of research for Andersen Consulting	Secretary of State: Health Secretary of State: Trade and Industry
Senior executive, McKinsey	The head of No. 10 Policy Directorate
Partner, Deloitte	Director-General of NHS IT, and Head of CfH

Table 9.1. Movement of consultants into key government positions

Horrocks (2009) gives a number of examples of key decision-makers in the UK government who championed large consultancy projects but who had significant careers as consultants prior to their government positions. These are outlined in Table 9.1.

Both Horrocks (2009) and Craig and Brooks (2006) also detail a number of government advisers who moved to senior consultancy positions, usually after the "cooling-off" period imposed by the Advisory Committee on Business Appointments (ACOBA). The danger (and reality) here is that ex-ministers then lobby their former government colleagues on behalf of their new employers: arranging meetings, influencing policy, and setting agendas. As Horrocks points out, even the ACOBA admit that they see "a significant number of appointments being offered to former Ministers which will probably entail lobbying current Ministers or officials" (ACOBA 2004: 8). These "revolving-door" relationships, from government to consultancy, raise numerous ethical issues:

- Government officials appointed from consultancies often return from whence they came. This raises the question of whether ministers' decisions to outsource work to consultancies are motivated by efficiency or simply a desire to maximise their employability when they leave.

- These officials often maintain strong links with their previous employer, allowing that organisation preferential access to key decision-makers and thus to influence policy.

- The fact that the decision-maker has come from a consultancy background reinforces the "culture" of modernisation in the government by using the language, methods, and agendas of consultancy firms. This need not be intentional, of course, but consultants are trained from the beginning to focus on change, and its associated expenditure, rather than stability.

• The network of support these officials have will often mean that they use consultancies for free labour such as sponsoring conferences, training employees, secondments, and thought leadership papers. These, again, help set the agenda for consultancy projects.

Countering these claims, it could be argued that consultants, having developed strong working relationships with government and having attained expert knowledge of required systems, are ideal candidates for government positions. It is surely within the government's interest to employ the most qualified and experienced advisers available. The same argument can be used for government employees turning to the private sector. Having developed expertise in a certain area, it would surely be obtuse to prevent a minister from moving into private consultancy.

Government role	Consultancy role
e-Envoy: NHS IT strategy	Consultant at BT (responsible for delivering NHS IT Programme)
Head: Prime Minister's Delivery Unit	Expert principal at McKinsey
Director-General: BBC and Strategy advisor to Tony Blair	Consultant at McKinsey and Partner at Cap Gemini

Table 9.2. Movement of government decision-makers into consultancy roles

IT Companies

Over the last thirty years many consultancy companies have moved into the IT space (e.g. Accenture) and many IT companies have moved into the consulting space (e.g. IBM). The obvious reason for this is that there is considerable consistency between the two endeavours. From the consultancy perspective, it is important that IT solutions are aligned with the business strategy and business needs. Consultancies, therefore, are often asked by clients to assist in:

• Defining an IT strategy.

• Aligning IT to the organisation.

• Designing a business architecture to guide IT work.

• Selecting IT and outsourcing systems and providers.

• Helping ease the business change through IT implementations.

Whereas "pure" management consultancies usually hand over IT development or implementation to technology specialists, companies like Accenture retain the work for themselves. Their rationale for this is that they know best what the business wants and, therefore, would be better placed than a "pure" IT company to ensure that any implementation or development is aligned with the business need. Conversely, companies like IBM have traditionally had to tailor their IT implementation to business requirements identified by either the clients themselves or their appointed consultants. However, arguing that they know technology better than any "pure" management consultancy, these technologists have moved into the consulting space to provide advice on how best to fit business and IT together.

The difficulty with this arrangement, in terms of ethics, is twofold. First, there is the question of how a company that employs Accenture for advice on an IT implementation knows that it is receiving independent advice when Accenture has a vested interest in selling its own solutions. Whilst it is relatively rare for clients to use a service provider to give independent advice, these types of consultancies are capable of setting agendas indirectly. For example, if Accenture is asked to advise on cutting costs in an HRM department, it is likely that it will recommend an outsourced programme where Accenture ends up running the HR for the company. Whilst this practice is not necessarily unethical, there is a potential conflict of interest in the dual role of adviser and the solution provider.

The second issue with an IT/consultancy synthesis is to be found in what are commonly known as kick-backs. A kick-back is a secret rebate of part of a purchase price by the seller to the buyer or to the one who directed or influenced the purchaser to buy from such seller. In the consulting world this often refers to consultants giving "independent" advice to clients on the best IT provider for their problems, whilst receiving payments from that provider. It's like asking your mechanic which car to buy, when he's getting secretly paid by Toyota to advise you in their favour: you will probably not get the best deal and, what's worse, it will undermine trust between you and your adviser.

Kick-backs can occur in many different ways, either at the level of the firm or of the individual. For example, these are real cases which have occurred recently:

1. In 2006, BearingPoint, KPMG, BAH, and Ernst and Young paid around $25m in compensation to the US government who argued that rebates from consultancy fees, of up to 40 per cent, from travel and credit card companies weren't passed on to it. In other words PWC, it is alleged, was charging its clients full-whack expenses but getting rebates from hotels, restaurants, and credit cards that they did not pass on (DOJ 2006). It appears that this is a relatively common trick that consultancies use to maximise the income from their clients whilst minimising their own costs (Craig and Brooks 2006).

2. In 2001, a US army colonel called Moran was wined and dined and offered a job by a consultancy called ISS who wanted to install a global command and control centre. As a result Moran overturned the army evaluation board's recommendation and awarded the contract to ISS. Similarly, an air force official, Darleen, paid over the odds for some Boeing aircraft in exchange for jobs for her, her daughter, and her daughter's fiancé. Both Darleen and Moran ended up in prison (DOJ 2005).

A final ethical consideration with regard to consultancy's association with IT is their involvement in the dotcom bubble of the late 1990s. Many commentators believed that consultancies hyped dotcom companies in part to secure large fees from start-up companies. By 2001, the dotcom industry was patently falling far short of its promises to generate profits and shareholder value. The impact of the hype generated by consultancies, banks, and the press was felt by the whole IT sector and much of the rest of the economy as billions were wiped off the share price of companies that had dabbled in anything with e- or i- in front of a noun. Central to the hyping of the dotcom phenomena was the involvement of thousands of consultants paid for by venture-capital money to help start up and promote e-businesses.

Consultancies were accused (rightly or wrongly) of charging excessive fees, building unrealistic business cases, and contributing to the over-inflation of e-business generally, resulting in unsound investment and excessive share prices. Despite these allegations, it is unlikely that the hype expounded by consultants was any more excitable than that of the media or even the general public. However, perhaps they, more than anyone, should have known better.

We have seen, then, how ethical dilemmas can arise from the relationships between consultancy firms and audit, government, and technology stakeholders. Next we are going to examine the damaging impact of some of these relationships in the early part of this millennium and consider the effectiveness of the methods used to clear up the mess.

■ The Failure of Institutional Reform?

After the dotcom crash and the fall of Enron, the consulting industry was hit hard: growth evaporated, share prices plummeted, and the public image of the industry was tarnished. Arthur Andersen and AD Little collapsed, McKinsey was forced to ask its own partners for hand-outs, and many of the clients that had received advice took their consultants to court. There was, in the words of *The Economist* (31 October 2002), "a crisis of confidence in consulting". This was not simply a crisis in the financial sense, but also a crisis for the reputation of the industry. It is the latter, rather than the former, that has proved its longevity. Hoping to limit scope for unethical behaviour in the future, a number of policies were implemented or pursued which governments hoped would minimise the structural and institutional conflicts of interest which had so tarnished the reputation of the consulting industry at the beginning of the twenty-first century. However, unlike the audit profession, which was provided with strict regulatory processes in the Sarbanes–Oxley legislation, the consulting industry escaped relatively unscathed from the fallout of Enron. The following sections explore how consulting's institutional relationships to audit, government, and IT have changed in response to the crisis. If we examine these three categories, it is clear that whilst there have been some modifications, the industry still maintains some obvious conflicts of interest.

Audit

Although, as we have seen, the SEC encouraged audit houses to sell their consulting divisions, many of these companies had already begun to rebuild this capacity by 2005. This return to consulting was due to a non-competition clause which prevented the likes of KPMG and PWC from offering consulting services for up to five years after the sale of their consultancy arm. However, once this period had expired, all the consultancies quickly and successfully rebuilt their consulting capacity, by re-hiring senior consultants, taking over small consultancies, and (re)starting their graduate recruitment for consultancy.

Initially, competitors were sceptical of the chances of success of this re-entry. Blacksel, the CEO of CapGemini, stated that the audit companies which "can't provide the organisational wherewithal to be credible in execution as well as in advice, may well pick up some work, but they'll have limited aspirations". Accenture's CEO, Thomlinson, argued, "we clearly have much greater breadth and depth. It's not just based around providing advice and reports, but having the capability to deliver results" (Reed et al. 2007). Both predictions were proved wrong, however, when the new consultancy arms brought in significant profits in their first years and growth outstripped competitors during the 2008–9 recession.

So, has the current audit/consulting industry simply reverted back to its unfettered position of pre-Enron days? Well, not entirely. SOX (which only applies to US-listed companies) legislated for systems which prevent, for example, the sale of consultancy services to audit clients. For example, if the auditor of a client is KPMG, they cannot sell SOX consultancy to that client. Other controls have forced reporting and assurance to ensure auditor independence. However, as several critical commentators have pointed out, it is still legal for a company auditing a client to sell many other consulting services to that client and auditors can still refer consulting work to their consultant arms and, indirectly, benefit from this work in the form of bonuses. Moreover, the most common arbitrator of what is ethical or not is the firm's own audit committee. Much of the time, the consultant–client–audit relationship is so complex and confidential that external bodies find conflicts of interest hard to detect. For example, when Agilent Technologies decided to split up into three different companies, Deloitte had 200 people working in several different roles, advising on the IPO of one company, the supply chain of another, and the tax burden of another. Coincidentally, Deloitte also audited the company which was buying one of the spin-offs. The point here is not that anything untoward was necessarily done but that the complexity of achieving transparency in complex situations can mean that regulators find it hard to police these relationships.

Government

Since the year 2000, there have been some institutional changes in the relationship between consultancies and government but few of these have been significant enough to remove the potential for conflicting interests between ministers and senior consultants. The primary biggest change in Western countries has been in the growth procurement centres in the public sector which, as we witnessed in Chapter 2, help government departments control procurement costs and procedures. In the USA, the main procurement centre of expertise is the Office of Federal Procurement Policy (OFPP), whilst in the UK, it is the Office of Government Commerce (OGC), and it is this latter institution that we shall use as an example here.

Established in April 2000, the OGC has developed best-practice principles which govern the procurement of consulting services. Amongst other things, these best-practice policies are aimed at:

- Minimising cosy relationships between business owners and consultants.
- Promoting clear aims and objectives which avoid scope-creep.
- Managing projects effectively to prevent overrun on costs and hours.

Talking to business development (sales) departments in consultancies, it is a common observation that clients, especially in the public sector, have become more sophisticated in their procurement of consultants and that projects are managed more tightly than pre-2000. However, take-up of OGC services remains low in government and consultancies still remain effective at avoiding procurement processes where possible. Interviews with consultants reveal that it is much easier to avoid procurement if one is already working on an existing project within a department. For example, if you are a consultant working in a department on some strategy work, and you know another project is coming up, it is often possible to talk informally to the business owner so to avoid procurement processes.

Moreover, the importance of agenda setting should not be underestimated: when a consultancy is working within a department, they have ample opportunity to influence the direction and requirements of that department to make it more likely that their consultancy will be used in the future. For example, if consultancy X has a strong security department compared to its competitors it is likely to push the agenda of security with its existing clients by providing "free" talks, research, training, conferences, and white papers on the need for security. This is a relatively common but very under-researched method by which consultancies can influence the thinking of their clients.

However, the improvements in objectivity and independence engendered by the OGC have been neutralised by the unwavering relationship between consultants and ministers in central government. The "modernisation project" of central government from 2000 has accelerated rather than slowed and consultancies are increasingly central in setting the agenda of governments, advising on policy, and guiding the hand of ministers. Thus, the vast majority of government IT projects since 2000 have involved senior consultancy figures, not just in delivering the work but also in developing the business case, attending meetings, and steering the agendas. It is no coincidence, therefore, that the fastest expansion of government spending on consultants occurred during the 2000–7 period.

What makes this more galling to opponents of the expanding role of consultants in government is that the inquiry set up by Tony Blair into the relationship between ministers and consultants was chaired by Sir Patrick Brown. Brown was a former Permanent Secretary at the Department of Transport who had moved to non-executive chairman at one of the largest public transport companies. Indeed, it was only the loud protests of the Public Administration Select Committee (PASC) that prevented the removal of the rule that ministers should seek approval for their business appointments (Hencke 2004).

One can understand why, of course, governments wish to turn to experts in e-business, privatisation, and change when attempting to modernise public services. However, there are several outstanding questions which give commentators the chance to suggest that there are opportunities for (if not actual) conflicts of interest:

1. Why does the government not develop internal consultancies to manage common types of modernisation projects?

2. Why are there so many instances of senior consultants moving into executive government roles and vice versa?

3. How can the public be sure that there are no conflicts of interest, both in actual decision-making and in agenda setting about the use of consultants in government departments?

4. Should the committee that oversees central government appointments to the public sector be funded by the central government?

If one wished to be cynical in seeking to understand why governments have not done more to prevent conflicts of interest in this sphere, one could point to the financial interest that many of the public officials have in these consultancies. Several of the major consultancies undertaking government work have either directly or indirectly made donations to the party in power. The Capita chairman, Rod Aldridge, for example, was forced to resign when it was discovered he had donated £1m to the Labour Party. Furthermore, several key public decision-makers, such as the ex-chief executive of the Immigration and Passport Service (IPS), the ex-head of personnel in the Cabinet Office, and the ex-director of Border and Immigration Control, had shareholdings worth several million pounds in the consultancy companies which worked in their departments. Finally, many decision-makers have received significant benefits from consultancies, ranging from fees for speaking, to hospitality, or payment for advisory services (Craig and Brooks 2006).

IT

The relationship between IT provision and management consultancy has, if anything, intensified since 2000. This is despite three of the Big Four accounting firms refusing to make inroads into the IT market. Deloitte, the one firm that kept its advisory arm when the others were divesting, has uniquely retained both its outsourcing function, its systems integration group, and its IT advisory arm. This potentially creates potential conflicts of interest in that clients paying for independent advice on IT strategy may not be aware that the consultancy has a vested interest in selling its own solutions.

Despite internal ethics officers and Chinese walls, Deloitte, like all other dual IT–consultancy companies, has been plagued by lawsuits concerning potential conflicts of interest. It is becoming increasingly clear that the lessons of Enron were short-lived. For example, in 2007 IBM, PWC, CSC, Accenture, Hewlett-Packard, and Sun Microsystems were all charged by the US Department of Justice with making and receiving improper payments to vendors and suppliers whilst working for the US government (DOJ 2008). The payments, it is alleged, were made by systems integrators for preferential treatment in dividing up government contracts. IBM, PWC, and CSC all settled by paying several million dollars. HP, it was suggested, made payments to BearingPoint, CapGemini, Electronic Data Systems Corp., Science Applications International Corp., and other companies, while Sun purportedly made payments to Accenture, PricewaterhouseCoopers Technology Integration LLC, World Wide Technology Inc., Northrop Grumman Corp., and other companies. In a bigger case, in 2005, PWC paid $41.9m to settle a claim that they had defrauded the Department of Defense, the Justice Department, the Environmental Protection Agency, the Securities and Exchange Commission, the Peace Corps, the Department of Education, and the Department of Veterans Affairs. The alleged fraud was focused on rebates PWC had received on its travel expenses from credit card and travel companies, airlines, hotels, and rental car agencies (DOJ 2005).

Many of these cases were uncovered only due to a clever piece of legislation in the USA called the False Claims Act (1987), which allows whistleblowers to collect between 15 and 20 per cent of the damages recovered in claims against improper action. The sheer volume of these legal cases seems to suggest an inherent conflict in the very nature of such dual-purpose consultancies. Moreover, such numbers also speak to the difficulties faced by regulators in tackling these tensions. For the most part, the policy taken is *caveat emptor*—buyer beware—but this reliance on clients to ensure that their systems are free from potential kick-backs, biased advice, and other conflicts is both an expensive and time-consuming job.

This section has argued that despite potential conflicts of interest between consultants and the institutions of government, IT companies, and audit firms, there have been few attempts to tackle these at a fundamental level. Instead, an institutional tinkering has been undertaken which at best reduces rather than eliminates institutional conflicts in ethical practice and at worst simply provides a rhetorical device to disguise unethical, and sometimes illegal, practices. In the next section, it is argued that parallel to the failure of institutional reform has been the rise of an individualisation of ethics.

■ The Individualisation of Ethical Responsibility

Understanding Individualisation

What appears to have happened to the *responsibility* for ethical practice in consulting (as well as other areas of the economy) is that emphasis has shifted away from the institution and onto the individual. This is not to say that organisations are no longer held accountable by the courts when illegal activity takes place (though these cases are increasingly targeted at key personnel), but that not enough emphasis is placed on the systems which encourage individuals to act in an unethical manner.

As we will discuss later in the book, a successful consulting career is often based on maximising income both for the consultant and the consultancy. This means that, without checks and balances, the system can encourage consultants to sell products and services which clients don't necessarily need, to elicit payments from providers who have work sent their way, and to divert economies of scale to the consultancy rather than pass them on to the client. It is argued below that the consulting industry currently resists systemic or institutional solutions to ethical issues and instead focuses on the individual as the prime point of responsibility. Such a focus will be recognised by followers of free-market economics as *homo economicus*—a free-thinking, unsocialised, and rational individual who is aware of all information and will make logical choices based on assessing the rewards and constraints of any course of action.

The assumption behind this individualisation is that if consultants themselves are ethically responsible, then consulting practice will be ethical. To borrow a consulting phrase, this is a form of outsourcing of ethics. Ethics, as a concern, is removed from institutional or systemic operation and is, instead, imposed upon individuals or groups that can be held responsible when things go wrong. The benefit of this for the organisation is high. Where unethical practice does take place, the metaphor most commonly used is that of the "bad apple", an errant individual who failed to practise ethical standards. Such a convenient scapegoat relieves both the company and regulators from undertaking a more time-consuming and expensive assessment of the reasons why the institution grew the "bad apple" in the first place.

These processes fit with Beck's conception of individualisation as a feature of late modernity: because organisations, experts, and governments "dump their contradictions and conflicts at the feet of the individual" (Beck 1992: 137), he or she has to find personal ("biographical") solutions to handle risks. The burden for assessing and managing the risk is placed firmly on the individual. The problem with this individualisation process is that it "is driving risk experts and professionals to focus more on their personal, legal and reputational risks, rather than on the primary risks embodied in their formal mission" (Power 2004: 15). Thus, the identification of risk is focused at the individual level rather than at the institution. In reality, however, whether we are talking about Enron, Abu Grahib or Barings Bank, "unethical" individuals are simply manifestations of bureaucracies that are not adequately constrained by the legal and political structures that should police them.

In the consulting world, then, the process of individualising ethics can be evidenced in three ways: first the development of ethical codes of practice, second, the segmentation of ethical work, and finally, the professionalisation of consultants. These are now examined in turn.

Ethical Codes of Practice

Since Enron, a vast amount has been written on the ethics of consulting. Concurrently, the industry itself has carefully cultivated the impression that both consultants and consultancy companies adhere to the highest ethical standards. Management Consultancy Association (MCA) in the USA for example has a (voluntary) code of conduct which stipulates that its members shall:

- Only accept work for which they are qualified and which they have the capacity to undertake.

- Act with fairness and integrity towards all persons with whom their work is connected.

- Reject any business practice which might reasonably be deemed improper.

This type of code is mirrored, in different ways, in all the major consultancies. Accenture, for example, has a 44-page Code of Ethics with an *Ethical Fitness Decision-Making Model* amended from the Institute of Global Ethics. While all the major consultancies have similar codes, most have also adopted schemes designed around work–life balance, corporate citizenship, and work in the community.

Now, there are various flaws in ethical codes, and these are worth visiting briefly before exploring how they add to the individualisation. Three flaws stand out. First, these codes and practices are primarily voluntary activities within the industry—they were not imposed by governments with relevant legal sanctions. Thus, breaking these codes and practices is not illegal unless it contravenes other legal restrictions. Second, the codes are often vague, leaving plenty of room for interpretation and subjectivity. The Institute of Business Consulting Code of Professional Conduct and Practice states that a member:

> will put client interests first, doing whatever it takes to serve them to the highest possible standards at all times. (p. 3)

This, and other similar statements, can easily be interpreted in many different ways. For example, who is the client: the business owner, the funder of the project, or the shareholders? Should "the highest possible standards" include considerations of time and cost? Much of consulting activity is complex, political, and interpersonal—areas which are difficult for "codes" to legislate.

Finally, there is ample evidence that codes are sometimes, and possibly frequently, ignored by consultants. If one examines personal accounts, blogs, lawsuits, and the press, one frequently encounters examples of illegal and unethical practice. If one assumes that the majority of these practices go unobserved or unreported then this points to a number of individuals ignoring their organisation's ethical code.

These company codes are central to the individualisation of ethics because they make the individual responsible for the ethical operation of the consultancy. The employee must know, remember, and understand how and when to use a code designed and delineated by the employer. The difficulty for the consultant is that the ethical code can conveniently ignore processes (such as promotion or bonus criteria) which may implicitly encourage unethical behaviour. The benefit for the organisation is that they can apportion blame on the individual rather than accepting it themselves. Enron, for example, had a 65-page Code of Ethics; yet when things went wrong, it was Jeff Skilling and Ken Lay who were imprisoned, but the systems that produced and incentivised their behaviour in the industry generally were left virtually untouched.

Segmentation of Ethical Behaviour

A recent trend by consultancies in presenting an ethical face to the media and potential recruits is to provide "ethical work" for their employees. This usually consists of providing consultants with time to engage with ethical work which is supported and publicised by the company. Here are a few examples taken from the websites of various consultancies:

> Accenture's Community Teach Program . . . will place select Accenture executives in teaching roles and other educational activities at local community colleges.

> The pilot program will leverage the skills and experience of Accenture executives to bring their real-world experience to benefit the students.

> Deloitte's Community Days provide an opportunity for teams of Deloitte people to get involved in their local community for a day in the firm's time. In 2006 over 1,500 of our people have undertaken a variety of highly enjoyable and rewarding indoor and outdoor community and environment projects.

> PWC offices in Scotland organised a number of team volunteering days, one of which included a team of volunteers from the Edinburgh office working at Pentland Hills Regional Park. Fifteen volunteers took part in the challenge, which was to rebuild and replace a series of steps close to the entrance to the park.

In interviews with consultancies, it is clear that these programmes help improve the image of consultancies not only with potential recruits concerned with social responsibility, but also with the wider public. However, beyond this, this type of work provides both a segmentation and an individualisation of ethics by which the ethical concerns of the individual about their day-to-day work can be assuaged by their involvement in "good" projects. The provision of such "ethical time" encourages the employee to perceive their company as socially responsible and, therefore, broadly "good". This is not to say that consultancies don't pay a premium for this kind of work, or that it is not a good thing; however, it does contribute to the responsibility of the individual for the firm's ethical reputation.

Professionalisation

The final method by which ethical concerns in consulting have been individualised is through the process of professionalisation. As Chapter 2 detailed, the International Council of Management Consulting Institutes (ICMCI) has become a significant institutional force in recent years as its membership has increased through the process of professionalisation. As of 2008, the ICMCI is represented in forty-five countries, and has a membership of over 30,000 consultants through its local representative institutions.

As in many professions, the professionalisation of consultants takes place at the level of the individual rather than the firm. Thus, whilst it is possible, for example, for KPMG to become a member of the British arm of the ICMCI, the IBC, this does not mean its employees become members. Instead, individual consultants are encouraged to become members. This means that each individual needs to provide evidence of competence and experience, abide by the profession's guidelines, and pay an individual membership fee.

With regard to ethics, the individual consultant, rather than the firm, is held accountable for professional misconduct, even if the firm has encouraged the individual to act in an inappropriate or unethical manner. However, as it is virtually impossible for any institution to audit the day-to-day ethical activities of a consultant, membership of a profession is usually only withdrawn when bad practice is made public. Moreover, as it is not compulsory for a consultant to be a member of a profession in order to practise, even the ethical standards encouraged at the level of the individual are not necessarily uniform across the sector. By encouraging sanctions and controls, however limited, at the level of the individual, these professional bodies foster an atomistic model of the industry: the sum of the industry is equal only to the parts of the individual consultants within. Such a reductive representation fails to acknowledge the ways in which systems, cultures, and procedures can influence the ethical practice and perception of individual consultants.

McKenna argues that the rapid success of both the consulting and investment banking industries contributed to their ability to avoid professionalisation, a process he argues helped develop professional ethics in the fields of medicine, journalism, and law (McKenna 2006). The outcome is described by Kipping et al. (2006) as "corporate professionalism" where responsibility for ethics and standards remains with the firm rather than with the state or an external body. In the consulting industry, the lack of an industry-wide regulatory body which could provide an external audit of consultants' operations means common standards are difficult to define and impossible to police.

Furthermore, it should be noted that the individualisation of ethical practice focuses on the conflict of interest between the individual and the client, not the consultancy and the client, or indeed the consultancy and the consultant. In Figure 9.1, four stakeholders are represented as playing a part in the ethical practices of the industry. However, out of all the possible relationships between these stakeholders, it is only the relationship between the consultant and the client which is bound by professional ethics. The relationships between the consultancy and the client, the consultancy and the consultant, or the consultancy and society are virtually ignored by ethical codes or industry legislation.

Up to now, this chapter has argued that the management of ethics in the consulting industry has been hampered by lack of institutional reform and by the individualising of ethics in the industry. The next section considers the charges that have been made against the industry with regard to ethical practice and assesses the validity of their claims.

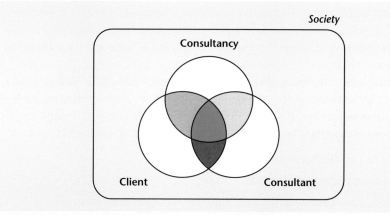

Figure 9.1. The ethical stakeholders in the consulting industry

CASE 9.2

The NHS NPfIT

The world's largest non-military IT project, initiated in 2002, is the National Program for IT (NPfIT)—an initiative by the Department of Health in the UK, to create a single, centrally controlled system for managing and connecting NHS patients and GPs in the UK. As there are 60m NHS patients, 30,000 GPs, and 300 NHS hospitals, this was no small undertaking.

The project was run by an agency called Connecting for Health (CfH) and deliverables included "The Spine": a national data set of patient information and six regional local service providers run by different consultancies/service providers. The man running the project was Richard Granger, head of NPfIT, a previous employee at Andersen Consulting (which became Accenture). Originally very proud of the stringency of the contracts with consultancies and service providers, Granger stated:

> Managing the NHS IT suppliers is like running a team of huskies. When one of the dogs goes lame, it is shot. It is then chopped up and fed to the other dogs. The survivors work harder, not only because they have had a meal, but also because they have seen what will happen should they themselves go lame.

Originally estimated to cost £2.3bn over three years, overruns, escalations, and delays have increased this estimate to £20bn over twelve years. In 2007, the Public Accounts Committee released a report stating that "the biggest IT project in the world . . . is turning into the biggest disaster" and that "it is unlikely that significant clinical benefits will be delivered by the end of the contract period". In 2009, they stated that "the current levels of support reflect the fact that for many [NHS] staff the benefits of the Programme are still theoretical".

Accenture, one of the four regional contractors for the programme, withdrew from the contract in September 2006 saying that its failure to meet various deadlines would cost the consultancy £260m. Accenture blamed much of the delay on its software supplier iSoft. Despite robust contracts which allowed the government to fine Accenture up to £1bn for their exit, the consultancy was eventually fined only £63m after agreeing to hand over their operations to CSC and not to sue either the government or iSoft.

Granger left his role shortly after the PAC report was made public stating "I think that with a bit less whingeing and a bit more support, we might have even got the programme done quicker" (*Guardian* 2007). The first trusts to implement the new IT systems have encountered several problems with the systems which had:

• failed to flag up child-abuse victims;

• not identified patients with MRSA;

• cancelled 272 operations at the last minute for non-clinical reasons;

- delayed the assessment of potential cancer patients;
- failed to track and readmit patients needing follow-up treatment;
- forced the manual amendment of 12,000 patient records.

    In 2008 the withdrawal of Fujitsu, one of the three remaining service providers, over contractual issues, caused more problems for the project and, at the time of writing, the project is expected to be delivered at least five years late, costing billions more than was originally suggested.

- What are the pros and cons of a client treating consultancies "like huskies"?

■ Considering the Charges

The lack of serious reform in the consultancy sector has done little to improve the reputation of an industry which has never enjoyed the unqualified commendation of society. Suspicions clearly, and sometimes understandably, persist regarding the ethical status of consultants and the consulting industry. The list below details the most enduring charges that are aimed at the world of consulting. In the following sections these claims are considered and assessed against evidence from the sector. The charges, in no particular order, are as follows:

1. Consulting advice isn't value for money and doesn't work.
2. Consulting solutions are either fads or "boiler-plated" templates.
3. Consultants can't be trusted.
4. Consultants prey on the insecurities and ignorance of client managers.

Charge 1: Consulting Advice Isn't Value for Money and Doesn't Work

> A consultant is someone who saves his client almost enough to pay his fee. (Arnold H. Glasow)

In recent years, several critiques of consultancies have appeared claiming that the money that is spent on consultants isn't recouped in efficiency savings (or growth in profits). In the UK, for example, a recent book entitled *Plundering the Public Sector* (Craig 2006) argues that consultants have charged excessive fees to public sector companies and the UK government. A recent attack on the industry by Liberal Democrat Shadow Chancellor, Vince Cable, stated that consultancy in the government sector was a "gravy train" (Reed 2008). Other writers have focused on the high failure rates associated with consulting interventions. Examples include:

Child Support Agency system. The system was declared months behind schedule (due to go live April 2003), functionally not fit for purpose (due to unspecified "technical problems"), and £50m over budget (original cost estimate £200m).

NHS Medical Records system. The real cost of the new programme is quoted at £12bn over ten years, not the £6.2bn originally quoted at the outset. It now appears that despite this extra expenditure some key features of the system are virtually unworkable.

As a consequence both the Public Accounts Committee (PAC) and the National Audit Office complained vociferously about the amount of money public bodies were spending on consultants and suggested that better management and consideration of consulting projects would help reduce the massive spend. The result has been the implementation of public procurement services to recruit and manage consultants and tighter controls on benefits management.

Charge 1: Consideration

Whilst it is true that there have been considerable criticisms regarding the value of consultancy interventions, it should be pointed out that few have attempted to measure the benefits of this advice. In part, this is because some interventions are notoriously difficult to measure. Even so, it should be noted that consultancies have been involved in a number of highly successful projects—even in the public sector.

It should also be noted that *all* change interventions have a high failure rate, not just those implemented by consultancies. For example, research shows that failure rates in change management, merger and acquisitions, process re-engineering, and IT implementation can approach 80 per cent regardless of whether consultants are involved or not. Thus, it is much more likely that projects fail for reasons other than the involvement of management consultants.

In addition many consultants would also retort that the key reasons for project failure usually include those associated with clients, especially in the public sector: poor leadership, resistance to change, no management buy-in. Even the PAC and the NAO pointed out that it was not necessarily the consultancies' fault that projects overran. Public sector managers have, in the past, been notoriously bad at defining what they want and providing consultants with clear objectives. The outcome of these badly managed projects is that boundaries change and scope begins to creep—resulting in increased costs and overruns.

However, surveys which ask clients how useful their consultants have been often support the charge. A survey by Cranfield University in the 1990s, for example, found that only 36 per cent of clients believed consultants added value to their organisation (compared to 70 per cent of consultants). Coincidentally, the 36 per cent figure was repeated in an survey which asked clients if they were satisfied with the results of consulting projects (Czerniawska 2006). Interestingly, the survey also found that as respondents went down the organisational hierarchy, they were increasingly less satisfied with the engagements: 48 per cent of senior decision-makers were completely satisfied compared with only 28 per cent of project managers and 17 per cent of end users. Another survey by IPSOS/MORI in 2007 found that 53 per cent of clients questioned about consulting projects believed they had not improved the performance of their business. Not a promising statistic.

Charge 2: Consulting Solutions Are Fads or "Boiler-Plated" Templates

> It is hard to determine who is more interested in fads, the academics who write about them, the consultants who sell them, or the managers who use them. (Whitney Gibson, Tesone, Blackwell)

There has been a copious amount of academic writing suggesting that consultancies are key to the production and dissemination of management "fads" (Abrahamson 1996; Grint and Case 2000; Newell et al. 2000). In critical consulting literature, a "fad" is usually a disparaging term for a "standardised" change programme that becomes very popular and then quickly disappears. Examples are TQM, BPR, SCM, and Management by Objectives. The implication of this word is not only that these programmes have short life-spans, but also that they don't actually work. As ten Bos (2000: 5) writes, "the fashionable is never authentic or robust, but always untrustworthy, unpredictable, fickle and capricious".

Other critical academics have argued that consultants often use templates that they have developed for other clients and simply change the name on the front of the document. This "one size fits all" approach to change, they suggest, is one reason why so many consultancy interventions fail.

Charge 2: Consideration

At first glance, there is evidence to support the claim that consultants sell fads. An examination of the citation of, say, BPR in academic and practitioner literature or corporate press releases, shows a very definite life-cycle, with a rapidly growing rise in citations in the first few years, followed by a slow reduction as the fashions become less popular (Heusinkveld and Benders 2001; Spell 1999). However, there are many reasons for this which are not necessarily related to the impotence of the "fashion". For example, some programmes, like BPR, are rarely implemented more than once, so they are not likely to feature in the company literature once they have been installed. Other times, a word may go out of fashion but the actual practice may continue. For example, lean management, TQM, Japanese Management, and Quality Initiatives can all loosely refer to the same thing, but the terminology which is used will vary depending which decade one looks at. Another view is that the original programme has evolved into something else. Through the process of variation, replication, and selection some ideas evolve into different forms with different names (O'Mahoney 2007). This process does not mean the idea didn't work but simply means that it changed when its environment changed.

The charge of boiler-plating, in my view, misses the key point about consultancies. A consultancy's unique selling point is its experience with other clients. This means that, over time, a consultancy will experience challenges (e.g. outsourcing) hundreds of times that a client will only ever face once or twice. This enables them to build up best practice which is, actually, often generalisable across organisations. To extend the outsourcing example, most organisations' payroll and HR outsourcing efforts will be 90 per cent similar. By reusing "best-practice" knowledge that they have developed over years, consultants are not only ensuring that their clients get the best advice possible, but also ensure that they are getting it more cheaply than if the consultancy had to start from scratch.

Charge 3: Consultants Can't Be Trusted

> [Consultants] are people who borrow your watch to tell you what time it is and
> then walk off with it. (Robert Townsend)

There is a general view of consultants amongst the more critical sections of the press that
consulting ranks with lawyers and car salesmen as one of the least trusted professions. The
reasons for this distrust generally concern the tendency of some consultants to maximise
the length and cost of projects at any costs. This might include:

- Exchanging expensive senior staff with cheaper less experienced consultants.
- Exaggerating problems so as to increase the chance of selling bigger solutions.
- Befriending key decision-makers to increase the likelihood of sales.
- Making the consultants indispensable to the company operations to prolong projects.

Charge 3: Consideration

It is certainly true to say that levels of trust between consultants and clients are not particularly high. The 2007 IPSOS/MORI survey found that 40 per cent of clients would not
describe the consultants they use as trustworthy. Given that this group had already selected and employed the consultants they are describing, this is a very worrying statistic. However, compared to other professions, consultants do not fare too badly. A survey by IMC
USA (2007) found that compared to other professions, consultants ranked about mid-way,
below nurses, doctors, teachers, and accountants, but above journalists, politicians, sales
representatives, and business executives.

It is also true that there is considerable evidence contradicting the image of the consultant as the "trusted adviser" who places the interests of the client's business ahead
of their own. If one examines blogs, books written by ex-consultants, court cases, and
academic articles, there are a number of cases from virtually all the major consultancies
which point towards unethical, and potentially illegal, behaviour. The extent to which
this is systematic or exceptional may be debated by industry representatives, but it seems
fair to say that what has been detected and made public is probably the smaller part of
what actually happens.

However, it is also true to say that client spending on consultants increased by around
10,000 per cent between 1980 and 2007: how does this increased reliance on consultants fit
with the argument that they are generally not trusted? There are three things to say here.
The first is that often companies have no choice but to bring in consultants. In the same way
that you may have to use a used car salesman or a lawyer who you don't particularly trust,
companies needing to implement an IT system, cut costs by 30 per cent, or enter a new market are all but forced to turn to consultants regardless of whether they trust them or not.

Second, decreasing levels of trust in consulting are not necessarily the fault of consultants.
As clients have grown increasingly sophisticated and procurement departments have
become responsible for the consulting relationship, the interpersonal trust that was often
present between senior consultants and senior client managers has eroded. Additionally,

if clients run procurement processes which select the lowest-cost offer, it should not be a surprise when projects do not always deliver on what they promise.

Finally, whilst consultants are incentivised to maximise income for themselves and the firm they represent, there is also an incentive not to rip clients off too obviously. In many cases, consultants are reliant on clients for repeat business, so making a mess of a project whilst charging extortionate fees will not incline the client to consider the consultancy for subsequent projects. Indeed, Andersen Consulting were, in effect, barred from government projects in the 1980s after the then Prime Minister Margaret Thatcher perceived them to have acted unethically as auditors to Delorean (Foot 2000). Low levels of trust, therefore, are avoided by most consultancies at all costs.

Charge 4: Consultants Prey on the Insecurities of Client Managers

> Wall Street is the only place people ride to work in a Rolls Royce to get advice from people who take the subway. (Warren Buffett)

Huczynski (1993), Jackall (1988), and Kieser (2002) argue that many managers are insecure individuals who use consultants as psychological and epistemological crutches. The implication of much of these authors' work is that this insecurity creates a demand for "secure" knowledge in the form of management fads and fashions which consultants can sell. As Kipping and Saint-Martin (2005: 454) state:

> [Consultants] allow management to shy away from its own decision-making responsibilities and, if necessary, blame mistakes on somebody else . . . these fashions appeal to managers because they reduce their insecurity and provide them with the perception of control. But they are soon replaced by new fashions, which managers need to adopt again to maintain (or regain) their competitive advantage.

Of course, insecurity need not be a deep-seated psychological anxiety on the part of managers; instead it is often portrayed as a need for confidence and certainty which reflects the "scientific" inclination of capitalism in an age of constantly shifting and unstable patterns.

Charge 4: Consideration

In interviews with consultants, I have found a common retort to this charge is that it is the consultant who gets blamed for the condition of the manager. As one senior consultant comments: "this is akin to blaming the shop when a customer buys too many, or the wrong type, of products". Whilst this counter argument has some validity, the metaphor isn't exactly appropriate. In the consultancy case, the shop may exaggerate the quality of the product or the customer may find the product costs more than advertised when they reach the till.

The "insecure manager" story is, however, essentially unconvincing, especially in the twenty-first century (Kitay and Wright 2004). Most large companies now have experienced and highly qualified individuals (often ex-consultants) in charge of the procurement and management of consultancy work. Those senior enough to recruit and pay consultants are usually hard-nosed and experienced enough to deal with them. Indeed, in some projects, the client managers are so tough that it is the consultancies who are left out of pocket.

In recent years, academics have moved away from the "insecure" model of managers. Sturdy (1997), for example, argues that this view of clients ignores the fact that "managers are often critical of, and resist, consultants and new ideas and, in turn, consultants respond to and seek to anticipate such concerns . . . [that] consultants tend to be portrayed as confident and 'in control' rather than being subject to similar pressures and uncertainties has emphasized instead the interactive nature of the client–consultant relation and consultancy itself as an 'insecure business'". O'Mahoney (2007), for example, emphasises that many consultants are in a much more precarious and insecure position than that of the clients which whom they engage. It is the personal implications of this which the next section considers.

■ Chapter Summary

This chapter has examined the causes and effects of unethical behaviour in the consulting industry. It:

- Outlined the institutional conflicts of interest that contributed to the "crisis" of consultancy after the turn of the millennium.

- Argued that attempts to tackle unethical behaviour have focused on the individual rather than dealing with institutional conflicts of interest.

- Showed that one result of the failure to make significant institutional reform is that many (though not all) of the claims of unethical behaviour in consulting still stand.

- Suggested that ethical problems in consulting are complex and cannot be tackled simply by giving students "ethical dilemmas" to resolve.

Student Exercise

Deloitte consulting is, amongst other things, a story of how successful strategy is often determined by luck. While all the other audit houses were being persuaded to divest their consulting arms, Deloitte was seeking funding to finance a leveraged buy-out of their own consultants. However, after Enron and the collapse of Andersen Consulting, the cost of borrowing made it too expensive for Deloitte to spin off their consulting arm, so they withdrew from the deal.

As the only audit house to retain their consulting arm, Deloitte filled an obvious gap in the market, despite moving away from delivery and towards pure advisory work. Ironically, much of this consulting was the implementation of Sarbanes–Oxley legislation. As they only audited about 25 per cent of the Fortune 500, this left them with a considerable number of potential clients for their consultancy services. Demand for Deloitte's unique combination of financial and business expertise rocketed, leading to their acquisition of a number of consultants and units from other companies, such as Andersen Consulting.

Unsurprisingly, consulting profits at Deloitte soared, and by 2006 they accounted for almost half of the firm's income. It was unsurprising, then, that by 2005 all the other large audit firms had begun rebuilding the consultancy divisions that they had divested a few years previously.

In groups, discuss the following questions:

1 How much of a role should government institutions play in intervening in businesses?

2 If a consultant is rewarded for making sales but is found to have used audit information to achieve this goal, who, or what, is at fault?

Discussion Questions

• Why has ethics become so important to society and to consultancies in recent years?

• Do ethical policies make consulting practice more ethical?

• Is the prevalence of ethical policies mere "window-dressing" or is it more substantial?

• Should clients be entirely responsible for ensuring their consultants do not over-promise and under-deliver or does the consultancy share the responsibility?

Further Reading

There are various kiss-and-tell or airport style books which detail the unethical behaviour of management consultants. Many of these exaggerate their point and simplify the debate to a mere "consultancy equals bad" equation which does not do justice to the complexity of ethics. However, two well-researched books which are both fun to read and very informative are:

• Craig, D. (2005). *Rip Off: The Scandalous Story of the Management Consulting Money Machine*. London: Original Book Company.

• Craig, D., and Brooks, R. (2006). *Plundering the Public Sector*. London: Constable.

The second is better researched and deeper than the first, but Craig's background as a journalist clearly comes out in his easy-to-read style and rigorous research. If fun is what you are looking for then you may also wish to visit the Enron Code of Ethics at: www.thesmokinggun.com/graphics/packageart/enron/enron.pdf. It gives a good illustration of why ethical guides and training are simply not enough to ensure ethical practice if there is no institutional reform.

There are a few excellent academics worth reading who give a more balanced view of consulting practices. Two articles I would recommend are:

• Sturdy, A. (1997). The Consultancy Process: An Insecure Business. *Journal of Management Studies*, 34 (3): 389–413.

• Armbrüster, T., and Glückler, J. (2007). Organizational Change and the Economics of Management Consulting: A Response to Sorge and van Witteloostuijn, *Organization Studies*, 28.

The former is an excellent critical academic, whose writings on consultancy are all worth checking out for their sensible arguments and rigorous thinking. The latter are German professors who approach consultancy from a sociological and economic perspective with some interesting results.

If you want an insider's view on the treatment of consultants in the industry, then my own article, printed a few years ago, provides this in a relatively accessible format:

• O'Mahoney, J. (2007). Disrupting Identity: Trust and Angst in Management Consulting. In S. Bolton (ed.), *Searching for the H in Human Resource Management*. London: Sage.

For a good insight into the Enron case, you may wish to read "The Downside of Rank and Yank" in What Went Wrong With Enron? by Fusaro et al. (2002) or watch the *Enron: The Smartest Guys in the Room* DVD.

References

Abrahamson, E. (1996). Management Fashion. *Academy of Management Review*, 21: 254–85.

ACOBA (2004). *Sixth Report 2003–4*. London: Cabinet Office.

Beck, U. (1992). *Risk Society: Towards a New Modernity*. London: Sage.

Craig, D. (2005). *Rip Off: The Scandalous Story of the Management Consulting Money Machine*. London: Original Book Company.

——and Brooks, R. (2006). *Plundering the Public Sector*. London: Constable.

Czerniawska, F. (2006). *Ensuring Sustainable Value from Consultants*. MCA/PWC.

DOJ (2005). US Department of Justice, Press Release, 25 July.

——(2008). US Department of Justice, Press Release, 13 May.

Foot, P. (2000). Medes and Persians. *London Review of Books*. 2 November.

Frankel, R. M., Johnson, M. F., and Nelson, K. K. (2002). The Relation between Auditors' Fees for Nonaudit Services and Earnings Management. *Accounting Review*, 77.

Fusaro, P., Miller, R., and James, T. (2002). *What Went Wrong at Enron?* New York: John Wiley and Sons.

Guardian (2007). Ailing Project at Heart of NHS. 19 June.

Gladwell, M. (2002). The Talent Myth. *New Yorker*. 22 July.

Grey, C. (2002). The Fetish of Change. *Tamara: Journal of Critical Postmodern Organisation Science*, 2 (2).

Grint, K., and Case, P. (2000). Now Where Are We? BPR Lotus-Eaters and Corporate Amnesia. In D. Knights and H. Willmott (eds), *The Reengineering Revolution: Critical Studies of Corporate Change*. London: Sage.

Hencke, D. (2004). Plan to End Whitehall Sleaze Rule: Path Eased to Private Sector Jobs, *Guardian*. 16 August.

Heusinkveld, S., and Benders, J. (2001). Surges and Sediments: Shaping the Reception of Reengineering. *Information and Management*, 38: 239–51.

Horrocks, I. (2009). "Experts" and E-government: Power, Influence and the Capture of a Policy Domain in the UK. *Information, Communication and Society*, 12 (1): 110–27.

Huczynski, A. (1993). *Management Gurus: What Makes them and How to Become one*. New York: Taylor and Francis.

IMC USA (2007). *The Consulting Survey*. www.imcusa.org .

Jackall, R. (1988). *Moral Mazes: The World of Corporate Managers*. Oxford: Oxford University Press.

Kieser, A. (2002). Managers as Marionettes? Using Fashion Theories to Explain the Success of Consultancies. In M. Kipping and L. Engwall (eds), *Management Consulting: Emergence and Dynamics of a Knowledge Industry*. Oxford: Oxford University Press, 167–83.

Kiln, M. (2005). *House of Lies: How Management Consultants Steal your Watch Then Tell You the Time*. New York: Imported Little.

Kipping, M., and Saint-Martin, D. (2005). Between Regulation, Promotion and Consumption: Government and Management Consultancy in Britain. *Business History*, 47 (3): 449–65.

——Muzio, D., and Kirkpatrick, I. (2006). Overly Controlled or Out of Control? Management Consultants and the New Corporate Professionalism. In J. Craig (ed.), *Production Values: Futures for Professionalism*. London: Demos, 153–65.

Kitay, J., and Wright, C. (2004). Take the Money and Run? Organisational Boundaries and Client Roles. *Service Industries Journal*, May: 1–19.

McKenna, C. (2006). *The World's Newest Profession*. Oxford: Oxford University Press.

McKinsey Quarterly (2007). The Atomization of Big Oil. 22 March.

McLean, B., and Elkind, P. (2004). *Smartest Guys in the Room: The Amazing Rise and Scandalous Fall of Enron*. Portfolio Hardcover.

Newell, S., Robertson, M., and Swan, J. (2000). Management Fads and Fashions. *Organization*, 8 (1): 5–15.

O'Mahoney, J. (2007a). The Diffusion of Management Innovations: The Possibilities and

Limitations of Memetics. *Journal of Management Studies*, (43) 8.

—— (2007b). Disrupting Identity: Trust and Angst in Management Consulting. In S. Bolton (ed.), *Searching for the H in Human Resource Management*. London: Sage.

Power, M. (2004). *The Risk Management of Everything: Rethinking the Politics of Uncertainty*. London: Demos.

Reed, K. (2008). Consultants Move to Dispel their Gravy Train Reputation. *Accountancy Age*, 24 September.

—— Wild, D., and Perry, M. (2007). Consultants Dismiss Big Four Challenge. *Accountancy Age*, 17 May.

Saint-Martin, D. (1998). The New Managerialism and the Policy Influence of Consultants in Government: An Historical-Institutionalist Analysis of Britain, Canada and France. *Governance*, 11 (3): 319–56.

SEC (2001). Accounting and Auditing Enforcement, 1405, 19 June. File No. 3-10513.

Spell, C. (1999). Where Do Management Fashions Come From, and How Long Do They Stay For? *Journal of Management History*, 5: 334–48.

Sturdy, A. (1997). The Consultancy Process: An Insecure Business. *Journal of Management Studies*, 34 (3): 389–413.

ten Bos, R. (2000). *Fashion and Utopia in Management Thinking*. Amsterdam: John Benjamins.

Do Consultants Get Results?

David Craig, author of *Rip-off* (2005) and *Squandered* (2008)

The big question to answer about management and IT systems consultancy is whether clients actually get, and believe they get, value for the billions they pay to their consultants. There has only been limited research into success levels of management and IT systems consulting, but the figures are worrying. Indications are that around 30 per cent of management consulting is successful—for IT systems consulting, the success rate is well below 20 per cent.

There are many very talented management consultants who are dedicated to providing the best possible results for their clients. Yet too often they are prevented from delivering value and are even put in ethically questionable situations by the way the consultancy industry works. I have found that there are about six main reasons why so many organisations get disappointing results from their consultants.

■ 1 Utilisation Targets

In many consultancies, executives' bonuses depend on them reaching certain "utilisation" targets—usually about 70 per cent. This means that 70 per cent of their consultants' time must be sold to clients, whether clients have problems to be solved or not. Failure to achieve the utilisation target can result in a consultancy director losing several hundred thousand pounds of bonus. So consultancy directors are under tremendous pressure to sell their people's time. Thus many consultants find their talents wasted by being put to work on projects that are just lucrative "billing slots" sold to keep utilisation levels up, but with little practical value for their clients.

■ 2 "Warm Bodies"

Many consultancies have just a few experienced experts in each of their areas of work, while most of their employees are what we called "warm bodies" or "billing fodder". The consultancy's profitability depends on being able to sell teams mostly made up of lower-paid "warm bodies" with their more highly paid experts working on several projects at the same time and only visiting each project occasionally. Of course, with proper direction from the experts, the "warm bodies" can provide good work, though sometimes, the warm bodies may be of dubious quality. As a consultant at one of the world's largest consultancies wrote on meeting the latest intake of recruits (green beans), "The green beans have arrived and oh my god I suggest you start shorting your stock—these new hires are absolute monkeys. These new people are absolutely stupid. What the hell was HR thinking?" Normally clients would get much greater value if their consulting teams were mostly made up of more experts and less billing fodder.

■ 3 Product Sales

Quite a few consultancies are "product-focused" rather than "solution-focused". This means that they are interested in selling you their "product"—the services that they know how to deliver. This focus on selling their product can prevent them actually trying to find the right solution for your particular organisational issues. Moreover, if your consultants are part of an IT systems supplier, they will probably be under huge internal pressure to sell you IT systems work even if you don't really need it. So good salesmanship can often lead to clients implementing organisational changes and new computer systems that give them relatively little value and are not what they ought to have bought.

■ 4 Wrong Issue

One problem facing organisations that buy consultancy is often a lack of capability in the top management team. However, there are few top management teams that will be honest enough to admit that they are not up to the job. So, when faced with difficulties, they will tend to blame other factors like their employees, their computer systems, their organisation structure, and so on. Clearly in such situations, if a consultancy takes millions for providing new organisation structures, new IT systems, or employee training without solving the weaknesses at top management level, their interventions will be of limited value.

■ 5 Contract Structure

Too much consulting and IT work is still done on what we call "Time and Materials" contracts. On Time and Materials contracts, the supplier is paid on the basis of how much time and resources they use—so the more time and resources they use, the more money they get. Thus they have no strong incentive to finish within a tight timeframe or with carefully controlled use of resources. If they were on contracts with a fixed price and penalties for cost and time overruns, then many more consulting projects and IT systems might be completed faster and at much lower cost than is the case now. Other projects may appear to be based on a fixed price and being completed within a fixed timeframe. However, when you look at the small print, you tend to find a whole series of "Get out of jail free" clauses that allow the consultants to continuously increase the cost of the project and the time taken. Hence we see many systems providers, especially on public sector projects, making stupendous profits year after year in spite of the fact that many of their massive projects end up as fiascos costing hundreds of millions more than initially budgeted and taking years longer than initially planned.

■ 6 Reinventing the Wheel

Although their products or services may be very different, most organisations do fundamentally similar things. They make/buy something, put it in a box, and sell it. Or they make/buy something, put it in a shop or website, and sell it. Or they take some skill/knowledge (cancer surgery, accountancy, law), provide it to customers/patients, and manage their costs and budgets. Or they transport passengers. Or they handle their money. So most organisations need similar things from their systems—acquiring products or skills, identifying and attracting customers, managing information about customers, cost control/billing, HR management, financial accounting, and so on. So whatever the system you require, the basic elements probably already exist somewhere in the world and could be easily adapted to your needs. However, your systems supplier will usually try and convince you that your system is unique and requires them to build a new system from scratch. Normally doing a new system build is much more risky and will cost ten to twenty times as much as adapting existing technology.

PART 4

The Career Perspective

10

The Consultancy Career

Chapter Objectives

This chapter answers the question, how do I succeed in the consultancy career? To answer this question, the chapter:

- Describes the consultancy career and the options associated with it.

- Explains the access points to consultancy and provides help in being recruited successfully.

- Describes the challenges of moving up the consultancy ladder.

- Examines reasons why consultants leave and the options available when doing so.

- Answers the questions that students frequently ask when facing the challenge of applying to consultancies.

■ An Overview of the Consultancy Career

Management consultancy is the top career choice of MBA students (Wong 2008) and McKinsey held the "most preferred employer" title for twelve years in MBA surveys before being dislodged by Google in 2007 (Universum 2007). One would, therefore, expect MBA courses, especially those in management consultancy, to educate students about the consultancy career and how they might get into it. However, this is rarely the case. The unusual style of consultancy career entrance and progression often means that this expert knowledge falls between the gaps: professors keen on teaching critical and sociological issues assume that the generic "CV and interview practice" provided by the careers service provides students with all they need, whilst the careers service often lacks the specialist knowledge to help with the case interview, consulting competences, and terms such as "leverage" and "utilisation".

This chapter, therefore, aims to answer the hundreds of questions I get each year from students who feel lost when it comes to understanding the consultancy career. It specifically seeks to demystify the unique complexities of consultancy companies when it comes to recruitment, selection, and career progression. To achieve this, it first outlines the specifics of the consultancy career: the unusual firm structure, the standard career progression, the job titles, and associated salaries. It then provides advice on getting into the consulting industry: the entry points, what to look for in a good employer, and how to conduct a strong interview. The central core of the recruitment process, the case interview, is dealt with separately in the next chapter.

This chapter then moves on to what happens once an applicant has been accepted by a firm: how they get promotions, what competencies they need to excel at, and what their career options are. Finally, the chapter examines what happens when consultants leave: why they decide to go, what they do when they hand in their laptop and cash in their Airmiles, and what consultants say about the whole experience. This is especially important to read as many students are often blinded by the hype and rhetoric of the business world into thinking consultancy work is always a positive experience—some would argue otherwise.

■ The Consulting Career

The Dominance of Consultancy

Compared to other professions, such as accountancy, law, and medicine, consultancy offers the graduate a number of advantages. It has no compulsory professional training, there are no mandatory tests, and the advancement to senior positions is often much faster than comparable jobs. A 21-year-old graduate moving to a good strategy consultancy can expect to start on £50,000 and within six years, as an associate consultant or project leader, achieve a salary in excess of £100,000. From that point on, consultants can choose to stay in the career, aiming to become partner, or move to industry where their experience will land them senior positions far more quickly than if they had progressed through the standard management structure.

An article by *Fortune* magazine (Colvin 1999) compared the relative successes of CEOs from McKinsey and General Electric, then the world's largest company. They found that the partners at McKinsey "produced many more CEOS, and far more quickly, than the executives in General Electric ... the total market capitalisation of the five companies managed by CEOs who had started at General Electric was less than 15 per cent of the value of the five companies controlled by former consultants at McKinsey" (McKenna 2006: 4). Simply put, the training, experience, reputation, and, perhaps, mystique offered by the top consultancies puts them in a different career league from even the best performing blue-chip companies.

Furthermore, as the *Financial Times* (2007) pointed out, consultancy offers a good opportunity "if you don't know what to do". In other words, general management consulting routes give the graduate an opportunity to get a strong overview of how businesses work in many different areas. These experiences are attractive to employers should the graduate wish to specialise later on.

More Business—Less Professional?

In the 1950s when consultancy was developing as an industry, it sought credibility by mimicking the established accounting and legal partnerships that enabled higher fee rates (McKenna 2006). This professional model was also given credibility by recruitment from the top MBAs and the development of a strong professional identity in the top firms (Alvesson and Robertson 2006). This formula not only produced recruits that were controlled through the strong management of process, culture, and competence, but also, as Armbrüster (2006) argues, helped provide credibility in the face of sceptical clients. In other words, it signals to the market an "elite" group who have a common language, culture, and personality that the client often lacks.

For the potential recruit to the consulting industry, this "professional" image meant a number of common characteristics to their job:

- A reliance on MBA recruitment, especially at the top business schools.
- An "up or out" culture which fostered competitiveness and ambition.
- A higher salary than most other graduates.
- A strong corporate culture producing conformity and an elite identity.
- The use of the "case method" to test the business knowledge of recruits.
- The ultimate aim being partner level where firm ownership was possible.

Whilst these characteristics still remain in the older partnership firms, it is increasingly common for consultancies to be publicly traded rather than privately owned. Indeed, in the last fifty years the proportion of the top consultancies which are privately owned partnerships has declined from around 85 per cent to around 40 per cent (Kennedy Information 2007; McKenna 2006). In an excellent but rarely cited paper, Adams and Zanzi (2005) outlined the effect of this transition on the career of consultants joining the firms. Central to their paper is the argument that publicly traded firms such as IBM and Accenture must focus more sharply on short-term returns to shareholders rather than sustainable, long-term growth. When they examine the levels of morale amongst employees of the different companies, and the reputation of firms amongst MBA students, they find that it is the privately owned partnerships rather than the publicly traded companies that have the highest morale and the best reputations.

The increasing number of publicly owned firms means that the traditional professional career structure of consultants is under pressure. They are increasingly influenced by the structures of the IT and outsourcing companies that own them and are, therefore, more likely to be more like a "standard" organisation. What this means for the aspiring MBA student or business graduate is that whilst publicly traded firms have brought different practices to recruitment and competence management, the "ideal" model developed over fifty years ago in McKinsey remains virtually unchanged in what are considered the top consulting firms.

Reasons for Joining

Regardless of the changes to the structure of the consulting industry, it has remained top of MBA career wish-lists for many years. To some extent, this should be no surprise, as the growth of the MBA in the 1950s and 1960s was primarily driven by the demand from management consultancy recruiters (McKenna 2006). This said, the variety of reasons students give for wishing to join the consulting industry are varied: the salary, the opportunity to learn, the flexibility, and, sometimes, the power are all mentioned as reasons for becoming a consultant. Depending on their perspective, they all have different aims and career goals (see Table 10.1).

I want to:	I will aim at:	My career will focus on:	I will leave when:
Earn as much money as possible.	The highest-paid consultancies; the fastest promotion; the biggest bonuses.	Making myself invaluable to the company; building connections with expensive clients; focusing on strategy or financial consulting. Preferably both.	A client or consultancy offers me more money.
Learn as much as possible.	The most training; The best mentors; The most interesting clients.	Developing a diverse and interesting skill-set, supported by job rotation, moving frequently between industries, clients, and consultancies.	A more challenging and interesting job becomes available.
Get a good work–life–pay balance.	Being as flexible as possible so I can fulfil my needs.	Finding a firm, or an arrangement, that allows me to work the hours I wish. This may involve being an associate or a contractor at different points.	I cannot maintain my work–life balance.
Get as powerful as possible.	Getting control over as many people and resources as possible.	Building empires though Machiavellian realpolitik.	I get sacked for empire building or retire as partner.

Table 10.1. Reasons to enter consultancy

Career Structure

Defining Roles

Whilst the formal nomenclature of different career titles varies considerably from firm to firm, the actual content of the jobs at different levels remains remarkably similar. In Table 10.2 the different terms for positions in the "pure" consultancy firms are outlined. In this chapter, the definitions on the right-hand side are used as these are most common in consulting firms and are descriptive of what each role does.

In many texts, the first two levels are referred to as the "grinders", the middle two are the "minders", and the last two are the "finders". The grinders are responsible for doing the work, the minders are the people who ensure the work gets done, and the finders are the people who find new work.

Descriptions of what the different roles do are outlined below.

Analyst

Analysts are the workhorses of consulting firms. It is they that perform the research, gather information, crunch numbers, and prepare reports. They often spend long periods of time processing data and putting together presentations for more senior consultants and, for this reason, are often known colloquially as Excel-jockeys or PowerPoint-monkeys. Whilst such teasing is common amongst more senior consultants, there are few who could survive without their research skills, which are valued at all levels of the firm.

This role needs to have the capability, rather than the actuality, of being a skilled analyst. Due to the analytical focus of these roles, graduates from engineering, mathematical, and science backgrounds tend to find these jobs easier. However, the potential for moving up to

McKinsey	Bain	BCG	BAH	Oliver Wyman	THIS BOOK
Business Analyst	Associate Consultant	Associate	Consultant	Analyst	**ANALYST**
Senior Business Analyst	Senior Associate Consultant	Senior Associate	Senior Consultant	Consultant	**CONSULTANT**
Associate	Consultant	Consultant	Associate	Associate	**ASSOCIATE CONSULTANT**
Engagement Manager	Case Team Leader	Project Leader	Senior Associate	Senior Associate	**PROJECT LEADER**
Associate Principal	Manager	Principal	Principal	Principal	**PRINCIPAL CONSULTANT**
Partner	Partner	Partner	Partner	Director	**PARTNER**

Table 10.2. Standard hierarchy in a large consultancy firm

less data-driven work means that consultancies widen their horizons to arts subjects when recruiting for these positions. Analysts will usually be recruited directly after their under-graduate degree; however, an MSc or work experience in a good establishment will boost an individual's chance of being accepted.

Consultant

The consultant is an experienced analyst. They will either be an analyst who has a couple of years' experience or an MBA graduate, usually with a year or two's work experience under their belt. The consultant is expected to "do the work" and to use analysts to support them in achieving this. As part of their remit, the consultant will develop the skills of the analyst, ensuring that they learn the ropes of the firm and understand the basics of being a consultant in the firm. The consultant will usually be responsible for producing the work: designing the processes, completing the analysis, or producing the report.

The consultant needs to be a skilled designer as well as an analyst: they must not only be able to find, crunch, and map data but must also be able to construct and present them in a way that is pleasing to both the client and the associate they work for.

Associate Consultant

The role of the senior consultant is to ensure that the work gets done. This means supervising, editing, and pulling together the work of the various consultants and analysts working on any project into a coherent and client-facing deliverable.

The associate will usually have started as a consultant with an MBA, or as an analyst with a degree, and have 2–4 years' work experience. The latter will allow them to have mastered all the technical analytical skills of the roles below them, but also to understand the politics and processes of client interaction.

As such, the associate consultant needs to have two outstanding skill-sets. The first is project manager: bringing together, supervising, and editing the work of the various con-sultants and analysts on a team to ensure that a coherent deliverable is produced in time for the client. The second is client-facing and marketing skills: to be able to understand what the client wants and deliver it in an effective manner. In addition, the associate consultant will sometimes have a higher or specialist qualification in their area such as a PhD.

Project Leader

The project leader, unsurprisingly, will lead a client engagement project and provide the main point of contact between the client business owner and the consultancy team. Typically with 3–6 years' experience, the project leader will have proved his or her ability at interacting with clients and managing the delivery of projects and will have a number of direct reports whom they will coordinate, manage, and develop.

The project leader will act as manager on smaller projects or on smaller parts of larger engagements. They are responsible for integrating projects to provide client solutions, ensuring quality, and strengthening the client relationship.

Principal Consultant

Although all members of a consultancy firm are responsible for selling, this is primarily the responsibility of principal and partner levels. The principal consultant will begin to develop their own contacts with potential clients, building a network that will enable them to progress to partner level. This role will often involve managing the on-going relationships with existing clients and overseeing all the projects associated with that client. This will often mean acting as an adviser to the firm, even when there are no billable projects active.

As part of their marketing focus principals will develop the intellectual capital and the products of the firm by monitoring client demands and using their sector expertise to innovate and experiment. This enables them to take an active role in selling to clients. With respect to their own reports, they will be responsible for coaching and developing their project leaders.

Principals will usually have 10–12 years' experience of consulting or significant senior experience in another professional context.

Partner

The partners of a company own the firm and are primarily responsible for developing new business and strengthening existing client relationships. Partners will have a strong reputation and a large number of contacts in their field and act as strategic advisers to senior clients. Partners have the responsibility for setting the strategic direction of the company and are primarily responsible for the growth and success of the firm.

The partner will typically have 15+ years' experience and will be promoted primarily on their ability to bring new business into the company. Often principal consultants, frustrated by the lack of opportunities in their own firm, will jump to a partnership in a competitor's business, taking their contacts and networks with them.

The independence of partners and the value they necessarily attach to their contacts makes them, in many firms, poor team-players. Whilst a minimal amount of cooperation is necessary for a partnership to work, the value (and salary) of a partner is, to a great extent, dependent on the business they can pull in from their contacts. This, in the words of Lowendhal, makes their strategic cooperation akin to "herding wild cats" (2005: 69).

Salaries

There are dozens of salary surveys which "predict" what can be earned as a consultant. However, your salary as a consultant will depend on a number of variables that are virtually impossible to predict. These include, in loose order of importance:

- Your position in the company: partners are, of course, paid more than consultants.

- The firm: bigger firms tend to pay more, though there are exceptions. Niche strategy firms such as McKinsey and Bain pay considerably more.

- The type of consultancy you do: strategy consultancy in the finance industry earns much more than IT consultancy in the public sector.

- Where you graduated from: the average post-MBA consultancy salary at Harvard in 2008 was $125,000 with a signing bonus of $35,000. At weaker schools, it will be considerably less.

- The competition: in the 1990s, consultants could charge a premium for IT advice. Now that much IT work can be done by Indian companies for a lower wage, pay in this area has plummeted.

- The economic conditions: in a recession, demand for consultancy falls and consultants freeze recruitment and wages.

- Your negotiation skills: good negotiators who ask their boss for a raise and are constantly on the lookout for a better-paying job will earn a lot more, regardless of their talents.

Our top competitor for talent isn't BCG or Bain, it's Goldman Sachs.

(McKinsey recruiter)

The average pay of a consultant in the UK is £52,000 (ONS 2007). However, wages vary considerably according to the level that the consultant works at. In order to give some account of the variation, Table 10.3 provides the approximate average salary of a strong position and a weak position. The former might represent a strategy consultant in a generous company who is a strong negotiator. The latter might represent an IT consultant in a mid-ranking firm. The data are based on an average of a number of sources which include several surveys from Wetfeet (2008), Vault (2008), the Bureau of Labor Statistics (2008), Woodhurst (2007), and BLT (2009). The averages are rounded up to the nearest £5,000.

Job title	Average salary	Strong average	Weak average	Average bonus
Analyst	£30k	£45k	£20k	£3k
Consultant	£45k	£80k	£35k	£10k
Associate Consultant	£65k	£100k	£45k	£15k
Project Leader	£80k	£120k	£70k	£20k
Principal Consultant	£120k	£300k	£95k	£55k
Partner	£200k	£1.5m	£150k	£100k

Table 10.3. Consultancy salaries and bonuses 2007–9

As can be evidenced from the table, the variation in pay is considerable, especially at the higher levels of a firm. The same is true of bonuses which can vary from nothing in some years (2009 being the worst for some time) to up to 40 per cent of the base salary in good times. In addition, consultancies may also offer:

- A signing bonus of 10–25 per cent of the joining salary.
- Repayment of MBA fees over three years.
- A company car.
- Health insurance.
- Training for professional qualifications.

It should also be noted that, in recent years, whilst consulting revenue has grown, profits have not kept up as clients have put pressure on their procurement teams to reduce consultancy spend. This trend has not been helped by the 2008–10 recession, nor the spiralling salaries offered in the finance sector. Wages for consultants have, therefore, remained relatively static since 2008. It is likely that this stagnation in salaries will continue for some time.

In addition to these packages, larger consultancies offer a "menu" of additional benefits so the employee can chose options which suit their lifestyle best. However, before spending too long considering the rewards of consultancy, one must first understand how to get a job in the industry.

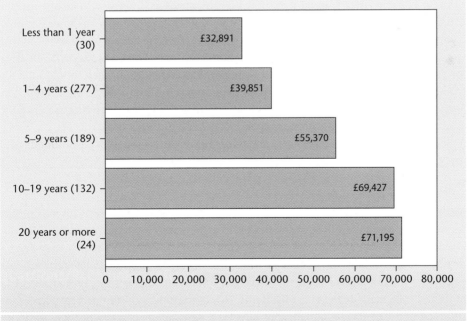

Figure 10.1. The relationship between experience and salaries in consultancy

■ Points of Entry

Getting into consulting is hard but the work, as one successful McKinsey applicant told me, is done long before you ever get to interview. If you're reasonably bright, have worked hard through your educational and career years, and have done your homework with your application you should be in a position where many consultancies would see you as an asset.

However, if you don't have a first from Harvard and work experience at Boston Consulting Group, all is not lost. You should not think that because you have a third-class degree from a minor university entry into consultancy is impossible. Consultants come in all shapes and sizes: I know several people in top consultancies who went to relatively poor universities and graduated in the bottom half of their classes. Many successful independent consultants don't even have a degree. It should be noted, however, that many of these hires were experienced and had put themselves in strong positions through wise choices in their careers.

Fortunately for less-qualified candidates, recruiters often do a simple cost–benefit calculation and, looking at the applicant's experience and qualifications, worked out if they could sell them for a certain percentage more than they could hire them.

In general, therefore, how you can enter consultancy will depend very much upon when in your life you have "added value" to your employability. If you have a third-class degree from a third-class university and no work experience, you won't even get an interview at most consultancies. However, this section is aimed at giving you the information and skills that will enable you to maximise your chances of getting a good job within the constraints that you have.

There is some international variation on this message, however. In many smaller countries, getting a good blue-chip job is quite difficult because only the multinational companies offer graduate recruitment positions, and these are rare. In an interview with a Greek consultant from Deloitte, she suggested that work experience was a key differentiator for young graduates getting onto these schemes. She argued that "they should look for work experience in the area they are interested, even if it is not paid, for a few months". Networking is, of course, especially important in these situations: attending careers fairs, seminars, and other events where a rapport can be built on a face-to-face level.

Below, the different points of entry and what they mean for job roles are outlined.

Degree

A degree-holder will normally enter a consultancy at the analyst position. This means that the application will need to have and be able to demonstrate analytical capabilities as well as strong interpersonal and teamworking skills. Students often ask whether they need a degree in business studies in order to enter the consultancy industry. The answer is an emphatic "no". In fact business studies comes in behind engineering and mathematics in terms of the main degrees of consultants. However, students without these degrees are still recruited. The ideal graduate applicant for a top strategy consultancy will have the qualities shown in Table 10.4.

Ideally	At the worst
A first class degree (top 5%)	A 2:1 (top 20%)
Degree in a numerate, problem-solving subject	Any degree with an analytical aspect
Studied at a top-rated course at a top university	From any university
An MBA from a top university	No MBA
Work or placement in a blue-chip company	No work experience

Table 10.4. Graduate applicant qualities

Smaller consultancies are more difficult for graduates to get into because these companies often rely on highly skilled experienced individuals, and graduates often have little work experience. However, these firms often need a "work horse" to prepare reports and slides, and this can be a good learning experience. Applying to these firms is usually a matter of sending off a covering letter and CV to any firm you can find information on. Often these firms don't have the budget or time to advertise roles and welcome speculative applications.

The graduate recruitment process is, however, incredibly competitive. In 2006, 10,000 graduates applied for jobs at Accenture UK but only 5 per cent of these were offered jobs. The odds are much greater at famous strategy houses such as McKinsey and Bain.

MBA

MBAs have traditionally been perceived as the entry point to management consultancy, and the exponential rise in MBA courses and students was in part due to the massive recruiting drive by strategy consultancies from the top business schools from 1950 to 1990. However, in recent years things have changed. As clients have become more sophisticated, they are increasingly unhappy with paying £750 a day for an MBA graduate with little practical expertise and have pushed for more experienced project teams.

This pressure has trickled through to the recruiters for large consultancies who are cutting back on MBA recruitment in favour of specialists with 10–15 years' work experience. This trend has been exacerbated by the drying up of pure strategy work which favours bright analysts with client-friendly faces, and the increase in implementation work which needs more experienced hands.

This said, MBA graduates are still the highest paid in the world (Quacquarelli 2008) and the generalist skills that the MBA provides create a rounded individual capable of turning their mind to any sort of business problem. For this reason, the MBA is still the pre-eminent qualification for consultants around the world. In an effort to retain this status, and perhaps in recognition of the changing recruitment patterns, many business schools, such as MIT, Wharton, and Haas, are offering students a specialisation in anything from Finance or Management Consultancy to e-business or sports management.

In terms of recruitment, consultancies actively target the top MBA courses and will run career fairs, workshops, or undertake interviews on campus to raise their own profile. Most consultancies allow MBAs to come in at the consultant level rather than the analyst level, and will provide them with a premium in pay and benefits: "a typical MBA graduate is most likely to have three or four years' work experience, be hired by a US consulting firm, acquire a mid-level position, and earn a salary that is almost double that of a recent graduate" (GMAC 2008). Many consultancies will, if you negotiate well, offer to reimburse your MBA fees. This will usually happen over a three-year period so that you are tied into the firm for some time.

Experienced Hires

As clients become more discerning and sophisticated in their recruitment of consultants, so too have consultancies become more aware of demonstrating value to the client. Part of this effort has been to recruit experienced workers with specialist skills in relevant sectors. Experienced hires now account for around 25 per cent of all recruitment to the top consultancy firms and they will usually join at Associate or Project Leader level depending on their experience (Wetfeet 2008). If the hire is at director level and has a number of useful contacts, they are occasionally recruited at principal, or even partner, level.

I wouldn't have thought about consulting when I was younger. To be honest, I wouldn't have been confident enough. Now I know my trade I'm happy to advise.

(McKinsey experienced hire)

For many, joining a consultancy as an experienced hire makes good sense. As the average consultancy career lasts only seven years, some believe it is better to have this stint at a more senior level rather than as an analyst or a junior consultant. Moreover, many experienced hires would not have got into a good consultancy when they were younger due to poor grades or lack of solid experience. Several hires I interviewed said that they didn't think about consultancy as a career until they worked alongside consultants who were doing the same job as them but on double the money.

The recruitment process for experienced workers is the same as that of all other levels; however, the opportunities vary considerably. One month, AT Kearney may have a drive to recruit supply-chain specialists in an attempt to bolster its position in the retail industry, another month McKinsey may be recruiting healthcare experts to take advantage of deregulation in Europe. There is, therefore, a fair amount of luck as to whether your specific skills would be in demand at any given time, and a reasonable amount of monitoring the consultancy websites and recruitment agencies is advisable.

CASE 10.1

A Delayed Entry

Claire wanted to get into consultancy when she left university, but the economy wasn't in great condition and, despite several applications, she failed to get further than the interview stage. She eventually got a graduate job with a large public sector health firm and spent ten years working in procurement—the buying of equipment and services.

Claire's career progression was slow but she eventually became a senior manager in a procurement department that was expanding in both size and importance. As hospitals increasingly used consultants and as procurement was increasingly bound by complex regulations, Claire became more of an expert in knowledge work and eventually became responsible for creating, managing, and delivering the procurement of consulting services.

As a result of working closely with consultancies and developing skills and knowledge that might be valuable to a consultancy, Claire was approached by a consultancy keen to improve their sales to the public health sector. Claire was interviewed by the consultancy and was offered a job on a salary which doubled her current income. Claire's new role focused on writing proposals and giving presentations for consultancy projects in the public sector.

However, after two years in consultancy, Claire decided to take a pay-cut and move back into the public sector. I interviewed her shortly after her decision to return. Some of her comments are summarised below:

> At first I found it strange that all these young consultants with little experience could be sold in at these enormous rates, but then you realise that their skills don't have to be experience based ... It was good for me being an expert in this area as I could help them with areas they didn't know about and vice versa....
>
> Consulting was much faster than working in the public sector—you're expected to learn incredibly fast and work longer hours and more intensively than those round you. Of course, that's what you're paid for. The whole "selling" thing is entirely different as well. You don't just do a good job, but you show that you've done it too....
>
> Eventually I think the culture shock was too great. I only saw my family three nights of the week and even then I was pretty exhausted ... I learnt a huge amount but not many people can keep that level of work up indefinitely.

- How could consultancies reduce the stress that causes so many consultants to leave?

Internships

An internship is an opportunity for students to do a short, often three-month, placement in a consultancy to get a better understanding of how the company operates and what a job there would entail. For the consultancy, it is a way of engaging more deeply with good applicants, assessing their suitability for the job, and also a way of getting quality labour relatively cheaply.

Around 60 per cent of companies take interns and virtually all large consultancies have an internship scheme (GMAC 2007). Additionally, 70 per cent of those who successfully get a place are eventually offered a job with that company. However, competition for intern places is just as competitive as that for normal positions within a consultancy and the recruitment process can be equally severe.

Associates

Associates are contractors for the consulting industry. They are a bank of skilled individuals with consultancy experience that the firm can call on for short periods of time. For the consultancy, this offers a flexibility of employment which can reduce permanent headcount in times of recession. Some consultancies, such as Eden McCallum, have built up their entire business model on the back of associate consultants.

For the associate, this offers a flexible form of work whilst attracting a premium rate for the work they do. On the downside, associates are less profitable for the consultancy, with between 35 and 45 per cent of the fee charged for an associate being reimbursed to them and the consultancy taking the rest. In addition, consultancies may often find that their associate is working on another project for another firm when they want them most, and that it is difficult to develop a shared culture, brand, or methodology for clients to recognise. For the associates, some may find the unpredictable nature of demand difficult to plan around.

■ The Recruitment Process

Now we have taken a closer look at the different types of consultant and the different routes for getting into a consultancy, it is worth paying closer attention to the recruitment process itself. Consultancies rely on their people much more heavily than any other industry because this is their primary asset, their most tangible product. As Armbrüster (2006) argues, having the best people not only means that the work may be done better but it also sends a signal to the market as to the, very often intangible, value of the work that is done.

Most large consultancies have a standard application process for all levels up to partner. This usually involves one or more of:

- A CV and covering letter, *or* an application form.
- A telephone interview.
- A face-to-face interview.
- An assessment centre.
- The case interview.

As the case interview is a fairly complex and unique method of recruitment it is covered in more detail in the next chapter. However, below the other stages are introduced and various tips are provided for applicants that are considering a consultancy career. There are thousands of resources for tackling the recruitment process online (see Further Reading) so these sections will focus on what is specific for management consultancies.

Area	Competence	Primary/secondary test
Analytical Ability	Problem solving	Case interview, assessment centre
	Competence with numbers	CV, case interview
	Applying a structured methodology	Case interview
Client-Facing Skills	Verbal communication	Interviews, Case interview
	Written communication	CV, letter, assessment centre
	Interaction and rapport	Interviews, case interview
	Calmness under pressure	Interviews, assessment centre
Team-Working Skills	Ability to work with others	Interviews, assessment centre
	Leadership	Interviews, assessment centre
	Persuasion and influence	Interviews, assessment centre
Personal Excellence	Motivation	Interviews, assessment centre
	Energy	Interviews, assessment centre
	Fit with the culture	Interviews, assessment centre
	Trustworthiness	Interviews

Table 10.5. Consulting competences and assessment methods

Throughout the recruitment process, consultancies are trying to assess the candidate's competencies. A competence is a capability or an aptitude for performing a specific skill-set. Table 10.5 lists the typical competencies that consultancies look for in applicants and where they are usually tested.

Both the competences looked for and the methods by which they are assessed vary from consultancy to consultancy. For example, pure consultancies tend not to use assessment centres, whereas virtually all of the Big Four firms do.

The key focus is not simply to have the ability, but to be able to demonstrate it both in the tasks you are given in the selection process and in your previous experience. Throughout all of the selection process you should remember that consultancies tend to be conservative employers. Sarcasm, risky humour, and too much individualism are often frowned upon. The ability to fit in, demonstrate reliability, and to work hard are key in all stages of the process.

Covering Letters and CVs

Covering letters and CVs for the consultancy industry should be guided by the same principles as those which apply to most other professional industries. The covering letter should be brief, expressing the position you are applying for, why you are applying for it, and a few key points as to why your experience and achievements would make you a suitable candidate. A sample covering letter can be seen in the Online Resource Centre.

CVs should be two pages long unless the recruiter has asked for a different length or unless your experience will not fill two pages. The CV should emphasise the experience and achievements that demonstrate the competencies in Table 10.5.

Many applicants make the mistake of simply stating their role and formal duties. For example:

Summer 2009: Chef, The Grand Inn, London.
  • *Cooked lunch and dinner, including vegetarian options.*

Instead, the consultancy is going to be much more interested in what competencies you demonstrated and any achievements you had. For example:

• Sourced a new supplier of vegetables, saving the Inn £12k over 3 years.

• Managed two sous-chefs to prepare meals for up to 70 people in high-stress environment.

• Conducted customer satisfaction survey and consequently improved the menu, creating a 12 per cent hike in customers and a 15 per cent hike in revenue.

You can see how this different style shows that you know how to think like a consultant by focusing on what can be improved and also demonstrates a familiarity with business needs, showing several competencies that would otherwise have been missed.

Competency-Based Interviews

Consultancies are relatively unique in placing so much emphasis on interviews. To some extent, this is hardly surprising, as communication and analytical skills can both be tested. The case interview, covered in the next chapter, is a common method of testing both of these. However, another form of interviewing is the competency-based interview.

Undertaken over the phone or face to face, the competency-based interview seeks to understand an applicant's past demonstration of competencies in the hope that they are a reliable predictor of their ability to perform. There are, of course, several weaknesses with this approach: candidates can simply make up their answers and there is little evidence that the ability to tell a convincing story is evidence of future performance. However, these interviews are used in around a third of recruitment processes in large companies and are, therefore, worth understanding in some detail.

At What Stage Is the Interview Undertaken?

The competence interview is usually the second line of selection after receiving and vetting the CV or application form. It is usually undertaken before any case interviews, presentations, or group work because it is a more cost-effective way of reducing the numbers of applicants. Sometimes, the application form will incorporate competency-based questions, but this will not stop the company asking you questions about the answers you put down. For this reason, it is always important to photocopy whatever you send to them.

This interview is sometimes undertaken over the phone and often by recruitment agencies that specialise in this type of work. The important thing to remember is that your interviewer is not interested in you telling them how great you are but is simply looking for certain examples that will demonstrate that you have the competencies the company requires. The competencies that are looked for in competence-based interviews are varied, but usually include: supporting teamwork, achieving excellence, showing leadership, solving problems, and managing communication.

Give Me Some Examples

Often questions will be asked with follow-up questions to prompt you to expand on what you did or didn't do:

- Give me an example of a time you worked in a team to achieve a specific goal. How did you help the team achieve it?
- Tell me about a time when you persuaded your boss of the merits of an idea that you had. How did you deal with his or her objections?
- Tell me about when you had to present to a large group. What did you do before the presentation?

Of course, the questions can always be asked in the negative:

- Tell me about a time when you failed to get buy-in from your boss. How did you deal with him or her?
- Give me an example about a time when you really didn't get your point across well. What would you do better next time?
- What was your biggest failure? How did you deal with it?

What Should my Answer Be?

The marking criteria vary from consultancy to consultancy but you will be awarded points when you say something to demonstrate the competence which they are measuring.

However, it is important not simply to focus on the single event that demonstrates your competence (e.g. that you are a good communicator or a persuasive person) but to break down the story to demonstrate this in several different ways. For example, with the persuasion competence, you will not simply be expected to tell a story about influencing someone, but also to tell:

- That you used a range of approaches.
- That you got some other people to argue your case.
- That you considered the other person's perspective.
- That you enabled that person to benefit from the solution.

You might also be marked down if you displayed undesirable characteristics such as:

- Inappropriate forms of influence (e.g. undermining or attacking them).
- Using command and control techniques on subordinates (this isn't persuasion!).
- Failing to get buy-in.

	Positive behaviours	Negative behaviours
Supporting Teamwork	Selling the team to individuals Seeking the views of all Valuing different contributions Involving everyone Sharing information and ideas Connecting the team and the organisation	Being divisive Not involving people Creating cliques
Achieving Excellence	Finding out expectations Setting goals Making plans Monitoring against plan/benchmarks Overcoming problems and issues	Not understanding the goal Not maintaining focus Ignores goals, quality, or milestones
Showing Leadership	Assessing appropriate leadership Being charismatic Communicating clearly to all Building personal loyalty Setting clear direction and goals Coaching individuals who need help Setting clear milestones Provide praise and constructive criticism	Being weak and not setting clear direction Riding roughshod over people's objections Not communicating clearly
Solving Problems	Clearly identifying the issue Understanding implications of problem Gaining insight from others Generating many potential solutions Testing potential solutions Selecting best solution Understanding implications of solution	Not comprehending problem Not involving others Jumping to implementation too quickly Not selecting the best solution
Managing Communication	Uses appropriate comms channels Chooses appropriate style Seeks to understand audiences Focuses on key messages Adapts style and method depending on feedback Encourages questions and feedback	No sensitivity to audience Uses inappropriate language Comms lack clarity Wrong message to wrong people

Table 10.6. Behaviours for different competences

In short, when faced with having to provide evidence for a competence, think about the best possible way in which it is possible to do that thing, not simply just doing it. There are several examples given in Table 10.6.

Ensure that you think of all aspects of the competence, not just the "doing it". Don't assume that the interviewer knows anything at all and ensure that you spell out everything that could look positive in the way you handled the situation.

How Should You Prepare for a Competency-Based Interview?

Use the list of questions in Table 10.7 to write down some general examples of you demonstrating a competency in recent years.

	Positive behaviours
Supporting Teamwork	Have you worked with others to achieve something? When did your teamwork fail? How would you manage a team to cross a desert?
Achieving Excellence	Have you ever introduced an improvement to something? Have you ever fallen short of performance standards? What is your greatest achievement?
Influencing and Persuasion	When have you had to win buy-in from other people? What was the hardest bit of persuasion you've done? How do you influence your boss?
Showing Leadership	When have you led a team to success? When have you led a team to failure? How would you lead this consultancy?
Solving Problems	Tell me about a time you solved a hard problem. Have you worked in a team to solve a problem? What's the trickiest decision you've ever had to make?
Managing Communication	Tell me about when you dealt with a difficult situation that required extensive good communication. What was the hardest presentation you ever gave? Give me an example of how you dealt with a difficult person?

Table 10.7. Typical competency based interview questions

You should ensure that you have answers for both positive questions (when did you show leadership?) and negative ones (when did you fail as a leader?). Both answers should show your awareness of all the right things to do, though your "failure" examples might hinge on things that were out of your control. You should, in these cases, show how you dealt with failure to ensure it didn't happen again. As with all interviews—don't be afraid to ask the interviewer if you don't understand.

One of the key things to work on in interview preparation is practice. You should get your friends, colleagues, and university to organise several practice interviews so that by the time you do it for real, you feel comfortable, prepared, and relaxed.

Asking Questions

An interviewer will usually ask you if you have any questions at the end of the interview. You should try to avoid asking questions that show you may not be entirely committed to the company or to working hard. For example, how much holiday will I get? Do I get a sabbatical? Do I get to fly first class when I travel? You should also avoid asking questions that you can easily find the answers to elsewhere as this may indicate that you haven't done your homework. For example, how much profit did you make last year? How many consultants do you employ? What has your growth rate been?

This is a chance to get some useful information about the firm and the job you might end up doing. Should you be in a position to choose between several offers, the information you get here will help you make up your mind. On top of questions that may be pertinent to your own special interests, you might also ask:

- What projects do you have on at the moment which I would typically be asked to work on?

- What types of training would I typically receive in my first two years?

- Is it possible to specialise, say, in finance or strategy later on?

In addition, you can ask questions that, as well as eliciting useful information, also show that you have a good understanding of how consultancies work. For example:

- What is your average revenue per consultant at my level?
  The answer to this question will help you understand what the consultancy typically charges its graduate-level employees out at. Generally speaking, the higher the rate, the more skilled work you will be undertaking, the better salary you will be able to command, and the better the reputation of the firm. Bain, for example, might have an average daily rate which is almost twice that of, say, Accenture.

- What is the ratio of partners to consultants?
  This will help give you an idea of the promotion opportunities in the firm and also the chances that you will have to work with senior consultants and partners. If the ratio is high, it is possible that you may find yourself working amongst lots of other graduates and having significant competition for promotions.

- What percentage of your income comes from strategy work?
  Strategy work has decreased considerably over the last ten years. However, many firms are keen on presenting themselves as having a foothold in the strategic market when in reality a vast majority of their work is implementation. Finding out the proportion of strategy work will help you to discover the likelihood of you working on implementation projects.

- What do you like and dislike about the firm?
  This question enables you to strike up a more personal relationship with your interviewer as you have asked them about them rather than the firm. It is also likely that they will be honest in giving you an answer which will be useful in understanding the informal side of the organisation.

Assessment Centres

Assessment centres for consultancies are usually only used in firms that are primarily IT or accountancy companies. In these cases, the assessment centre is very similar to the type that you might experience with any other blue-chip company.

Usually one- or two-day programmes, most assessment centres involve two or more:

- Interviews

  Usually two interviews: one with the HR manager who will try to assess your competences in different areas, often with a competence interview. The next with a senior manager or partner who will assess your fit with the organisation.

- Group exercises

  These assess how well you work in a team. For this reason it is important not to dominate the group or be too aggressive. Provide leadership when you can, but also support other members by asking them what they think and building on their ideas. Try to provide structure for the group: how long should you allocate to tasks? How should you solve the problem? How should you make decisions as a group?

- Presentation exercises

  Consultants will usually need to present slides to clients, so this test is designed to assess your public speaking and your confidence in dealing with awkward questions. You should practise this before going to an assessment centre. Remember to make eye contact with your audience and speak in a clear, confident voice. Keep messages simple and don't be afraid to say "I don't know, but I can find out for you" when stumped. Finally, don't get angry or snappy when they try to put you under pressure.

- In-tray exercise

  These provide "realistic" work problems that you may have to face as a consultant: for example, a lot of information that you have to sift through for a client. These will usually test your analytical skills. You should practise your maths for a while before coming on an assessment centre.

- Numerical/verbal tests

  The only way to improve these is with practice. There are dozens of tests that you can do on the internet to develop your skills for this.

- Psychological profiling

  Personality or psychological tests will not "make or break" an assessment centre. They are usually used by recruiters to see what type of role you would be most suited to. As there are many different types of role, it is usually best just to answer the questions honestly and consistently so that you get matched with what you are best at.

Dealing with Rejection

Unless you are incredibly lucky you should expect to be rejected from many, if not all, the applications that you put in. The simple maths show that if only 5 per cent of applications are eventually accepted by companies such as Accenture, the odds are never going to be in your favour. However, despite knowing this, many students take it very personally when they are rejected.

When you get a rejection there are two important things to remember. The first is that there is a vast amount of luck involved in getting recruited. Recruiters often tell me that they are frequently faced with five applicants, all of whom would do an excellent job, but they can only offer it to one of them. The recruitment process is not a science and there is plenty of room for error. One medium-sized consultancy I am familiar with found out that its HR person had been sifting through applicants and filling places alphabetically, so that applicants whose surnames began with A or B were much more likely to get recruited than anyone else.

It is also important to remember that consultancies are looking for a certain type of person. That type of person is not better or worse than anyone else in any moral or human respect. They may well have strong analytical skills but they also tend to be conformist. Not fitting into the box that somebody else has defined for you should never be a measure for your success.

■ Getting On

If and when you are accepted for a consultancy position, your focus will usually be on getting promoted, especially if your firm has an "up or out" policy where there is an added incentive to have made the grade after a certain period of time. This section provides commentary on how to make good choices when climbing up the career ladder of consulting.

Setting your Career Strategy

Much of your success as a consultant will depend on positioning yourself in the right company, at the right time, and doing the right thing. For example, if you position yourself as an IT consultant in the manufacturing sector, in say IBM or Accenture, your career trajectory in the 2009–12 period is likely to be less dramatic than, say, a strategy consultant in the Finance sector working for Bain. What should be noted here is that different industries and specialisms are popular at different times. BPR, for example, tends to be popular in recessions when costs need to be reduced. Strategy tends to be popular in times of economic boom. Understanding the consulting market and the areas which are growing will enable you to position yourself better.

Your career planning should be structured by your long-term goals. Do you want to eventually start your own consultancy? Do you want to become a partner? Do you want to jump into industry? Of course, it is impossible to predict what will actually happen, but having an idea of where you want to end up will help you structure and prioritise your options.

It is important to establish this *before* you accept your job as much of the influence you have on what you do, especially at junior levels, will need to be negotiated prior to you joining. Your specialism, training, mentoring, and industry focus should all be discussed with the company after you have been offered a job but before you accept: the time when you, as an applicant, have the most power.

Finally, you should also have an idea of the constraints and opportunities to promotion in the company you are seeking to join. What is their leverage ratio? Do they have an "up or out" policy? What are promotions based on? What is the average tenure at your level before promotion? What opportunities are there to move to other industries or specialisms? Do they have a sabbatical policy? Will they fund external training courses? These questions will give you an idea of the institutional structures which will enable or prevent your early promotion and career development.

The Formal and Informal

Once you understand the market and institutional constraints and opportunities to your career, it is then down to you how you manage things. In terms of getting on in the company, there are the formal things to consider such as performance ratings, promotion policies, and appraisals, but in some companies the informal factors are equally, if not more, important.

The key factor to consider on the formal side of things is how your appraisal and performance rating are determined. This usually focuses on your contribution to the projects you have been working on and your contribution to the firm. The former is usually judged as more important and will include your performance on deliverables, teamwork, taking the initiative, and interaction with the client. At higher levels this will increasingly be focused on your ability to manage other consultants but primarily your ability to sell work to clients. Often, your appraisal will be based on "360 degree" feedback: from those working below you, above you, and with you. This will often include the client team as well.

The informal side of things will again vary from consultancy to consultancy. However, a number of factors are usually important, such as building strong relationships with those senior to you, developing strong client-facing skills, and, not least, being seen as a predictable, reliable, and trustworthy colleague. This also involves a number of cultural things that you should be aware of in your firm. For example, turning up in jeans to work would be a big problem at, say, McKinsey, where uniformity and conformance are quite important.

Mentoring

It is very difficult to get a promotion without sponsorship from either your boss or a mentor. Both roles are highly influential on your career. Often a consultancy will assign you a mentor in the firm, especially if you are a junior consultant. You should develop a strong relationship with this person as they can often help you out when your boss will not. A personal vignette demonstrates this point well.

The first consultancy I joined was a new, expanding company, but unfortunately, my immediate boss was incredibly bureaucratic and risk-averse. Despite having built up good experience as a private consultant and having just completed a Business Doctorate on one of the highest rated programmes in the world, I was put on "admin duty" checking other people's documents for grammar. Fortunately, I built up a relationship with a senior director called Simon Forge, who went round my boss and gave me my first big break in consulting, where I ended up on a large, exciting project, taking responsibility for things that really stretched my skills and enabled my career to take off.

The mentor you develop a relationship with does not have to be the "formal" one provided to you by your firm; however, you should definitely spend time and effort developing strong relationships with a couple of senior people. You never know when you will need them. Additionally, senior consultants change company frequently, and having good contacts with them may provide you with an opportunity to jump ship if things don't work out in your original firm.

Planning a Promotion

It is a great misconception of consulting recruits that a promotion will come when you deserve it. As we saw in Chapter 7, consultancies need to retain their leverage ratios. Consultancies will only promote you if there is an available position or they don't want to lose you to a competitor. For this reason, it is important to plan a promotion as you would any other important project. Key tips for this include:

- Ensure you are in a reasonable position to ask for a promotion. It is unlikely that you will be promoted if your more able and experienced peers deserve it more. Ensure that you are clear what the promotion criteria are and that you have evidence that you have achieved this.

- Have a good idea of what you are worth on the market. Have a look at consultancy websites to assess the buoyancy of the recruitment market. Talk to agencies, friends at other consultancies, and apply for a couple of external positions.

- Prepare your boss for your request. You should have already raised the matter of promotion in your review and asked what you would have to do to achieve the criteria for the next grade. Mention it a few times to your boss, your mentor, and anyone else you think might have some influence. Be inquisitive rather than pushy.

- Find a sponsor, ideally your boss, and ask them to sponsor you. They may simply say "I don't think that you're ready", in which case you can ask for some development advice. In the next few months, try to prove to them that you have achieved what they are asking for and communicate this to them. Approach them again when you think that you have achieved what they asked for.

- Show willing. There are a number of things you can do outside your main role to show that you make a good contribution to the company. Run a couple of talks on an area that you're interested in, initiate a project discussion, or run an internal focus group. Anything to show that you're keen, motivated, and useful.

- Most importantly, begin acting like the level that you want to be promoted to. If you behave and perform like the person you want to be, your seniors will take you more seriously when you apply for a promotion.

When a promotion is turned down, some consultants resort to threatening to leave in order to force their employer's hand. This can be a disastrous move if handled in a bad way, especially, as has been known to happen, if the consultant can't find another job and has to renege on their threat. If you are going to threaten to leave it is absolutely imperative that you have a firm offer in your hand before doing so. However, even this can backfire. A close and able friend of mine had his salary doubled by a firm that he jumped to after his request for a promotion was denied. However, after one month in the new job, the recession bit and he was told they would be making him redundant because the firm had a "last in, first out" policy. In his previous firm, his job would have been much safer as he had been with them for some time.

Additionally, if you are going to force your employer's hand, ensure that you leave them on good terms as you will need to rely on them for references, may well work with them again, and may rely, in the future, on the relationships you develop while you are there. Be polite and explain to them exactly why you're leaving. Your resignation should not be a shock to them and should be part of an on-going conversation with them about your prospects.

Your employer may well offer you the position that you wanted after you tell them you've been offered an alternative position. Whether you accept this or not will very much depend on what you think of the relative merits of both firms.

■ Getting Out

Why Consultants Leave

For one reason or another, the vast majority of consultants leave the industry, generally after less than ten years. There are no aggregated figures concerning the number of consultants leaving the industry each year, though Top-Consultant (2008) estimates that the annual attrition rate from individual firms is around 20–30 per cent, almost double that of standard management roles.

As we can see in Table 10.8, most of those who leave consultancy leave to go into industry.

Of course many of those who leave go to other consultancies. According to Top-Consultant (2009) the main reasons that consultants give for leaving to go to other consultancies are:

- Pay.
- Not being involved in selecting projects.
- Long and inflexible working hours.
- Extended periods away from home.

	Another consultancy	Industry	Other (e.g. retirement)
Partner	19	55	25
Director	25	66	9
Senior consultant	28	61	12
Consultant	22	59	19
Analyst	20	22	39

Table 10.8. Reasons consultants leave
Source: Consulting Magazine (2009).

Interestingly, however, whilst pay is the biggest reason consultants leave to join other consultancies, when asked what would tempt them to an industry employer, their answers are, in order of importance, more flexibility, more interesting assignments, and money (*Consulting Magazine* 2009).

A survey by *Consulting News* (2007) found that 36 per cent of consultants spend more than 76 nights away from home each year. Most spent more than 50. A new hire can expect to be home two days a week if they're lucky. If they're unlucky a nine-month stint in a windowless office in Slough is what some of my colleagues were faced with. According to *Consulting Magazine* (2009) analyst-level employees took an average of ten days' holiday a year. The average workload of a consultant is 60 hours a week (Bernstein 2004) and in heavy times, this can reach up to 90 hours. In recent years, to make things worse, lower profit margins have led to increased utilisation rates and hours worked, whilst time off, training, and morale have all slipped considerably (*Consulting Magazine* 2009).

Generally speaking, the vast majority of consultants who leave the industry do so to shift down a gear so they can be based at home, see more of their friends and family, and avoid the stress of having to work long hours and constantly travel.

Other consultants leave because they want to have ownership and end-to-end control of a project. In interviews I conducted, many consultants stated that they were getting tired of constantly being involved in just one part of a project and not having responsibility for decision-making or ownership. For this reason, consultants often jump to clients that they have worked with and built a good relationship with to manage projects that they were involved with.

The Personal Cost of Consulting

Of course, not all reasons for leaving can be adequately captured on a spreadsheet. Some consultants feel that by accepting payment to implement pretty much any project and by being involved in some of the dubious practices outlined in Chapter 9, they are selling out. A consultant in the UK, for example, kept a blog called "The Prince". After nearly a decade blogging about his experiences in the industry, this was his final post:

> Today is the day. I am leaving this firm. I have spent (I can't say if it was "invested", "endured", or what) almost nine years destroying my soul with this company and today it stops. Today, I choose authenticity. Today, for no particular reason that anyone will be able to put on an HR database, I will resign. No one will expect it. That, I think, is the most marvellous thing about it—nobody expects someone to resign because he is being destroyed, existentially, by working with this company. Nobody—except, perhaps, my HR department who will quite possibly have a "reason for leaving" code on the database: Existential Self-Destruction.

It is a fair claim that unless you're quite an unusual person, the consulting experience will change you both for the better and for the worse. You will be richer, you'll know more about business, and you'll be a more confident and articulate presenter. On the other hand, you may well develop traits that you would once have deplored, your family life may well suffer, and you may leave, five, ten, or twenty years later, burnt out. All these things need to be considered when weighing up the options to join the business.

Beyond the practice of consulting, potential recruits should consider the personal effect it may have on them. In this respect, there are two key charges:

- **Consultants are, or at least become, unethical:** consultants are encouraged by companies to develop unethical practices. This may range from expanding projects, over-billing, up-selling junior consultants, and under-delivering. The lifestyle encourages employees to act as "prostitutes"—doing any work so long as it pays well.

- **Consultants have a poor work–life balance**: this is a fairly universal criticism of consulting, but one that not only hits the consultant with stress and overwork, but also affects their family, friends, and colleagues.

The title of Chris McKenna's (2006) book, *The World's Newest Profession*, makes an allusion in its title to the world's oldest profession, prostitution. Indeed, it is not unusual for graduates to tell their peers they're *off to sell their souls* or for current consultants to talk about *whoring themselves out*. The assumption behind the metaphor is that in order to get paid a consultant will do things that a "normal" person would not.

However, such a characterisation is, in my view, unrealistic and simplifies the complex experience of being a consultant. Most consultants I have spoken to and worked with believe that what they do is for the good of the economy generally. When I asked a consultant from Accenture for his opinion on this he told me the following:

> I have no qualms about recommending the sacking of people and things like that. If businesses can be made more efficient, even at the cost of redundancies, then it means our country is more competitive, the public are getting cheaper goods and the person who paid for my advice is saving themselves money.

It should also be said that when it comes to questions of ethics, most consultancies are keen to accommodate the needs of their consultants. They simply can't afford to have someone leave because they feel their ethics are being compromised. For example, a colleague who I once worked with refused to work on an ERP implementation at a major tobacco company on the grounds that he didn't like what they stood for. Rather than making him an ultimatum, they simply moved him onto another project. This said, another colleague of mine refused to go on assignments more than four hours from her home as she didn't want to leave her cat alone. She didn't last long.

Generally speaking, the personal cost of being a consultant is not to be found in moral or ethical degradation but more in the sheer stress of the job. This isn't simply down to the long hours (which can be pretty awful) and the international travel (airport lounges and hotels stop being sexy after the first month). Day after day, this takes its toll on individuals. They lose meaningful social ties which can affect some people both morally and psychologically (O'Mahoney 2007).

Where Consultants Go

Sixty-five per cent of employees born after 1982 stay in a job, on average, for less than two years, 54 per cent have had three or more jobs already, and 30 per cent believe they will be working in a completely different industry within five years (*Management Today* 2008). If these figures are added to the normal stresses and strains of a consulting job, it is no surprise that more than half of all consultants leave the industry before seven years are up. The good news for consultants is that they probably have more options than any other career when it comes to moving on. Their general business skills and varied experience make them suitable for pretty much anything where management is involved.

The majority, around 51 per cent, of leavers in the UK tend to go to other consulting firms (Top-Consultant 2009), though internationally, the majority move into industry (*Consulting Magazine* 2009). A minority, around 10 per cent, go and work in similar city jobs such as investment banking or venture capital. Below, some of the more popular career choices for ex-consultants are covered before examining a new type of employment that I have termed "the merry-go-round".

Jumping to Industry

A move to industry is always attractive for a consultant. Their skills and experience mean they can often fast-track to a senior position much more quickly than if they had been in the company from the start. They also usually get reduced hours and less travel whilst also being able to take ownership of projects from beginning to end—something that is very rare as a consultant.

As consultants experience so many client projects it should not be surprising that they occasionally find an employer that they find more attractive than their current one. However, consultancies are always aware of the fact that, for a client, it would usually pay to recruit a consultant as a full-time employee to save paying them consultancy rates. For this reason, they usually have a clause in the contract stipulating that a client will need to pay a penalty if they recruit a consultant directly.

Now, for a good consultant, a client is often happy to pay this fee. A consultant friend of mine, for example, joined a famous US strategy house and shortly after arranged to jump ship to a client. The client was so desperate to get him that they agreed to pay a $250,000 penalty and pay off the consultant's $50,000 MBA fee. However, there are often ways for clients to avoid such a fee. For example, I once jumped from a consultancy to a client. For the client this made sense because they wanted me to work on a two-year project which would have cost them around £500,000 in fees, and my full-time salary was much less than this. The consultancy decided to waive the fee because the client threatened to release the forty other consultants they were employing from the same firm. Thus it made sense for the consultancy to "take the hit" of losing two or three consultants to the client, in exchange for the fees on the project which totalled around £30,000 a day.

Charity Work

Whilst published figures are not available, the number of consultants involved in charity work is extremely high. Having spoken to many consultants who either volunteer as part of a work-related scheme or have left consultancy for charity work, many feel that the profession sometimes made them feel "morally bankrupt", in the words of one leaver. Involvement in charity work, paid or otherwise, was their way of making up for this.

As charities have become more business-like in their recruitment, fund-raising, and advertising, the opportunities for consultants to join has expanded considerably in the last ten years.

After a few years bleeding the public sector purse, and feeling pretty rotten about it, I decided to give something back.

(Ex-consultant, now volunteering for CAFOD)

Start-Ups

Many management consultants, driven by a desire to have ownership of a project for a significant amount of time, decide to start up their own company, usually in partnership with a number of similarly qualified and experienced people. The remunerative benefits of being a consultant often mean that after several years in the industry, they have savings which, when pooled, can add up to a serious sized investment.

Of course, many consultants also decide to start up their own consultancy company (see Chapter 7), having spotted a gap in the market or simply believing they can do a better job than their parent company. A big risk some consultants decide to take is to "steal" the clients that they were already working with from their current consultancy. Whilst this practice is usually forbidden in terms of the contract that the consultant has with his or her employer, it is still, nonetheless, reasonably common.

The Merry-Go-Round

There is an interesting career pattern that I have noticed many of my colleagues have pursued over the last fifteen years which involves a constant transition to jobs which include, and are similar to, management consultancy. I have termed this the merry-go-round which I define as: the transient, nomadic, and non-standard career pattern of a loose grouping of individuals with informal, personal, and supportive ties. It may apply to other career patterns, but in consultancy, it usually involves:

- Temporary periods in variations on consultancy jobs: interim management, contracting, executive assistance, consultancy, associate consultancy, and temporary directorships.

- The frequent movement, voluntary or otherwise, between different patterns of employment and different companies.

- The maximisation of income through a strategic use of bonuses, redundancy payments, golden handshakes, the use of share options, the sale of companies, and, less commonly, kick-backs.

- The use of informal ties, personal recommendations, and trusted ex-colleagues to "bring each other in" to companies. This "recommendation system" usually results in "finder's fees" being won by the applicant's friends.

To help illustrate this, examine the end of chapter case on Paul, who I worked with in a previous consultancy.

This form of working may not be entirely strategic but may be the result of the opportunities offered by informal relationships and the easiest way to ensure the recruitment of skilled individuals in companies which require flexible but skilled individuals for short periods of time. Either way, it is an incredibly profitable way of working and, ironically, one that does not require the individual to be great at their job. As many of his references are written by Bill's friends and as his CV incorporates senior positions in several blue-chip companies, few recruiters would doubt his ability. It is Bill's ability to manage his career and his image that has led to his wealth, not necessarily his performance in the job.

CASE 10.2

John and the Merry-Go-Round

After six years working in telecom companies, John applied for a consultancy job with a large UK consultancy. He got it and was placed in a large team working with his old employer. Whilst he was there, he encouraged a number of his old colleagues to join him with his new consultancy and won "finder's fees" from the company for his efforts. After three years of working together, John and many of his new colleagues left to start their own strategy consultancy in the growing telecoms sector. This company grew, and four years later was bought by a larger consultancy, providing all the founders with a large pay-out.

A few months later, one of John's co-founders was head-hunted for a directorship at a telecoms start-up which was looking to grow fast. The co-founder recruited John and several of the old team, all of whom received large "golden handshakes" for joining and director-level salaries. One of the recruits still headed up his own spin-off consultancy, which he brought in to help the company with its expansion plans.

Two years later, John and several others were made redundant, which again provided Bill with a significant pay-out. John then contracted for six months, before becoming an interim manager with a digital media company. As interim manager, John called in several of his old colleagues as permanent employees, contractors, or consultants. John was eventually recruited as Director of Change Management where he brought in a consultancy started by his old colleagues through his discretionary budget.

• What are the costs and benefits of this "Merry-go-round"?

■ Key Career Questions

Students tend to ask me the same questions year after year with regard to their careers in consultancy and other professions. I have collected these together below. It should be noted that these are simply my own views and that the advice of the careers service, professors, and the recruiters themselves should be sought before making any life-changing decisions.

What Degree Should I Do?

Consultancies tend to recruit from analytical degrees that involve a form of problem solving: for example, engineering, physics, mathematics, and business studies. However, there is no reason why a good degree in any subject from a good university shouldn't be considered for a consultancy position. It is less likely you will be considered for a graduate position if you have studied textile design or sports science, but recruiters I have spoken to rarely write off any discipline. Social sciences such as sociology, applied sciences such as psychology, and cultural sciences such as history, English, or philosophy are all also commonly recruited, especially from the top universities.

When choosing your degree, it is important to get a good balance between what you enjoy, what you are good at, and what will give you the best prospects for the career you want. Fortunately, these often coincide. If you are an excellent horticulturalist and love gardening, it is unlikely that you'll want to spend your career in front of a laptop and living out of a suitcase.

Why Should I Choose Consultancy as a Career?

There is a huge amount of research demonstrating that, after one has adequate income to cover basic costs, increased income is not correlated with increased happiness. What studies find does correlate to increased happiness levels are social factors such as being part of a local community, having close friends and family, and living in a society that is relatively equal (Wilkinson and Pickett 2009). For this reason, I rarely urge students to pursue any career path other than that which they most enjoy and they think will make them happiest.

This said, the consultancy career has a number of benefits above others. It is varied, allowing you to accumulate considerable experience in different environments very quickly. It will develop your core analytical, sales, and presentation skills faster than many other comparable careers. It is also a good step if you are unsure where you wish to specialise as industry recruiters are particularly keen on ex-consultants. It doesn't hurt that the money is quite reasonable too. On the down side, expect considerable instability, high-stress deadlines, and often a lack of workplace camaraderie.

Should I Do a Postgraduate Degree?

If you want to be a management consultant then apply a few months before you finish university. Also apply to some good blue-chip firms. If you fail to get a position in consultancy, then you are better off taking the blue-chip role and building up some experience before applying for consultancy roles later. However, if you get neither the consultancy job you want nor a good blue-chip position, you might consider applying for an MSc, an MA, a PhD or perhaps a professional qualification such as one in finance or accountancy. Again, your choice should be based upon what you are interested in, what you are good at, and what type of career you want.

An MSc in a relevant area, such as IT Strategy, Finance, or Consultancy, will definitely help your career prospects providing it is done at a good institution. Given that these courses often cost in excess of £10,000, I would not recommend doing one unless it was at a good university. This is not simply because you will get better training there, but also because consultancies, and other employers, will actively target the better institutions with careers fairs, seminars, and meetings when they recruit. Outside the top five universities in each country, it doesn't really matter to the recruiter where you get your Master's.

Master's degrees in non-business areas will not do your chances any harm, especially if they include an analytical, numerate, or problem-solving focus. However, a non-analytical Masters will probably not boost your chances significantly either. This said, so much of the recruitment process is based on the case interview that a graduate from any discipline stands a strong chance providing they can score highly in skills assessments. Whilst a typical MSc student with two or three years' experience will generally join consulting at the analyst, rather than the consultant, level, they will generally demand a salary up to 30–40 per cent higher than that of a graduate (GMAC 2008).

A PhD is a slightly different matter. A doctorate in any discipline provides three additional benefits to a consultancy recruiter. First it demonstrates that the applicant has the discipline to study methodically for at least three years. This is, therefore, likely to be a dedicated and hard-working individual. Second, it is likely that the applicant has extensive research skills and experience that might come in useful in a consultancy context. Finally, a "Dr" in front of a consultant's name often builds credibility in the eyes of a client and usually means that they can be charged out at a higher rate.

A vocational qualification such as the Chartered Institute of Management Accountants (CIMA) or the ITIL is a good way to develop a specialism which will make a candidate more attractive to a recruiter. However, it should be said that not all professional qualifications

	4 yrs Experience (no Masters)	Masters	PhD	MBA
Consulting/Prof. Services	$66,271	$48,500	$64,953	$101,137
Energy	$66,461	$50,325	$60,851	$84,701
Financial Services/Banking	$80,236	$43,176	$65,682	$89,169
FMCG	$54,898	$39,723	$50,111	$80,209
Manufact./Automotive	$71,013	$46,720	$66,309	$90,435
Media/Entertainment	$63,745	$45,430	$60,390	$97,295
Pharma./Healthcare	$74,999	$54,321	$71,847	$96,014
Telecoms/High Tech	$74,378	$42,230	$68,480	$106,142
Transportation/ Distribution	$60,706	$41,376	$57,853	$82,993
Travel/Leisure	$61,508	$33,550	$59,272	$86,523

Table 10.9. Average salaries in EU and North America, by level of higher education
Source: From www.topmba.com.

are equal. It is always a good idea to ask what the failure rate is of the qualification you intend to take. If the failure rates are low, it is likely that the employer will not rate it. Most specialisms have some form of professional accreditation, but it is worth speaking to a consultancy before signing up for one.

Where Should I Apply for a Consultancy Job?

In short, if you really want a job, the answer is "everywhere". All the big companies have recruitment opportunities posted on their websites and many of the questions that you are asked on forms are very similar. It is worth keeping a copy of your answers so you can reuse and improve them for different applications. In addition, it is worth finding a list of all medium-sized consultancies and sending them a CV and covering letter. Such lists are often available in library databases, on the internet, or on the websites of the various consulting institutes.

If you don't get into the consultancy profession it is something that can wait. Maximise your work experience in a good, blue-chip company and try to develop the skills and experience that would be useful to a consultancy. This may then allow you to apply as an experienced hire later on in life.

How Should I Choose Between Job Offers?

The only advice I give to successful applicants who have a choice of careers is not to follow the money. Whilst an extra £5,000 or so may sound attractive when you first join, what is much more important for your career, and therefore your future earnings, is the company you will be joining and the type of work you will be doing.

Once you have decided which company suits your career trajectory best, by all means attempt to negotiate a higher salary with them using the other offer(s) as a benchmark. However, do ensure that you have a clear idea of the work that you will be doing before you sign up. I am aware of a number of students who have successfully won a place at a management consultancy only to find that the process or IT work they are doing is much more commodified and bureaucratic than they thought it would be.

I Plan to Get Out of Consultancy after Making Some Money

> Before chasing my dreams, I will earn myself some money and get myself some skills so that the pursuit of my dreams is made easier. If I have £100,000 in the bank, I will be able to take time out, buy assets and fund training that I would not be able to do if I didn't spend a few years in consultancy.

This was emailed to me by an MBA student who, whilst fully accepting that they did not want to do the job, aimed to make a lot of money and *then* "pursue their dreams". As an MBA teacher and as a consultant, this is one of the most common, and unreliable, sentiments I hear from new recruits.

Unfortunately, two things happen to stop this occurring. First, the graduate's identity shifts. Either intentionally or unintentionally companies have their ways of making the abnormal appear increasingly normal over time. Thus, the long hours, stress, and travel are increasingly accepted as the norm in consulting life as is the pursuit of wealth and the accumulation of good suits, nice cars, and other items. Moreover, the consultant often slowly adopts an "elite" identity as a consultant (Alvesson and Robertson 2006) which makes it difficult for them to envisage life in any "lesser" occupation.

Additionally, what seems like a fortune in your early twenties very quickly seems like not enough. Many consultants I know would have been amazed at their luck if they had known, as graduates, that they would be earning £60,000–100,000 a year. Incredible as it sounds, however, your spending will usually slowly expand to dissolve your monthly income regardless of what it is. Additionally, the consulting lifestyle is an expensive one and you quickly become accustomed to luxury tastes.

So, whilst it is true that the experience that consultants accumulate makes it easy for them to enter other businesses, it is rare to find an ex-consultant who will admit that they have found it easy to downsize their salary.

■ Chapter Summary

This chapter has covered the basics of the consulting career and the options available to you. Specifically, it has outlined:

- The consulting career structure and the salaries you might expect.

- The different entry points to the career.

- How to succeed in the recruitment process.

- How best to land a promotion if you manage to get into the consulting profession.

- What the options are on leaving the consultancy industry.

The chapter has also stressed the difference between a lucrative career and a successful career which often confuses young graduates. The former is one where you gain a lot of wealth. The latter is one where you are happy and have time to do the things you value. The two are occasionally the same thing, but very rarely.

Student Exercise

Before undertaking any life-changing decision you should be clear about why you are doing it. At the least you should have a clear idea of your values. Your values are the things that are most important to you (whether saving the planet, time with family, or ruling the world). Your values should drive your goals. Once a year it is worth sitting down and making a list of your goals for the year and ensuring they meet your values. Always remember the treadmill of business work can speed up so imperceptibly that you often don't notice. It is only you that can press the stop button.

1   What are your three main values in life? What do you think are the most important things to do in life? For example, having a successful career, respecting the environment, having new experiences, or having close relationships with your family.

2   What specific long-term goals follow from your values? What would you like to have achieved in your lifetime which will mean that your values will have been followed? For example, having contributed to charitable work, being a successful artist, having created and sold an internet company, being married with children, or being able to run a marathon.

3   For each of your goals, break them down into five-year aims. What would you need to do in each five-year block in order to achieve your goals? For example, if you wanted to run for President, you might aim at joining a political party, developing a funding network, undertaking an MSc in Law or Politics, and socialising with the right people.

4   Finally, for your first lot of five-year aims, how will you move towards achieving them this year? Think of practical decisions that you can take, the resources that you have, the people that can help you, and the things you will need to do.

When done well and seriously, this exercise, whilst time consuming, may be the best time you spend in the year. It's a good idea to keep your plans in a journal so you can revisit them every year, marking any changes and plotting your progress.

Discussion Questions

- What two reasons explain the rise in recruitment of experienced hires?

- What are the pros and cons of the consultancy career?

- What competencies are consultancies likely to ask you to demonstrate?

- What are the main routes into a consultancy career?

- What is the merry-go-round?

Further Reading

The best place to go for advice on consultancy recruitment is the consultancies themselves. Not only do their websites offer advice, tips, practice questions, and even videos of good candidates, but at careers fairs and "milk-round" sessions, consultancies are happy to answer questions and give the informal view on the organisation. Especially good websites include those of McKinsey, Bain, Accenture, AT Kearney, and Boston Consulting Group.

In addition, there are several guides available which are written by top business schools, MBA recruiters, and consultancy agencies. These include:

- Beamant Leslie Thomas (www.blt.co.uk)
- Top Consultant (www.top-consultant.com)
- Mindbench (www.mindbench.com)
- Management Consultancies Association (MCA) (www.mca.org.uk)
- Wet Feet (www.wetfeet.com)
- Institute of Business Consulting (IBC) (www.ibconsulting.org.uk)

References

Adams, S., and Zanzi, A. (2005). The Consulting Career in Transition: From Partnership to Corporate. *Career Development International*, 10 (4): 325–38.

Alvesson, M., and Robertson, M. (2006). The Best and the Brightest: The Construction, Significance and Effects of Elite Identities in Consulting Firms. *Organization*, 13 (2).

Armbrüster, T (2006). *The Economics and Sociology of Management Consulting*. Cambridge: Cambridge University Press.

Bernstein, A. (2004). Guide to your Career. *Princeton Review*.

BLT (2009). *Management Consultancy Salary Survey*. www.blt.co.uk.

Bureau of Labor Statistics (2008). *Career Guide to Industries*. http://stats.bls.gov/oco/cg/cgs037.htm.

Chung, E., Herrey, P., and Junco, E. (2008). *Vault Career Guide to Consulting*. Vault.com.

Colvin, G. (1999). CEO Superbowl. *Fortune*, 140 (3): 238.

Consulting Magazine (2009). Retenion Survey. October.

Consulting News (2007). *Management Consulting Survey*. www.managementconsultingnews.com.

Financial Times (2007). Management Consultancy: Appealing if you Don't Know What to Do. 16 October.

GMAC (2008). *2008 Corporate Recruiters Survey*. Graduate Management Admissions Council.

Kennedy Information (2007). *Global Consulting Marketplace*. Kennedy Information.

Lerner, M. (2003). *The Vault Guide to the 50 Top Consulting Firms*. Vault Inc.

Lowendhal, B. (2005). *Strategic Management of the Professional Service Firm*. Copenhagen: Copenhagen Business School.

McKenna, C. (2006). *The World's Newest Profession*. Oxford: Oxford University Press.

Maister, D. (2003). *Managing the Professional Service Firm*. New York: Free Press.

Management Today (2008). *Work 2.0 Survey: My Generation*. FreshMinds.

O'Mahoney, J. (2007). Disrupting Identity: Trust and Angst in Management Consulting. In S. Bolton (ed.), *Searching for the H in Human Resource Management*. London: Sage.

ONS (2007). *Annual Survey of Hours and Earnings*. London: Office of National Statistics.

Quacquarelli, N. (2008). *MBAs are the Highest Paid Postgraduates around the World*. www.TopMBA.com. 8 December.

Top-Consultant (2009). *Recruitment Channel Report*.

Universum (2007). *The Universum IDEAL Employer Rankings*. Universumusa.com.

Wetfeet (2008). *Wetfeet Consultancy Career Guide*.

Wilkinson, R., and Pickett, K. (2009). *The Spirit Level: Why More Equal Societies Almost Always Do Better*. London: Allen Lane.

Wong, L. (2008). *The Harvard Business School Guide to Careers in Management Consulting*. Cambridge, MA: Harvard Business School.

Woodhurst (2008). *First Mover Advantage: Salary Survey*. www.woodhurst.com.

Recruitment

Don Leslie, Director, BLT

As consultancy has evolved over the last twenty-five years, so has the type of recruit changed.

"I remember our team's first £1m project win," says Alan Edwards, a former partner at KPMG. "It was such a big achievement for 1987 that we all went out to celebrate. Now, we would need to bring in multi-million pound projects all on our own, in order to justify our existence." Back in those days projects were "advisory", helping the client with small pieces of work. "It was preparing business cases to justify courses of action for the client," says Alan Edwards, who joined the consultancy arm of Coopers & Lybrand in 1987. Straight out of the public sector, he became a consultant on competitive tendering issues. Mark Lawrie, who joined Touche Ross (now Deloitte) just a few years later, and is now a senior partner for the Midlands, echoes his comments. He, like his fellows, was already experienced in a market sector or industry verticals. "We'd done it before." Clients wanted consultants who knew them and their problems.

In the 1990s, the emphasis started to shift towards systems integration, as IT issues gained greater prominence. Consultancies were selling ERP solutions such as SAP to organisations who needed help in aligning information technology to business needs. This also had an impact on the type of recruit hired by the consultancies. "We changed from being a small team of smart, been-there-done-it individuals, to something rather different," says Lawrie. Over the course of the next ten years, consulting teams grew in size to become large, multinational operations working across several continents.

"There was more emphasis placed on IT literacy at that point," says a former partner with a large audit consultancy; "we looked for project management and IT skills, rather than just the relevant industry background. Assignments became much bigger and more complex," he recalls, "and major systems projects led to large scale change programmes. And engagements became longer and longer, stretching out from just couple of months into year-long pieces of work."

A number of the larger consultancies, most notably the "Big Four", moved into partner-ship contracts with clients in the late 1990s, becoming supply-side providers of services. Relationships became multi-year contracts, spanning years rather than weeks or months. "We were able to sell our consultancy teams on these projects as clients simply couldn't afford to keep a large team of specialists on their payroll."

Firms such as IBM, Accenture, and other large consultancies placed greater emphasis on hiring graduates straight from university, as the need to man large IT projects with significant numbers of junior consultants changed the staffing model in these consultancies. "We looked for much greater systems orientation in their backgrounds," says Edwards, who at that time was moving across with the consultancy arm of the merged Coopers & Lybrand and PriceWaterhouse firm to IBM Global Services. There was also a "march to quality", he recalls, as firms demanded higher academic achievement from undergraduates. "To enter consultancy in the late 1990s you needed to have a good degree from a top-tier university," a trend that continues today.

From the early years of this decade Deloitte has moved to training up some 200 of its own people from the undergraduate level, rather than taking in experienced industry hires to the same extent as it did before. Mark Lawrie was the fourteenth partner to be appointed in the Deloitte Consultancy arm: there are now 120. Then, there were some 300 consultants: now, 3,000.

Other firms stuck to the provision of advice only, rather than service supply. "Clients relied on us for the external perspective," says Cath Hardaker. "The need to bring in specialist resource and scarce expertise to provide the unbiased advice was still a rich seam: as it remains with the smaller and medium-sized consultancies who have eschewed the back-office, offshore operations in India and elsewhere. PKF stuck to its policy of hiring only experienced, industry-specialist professionals who could bring inch-wide, mile deep knowledge of their market sector."

All agree that the propensity of organisations to buy consultancy advice will only increase. "Clients are buying not just capability, but also capacity to deal with the peaks in workload," says Lawrie. As the size and complexity of organisations increase, so consultancies see the demand for their services increasing. The industry has doubled in size since the recession of 2001–3. There's still a pressing need to bring in the consultants—and although discretionary spending may have slowed in the current economic climate, growth is expected again in 2010. Consultancies will continue to hire the brightest undergraduates, MBAs, and "work-experienced" managers and professionals they can afford.

11

Case Interviews

Chapter Objectives

The case interview is central to the consultancy recruitment process. This chapter aims to help students understand and practise the case interview in order to maximise their chances of being recruited into the consulting industry. Specifically, the chapter will:

■ Outline the history, purpose, and background of the case interview.

■ Detail the types, structure, and format of a typical case interview.

■ Show how the case interview is marked.

■ Provide guidance on how to approach, analyse, and answer a case.

The chapter then takes the reader through two practice cases providing guidance at each step and suggesting strategies for successful answers. Next, the chapter provides three further cases for students to undertake. Model solutions to these cases can be found in the Online Resource Centre.

■ Introducing the Case Interview

The case interview is the prime method of recruitment into the consulting industry. For decades, consultancies have used the case interview to identify those candidates with the strongest analytical, communication, and problem-solving skills. Whilst the case method is a fairly democratic method of selection, presenting an easily understandable scenario accessible to all, the case interview undoubtedly favours graduates of schools that teach using the case method, such as Harvard, where such cases form the basis of the teaching system.

This chapter aims to create a level playing field for those students unfamiliar with or unpractised in the case interview. In order to maximise your chances of success with these types of questions, practice is key, ideally with a fellow student or tutor who can act out the part of interviewer. Links to other case interviews are given at the end of this chapter and solutions to the cases here are provided in the Online Resource Centre.

What Is a Case Interview?

A case interview is a method of recruitment where the interviewee is asked to solve a business problem. The "case" is presented by the interviewer, either verbally or textually. Typically, the interviewee then clarifies the problem, requests further information, and presents their solution to the problem (Figure 11.1).

Cases are usually one of three types explained below: estimation, creativity, or business formats. The last is much more common and often incorporates the first two. For this reason most of this chapter will focus on business type cases.

Estimation Cases

These cases test how an interviewee breaks down a problem. They usually require you to make assumptions and utilise basic arithmetic. They might include questions such as:

- What is the weight of a Boeing 747?
- How much oil does BP sell each year?
- What is the Brazilian market for credit cards?
- How many ping-pong balls would fit inside the Empire State Building?

With such questions, you are unlikely to arrive at the "right" answer, but that is virtually irrelevant. The interviewer is interested in how you reach your answer by breaking the problem down logically and making solid assumptions. With these cases, you may be allowed to clarify the problem by asking follow-up questions. Alternatively, the interviewer might simply ask you to make assumptions based on your personal knowledge.

How, then, might you approach the issue of how many ping-pong balls would fit inside the Empire State Building? You might start by guesstimating the dimensions of the ESB:

I don't know how big the ESB is, but I know it's the biggest building in New York and around twice the size of One Canada Square in Canary Wharf. I've been to Canary Wharf and reckon that building is 200 foot wide and 50 floors high, which, at about 12 feet a floor, gives it a capacity of 24,000,000 cubic feet. Double this to get an approximate ESB size of 48,000,000 cubic feet.

You might then want to refine your answer a little:

I will take out room for 50 floors, at two foot high, and 70 desks on each floor, each taking up 30 cubic feet. This gives around 4,100,000 of space which can't be filled, leaving around 43,900,000 cubic feet that can. This can be converted to cubic inches by multiplying by 12 × 12 × 12, which gives, roughly, 76bn cubic inches.

You can then go on:

If I can assume each ping-pong ball is, say, three cubic inches, you could fit roughly 25bn ping-ping balls in.

If you were seeking to extend this answer, you might then note to your interviewer that ping-pong balls don't fit together perfectly so you may need to reduce your answer by a certain percentage. Or you might point out the ESB tapers as it goes up and explain how you might restructure the question to take this into account.

The key with estimation cases is to show your interviewer how you are breaking the question down, what assumptions you are making, and what calculations you are undertaking. Your interviewer will usually intervene if you go too far off track with your calculations. You should also show the interviewer that you know how to refine your estimate further given the time. The applicant is sometimes allowed to take notes and use a calculator, but often they are not.

Creativity Cases

Creativity cases are designed to show that you can think "outside the box". Anecdotal evidence from conversations with recruiters indicates that creativity cases are waning in popularity. As these cases are especially difficult to revise for, this decline is generally beneficial to interviewees. Typical questions might include:

- Name as many uses as you can for a tyre.
- Why are cans of beans cylindrical?
- If a tree falls in the wood and no one hears it, does it make a sound?
- How would you answer this question?
- How many different ways could you tell if the light goes off in a fridge when you close the door?

As with estimation cases, creativity cases aren't concerned with finding the "right" answer. Instead, the purpose here, even with the cans of beans question, is to test how creative you are in generating answers. However, as creativity cases are difficult to practise for the interviewee and hard to score for the interviewer it is not surprising that they are fading as a meaningful method of recruitment.

Business Cases

The most prevalent form of case is the business case. This usually takes place as an interview, lasting between 30–60 mins. During this time an interviewer tells you (or provides information) about a case and expects you to formulate a response. You will probably be allowed a pen and paper (sometimes a white-board and marker), though rarely a calculator. Most cases will supply a business problem in which you will need to:

• Ask questions to glean more information.
• Make assumptions.
• Produce estimates.
• Make recommendations.

The business case will often require you to make assumptions and estimates as above, but only as part of solving a problem for a business. The problems might concern:

• The value of a product.
• Improving efficiency.
• Addressing new markets.
• Growing a company.
• Starting a new business.
• Tackling competitors.
• Increasing sales.
• Increasing profits.
• Reducing costs.

The case interview relies on the candidate interacting with the interviewer through asking questions and clearly relating their thought processes. In turn, the interviewer will often provide additional information and sometimes (if the case is vague) tell the candidate if they are straying off course.

Cases can range from short, two-sentence questions to several pages. The longest case I have seen was given by EDS to one of my own students which included a presentation, two spreadsheets of financial data, and a three-page case summary. It was, however, provided in advance so the student had a week in which to prepare their thoughts. However, even with short cases, the student is encouraged to ask more questions to help with their analysis. For example, a short case might appear as follows:

> A manufacturer of confectionery has found that their profit margins have reduced by 20 per cent over the last five years. Why is this?

You would then be expected to raise intelligent questions about the client to aid your analysis. For example, you could ask about the manufacturer's products, competitors,

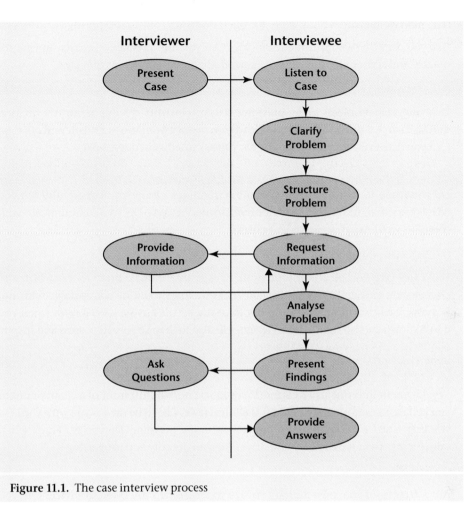

Figure 11.1. The case interview process

market, and costs. Your queries should be answered by your interviewer, who would then expect you to perform an analysis (not always quantitative) and provide answers in the form of solutions or recommendations. When seeking methods to generate ideas, students should refer to "Frameworks for Business Analysis" in Chapter 6.

How Is a Case Interview Marked?

The case interview is *not* aimed at getting the "right" answer, but at showing how the interviewee thinks about business problems and communicates under pressure. The interviewer (or occasionally, someone else in the room from HR) may take notes on your skills and competencies. These vary from practice to practice but may well include:

• Business knowledge

  Do you have a good general knowledge of the business area? Do you apply common frameworks to assist your reasoning? Do you consider the problem area comprehensively?

- Data management

  Can you perform basic arithmetic quickly? Can you interpret tables, charts, and graphs quickly and accurately? Can you estimate mathematical problems quickly?

- Problem solving

  Can you grasp problems under pressure? Can you identify the important information quickly? Do you think logically and clearly? Are your assumptions realistic and reliable? Can you deliver a thorough analysis? Do you ask intelligent questions?

- Communication

  Do you listen to instructions? Do you ask questions clearly and coherently? Do you adapt your style to different environments/interviewers? Do you communicate your thoughts well? Are you a confident talker?

- Dealing with ambiguity

  Few cases give you all the information. This is intentional. Interviewers will try to confuse you and make things difficult for you. You should be comfortable with not possessing all the information and not knowing all the answers. Keep calm when you don't know what is "right". Interviewers will also look to see if you possess and inspire confidence when giving your answers.

- Personality

  Would you fit into the firm's culture? Would you be "safe" in front of a client or might you behave inappropriately? Would the interviewer like to be on a plane with you? Do you keep a sense of humour and proportion under pressure? Do you get angry when criticised? Do you have energy and drive? Are you friendly and interesting?

- Self-awareness and flexibility

  Are you aware of your own limitations? Do you learn? Do you listen to advice? Can you change direction when prompted?

■ Managing the Case Interview

There are several steps involved in a typical case which are detailed below. Some of these steps may be missed in the case, but it is unlikely that any more will be added.

The key theme of these steps is communication. This entails relating your thoughts clearly and succinctly to your interviewer and explaining why you are approaching the problem in the way you are. This is important because it allows the interviewer to understand how your mind tackles problems. Good communication also means that you are more likely to receive accurate feedback from the interviewer regarding your particular method and approach.

Listening and Clarifying the Case

When the interviewer presents the case it can initially seem daunting and confusing. It is intended to be. Remember then to take clear and coherent notes that you can refer back to later on. Interviewers prefer you to be slow and methodical rather than fast and messy. If you need to pause for 30 seconds or so to consider the case, then ask them if that's okay, and do so.

At this stage it is a good idea to clarify exactly what is expected of you. As part of this, reiterate your understanding of the case to the interviewer and clarify any areas you are unsure about:

> If I understand you correctly, this company makes sweets and is unsure why its margins have reduced by 20 per cent over the last five years. Does the client just want to know what the problem is or do they also want solutions to the problem?

Your interviewer will clarify any questions you have. It is important that you take notes and respond to everything the interviewer says as they will often try to steer you in the right direction.

Structure the Problem

At this point it is a good idea to explain to your interviewer how you will approach the question. This will give the interviewer a chance to correct you if you're drifting off target and will also help clarify and communicate your thoughts. For example, with the confectionery case, you might say:

> I'm going to try and understand the declining levels of profit in this company by understanding their income, in terms of the price of their products and the quantity they are selling, and their costs, both fixed and variable.

You should use this structuring for your own analysis and begin writing down ideas that may relate to the case. I find that two things help here. First, many students use visual diagrams, such as mind-maps, issue-trees, or simple pictures, to structure their thoughts. Figure 11.2 shows an example issue-tree for the confectionery case. As more information

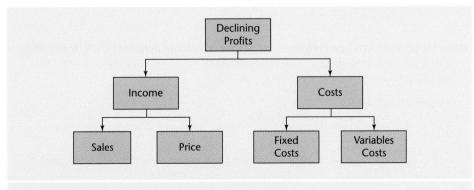

Figure 11.2. An "issue-tree" for declining profits

becomes available, the tree can be expanded and annotated. This also helps if your mind goes blank in the middle of an interview.

Second, I find it helpful to take a minute to really consider everything I know about the proposed industry. For example, in the confectionery industry, you may recall that consumers are becoming more health conscious, that advertising to children is increasingly restricted, and that ethical/organic companies have gained a growing market share over the last ten years.

These points should help you structure some general questions about the company which you can address to the interviewer. For example, in this case, you might ask:

> Could you give me some general information about the company, such as its market share, its market segmentation, its sales channels, and its sales trends?

Often an interviewer will prefer you to ask specific questions, such as those in the next section, but it never hurts to ask a general question in the hope that the interviewer will tell you everything they know without you having to ask all the right questions.

Requesting Specific Information

When tackling a case, you should first be sure what the client wants: what is the key question you need to answer when dealing with the case? You may find that you do not have enough information to answer this question which leaves you with two options:

- **Gathering more information**

  You will usually have to request additional information in order to properly tackle the case. In asking questions, you should be prompted by the frameworks you have learned in Chapter 6. For example, the 4Cs, the 4Ps, Porter's Five Forces, or Profit = Income (sales × price) – Costs (fixed and variable). For example:

  > I'm going to start with the basic notion that profit is what's left over when costs are subtracted from income. Let's start with income. What are the sales and pricing trends over the last five years?

  Your interviewer will either give you this information if he or she considers it relevant or will tell you if you are on the wrong track. It may be that a different framework is more appropriate to your case. Of course you may realise what framework is actually suitable, so just ask general questions about what the firm does, who its competitors are, and how its sales are doing until you feel you hit on a fruitful area—then explore it! Remember, however, in cases where the interviewer refuses to impart the information you need, you may need to make an assumption.

- **Making assumptions**

  Where additional information is not supplied, you may need to make assumptions. An assumption is different from a guess. The interviewer will expect you to base your assumptions on more than a gut feeling and will want to see detailed workings in support of your hypothesis.

  For example, you may be told that the confectionery company has 20 per cent market share of chocolate bars in the USA and that this line brings in £5bn a year, but the interviewer refuses to say what this equates to in sales and pricing. If you find you need this figure, you should be able to perform a quick estimate which assumes that, for example:

there are 300m Americans. Let's say, on average, they eat three bars a week. This equates to 900m bars a week and let's estimate 50bn a year. 20 per cent of this market would be 10bn bars, which means they retail at around 50 pence each.

With a more sophisticated analysis, you may need to break the market up into different age groups (for example, teenagers will eat more chocolate than the elderly).

Assumptions can often be graded according to their sophistication. For example, a recent question I read asked for the number of tyres in the UK. With this question, a weak interviewee would simply state their answer. A better one would take the population of the UK, estimate the number of families and the number of cars per family, and multiply this by four. An excellent student would also take into account the typical life of a tyre, the fact that most cars have a spare tyre, that different "segments" of family have different numbers of cars, and that there is a huge business market for tyres.

Analysing the Problem

Once you have the information you need (or at least, as much as you can get) and have identified any interesting patterns, you can then tackle the case. How you analyse the case will determine what type of problem you have been presented with. However, the interviewer will want to observe both logic in your approach and a general knowledge about business. There are, unfortunately, no perfect formulas for answering cases, but Table 11.1 provides a guide to facing different types of questions.

Most cases you will encounter will be too complex to solve in one go. This usually means that the problem will need to be broken up into smaller parts. For example, your attempt to discover why profitability is declining in the confectionery industry may well include:

- Using assumptions to provide an estimation of the numbers of chocolate consumers in the USA.
- Examining the balance sheets of competitors to identify the most likely threat.
- Analysing markets in different countries to assess whether expansion abroad is recommended.
- Analysing distribution logistics to understand if transport costs can be cut down.

You should keep each sub-problem separate until you need to bring them together to form answers and recommendations.

Remember, if you're stuck, use the 4Cs, the 4Ps, and other models to prompt questions that you can ask.

In addition, your interviewer will assume that you have a good understanding of business generally. They will expect you to know and understand techniques such as leasing, outsourcing, floating, loans, process re-engineering, training, merging, e-business, etc. . . . In other words, you should draw on everything you have learnt from your classes.

Client question	Factors to consider
What price should this product be?	Cost-based pricing? Price-based costing? Value on market demand? You can provide a ratio that is similar to other products. You should consider the competitors products' costs. What is the market segmentation? Who will buy the product? When? Will you offer discounts? Why? How? Price elasticity? Should you use loss leaders or traffic builders? Is price completely created though supply/demand?
How can we reduce costs?	What are the benchmarks of your costs and income? How can costs (fixed and variable) be reduced? Can functions be outsourced? Can some processes be removed? Do you have a lot of inventory? Are you making the best use of your assets? Are you focusing on your key competencies and adding value with everything you do? Can some activities be centralised or automated?
Should we enter a new market?	What is the size of the market (buyers, sales, turnover)? How is the market structured (trends, geography, segmentation, niche vs. mass)? Who are the competitors (see *Tackling Competitors* below)? What are the gaps in the market? What are the barriers to entry? How will you differentiate? Will you steal market share or grow the market? How loyal are customers? How will you enter (acquire, build, partner)?
What should our strategy be?	What is the industry structure? What determines success in the market (e.g. growth, size, brands, technology etc.)? What are the company's unique advantages? What trends are there in the market? Why are the competition successful? What are the opportunities for vertical (supply-chain) and horizontal (similar products/businesses) integration?
How can we better our competitors?	Is competition rational or based on other things? How many competitors are there? What is their market share? How would they react to another competitor? What are the competitions' strengths? What are your strategic advantages? Can you build a monopoly? What are your unique advantages? How can you build on them?
How can we increase sales?	Have you considered bundling products, encouraging loyalty or repeat purchases? Can new customers be attracted? Advertising? Is the brand effective? Improve channels to market? Position products better? Improve/increase sales outlets? Incentives for sales staff? Can existing products be modified for other markets? What drives a purchase? Acquire a synergistic firm?
How can we increase income?	How can income (sales and price) be increased? Regarding costs, are there opportunities for economies of scale, amalgamating suppliers, cutting labour, or automating, using e-business? Regarding pricing are there opportunities for increasing prices, producing specialist (differentiated) products, targeting market segments better? Price elasticity? Alternative Pricing?
Is this a good investment?	What are the potential costs? Up-front costs? Cash-flow required? What are the potential returns? What are the opportunity costs? Cost of capital? Net Present Value of investment? Risk involved? Can risks be mitigated? What are the benefits? Does it fit with company strategy? Will it impact other business areas (e.g. cannibalisation?).

Table 11.1. Factors to consider in case interviews

Sometimes, you will be presented with a huge amount of information (e.g. corporate accounts over ten years) and you will need to sift it quickly for useful information. When this happens you are usually looking for three things:

1. What is the useful information here? In other words, what information can you ignore? For example, on a statement of accounts, are telephone charges really important? Probably not. In fact, in a recent case I looked at which had 550 figures on it, only around 60 of them were worthy of closer attention.

2. What figures might be correlated? For example, in a case where a company has several branches, you might find a correlation between branch size and its economies of scale. If this is the case, it might lead to a recommendation to focus on larger branches. Perhaps profit is related to the seasons of the year, or sales are related to geographical location.

3. What are the unusual figures? If you are pressed for time, focus on what figures stand out as being far too large or too small. This might be anything from a badly performing product to a very volatile market. These figures can provoke additional questions, starting with "why is this happening?"

Very few cases will require complex mathematics. Instead, these cases test your ability to sift the useful information from the irrelevant data.

Presenting Findings

Your findings should be derived entirely from the facts given to you and the assumptions you have made. You should be able to prioritise the issues you discover and explain how you achieved your conclusions. For example:

> Based on the assumptions I made regarding pricing together with the profit figures you have given me, it seems likely that customers are buying fewer our products. Additionally, it appears, from the analysis which I performed on our pricing structure that some of our products are over-priced compared to the competition.

You should not be afraid to say that the information you have been given is incomplete and to suggest ways in which this might be rectified. For example:

> However, our competitors' sales are increasing, which indicates that some of our customers may be switching products. We would need to conduct some research to understand whether this is the case or whether these are new customers and not our own.

When explaining your findings, you should, if useful, draw charts or diagrams to support what you are saying.

Questions/Recommendations

Often the interviewer will ask you for recommendations after you have presented your analysis. Alternatively, recommendations may be asked for as part of your findings. Either way it is an opportunity to show your understanding of how business works and your creativity in finding solutions.

Many cases require recommendations for improving a situation. In these cases you should not simply list your recommendations but weight them, stating which improvements/recommendations you would undertake first and why. You should also consider the potential costs and implications of each solution, outlining the risks and stating what can be done to mitigate them.

Other cases might have asked for a quantification (an approximate price or some other metric). With these cases, you should not just provide the final figure but revisit your assumptions and explain the key risks and variables. For example, which of your assumptions are the riskiest? Which will have the biggest impact on your figures if it is changed? Why aren't you doing other things?

Hints and Tricks

There are a number of points that will help improve your performance in a case interview:

- **Follow the money**

  When swamped by facts, figures, charts, and balance sheets, it is easy to lose focus. When in doubt, concentrate on the bottom line. Even if you get the logic wrong a healthy obsession with making the client more profitable will never lose you friends in consultancy.

- **Red herrings**

  Interviewers will often offer irrelevant information to confuse your analysis. With every piece of information you ask yourself "is this relevant?" This will help you filter the data that are important and relevant. Try to spot "outliers"—data that stand out as unusual or which do not match the rest of the information you've been given.

- **Quicksand**

  You have limited time in which to complete the question, so don't get bogged down in one area unless your interviewer encourages you to do so. You are better off asking general questions early on in the interview to give you an overview of the company and its market. Detailed questions can be left until you know exactly where you should be focusing your attentions.

- **Practice**

  In terms of developing analysis skills, there is nothing like practise to get ahead of the competition. You should practise as many case interviews as possible and perform numerical problems every day for a month before the interview. In my first ever problem-solving test after university I scored 124, which was not enough to get through to the next round. When I re-applied the following year, I spent a month practising analytical cases prior to the interview and improved my score by 15 per cent, easily enough to advance to the next stage. You should also practise reading graphs, spreadsheets, and figures, so as to quickly understand and analyse any material presented in the interview.

- **Honesty**

  Get used to telling the truth. Nothing annoys a case interviewer more than applicants who attempt to bluff the interviewer. They've done this a thousand times and can spot a phoney a mile away. So be honest, be open, and tell them when you're unsure.

• **Calm**

Interviewers will often create additional pressure through aggressive questioning, feigning irritation, or asking provocative questions. They do this in order to see how you might react to a difficult client. Remain calm, polite, and good humoured as much as you can.

■ A Good Answer

In summary, a case is a good opportunity to demonstrate both your knowledge of business and your logical thinking. A good answer will:

• Focus on the core problem (don't get distracted).
• Start with general questions (focus on details later).
• Ask intelligent questions (prompted by different frameworks).
• Analyse the relevant data logically (showing you can sift).
• Make justified assumptions (realistic and supported).
• Provide a rigorous and detailed analysis (break down problems into component parts).
• Give detailed recommendations (evidence-based).
• Avoid vague generalisations (no bull!).
• Be confident and enjoy yourself.

■ Walk Through Cases

In the vast majority of case interviews, the interviewer will present you with a business problem that requires further investigation. Do not be tempted to jump straight to the answer as most of your marks will be awarded for your methodology.

The cases below are presented in a realistic format. In each case, the interviewer presents a problem. The "answers" provided should not be seen as definitive but as guides to help you define your own solution. Helpful hints are given in boxes. You should not move onto the next section until you have made an attempt at asking the right questions and completing the relevant analysis.

■ Case 1: Strategic Change at Mamouthe

Interviewer: Problem Statement

Your client is the Operations Director of Mamouthe, the largest furniture store chain in France. They have 200 stores nationally. In 2006 they made a profit of £28m on revenues of £200m. The client has, for some time, been the largest retailer in France which has enabled it to generate significant profits. The second largest retailer, Antopey, owns 150 stores and made a profit of £12m.

However, recently, a massive Scandinavian company, Ikron, has taken over Antopey and is planning to change all Antopey's outlets into Ikron stores. The Operations Director wants your advice on the extent of the threat and whether it can be mitigated.

Note:

The interviewer has given a direct clue as to where they want you to go: what are the risks for Mamouthe and how might you mitigate them?

Before this, however, you will need to ask some further questions. Don't assume that since you have asked one question, all relevant information has been given to you! What questions might you ask?

You: Asking the Right Questions

The questions you need to ask should focus on what might happen. If you're stuck for ideas, use the 4Cs or a SWOT analysis, but make sure you let the case, not the framework, guide your thinking. The threat will come from any changes that Ikron make to Antopey, so you need to find out how you think Ikron will change Antopey. You can do this by finding out more about Ikron's business in Scandinavia. For example, ask:

- Why is Ikron the biggest furniture store in Scandinavia?
- What strengths does it have?
- What has it done with stores it has taken over in Scandinavia?
- Will its strengths in the Scandinavian market transfer to France?

Additionally, in order to understand how the future plans of Ikron will affect Mamouthe, you need to understand Mamouthe itself, its strengths and weaknesses and its capabilities. For example, ask:

- How does Mamouthe make money?
- How did it get to number one in France?
- What strengths does it have?

Interviewer: Providing Further Information

In response to your questions, the interviewer provides you with the following information.

- Why is Ikron the biggest furniture store in Scandinavia?

  In the early days Ikron made its name by piling high and selling cheap. This strategy enabled it to capture customers from its competitors. Once this strategy had proven successful, Ikron took over competitor sites. Ikron has over 500 stores in Scandinavia and has cut costs in two ways. First by creating massive economies of scale in the production and distribution of its furniture. Secondly, by hammering down prices by suppliers. Its profits last year were £51m on revenues of £650m.

- What strengths does it have?

  Ikron sells a lot of goods very cheaply. It specialises in flat-pack furniture which customers build themselves which again reduces prices further. Its strategy is to undercut the competition and to provide goods at a low cost. It is a fairly "no frills" operation with minimal customer service and few high-quality products.

- What has it done with stores it has taken over?

  Ikron has built itself up by taking over competitors' stores and making them more profitable. It tends to replace more expensive lines with cut-price goods. It also has a policy of replacing staff with non-unionised workers and hiring temporary, flexible, and part-time workers (usually students).

- Will the strengths of Ikron transfer to the French market?

  Ikron can draw on massive economies of scale and there is no reason to doubt that it will exploit this in the French market. However, it will incur some costs in transporting goods from Scandinavia to France and in converting the Antopey stores. Additionally, as the Ikron brand is virtually unheard of in France, it may take time to build trust among potential consumers.

- How does Mamouthe make money?

  Mamouthe sells a wide range of furniture, from beds and sofas to foot-rests and plant pots. Its suppliers manufacture and assemble the goods, which Mamouthe then sells in its stores for a 50 per cent mark-up.

- How did it get to number one in France?

  Mamouthe's stores are roughly the same size as the competition and it sells similar products of both the cheaper and the higher-quality variety. It does have more stores than the competition but, as you can see from the figures given in the problem statement, its profit per store is significantly higher. Why is this?

  Well, primarily because it sells more than its competitors (not because its costs are lower). This is because of its excellent customer service which comes, in part, from the fact that it is primarily owned by its employees. The store has excellent HR policies which encourage older workers, career progression, and share ownership. Additionally, the manager of each store retains a proportion of the store's profits for their bonus.

- What strengths does it have?

  Mamouthe prides itself on excellence of service. The employees are knowledgeable and committed and the stores are well maintained and clean. Additionally, Mamouthe has a strong brand: it was recently voted third in a poll of the best places to work in France and has high customer feedback in terms of quality of service and brand loyalty.

You: Outlining the Risks and Mitigation

Risks

There are two key risks that you should have identified. However, these should be more than a simple list—you should provide a qualitative assessment so that the director knows the significance of each risk. If you named the following you are doing well:

1. Cheaper goods

   The Ikron takeover, according to their established pattern, would result in the old Antopey stores providing cheaper goods. Eventually, this would have some impact on

Mamouthe's cheaper product lines. However, it may take some time before the brand of Ikron catches on and customers are tempted away.

2. Market penetration

The takeover may result in Ikron winning some market share from Mamouthe. Indeed, this may be inevitable given the resources of the larger company.

Mitigating the Risks

What can be done to mitigate these risks? These recommendations are in order of utility. It is likely that those towards the bottom may be counterproductive.

- Remove the cheaper lines and concentrate on the higher ground. This would consolidate the brand reputation for quality.

- Market the "quality" and "customer service" angle of Mamouthe. This should attract customers who are willing to pay higher prices for good service. The "made in France" label should be exploited. A good guarantee for goods would help consolidate this image.

- Cut the cheaper lines where Mamouthe could not compete against the economies of scale provided by Ikron. However, this should only be done on low-margin goods. The Ikron label may still add value to goods which are high margin (e.g. decorations).

- Look for a potential partner to maximise economies of scale and compete more effectively in the cheaper market. However, this may have serious corporate implications.

- Introduce loyalty schemes (note this may have some drawbacks, e.g. rewarding customers who would have remained loyal anyway).

- Cut the prices of goods (although this may decrease profit).

Note:

It is likely that the interviewer will ask you follow-up questions. For example:

- *What do you think a loyalty card scheme would cost?*
- *What do you think we would lose by removing our five cheapest lines?*
- *We are thinking of taking over a medium-sized business. What do you think it should be?*

■ Case 2: 3G in China

Interviewer: Problem Statement

You have been hired by SinoCall in China to assess whether or not they should bid for a 3G licence in the upcoming government auctions. SinoCall is an existing telecoms operator (like Vodafone or T-Mobile) in China which runs 2G networks on the south-east coast (providing text messages and calls). The 3G licence would allow them to provide customers with new products such as video, music, and location services throughout the whole of China. The company wants your advice on whether it should bid for a licence, and, if so, how much they should pay.

Note:

This is, at heart, a profit question. In simple terms, you need to determine how much income SinoCall could make out of this business proposition and how much its costs would be. The answer would allow you to gauge roughly how much it could afford to pay for the licence.

You: Asking the Right Questions

Possible frameworks to guide the questions you ask might include Profit = Income – Costs, the 4Ps, and the 4Cs. You are basically being asked to build a business case to assess the viability of this purchase. Some potential questions are listed below, but you should note that most interviewers will encourage you to make informed guesses as to the answers.

- Costs
  - What are the fixed costs associated with this venture? (You might guess that buildings, staff, the 3G licence, the radio network, and digital content might comprise some of these costs.)
  - What are the variable costs? (Again, you might be asked to guess at these. They could include new mobile phones, marketing costs, and usage costs.) Later, these costs will need to be multiplied by the number of customers SinoCall projects it will capture.

- Market
  - Will the company continue to focus in the south-east or expand to the whole of China?
  - How many competitors are there in the 3G market? How many licences are being sold?
  - What is the potential market? (To show your interviewer that you have a good understanding of markets, you might also ask—or guesstimate—market segmentation, market maturity, and market trends.)

- Income
  - What is the disposable income of different segments?
  - What do customers spend on similar products (e.g. broadband, 2G phone calls, media, and entertainment)?
  - What do similar markets in other countries tell us about the likely income in this area?
  - What prices will the market support?
  - What products will you be able to sell (e.g. music, video, GPS, Roaming, Mobile Broadband)?

- Other
    - How long is the licence for?
    - Can the licence be leased/sold on to other companies?
    - What is the cost of capital for SinoCall?
    - What is the Net Present Value of future income?

There will, of course, be other questions that you can ask, and where the interviewer does not provide answers, you may need to make a guess to have a complete financial projection. It is important to acquire as much relevant information as possible so that you might build a realistic picture of this new opportunity.

Interviewer: Further Information

China has a population of 2 billion people and SinoCall is the fifth largest operator in the market, with a market share of 14 per cent and a customer base of 14 million people. The average monthly spend per customer is around $15. Mobile telecommunication services have been developing faster in China than any other country in Asia and year-on-year customer growth for the last five years has averaged around 20 per cent. Average revenue per customer has also increased over this period but is levelling out.

SinoCall is a cash-rich business with reserves of over $15bn. They have also been offered loans by banks of $15bn at an attractive interest rate of 5 per cent per year. If successful, SinoCall would offer four new products to customers. These would include:

- Video-calls (mobile calls with which you can see a live video of the person you are calling).
- Sports clips (downloadable video clips of customer's favourite sports).
- Music downloads (downloadable music).
- Place finder (interactive location maps which give directions to where you want to go).
- News clips (hourly news updates in the form of video clips).

The licence that is being bid for is one of four twenty-year licences offered by the Chinese government. The licences cannot be sold on once they have been purchased. Instead they have to be handed back to the government if the operator goes bust or decides not to use them. In other words, the cost is non-refundable. However, the successful bidders are allowed to lease bandwidth to other operators to use, if they wish. The licence would simply be that; operators would also need to build a 3G network infrastructure at a cost of around $100m per ten million customers. They would also need to purchase (or produce) content to provide to customers and upgrade customers to new 3G mobile phones.

You: Making a Credible Case

The provided information, together with your estimates, now allows you to formulate a reasonable breakdown of potential income, costs, and profits. You will achieve marks based upon the sophistication of your analysis. A weak candidate will say something along the lines of:

> there are 2bn people and 4 licences. This gives 500m people per operator which, multiplied by a spend of $15/month, gives income of $1.8 trillion. The costs are $100m × 50 = $500m. So the profit, and the amount payable for a licence, is $1.8 trillion—$500m . . .

Whilst this person has used the Profit equation, they have done so with little sensitivity. A more sensitive and useful analysis would take the following into account:

- **Market**

  It is true that the maximum potential market is 500m people. However, anyone with a basic knowledge of China will know that much of the population is very poor, technologically unsophisticated, and with virtually no disposable income. It is unlikely that the new network will be rolled out to rural areas. Moreover, many customers may be satisfied with 2G and not wish to pay more for additional products. Finally, it should be noted that market penetration is never 100 per cent in year one—more customers may join up each year. All of these factors should be taken into account to produce an estimate of what percentage of potential customers could afford, use, want, and access 3G products. This could be as little as 1 per cent of the potential market, growing to 5 per cent in twenty years.

- **Income**

  The spend per customer is based on 2G and in no way reflects what 3G might bring in. It may be preferable to make a guess, by product, based upon what a typical customer might spend on similar products per month (e.g. CDs, Sports, Maps, and TV) and to take a small percentage of this as a guide. You might also note that 3G is often paid through a subscription, and that even in well-developed countries, this is around £35/month (which includes standard 2G products). You might suggest that the 3G premium in China might only be worth around $5 per month per user.

- **Costs**

  Costs not only include the roll out of the network, but also the maintenance and upgrade of that network. Content costs could be guesstimated according to your own knowledge (e.g. the cost of music downloads). In addition, there are numerous other costs which should be taken into account, including sales, marketing, customer service, and all the normal operational costs a company incurs.

  An excellent answer will also take into account the cost of capital. This isn't simply the loan that the bank will be giving the licensee: SinoCall would be paying for the licence up front but not receiving any income for perhaps a year or two afterwards (in Europe, the 3G operators took at least three years to get their first handsets on the market).

  You should also remember that the point of comparison for this product is not zero income. In other words, if SinoCall simply put their cash in the bank, in twenty years' time, the interest may treble the value of their investment. Any potential profit that you calculate would, in a good answer, be compared against other returns.

Anything Else?

This is the type of question that many interviewers ask once you have presented a quantitative analysis. They are looking for an awareness of the broader strategic issues that may influence the decision whether to bid or not. Things you might consider are:

- Are there any replacement products that could threaten 3G? For example, some phones are now using WiFi technology to connect and route calls through free (or low-cost) local networks. What about 4G, satellite phones, and other threats?

- What are the implications of not buying the licence? Could a non-licensed SinoCall compete as a mobile operator in a 3G future?

- Are there any legal considerations to consider? China can be an interesting place to do business and the government has considerable executive power.

- Any additional knowledge you can throw in is always worthwhile. For example, in the European auctions, many operators felt they bid too much for the licences and were either forced to write off the costs or were taken over by competitors due to weak balance sheets.

■ Practice Cases

These cases are each in two parts. The first part contains a brief statement of the problem which an interviewer would give you. After studying this, you should think about:

- What questions would you ask to obtain the information necessary to answer the problem?

- What structure/approach you would use to answer the question?

■ Case One: McDobbles

Part One

McDobbles is an international fast-food chain specialising in cheap food for eat-in or take-away customers. The chain is run by McDobbles and all of the 20,000 locations are owned solely by McDobbles. The company is listed on the New York Stock Exchange and in 2008 generated profits of $3bn on revenues of $11bn. The stores, which employ around 200,000 staff, sell milkshakes, burgers, salads, coffee, chips, desserts, and breakfasts.

McDobbles has two main international competitors who compete with it globally: HamKing and Weakling. Their relative performance over the last five years has shown the two competitors gaining significant market share over McDobbles. McDobbles have asked you to undertake research into their declining profits.

What questions would you ask the interviewer?

	2003	2004	2005	2006	2007	2008
McDobbles	4.4	4.1	4	3.8	3.3	3
HamKing	2.2	2.4	2.6	2.8	3	3
Weakling	1.4	1.6	1.4	1.8	2.1	2.3

Table 11.2. World fast-food profit (bn)

Part Two

After you ask your questions, the interviewer gives you the information in Table 11.2.
You are also given excerpts from two interviews with directors:

Director of Sales

. . . Despite the competition in the US, we'd done well in expanding our restaurants until the year 2000 in other parts of the world. In the 1980s and 1990s, the big area for expansion was Europe, as this area became saturated, we began to look to developing countries which we are still expanding in. However, the profit margins in developing countries are usually smaller than the EU or the US because people tend to prefer traditional food and don't necessarily have the disposable income available. Despite what people said in the press, our customers didn't really like our healthy options, and if they came into our stores, even if they were looking for something healthy, would usually end up getting a burger and fries anyway. We're probably reaching the limit on the number of stores that the market can sustain now. We're also a little concerned by new forms of fast food. You're getting increasing numbers of alternative stores which do bagels, sushi, soups and the like, as the market gets more diverse and specialised. This said, our food is a lot cheaper. We've tended to go for the pile 'em high, sell 'em cheap option. The press complain about us sometimes, but we do offer a completely safe, tasty meal for under five dollars and how many other people do that? We find that if we put our prices up the customers go away, they're very price sensitive. We do try to keep our menus localised but I think too much diversification may hit our core product and our brand. We are, after all, an American company . . .

Director of Finance

. . . well, we're going to need to do something because at this rate we'll lose our number one slot. Our profits have been declining year on year for some time and, to some extent, that's the difficulty you have when you're at the top: the competition have the luxury of trying new things. I don't know if we've perhaps become a little bureaucratic and are a bit too slow at taking decisions and breaking out of the mould. Maybe we need a new sales director. I don't know. I guess you're more interested in the financial side of things anyway. There's not much room for manoeuvre, that's the trouble. Our labour costs, for example, are pretty much as low as we can pay given things like the minimum wage, labour laws, and national insurance. The same is true of building costs: there are so many health and safety laws now

	2003	2004	2005	2006	2007	2008
McDobbles	10.6	10.6	10.7	11.1	10.8	11
HamKing	6.3	6.7	6.9	7.3	7.8	7.9
Weakling	4	4.2	4.4	4.8	5.4	5.8

Table 11.3. World fast-food income (bn)

associated with the infrastructure of food sales that it's all become quite expensive over the years. Insurance has gone up, as have distribution costs of raw materials because the price of fuel has been so high. I've got a good team on top of these fixed costs who are quite good at hammering down prices wherever they can.

Given the information you have been provided with here, what do you think the main problem is at McDobbles?

In brief, what types of solutions might you consider exploring?

Part Three

The interviewer tells you that you have been asked to head a small team looking at potential cost saving measures in the McDobbles restaurants. They have asked you to take a closer look at the cost savings involved with certain ideas that the team has generated.

1. Instead of customers helping themselves to condiments such as mustard, sauce, salt, and vinegar, which are currently provided in squeezable containers at the tables, McDobbles are considering putting small plastic sachets behind the counter for staff to hand out. They believe this will encourage customers to use a smaller quantity of each condiment.

2. In the toilets, customers currently take paper towels to dry their hands. A member of the team believes that hand air-dryers may save money.

3. Customers currently help themselves to napkins/serviettes with their meal. They often simply grab a handful. A team member has seen a machine for sale that dispenses one napkin when a customer pulls a lever. They believe this will encourage customers to take fewer napkins.

Using assumptions, estimate the potential cost savings (or increases) for each idea for McDobbles worldwide. Detail both your assumptions and your calculations.

What issues or challenges might you need to consider before implementing any of the solutions?

■ Case Two: The Olympics

Part One

CPC, an international broadcasting company, is thinking about bidding for the rights to broadcast the 2012 Olympics on television. CPC have asked your consultancy, Xantox, to advise them on the bid. They want to know how much the licence is worth to them with a view to providing an upper limit to their bid (i.e. the most they should pay for it).

What questions would you ask the interviewer?

Part Two

After asking your questions, the interviewer has given you the following information:

- **Company**

  CPC is a large international broadcasting company which broadcasts on digital channels in Europe, the USA, and South America. CPC is a privately owned company with solid and consistent financial performance. Their turnover last year was £1.7bn and their profits amounted to £749m. The company has employees in each country that it broadcasts in. The employees are unionised but worker–manager relations are good.

  CPC broadcasts eighty channels which are a mix of own brand content (e.g. news, weather), commentated sports (e.g. football, boxing, motor-racing), and third party content (e.g. sitcoms, soap operas, films). Several channels are purchased by CPC from other companies (e.g. BBC News) and several are dedicated to different themes (e.g. history, sport, entertainment). There are four sports channels which CPC has complete freedom over.

	Total profit	Europe	S. America	USA
CPC	£749m	Yes	Yes	Yes
SKY	£889m	Yes	Yes	Yes
Virgin	£412m	Yes	No	Yes
Sander	£452m	Yes	Yes	No
BoxTV	£122m	Yes	Yes	No
Foxy	£188m	No	Yes	Yes
NBBC	£955m	No	Yes	Yes
Atalos	£514m	No	No	Yes

Table 11.4. Profits and presence of CPC competitors

- **Business models**

  CPC makes money in three ways. First it sells television subscription packages to households (basic, medium, premium). These cost £10, £25, and £40 per month (in Europe, the USA, and S. America are discounted 10 per cent, 20 per cent, and 50 per cent respectively). The higher subscriptions get premium channels. For an extra £5 per month this service can also be bundled with a high-speed internet connection, also provided by CPC.

  Second, CPC offers pay-per-view for important events such as high-profile boxing or football matches. This enables customers on the two cheapest packages to buy one-off access to important events. Customers on the £40 package have all these events included in their subscription package.

Finally, advertising. Advertising revenue depends on how many people are watching a programme. The rate card is £250,000 for each 20-second commercial at prime time (6 p.m.–10 p.m. GMT) and £100,000 for each 20-second commercial at all other times. Contractual regulations demand that a maximum of 10 minutes per hour is devoted to adverts.

In order to receive CPC, the customer requires a set-top box which decodes and presents the channels. Each box costs CPC around £30 to manufacture and install. The customer is not charged for this.

- **Market**

In total, CPC broadcast in thirty-one countries with a total population of 490 million. The average disposable income of each customer varies greatly from region to region with the USA being highest, followed by Europe and S. America.

- **The licence**

The Olympic Committee sells the following licences: USA, Europe, S. America, Canada, India, China, Japan, Africa, Australasia, S. America. The auctions will be held in 2010. There is an auction for each geographical area. Bidders can bid for one or more licences. The licence provides each successful bidder with the rights to broadcast live and recorded material from the Olympics on television. They may sell the material on to other companies to broadcast on television but not for "live" usage. Non-licensed companies cannot broadcast Olympic material unless it has been bought directly from a licence holder.

There will be two successful bidders in each geographical area. The bidding is a closed-envelope bid. This means that bidders make one bid to the Olympic Committee. They do not know what anyone else bids.

- **Competition**

There are different competitors from CPC in different countries. All the competitors are the same type of business as CPC (i.e. broadcasting television). Last year, the competitors made profits as shown in Table 11.4.

- **Costs**

There are many costs associated with CPC's potential involvement in the Olympics. The operational costs for the production and distribution of the Olympics, which include acquiring and using filming and editing equipment, hiring key staff (including hosts), advertising, management, etc., are estimated at around £62m.

- **The product**

The Olympics lasts for 28 days (from 9 a.m.–10 p.m. GMT) and is being held in London. In addition, there is an opening and closing ceremony, each lasting for three hours.
     What advice would you give to CPC?

Final Question

The client wants to know if there are any further avenues or issues they should consider before starting the bidding process. What are your thoughts on this?

■ Case Three: Market Share at Netcom

Part One

Your client is NetCom, a software provider of "back-office" systems (primarily payroll and HR) for the emergency services (police, fire brigade, and ambulance). Similar to most ERP providers NetCom focuses on managing employee information and ensuring that the employees are paid each month.

Despite cutting their operating and supplier costs down to a minimum, NetCom have noticed that whilst their sales are not declining, their market share and profitability is diminishing. They are not retaining their share of what they believe is an expanding market. The CEO of the company has asked you for your advice on how to increase their profits.

What questions would you ask the interviewer?

Part Two

In response to your questions, the interviewer provides you with the following information, and a set of tables.

- **What other software is bought by the clients?**

The Emergency Services tend to buy two additional types of software:

1. Geographical Location Systems (GLS): these use GPS technology to provide specific support for officers. For example, they might alert nearby teams to an accident, help locating an incident, monitor the location of a unit, or track the movements of a suspect.

2. Client Record Systems (CRS): these systems are used to manage the information provided by the general public calling the emergency services. For the police, they manage the information in the National Criminal Records Database (such as fingerprint identification, reporting software, and data-mining), for the fire service, they manage the records of locations with their fire-safety and history records. For the ambulance service, the systems manage the records of patients and locations that have used the service.

- **Who does the buying and how has this changed?**

There has been increasing pressure in recent years for the emergency services to work together and achieve economies of scale with their purchasing. Increasingly they are being amalgamated into five regional districts where most of the purchasing occurs. Purchasing for all software systems tends now to be undertaken by the same committee/vendor selection department, although the final decision is taken by different people. There are now likely to be fewer but larger purchases.

The other big trend has seen supplier services competitively tendered (i.e. different suppliers bid to provide the services in a competition). This has driven down costs

Company	Share (%)	Sales (£m)	Growth (%)
NetCom Ltd	49	300	3%
Xantax Ltd	8	50	10%
Minime Ltd	3	20	12%
Pretam Ltd	5	30	20%

Table 11.5. Back-office market for emergency services (top four)

for the police and put pressure on the profits of suppliers. However, security concerns mean that suppliers require (expensive) Government Security Certification (which NetCom possesses). More and more services are upgrading their software to competitors' products.

- **What is the market for this kind of software?**

Table 11.5 provides a breakdown of the market share in the back-office systems for the emergency services.

- ○ This market is growing at around 4 per cent a year (averaged over four years).
- ○ The profit margins for this market are around 20 per cent.

Tables 11.6 and 11.7 provide a breakdown of the market for Geographical Location Systems (GLS) and Client Record Systems (CRS) for the emergency services. NetCom do not have a presence in either market.

- ○ The GLS market is growing at around 18 per cent a year (averaged over four years).
- ○ The profit margins for this market are around 20 per cent.
- ○ The CRS market is declining at around 2 per cent a year (averaged over four years).
- ○ The profit margins for this market are around 35 per cent.

Company	Share (%)	Sales (£m)	Growth (%)
ICIM Ltd	35	100	20%
Xantax Ltd	23	50	10%
Powerdata Ltd	7	40	16%
Minime Ltd	35	40	30%

Table 11.6. GLS market for emergency services (top four)

Company	Share (%)	Sales (£m)	Growth (%)
ChopChop Ltd	20	75	5%
Xantax Ltd	10	50	−2%
Minime Ltd	8	20	−8%
Rankin Ltd	8	75	0%

Table 11.7. CRS market for emergency services (top four)

By talking to some customers the following things were noticed about NetCom's products:

- They are seen as quite cheap and basic, without the bells and whistles of other competitors' products. They are the Ford Escort rather than the Porsche or the Rolls Royce of the sector. Other competitors have add-on products and better functionality.

- NetCom is hampered by bad after-sales services. Its training and support services for clients are perceived as weak compared to the competition. Several clients complain that it is difficult to get through on the telephone when things go wrong and that the implementation is often left incomplete.

- **How are the products sold?**

  Sales teams are organised by UK regions (i.e. South-West, North-East, etc.). Each team takes responsibility for targeting the emergency services within its territory.
  What advice would you give to NetCom?

■ Chapter Summary

The case interview is the most prevalent recruitment tool of the consulting industry. In this chapter, we have:

- Explained what the case interview is and why consultancies use it.
- Shown how to tackle the case interview by deconstructing problems.
- Walked through a number of case interviews and given tips on how to answer them.
- Provided three realistic case interviews for you to tackle alone. Suggested answers to these are provided in the Online Resource Centre.

Success with cases rests on logically analysing business problems and communicating your thinking clearly to the interviewer. The more you practise this, the better you will become. Good luck!

Further Reading

Becoming effective at case interviews has very little to do with natural skills and much to do with preparation and practise. This means not just practising cases, but also practising your mental arithmetic and your other problem-solving skills.

There are a number of free guides on case interviews available on the internet. Most of these include different cases that can be practised. Several consultancies offer business-case advice and practice tests on their recruitment websites. To find good cases and examples provided by consultancies, it is worth exploring the websites of Bain & Co, McKinsey, AT Kearney, Accenture, and Boston Consulting Group.

There are also a number of organisations that offer free, or cheap, access to cases. These include the following:

- Kellogg Consulting Club: Get off my case

- Johnson School Consulting Club: Big Red Consulting Book

- Marshall Management Consulting Club: Practice Case Workbook

It is also worth looking at the websites of Vault, Wetfeet, and Top-Consultant. New sites appear so quickly it is always worth simply typing "case interview" and "consulting" into a search engine and seeing what comes up.

INDEX